I0214389

The Lie
That Changed
The Modern World

A Refutation of the Modernist Cry:

"Poly-Scripturae"

H. D. Williams, M.D.

THE BIBLE FOR TODAY PRESS
900 Park Avenue
Collingswood, New Jersey 08108

B.F.T. #3125

Published by

THE BIBLE FOR TODAY PRESS
900 Park Avenue
Collingswood, New Jersey 08108--U.S.A.

BFT Phone: 856-854-4452
Church Phone: 856-854-4747
Orders: 1-800-John 10:9
E-mail: BFT@BibleForToday.org
website: www.BibleForToday.org
FAX: 856-854-2464

**We Use and Defend
the King James Bible**

**July, 2004
BFT3125**

Copyright, 2004
All Rights Reserved

ISBN #978-0-9985452-7-1

Publisher's Note
July 1, 2004

It is with great pleasure that the Bible For Today has been able to publish *THE LIE THAT CHANGED THE MODERN WORLD*. I have worked with Dr. Williams for some time now, as we have sought to get all the details of his book in readiness for publication.

At first, Dr. Williams published this in an 8.5 by 11" format. We have changed it into a 5" by 8.5" format to be more easily read and used throughout the world.

Due to various computer failures, this work has been delayed for many months. The time has now come to put this in print as it now stands. Granted, more work of editing and arranging could be done, but this will be left for a second edition. Time is of the essence.

The author is a medical doctor, now retired, who has researched this important topic thoroughly. Though he has not had the benefit of formal theological or seminary training, he has proved to one and all that so-called "lay" people who have a desire to understand this important subject can do so by diligent study, as Dr. Williams has done.

May the Lord Jesus Christ use and honor this study in the days, weeks, months, and years ahead until our Lord Jesus Christ returns. It should be in every layman's library, every Pastor's library, every church library, every college library, every university library, and in every theological seminary library.

Sincerely for God's Preserved Words,

D. a. Waite

DAW/w   Pastor D. A. Waite, Th.D., Ph.D.
Director, The Bible For Today, Incorporated

Copyright © 2004
The Bible For Today, Incorporated
900 Park Avenue, Collingswood, New Jersey 08108, U.S.A.
All Rights Reserved
Printed in the United States of America

Disclaimer

All quoted material was edited for spelling. This work does not claim to have caught all errors in quotes which are obvious 'spelling errors.' Many quotes have inserts in brackets to emphasize concepts and are not intended to change the meaning. Many quotes have material which has been placed in bold, italics, and font changes to emphasize ideas, concepts, and material. No attempt to modify their meaning was made.

ISBN #: 1-5848-042-3

All Scripture quotes are from the King James Version except those verses compared and then the source is identified.

No part of this work may be reproduced without the expressed consent of the publisher, except for brief quotes, whether by electronic, photocopying, recording, or information storage and retrieval systems.

Address inquiries to:
The Bible For Today, 900 Park Avenue,
Collingswood, New Jersey 08108, U.S.A.
Phone: 856-854-4452; FAX: 856-854-2464
Web: BibleForToday.org; e-mail: BFT@BibleForToday.org

Dedication

I dedicate this work to the Lord Jesus Christ, my Saviour, who is The I Am That I Am, The Alpha and Omega, The Bright and Morning Star, The El-Shaddai, The Son of God, Wonderful, Counselor, The Mighty God, The Everlasting Father, The Prince Of Peace, The Saviour, The Yahweh, The Bread Of Life, The Offspring Of David, The Bridegroom, The Adonai, The Jehovah-Jireh, The Son Of Man, The Jehovah-Elohim, The King of Glory, The Resurrection, The Jehovah-Shammah, The Surety, The Life, The Jehovah-Rohi, The Our Passover, The Key Of David, The Cornerstone, The Refiner, The Rock, The Jehovah-M'Kaddesh, The Firstborn, The Shiloh, The Rose of Sharon, The Emmanuel, The Door, The Jehovah-Tsidkenu, The Lord Of Lords, The Author And Finisher Of Our Faith, The Bishop, The Advocate, The Lion Of The Tribe Of Judah, The Anointed, The Righteousness Of God, The Baptizer, The Door, The Straight Gate, The Life, The Good Shepherd, The King Of The Jews, The Narrow Way, The True Vine, The Head, The King Of Kings, The Prophet, The Priest, The Seed Of David, The Way, The Truth, The Light, The Friend, The Lord Of The Vineyard, The Jehovah Rophe, The Love, The Holy One Of Israel, The Lord Thy God, The Horn Of Salvation, The Everlasting Covenant, The Lamb Of God, The King Of Israel, The Just, The Passover, The Heir Of All Things, The Holy One, The Apostle Of Our Faith, The Friend Of God, The Author of Eternal Salvation, The Forerunner, The Star, The Scepter, The Jehovah-Nissi, The Master, The Rabboni, The Branch, The Apostle And High Priest Of Our Profession, The Rod, The Root Of Jesse, The Ensign, The Covenant Of God, The Rod And Staff, The Holy One of God, The Desire Of All Nations, The Morning Star, The Messenger of the Covenant, The Covenant, The Nazarene, The Friend of Publicans And Sinners, The Prince of Life, The Lord of Lords, and

The Word

"Whose shoes I am not worthy to unloose" (Luke 3:16b)

H. D. Williams, M.D.

Some of the Names Explained

Elohim = The omnipotent, sovereign God
Jehovah = The Being who is absolutely self-existent
El-Shaddai = God Almighty
Adonai = Master
Jehovah-Jireh = The God who foresees and provides
Jehovah-Rophe = The God who heals
Jehovah-Nissi = The God who is my banner
Jehovah-M'Kaddesh = The God who sanctifies
Jehovah-Shalom = The God who is peace
Jehovah-Tsidkenu = The God who is our righteousness
Jehovah-Rohi = The God who is my shepherd
Jehovah-Shammah[1] = The God who is there
Yahweh = tetragrammaton (YHWH) usually translated Jehovah or LORD

---

[1] Stone, Nathan; <u>Names of God</u>; Moody Press, Chicago; 1944; ISBN: 0-8024-5854-8

Acknowledgments

The author of this work cannot put in words the appreciation for the following people:

1. My wife, Pat, who demonstrated the patience of Job, who spent hours reading the manuscripts, and who showed her continuing love and faithfulness by being the helpmeet she has always been.

2. My friend and confidant, **Thomas Eller**, Senior Deacon, Old German Baptist Brethren, who has contributed immensely to this work by sitting hours on end in our basement reading, editing, and encouraging this author.

3. **Danny Lynch**, Elder, Old German Baptist Brethren, encouraged this author more than he knows to finish the work.

The following authors who have "gone before" are due the biggest thanks and congratulations for the mammoth labor performed in the subject matter of this work. This author has used and quoted their works throughout this work. This work would not have been possible without them. Many of them are graduates of the best (or formerly best) postgraduate schools in the nation. In alphabetical order they are:

4. **David Cloud**, Director, Way of Life Literature, Port Huron, MI., whose writings, books, and other materials were used extensively. His electronic disc produced for defense of the Word of God is recommended to anyone who is interested in the subject matter of this work. His web site is: **www.wayoflife.org/**

5. **William P. Grady**, Ph.D., Th.M., M.Ed., D.D., whose works, *What Hath God Wrought* and *Final Authority,* are incredible. Dr. Grady, who came out of Catholicism into the "Light" and who demonstrated research capabilities that are irrefutable, deserves the highest praise and congratulations. Grady Publications, Inc. may be reached at P.O. Box 5217, Knoxville, TN, 37928.

6. **Edward F. Hills**, Th.D., whose classic work, *The King James Version Defended*, helped get me started on the road to understanding the issue of preservation of God's Words.

7. **Rev. Jack A. Moorman**, a missionary and Bible college professor, who wrote many detailed manuals for his students, needs to be honored for the many long hours he spent preparing his works. They were immensely helpful to this author. His books may be obtained from www.biblefortoday.org

8. **James Sightler**, M.D., has authored a number of excellently documented works that support the KJB. They were enormously helpful and appreciated. Dr. Sightler's works may be obtained from Sightler Publications, 25 Sweetbriar Road, Suite 1-A, Greenville, SC 29615.

9. **Pastor D. A. Waite**, Th.D., Ph.D., who is director of "**The Bible For Today**", 900 Park Ave., Collingswood, NJ, 08108, and who helped organize, and still serves the Dean Burgon Society as President, will never know how helpful his book, *Defending the King James Bible* and B.F.T. materials have been. His web site is www.**BibleForToday**.org/ Praise God for men like Dr. Waite who are willing to stand on the front line for THE TRUTH!

10.   **Dean John Burgon** who lived in the late 1800's, wrote, and defended the manuscripts received from the local independent churches in the New Testament era; whose name graces the Dean Burgon Society, can only be praised with the highest accolades. His works helped Dr. Waite, and many of us to see the truth concerning the issues presented in this work. Those who would try to dishonour him by negative comments should be ashamed.

11.   Many others have contributed in many ways. They are too numerous to list and some I am sure I have forgotten to acknowledge them on these pages. I wish to express my sincere thanks to all of them. You know who you are; may God bless you mightily. This work was not written to glorify any man, but the Lord Jesus Christ. So, if I have forgotten to mention you, don't be upset and purpose with me to pray that this work may influence at least one person to see THE TRUTH. [Jn. 14:6]

Foreword

THE SPIRIT SPEAKS: "SOLA-SCRIPTURA"

I.   Dr. Williams requested our review of his work from an editorial point of view early on. Thoughts in print expose purpose and conviction of the heart. It is one thing to "say something" and yet another to bare one's spirit with the "written" word. Time and memory fades the "spoken" while pen and parchment "extends" the written.

The "written" Word of God is the Spirit speaking by the prompting of "holy men of old". The preservation of the Word has taken astounding historical twists and turns. This work emphasizes the historical line of the *priesthood of believers* who protected the Truth transmitted in the *Textus Receptus* and translated into the *King James Version*.

Historically, the *priesthood,* first called Christians at Antioch, *always* has been energized by the Spirit prompting the refrain: "Sola Scriptura", "Sola Scriptura". The antitype cry in response to "Sola Scriptura" is the post-modern declaration "Poly-Scripturae" position. The post-modern assertion "whatever, whatever", meaning "whatever" is right for you, gave birth to the affirmation of "Poly-Scripturae". And by all means the postmodernist asserts: "Be true to your<u>self</u>"! He adheres to the modern textual critics pronouncement: "Bring on the 'politically correct' translations". The *priesthood* declares as a result of the "whatever" and "politically correct" thinking modes of the post-modernist: "Bring on confusion. Bring on the mixing of Church and State. Bring on the One World 'Bible'. Bring on the One World "**WHATEVER**", the One World "_____". So, as believers "fill in the blank" they essentially validate "The Lie" of the cry: "Poly-Scripturae".

THE PRIESTHOOD OF BELIEVERS SPEAKS: "SOLA-SCRIPTURA"

II.   In addition, Dr. Williams asked us to trace our Old German Baptist Brethren (OGBB) background. Through study and research in this work he has come to the conclusion that we (OGBB) have roots that go back to the *priesthood of believers.* Of course, this was no surprise to us.

Our "beginning" at Schwarzenau, Germany with Alexander Mack in 1708 was actually a regrouping of our part of the *priesthood.* With strong Waldensian influence, and a blending of pietism and Anabaptist principles, the "Brethren" cry was "Sola Scriptura, Sola Scriptura". Let the Word, and only (sola) the Word, be our creed! Let the simple sanctified life be the manifestation of this cry!

The regrouping led back to the Spirit Church; the Spirit, rather than the State, speaking regarding worship of God. And as the "Spirit speaking" through the written Word—with the "old brethren" it was simply *never* a question regarding the validity of the *King James Bible* (KJB). The "old brethren" used it; we use it today. It is the Word of God preserved in English. The SOAP work-up of "THE LIE"that came from modernists verses "THE TRUTH" of this work supports our stand regarding the KJB. Enough said!

Now, this stand (on the Word alone) has, through history, led to persecution, even to bloodshed. The *priesthood* pathway is bloody, but is it any wonder! Our path traces back to the foot of the Cross—and there was THE BLOOD, the sacrificial BLOOD of ultimate persecution, the BLOOD of Christ our High Priest, the first in the *priesthood* "blood line"! Indeed, our OGBB background traces back to the cross; but only so as we find ourselves trusting in the BLOOD that brings us to the saving faith in the Work of the Cross. And may our life in Him, then, "show forth His praise"!

Thomas Eller, R. Ph.

Biographical Sketch

Thomas Eller was born in Modesto, California and was saved at an early age in the Church that is the offspring of the United Brethren who are descendants of the Cathari (sufferers) and who are called the Old German Baptist Brethren (OGBB). He was active in his Church as a young person, and continued to serve in that capacity as an adult. After his formal education, he obtained a degree in pharmacy. He became the Director of Pharmacy at a large California hospital. His expertise allowed him to continue to be involved with youth through his Church by helping his community's drug treatment programs. He lectured and wrote on the subject of drug addiction. He moved to North Georgia about 19 years ago and continued working as a research pharmacist at a large national company. First elected to the position of Deacon in a large district of the OGBB Church in 1977 in California, he served in this capacity until 1985, when he moved his family to Cleveland, Georgia. He has functioned as Senior Deacon and as one of the initial organizers of the OGBB Blue Ridge District. The district continues to grow and "serve the Lord with gladness". He is married, and his wife has faithfully served next to her husband in his official duties. They have two daughters who are successful wives and mothers, and who also belong to the OGBB along with their husbands. They have four grandchildren.

H. D. Williams, M.D.

Preface

PRESERVED WORDS OR PRESERVED THOUGHT?

Do we have the actual words of God? God inspired the Holy Writings so long ago that *perhaps* the actual words have been lost? Perhaps all we have left of His inspired Words are inspired "thoughts," phrases, corrupted copies of His Words, or perhaps something close to what He said. But, since God is so great, perhaps anything written that is close to His words or thoughts would be satisfactory for man to understand "what He meant"? Could this really be satisfactory since man is a fallen creature? Can man adequately restate what God said in the original writings and make them perfectly true, or even useful? What does God indicate is His desire for His Words and His thoughts?

Jesus said in John 10:35b, "the scripture cannot be broken. " Of course He meant the thoughts or Words cannot be undone, restated, unfulfilled or lost. He also meant that the Scripture is true to the smallest detail [Mat. 5:17-18]. This is a clear reference to the infallibility of Scripture. Paul made it clear in his letter to the Galatians that even singular and plural nouns were important. Galatians 3:16 says, Now to Abraham and his seed were the promises made. He saith not, And to seeds, as of many; but as of one, And to thy seed, which is Christ." Jesus said in Acts 1:8 "But ye shall receive power, after that the Holy Ghost is come upon you: and ye shall be witnesses unto me both in Jerusalem, and in all Judaea, and in Samaria, and unto the uttermost part of the earth. Notice He did not say "parts." This demonstrates that even letters are important. Jesus said they were. Paul said they were. Peter said they were. [1Pe 1:21-23] Who is qualified to counter these men?

Another term used to exemplify infallibility to the smallest detail is to say the Scripture is inerrant. To make sure we understand this thought, Jesus Christ said, "not one jot or tittle shall disappear until all be fulfilled." [Mat. 5:18] This does not mean a word, but even the smallest part of a word shall not disappear until everything stated or prophesied comes to pass. In another place Jesus said, "Heaven and earth shall pass away, but my words shall not pass away." (Please notice the plural, words) So, the Word will be preserved "until all be fulfilled" because it is true and "cannot be broken". The concept of the preservation of every word, syllable, letter, jot, or tittle should be important to us! Why? Because Jesus said every word would judge us in John 12:47-48 "And if any man hear my words, and believe not, I judge him not: for I came not to judge the world, but to save the world. [48] He that rejecteth me, and receiveth not my words, hath one that judgeth him: the word that I have spoken, the same shall judge him in the last day."

John 17:17b says, "Thy word is truth." If preservation has failed then the Scripture is not "truth."

DOCTRINE OF PRESERVATION CAST ASIDE

Most denominations, most churches, most colleges, most seminaries, and most institutions have cast the Doctrine of Preservation of the Scripture aside. This is a grievous and growing evil that is contrary to Scripture and that has placed "Christendom" on a *broad road* leading to destruction. This road, called "The Rejection of Inerrancy, Inspiration, Infallibility, and Preservation of Scripture," carries one to the doorstep of a house called, "Apostasy." Inside the house many seats are waiting. One of the seats is called, "The Rejection of Moses' Writings called the Pentateuch." As one progresses around the room, another seat is called, "The Naturalist's Neutral Seat." Another seat has the name above it called, "The Denial of the Miracles," or "Denial of the Virgin Birth," or "Denial of Prophecy." Finally, the seat is reached that belongs to the owner of the house, and on top of his throne are the words, "The Denial of the Divinity of Jesus Christ." As one looks back through history and examines the lives and beliefs of those who have moved from one seat to another or who have stretched out across them, the root problem (disease) starts with that slippery road called, "The Rejection of Inerrancy, Inspiration, Infallibility, and Preservation of Scripture."

Close by stands another house, an opulent one obtained by the very lives of the saints. It is built on a road called "Tradition." This new house is called "The Philosophy of Men." Inside this new house are more seats. The first seat is called, "The Seat of Logic." The next seat has a name above it called, "The Seat of Despisers." Further around the room is found, "The Seat of the Inquisitor" or "The Seat of Authority." Last but not least is a large throne that tries to imitate the throne found only in the north regions, which is the one belonging to **The Ancient of Days**. Above the throne in this house, however, is the title, "The Angel of Light." The seat is occupied.

One should be asking by now, is it possible that these are the roads being followed in the last of the "latter" days? Have we really cast aside the Doctrine of Preservation , Inerrancy, and Infallibility of Scripture? The answer is a loud, "YES!" The roads above have become wider and wider. More and more people have jumped on the buses heading to the houses described above. This is not the opinion of someone who is "untrained," or someone who is not a textual critic, or someone who is not a linguist. This is a loud shout from some of the best scholars in history and from the faithful ones down through the last 20 centuries. The shout is coming from their pulpits, from their writings, from the fires, from the boiling pots, from the lion's dens, from the crosses, from the hangman's nooses, from the racks of torture, and from the graves of the faithful. The martyrs of the ages are crying out from their graves, "How long O Lord?" And a voice like many waters says, "Just a little while longer."

THE PURPOSE OF THIS WORK

The purpose of this work is to bring to "life" this "allegory of the houses." The thoughts recorded in this work are not original. The gratitude to those who have gone before cannot be expressed with words. Most importantly, thousands of men and women have given their lives to protect and pass on to their progeny the preserved Words.

They have understood the "Doctrine of Simplicity." "You must become as a little child to enter the Kingdom of Heaven." You do not have to be a great scholar, or highly educated, or a linguist to "get it." You do have to have "ears." But just in case you don't get it, we will quote and use the thoughts of some of the greatest scholars, linguists, and teachers of all time who became "as a child" and did "get it." Many of them are very respected in the field of textual criticism. Some individuals, who have been opposed to the idea of Divine Preservation, are starting to see a "glimmer" of light. Other individuals are men who have "seen the light" and have spent *years* studying the issue. They are graduates of Harvard, Princeton, Yale, Oxford, Cambridge, Dallas Theological Seminary and many other institutions of higher learning.

In spite of what you may be thinking, however, the Living Word was not preserved by the professors and administrators of the institutions of higher learning, but by the lesser known and often discredited *priesthood of believers*. It is *the priesthood of believers* guided by the Holy Ghost that keeps the local church, which is the pillar and ground of truth [1 Tim 3:15], on solid ground, and that protects, guards, and keeps the only sure foundation for the church, the Words of God. It is *not* the institutions of scribes, Pharisees, or scholars that guard, protect, and keep the Holy Words. Hopefully, this concept will be established in your mind and heart by the testimonies in this work. It is the local, independent churches of God that have maintained, guarded, protected, preserved, and kept the pure Word.

The Scriptures have not been lost and we do not need "editors" to "reconstruct" or "correct" the Bible.

1. It is not hidden. It is not secret. 2 Tim. 3:16 All scripture is given by inspiration of God, and is profitable for doctrine, for reproof, for correction, for instruction in righteousness.

2. It will never fail. Matthew 5:18 For verily I say unto you, Till heaven and earth pass, one jot or one tittle shall in no wise pass from the law, till all be fulfilled.

3. It is true. John 17:17 Sanctify them through thy truth: thy word is truth.

4. It contains no fables. 2 Peter 1:16 For we have not followed cunningly devised fables, when we made known unto you the power and coming of our Lord Jesus Christ, but were eyewitnesses of his majesty.

5. It is "more sure" than if God were to speak directly from heaven to us. 2 Peter 1:18-19 And this voice which came from heaven we heard, when we were with him in the holy mount. We have also a more sure word of prophecy; whereunto ye do well that ye take heed, as unto a light that shineth in a dark place, until the day dawn, and the day star arise in your hearts

6. It is not mystifying. Isaiah 45:18-19 For thus saith the LORD that created the heavens; God himself that formed the earth and made it; he hath established it, he created it not in vain, he formed it to be inhabited: I am the LORD; and there is none else. I have not spoken in secret, in a dark place of the earth: I said not unto the seed of Jacob, Seek ye me in vain: I the LORD speak righteousness, I declare things that are right.

7. However, it may be veiled to unbelievers. 2 Cor. 4:3-4 But if our gospel be hid, it is hid to them that are lost: In whom the god of this world hath blinded the minds of them which believe not, lest the light of the glorious gospel of Christ, who is the image of God, should shine unto them.[1]

Last but not least is Psalm 12:6-7, which underwrites all the above: Psalm 12:6-7 <u>The words of the LORD are pure words: as silver tried in a furnace of earth, purified seven times. Thou shalt keep them, O LORD, thou shalt preserve them from this generation for ever</u> and Psalm 138:2c which seals all the above: *Psalm 138:2c* <u>thou hast magnified thy word above all thy name</u>. Wow!!

---

[1]Cloud, David, Way of Life, The preceding 7 items in this work were used from www.wayoflife.org but the precise reference was lost.

CONCEPTS TO KNOW

In the course of reading this work there will be certain concepts and definitions which the reader needs to know and understand from the beginning. Many concepts overlap and are integrated. For this reason, some initial definitions and concepts are necessary. You may not understand everything in a section of this work, but keep reading. Don't give up. The topics covered in this work are critical for a believer, particularly in these final days of the last generation.

A manuscript may be a hand written document on 1) papyrus, a sheet something like paper made from a reed found primarily in Egypt, or 2) vellum, a specially made animal hide for writing. Vellum is more durable and was frequently made into codices, a book-like binding of layers.

The Bible was initially handwritten in large letters called uncials or later on in small letters called minuscules on these materials when the original autographs (writings) were recorded and the copies of those autographs were made. The 44 authors of the 66 books of the Bible wrote in the languages of Hebrew, Aramaic, and Greek. Their writings have not been lost, in spite of what you may have been told. Those authentic copies of the original writings in the languages of the Bible were passed down to us through the "plain" people or **the priesthood of believers**. The preserved copies of the original language manuscripts go by a number of different names but the most common are: the traditional text (TT), the received text (RT), the Textus Receptus (TR), the universal text, the Byzantine text, the majority text, the common text, the Antiochian text, the Ecclesiastical text, and the Constantinopolitan text. The corrupted copies of the original language manuscripts are often called the Alexandrian text, the Egyptian text, the Westcott/Hort text, the UBS (United Bible Society) text, the Nestle text, the Nestle-Aland text, the *critical text* (CT), and the Roman text.

This work will be structured like an epidemiological study. Everyone is probably familiar with the recent terrorist attacks on post offices and the capital buildings in Washington, D.C. using anthrax. The CDC (Communicable Disease Center) of the United States in Atlanta, Ga. and public health officials had a major epidemiological problem. Specifically, they had to do detailed contact studies to try to determine the origin and transmission of the anthrax spores and disease. In like manner, this report will list men and circumstances without lengthy particulars much like an epidemiological study. Charts and diagrams to assist you have been prepared to link individuals and their beliefs may assist you. They can be found in the rear of the work.

The doctrine of inspiration as defined in this work is: the entire text of Scripture, including *the very words*, is a product of the mind of God expressed in human terms and conditions. This may be theologically stated as the verbal and plenary inspiration of the Bible. In addition, the Bible is true in all it teaches or affirms. This extends to both the areas of history and science. It does not hold that the Bible has a primary purpose to present detailed information concerning history and science, but contains the information God wants man to know. Therefore the use of idiomatic expressions, approximations, and phenomenal language is acknowledged to fulfill the requirement of truthfulness. Apparent discrepancies, therefore, can and must be harmonized.[1] In light of the above, the Scriptures are infallible as to the very words, parts of words, and thoughts.

The very words, letters, and thoughts contained in the Received Text have been providentially preserved by an omniscient, omnipotent, omnipresent triune God who is the one and only God I call the OOO God. The accepted doctrine is that this God was able to create and is able to maintain the universe consisting of billions of galaxies with billions of stars and that He may at His will operate outside the laws of nature and time by miracles or providentially within the laws of nature and time as man knows them.

Jesus Christ through His Words, the Scripture, has asked us as believers to **persevere** by **proclaiming, preserving** and **practicing** his words and doctrine until he returns by **proving** we are His servants through obedience to His Words. We will as a **result** of **repentance** be **refreshed** at the "times of **restitution,**" which is His second coming, the restitution of all things, and the literal presence of the Prince of Life.

Acts 3:19-21 <u>Repent</u> ye therefore, and be converted, that your sins may be blotted out, when the times of <u>refreshing</u> shall come from the presence of the Lord; And he shall send Jesus Christ, which before was preached unto you: Whom the heaven must receive until the <u>times of restitution</u> of all things, which God hath spoken by the mouth of all his holy prophets since the world began.

Please be aware that one cannot read this material like a popular magazine or a modern book. Some quotes from ancient writings are difficult to understand. Many comments to assist in the interpretation are made in the middle of quotes to aid the reader, but are bracketed. Hopefully, this will not cause too much confusion.

---

[1]House, H. Wayne; *Charts of Christian Theology and Doctrine*; Zondervan Publishing House, Grand rapids, Michigan, 1992, p.24

LONG QUOTES ON PURPOSE

Lastly, there are many long quotes. There are many reasons for this: 1) To let the reader sense the complete meaning of the author of the quote 2) To get personal interpretation out of the way 3) To let the author of the quote present the information far better than the author of this work could 4) To save this author time and energy at the bench reconstructing the same information 5) To let the reader truly understand there are some very outstanding scholars who have studied these concepts diligently and 6) To show the reader there are some who have "missed the boat." Even though you may not understand everything in a quote, push ahead. As you learn definitions and concepts, you will begin to appreciate what a few faithful men have been crying: "Sola Scriptura" (Scripture Alone).

HOLD FAST TO SOUND DOCTRINE

The importance of the battle for the Words of God cannot be taken lightly. The rapid changes occurring in the thinking of modern man with the explosion of knowledge in the last one hundred plus (100+) years has caused spiritual insecurity for some, denial of truth for others, and false security for many people. The *rise* of immorality, relativism, lying, and even murder is probably linked to the turning away from the absolute preserved truth of God. Foundations are being built on the sinking sand of man who is rewriting the Words of God and claiming, "This is what God said." My prayer is that the sharing of this work with the help of the Spirit will assist some to develop a foundation so firm that turning back, giving up, or becoming apostate will be averted in the soon to come persecution and Antichrist era. Can you claim that you are so certain that you have the actual Words of God that you can cry out like the venerable old pastor of the church at Smyrna when threatened with wild beasts,

> "Call them. For repentance from the better to the worse is not permitted us; but it is noble to change from what is evil to what is righteous"? And when he was threatened with fire, he said, "The fire you threaten burns but an hour and is quenched after a little; for you do not know the fire of the coming judgment and

everlasting punishment that is laid up for the impious. But why do you delay? Come do what you will." And finally, Polycarp said, "Eighty-six years I have served Him, and he never did me wrong. How can I blaspheme my King who saved me?"[1]
Polycarp was discipled by the Apostle John.

Could you respond like this member of the **priesthood of believers,** Polycarp? I ask this question because I truly believe we are in the 'last' of the latter days. A pastor, Dr. Robert Massey, recently stated from the pulpit that there are three classic stages in a nation's history of Christianity. The 1st stage is establishment; the 2nd is repudiation; and the 3rd, extermination. He said, "We are well into the repudiation stage in this nation." And this author believes it is because of the 'changes' in Scripture that are now accepted as the "true" Word of God and the confusion wrought by these changes. We are drawing close to the time of extermination, and the need for a firm foundation, not sinking sand, is near. Again I state: My prayer is that the information supplied in this work will also encourage the faithful to "hold fast" to that which is good; to that which are the **Words** of God; and not to the "thoughts", or "opinions" as to what **man** thinks are God's Words. Paul says in 1 Thes. 5:21 "Prove all things; hold fast that which is good." God says in Isaiah 55:8 "For my thoughts are not your thoughts, neither are your ways my ways, saith the LORD. For as the heavens are higher than the earth, so are my ways higher than your ways, and my thoughts than your thoughts." The only perfect and good thing currently on the face of this earth is God's Words, which are *God's* thoughts. We have His Preserved Words, they do not need to be dug up from the sands of Egypt, or discovered in a cave or monastery, or a garbage dump.

While reading this work, notice how the subtle forces of Satan have turned from 1) trying to exterminate "men" who were members of **the priesthood of believers,** to 2) trying to exterminate the Word of God. He was not completely successful with the first method but remember he was not successful at the Cross of Jesus Christ either. Jesus is alive. Will Satan be successful with the second method, trying to exterminate God's Word? We know he will not be successful, but he will lead many to believe the liberal modernist textual critics who have severely weakened God's message in many corrupted Bible versions. Which side will you be on in this struggle? Again I pray the information in this work will help you decide.

I have tried honoring all those that have addressed the issue of the preservation of God's Words on all sides. It is not easy, because when issues that determine salvation, sanctification, and eternity are involved, emotions run

---

[1]Richardson, Cyril C.; *The Early Christian Fathers*; Collier Books, MacMillan Publishing Co.; New York, NY; ISBN 0-02-088980-1; 1970; pp. 152-153

high. Those on both sides of the problem who are not patient, or who cast disparaging remarks towards others troubles me. Hopefully, this work will honour our Saviour and reflect His personality.

THOSE WHO HAVE GONE BEFORE

Finally, this thought has consumed me with sadness as this work was being prepared: Our generation has forgotten those who have gone before us; who have entered "the strait gate"; who have suffered immensely; who have given their lives for "the King Eternal, immortal, invisible, the only wise God" and His Words. I was so surprised to find the following quote by the author of a book written in 1660 who had the same thoughts and who, I now know, had this same profound sadness.

"Yet that which more than all else caused my tears to flow was the remembrance of the sufferings and the death of Thy martyrs, who altogether innocent, as defenseless lambs, were led to the water, the fire, the sword, or to the wild beasts in the arena, there to suffer and to die for Thy name's sake. However, I experienced no small degree of joy as I contemplated the living confidence they had in thy grace, and how valiantly they fought their way through the **strait gate**."[1]

H. D. Williams, M.D.

---

[1]Braght, Thieleman J. van; *Martyrs Mirror, The Story of Seventeen Centuries of Christian Martyrdom, From the Time of Christ to A.D. 1660;* Herald Press, Scottsdale, Pa, Waterloo, Ontario, 1660, Reprinted 1949, Mennonite Publishing House from the Dutch edition 1660; p. 5

Table of Contents

Matthew 7:13-14

Enter ye in at the strait gate: for wide is the gate, and broad is the way, that leadeth to destruction, and many there be which go in thereat: Because strait is the gate, and narrow is the way, which leadeth unto life, and few there be that find it.

The Lie That Changed The Modern World

INTRODUCTION

SIGNIFICANT EVENTS IN HISTORY

There have been momentous, heaven and earth shattering events in history that have forever changed the future. The birth of Jesus Christ, Immanuel, "God with us", was undoubtedly the most far-reaching event in history. That one solitary life changed people, nations, cultures, and even the spiritual realms. On a lesser scale there are other examples. The development of the theory of evolution is one. The debates over this issue have raged for the last several centuries. A new religion, called Humanism, has sprung up because of belief in evolution's principles. Another example of an event that has significantly affected civilization is the development of the atomic bomb. The possibility of atomic warfare is producing a soaring anxiety among world leaders, alert citizens, and scientists, eclipsing concerns about any other public danger. This anxiety is driving the search for terrorists who have or may have weapons of mass destruction. This same anxiety drives the desire to control despots such as Saddam Hussein in Iraq and rogue nations like Iran and Libya. The necessity for control of atomic power is driving nations like Russia and the United States to openly cooperate with one another. Another example of an historic event, which is more recent and which has changed America and the world forever, is the terrorist attack on the World Trade Center and the Pentagon. All of these incidents have changed the future.

DISTURBING LIES

A most disturbing recent incident is the action taken by a politician, which has helped mold and solidify the moral relativism among the people of America, particularly our children. Can anyone forget the evening newscast when President William Jefferson Clinton stood before a television camera and pronounced, "I did not have sex with that woman, Monica Lewinski." The subsequent spin placed on the President's lie has encouraged teenagers and adults to believe that it is all right to lie about sex, because "everybody does" and that is normal. The ultimate consequences of his actions on the moral fabric of the nation and world are yet to be determined.

LIES THAT HAVE CHANGED THE WORLD

There have been other lies in history that have affected the world. These have led to wars, murders, mayhem and social corruption. Examples of these types of lies are 1. the fabrication of the Piltdown man discovery at Piltdown Common in Sussex by Charles Dawson, an amateur geologist, 2. the construction of a genetic basis for homosexuality by the liberal left to justify homosexualism, 3. the falsification of the truth that Islam is a violent religion, and 4. the persistent acceptance of the theory of evolution without any evidence of support. But the tenet of this work is the belief that the lie about to be revealed has changed the world adversely, forever. The change started slowly, but is now like a snowball rolling downhill toward a one-world religion, one-world "Bible", and one-world government and economy. The power that is pushing and pulling this snowball is not gravity, but rather the plan of enemy spiritual forces toward ecumenism.

The lie is not well known. There is no doubt it has changed our modern world and will continue to change it in the foreseeable future. It is built on *argumentum ad hominem* reasoning. This type of argument is built on a series of *surmises*. Those who use these kinds of arguments forget the difference between a conclusion based on facts compared to a conclusion based on theory, probability, and/or presumption. The strongest conclusions based on these types of arguments can never rise above a **probability.**[1] But to promote the conclusions as truth, which is not based on *prima facie* evidence known to the persons or individuals, becomes a **lie.** Two men participated in THE LIE, which this work proposes has been overlooked by most, and sadly pressed as truth into modern and postmodern higher and lower theological criticism. One of the men participating in this fraud was a bishop of the Anglican Church and the other was a professor at Cambridge near the turn of the 19th century.

PREREQUISITES BEFORE EXAMINING THE LIE

Before discussing this world changing deceit, I would like to consider some very important prerequisites and a lot of historical information. One's view of God is critical to the understanding of the consequence of this deceit. The Judeo-Christian God of the Bible has been considered to be omnipotent, omniscient, and omnipresent. There are those throughout history who have not accepted an Almighty God with these attributes. They have believed that He is limited in time and space. They have not believed that He is eternal outside of time, but eternal in longevity or age only. They have not considered God to be all-knowing, but that He is learning as time marches on.[2] They do not believe He is the creator of the universe and presuppose the universe to have existed eternally without a creator. Some of the recent discoveries of astrophysics have refuted the eternal existence of the universe and have pointed to a sudden creation.[3] The tenet of this work is that God has existed eternally outside of time, is not limited by time, and is the triune God of the Holy Bible who is all-knowing, all-seeing, and all-powerful. He is the Creator of the universe from "nothing."

God cannot lie. By His very nature He is holy and righteous. He is truth. Many Scriptures refer to this character of God, for example, Numbers 23:19, *God is not a man, that he should lie; neither the son of man, that he should repent: hath he said, and shall he not do it? or hath he spoken, and shall he not*

---

[1] Thompson, J.P.; *Barnes' Notes*; Baker Book House Company; Grand Rapids, MI; ISBN: 0-8010-0835-2; Reprinted from 1873 edition of *A Critical and Exegetical Commentary on the Book of Genesis with a New Translation;* p.VIII

[2] Murphree, Jon Tal; *Divine Paradoxes*; Christian Publications, Camp Hill, Pa.; ISBN:0-87509-771-5, 1998, p. 8

[3] Ross, Hugh; *The Fingerprint of God;* Promise Publishing Co.; Orange, Ca. ISBN 0-939497-18-2; 2nd edition, 1991; p. 39-50. The sudden creation was ***not*** the Big Bang, however.

make it good? And in this verse, Deut. 32:4 He is the Rock, his work is perfect: for all his ways are judgment: a God of truth and without iniquity, just and right is he. And finally, Titus 1:*2 In hope of eternal life, which God, that cannot lie, promised before the world began.*

Here are some examples that demonstrate God did not, cannot, and will not lie. He is truth, and He will fulfill His promises.

There are 330 prophecies concerning the first coming of Jesus Christ. He fulfilled them all to the letter. A case in point is the prediction in Micah 5:2 that Jesus would be born in Bethlehem. "But thou, Bethlehem Ephratah, though thou be little among the thousands of Judah, yet out of thee shall he come forth unto me that is to be ruler in Israel; whose goings forth have been from of old, from everlasting." The chances of one man having fulfilled 330 prophecies are one to the billions and billions according to mathematicians.

Although many doubted the following would ever occur, Israel was established as a nation again in one day on May 15, 1948 after being a nation without borders for nearly 2000 years. Isaiah 66:8 Who hath heard such a thing? who hath seen such things? Shall the earth be made to bring forth in one day? or shall a nation be born at once? for as soon as Zion travailed, she brought forth her children.

If you do not believe in this Almighty God, then you don't have to read any more. As harsh as it may seem, you are considered an enemy of God and part of a growing tumult. (Psa 74: 22-23) If you are willing to learn about the God of Abraham, Isaac, and Jacob, before reading further, turn to appendix one (1). If you are not sure whether you believe in God (an agnostic), or if you are sure (a believer), read on and listen to what this God described above says about His Words. I would caution you to remember 1 Cor. 2:14 But the natural man receiveth not the things of the Spirit of God: for they are foolishness unto him: neither can he know them, because they are spiritually discerned.

The following verse is pivotal to understand the following discussion, although there are many other verses and we will present them later. Psalm 12:6-7 The words of the LORD are pure words: as silver tried in a furnace of earth, purified seven times. [7] Thou shalt keep them, O LORD, **thou shalt preserve them** from this generation for ever. (Please see the comments below concerning this verse)[1] **Pure** in this context means God will keep His Words uncontaminated, unpolluted, clean, and untainted. He also says He will keep, guard, **protect,** and **preserve** them **forever.** This clearly does not

---

[1] White, James R.; *The King James Only Controversy;* Bethany House Publishers; Minneapolis, MN; ISBN 1-55661-575-2, 1998; p. 243 The attacks on this verse by people who want to destroy this reference are appalling. The comments on this verse by White are typical of "Alexandrians", which will be explained in this work.

mean He will keep or preserve words someone else chooses, or decides to change, or decides to subtract from His Words! He, the Almighty Jehovah, will keep and preserve them. If you don't understand anything else in this document, please understand PSA 12: 6-7. Some will say, "Well, how did he preserve them?", or "Why can't other words be used if they "mean" the same thing?", or "Why couldn't there be several different paths God used to preserve His Words", or "Aren't there many different wordings in the manuscripts; so, how do you know which one is right?" It is the purpose of this work to answer these and other questions.

This issue was stirred in my heart about 10 years ago when a sister-in-law called me at home and said, "I saw a lady, Gail Riplinger, on Action Sixties (a Christian T.V. program in Tampa, FL anchored by Herman and Sharon Bailey) this afternoon who said the new versions were corrupted and the King James Version was the real WORDS OF GOD." What a shock to me! I had been teaching a Sunday school class to middle aged men at the First Baptist Church in New Port Richey, FL, and had been using the New American Standard Version (NASV) of the Bible. My reaction was like so many others I have encountered since that time who have been shocked by similar statements. Their first reaction after the shock is to say one of two things. 1. "I'm not going to change the version I have been using." 2. "My pastor uses 'this new version' or 'that new version' so why should I change?" Obviously I was incredulous, also. I did not want to change versions. I had heard and thought the King James Bible (KJB) was "difficult to read".

I set out to investigate why someone would say that the KJB is the Words of God. After 10 years of study and reading as time would allow, I have come to some definite conclusions. Read on!

THE METHOD USED TO INVESTIGATE

The place to start in order to research a problem, question, or difficulty is with the Words of God. So many of us get this backwards. We start with a problem, jump to a conclusion, formulate a plan, and then turn to the Scriptures. What so often happens as a result is to look for verses that confirm our position. This is similar to a faulty scientific method, or reminds me of what happens in a doctor's office all too often. Let me explain an acronym, SOAP, that we often use to record patient's visits to a doctors office. When a patient comes to a doctors office with complaints we record those as subjective, the "S" in SOAP. After hearing the complaints, or symptoms, and taking a patient's present and past medical history, the next step is to collect objective information, the "O" in SOAP. This information is primarily a physical exam. This is the part where we listen with a stethoscope, push and pull the patient, and look **very carefully**. The next step is to form an assessment or a preliminary diagnosis, the "A" in SOAP. Based on these steps a physician orders a laboratory or x-ray examination called the plan, the "P" in SOAP. That's where SOAP comes from. If any of these steps are skipped, a physician risks making a wrong final diagnosis. Young doctors in training have a tendency to jump to the assessment or diagnosis before taking a careful history and examining the patient. The years that doctors dedicate to training help them to stay focused without skipping steps.

Another point I consider crucial to an investigation of the Words of God is to let the Holy Ghost act as an X-Ray. He penetrates to the deep things of God, revealing the truth, just as an X-ray penetrates deep within the flesh of a patient revealing hidden disease. Those of you reading this work, who are saved, will remember something astonishing. Before you were saved and received the Holy Ghost, understanding or discerning the Words of God was impossible. Paul said in 1 Cor. 2:14 "But the natural man receiveth not the things of the Spirit of God: for they are foolishness unto him: neither can he know them, because they are spiritually discerned." I plead with you to discern with the Spirit.

THE PATIENT

The patient in this work is the Bible. The subjective complaint is: "That the words of the Holy Bible have been corrupted or spoiled or changed, or added to, or removed or 'infected" in many commentaries, versions, or works. We know that infection spreads rapidly unless it is checked. Paul said in Galatians 5:9 A little leaven leaveneth the whole lump. and in 1 Cor. 5:6-7 Your glorying is not good. Know ye not that a little leaven leaveneth the whole lump? **Purge out** therefore the old leaven, that ye may be a new lump, as ye are unleavened. For even Christ our Passover is sacrificed for us: A physician knows that infection must be purged; that is it must be drained, cut out or destroyed by antibiotics. Similarly, leaven or sin influencing the Words of the Bible must be "drained," "cut out," "removed," "destroyed," "purged" or avoided to keep it from spreading, or influencing our lives, or the lives of others.

Returning to our patient, the Bible, we must determine if it has been corrupted or infected. We must take a history and do a physical. We must examine the Words **carefully** and see if they are sick. We must take a **very careful history** and vigilantly examine the Words just like you would want a doctor to scrutinize you in a matter of life or death because objective or physical signs are sometimes subtle. However, this exam is even more important than a doctor's examination of a patient, because if we get this wrong, someone may be effected for eternity. This is one reason I have such great respect for pastors. The seriousness of the subject matter they are handling would scare any reasonably thoughtful person.

CAREFUL EXAM

Gail Riplinger noted in the introduction to her book, *New Age Bible Versions*, the following quote by "Herman Hoskier, the world's pre-eminent manuscript scholar who observed:

> Rough comparison can seldom, if ever, be of any real use, the exact collation of documents, ancient or modern with the Received Text, is the necessary foundation *of all scientific criticism."[1]*

Why would he state that one must compare all documents with the Received Text for proper "scientific" textual criticism? Obviously, there must be a standard to compare, but he must believe the **Received Greek Text[2] (RT) of Scripture** is the gold standard. It's not surprising Hoskier trusts and believes the Received Text. Listen to some of the verses from the Bible version based on the RT text, which is accepted by many as preserving the text of the original autographs (writings). Psalm 119:89 For ever, O LORD, thy word is settled in heaven. If the Words are not being changed in heaven, then Jesus Christ did not change the Words when He gave them to us to be used on earth. As a matter of fact when Jesus Christ was here, this is what He said, Matthew 24:35 Heaven and earth shall pass away, but my words shall not pass away. Sounds to me like His Words will be around forever. He also said in another passage, Matthew 5:17-18 Think not that I am come to destroy the law, or the prophets: I am not come to destroy, but to fulfil. [18] For verily I say unto you, Till heaven and earth pass, one jot or one tittle shall in no wise pass from the law, till all be fulfilled. Please understand that Jesus did fulfill all that He was prophesied to fulfill, but there are other prophecies to be fulfilled that are still pending. There

---

[1] Riplinger, Gail A.; *New Age Bible Versions;* A.V. Publications, Munroe Falls, Ohio; ISBN 0-9635845-0-2; 4th printing, 1994; p. 4

[2] The Received Text is the original language text handed down from independent Baptist church to independent Baptist church

are "things to come".[1] He said not one jot or tittle shall be lost from His Words until all is fulfilled. A jot and tittle are the smallest marks in the Hebrew written language. He was affirming the preservation of the Bible to the smallest detail until "**all be fulfilled**". Jesus was also affirming the **Hebrew** Old Testament by the Words in this passage. (Mat 5:17) "The Law and Prophets" was a *phrase or idiom* used by the Hebrews to refer to the Scripture *received* by them. The "Law and the Prophets" was arranged as the Law, the Prophets, and The Writings. (We will discuss the Received Text passed along by the Priesthood of Believers and how it has been preserved in detail later in this work.)

Since God in Christ Jesus said these things and much much more about His Words, is it any small wonder Herman Hoskier said the above? Many others have also affirmed the preservation of God's Words by the churches throughout history, as we shall see.

Now, let's return to an evaluation of our patient and obtain a history.

[1] Pentecost, J. Dwight; *Things to Come;* Dunham Publishing Co., Grand Rapids, Mich.; ISBN 0-310-30890-9; 1958

HISTORY

THE SUBJECTIVE

The definition of the subjective when gathering information about a patient is broken down into the complaints (symptoms) or statement of the problem, and the history of the complaint. The duration of the complaint and the intensity of the symptoms are all important.

Statement of the Problems or Complaints

1. The Words of God have been challenged since the Garden of Eden.
2. There are conflicting manuscripts in Hebrew, Greek, and Aramaic, the original languages of the Bible.
3. Inspiration and preservation of the Scriptures are a matter of personal interpretation.
4. Unholy hands have been on the Bible.
5. Lies, fabrications, and deception have been involved in the effort to establish the "right" Hebrew and Greek texts based on the recent discovery of older manuscripts.
6. "King James Only" or "Only King James" scholars and supporters are inadequately trained and superficial and cultic.
7. Only unintentional errors are responsible for the manuscript differences.
8. There are no significant doctrinal differences between the new versions (such as NIV, NASB, New Living Bible) and the old ones such as the KJB.
9. Compiling all the changes made in the words of new versions seems to point to a sinister new age philosophy being introduced into the Scriptures.
10. All the new versions are bad.
11. One of the major reasons for the new versions is to make money.
12. People get saved reading the new versions so there is nothing wrong

with them.
13.   The Scriptures were providentially preserved.
14.   Modern scholarship is better because of better technology.
15.   The new versions have caused confusion in the churches.
16.   Many theories abound as to the transmission of copies of the original texts.
17.   The King James translators did not have enough knowledge or manuscripts to do a good job.

THE HISTORY OF THE PROBLEM

The above list consists of just some of the complaints, also called the statement of the problems, which I have heard or read. However, the list is adequate enough to begin an investigation or history into the questions and declarations concerning the text of the Scripture. The history of a problem is important, is sometimes long, and is sometimes boring, but is imperative to begin to understand "troubles."

Physicians need to know how long a complaint has been present, as well as the location of the "pain", the persistence of the "pain", and the radiation of the "pain". Similarly, if there is infection (corruption), what is the origin of the corruption, where did it spread, and where has it persisted. Family history is, also, very important. We want to know if the problem could have been "passed on" in the family. Did the patient have any surgery? Was some "part" cut out? If the physical "part" such as a gallbladder is gone then that helps answer a lot of questions about whether the complaints are related to that physical "part." The occupation of the patient is important in this situation for two reasons: 1. The patient may have been exposed to a chemical, an infection, or a toxic substance. 2. If the patient was exposed to adverse substances, then keeping others from being exposed becomes very important. The social history tells us a lot about the person. How has he adjusted to life? Does he have any addictions such as alcohol, cigarettes, or drugs? What is the quantity and quality of the exposure? Is he stable mentally?

And lastly, a "review of systems" is performed, whereby the physician asks numerous provocative questions. He literally starts with the head and goes to the feet and lists *positive* and *negative* responses to his questions.

WHERE DID THE PROBLEM BEGIN?

Now, in relation to the transmission and preservation of God's Words we want to know similar things. Were the manuscripts handled with care? Was any surgery done to them? Was there confusion related to their reproduction and transmission? Were they exposed to any toxic influence of evil forces? Were the manuscripts exposed to scribes, philosophers, or teachers who had drug, alcohol, or mental problems? Many problems are caused by addictions and their influence on society. These kinds of problems (addictions) would undoubtedly have an influence on proper handling of the manuscripts themselves as well as their translation. Drunkenness is another form of leaven mentioned in the Bible. What was the occupation and experience of those involved in the history of the manuscripts? Were the manuscripts exposed to the infection of sin (leaven) known as heresy? The history of the problem will examine the ancient men and manuscripts; then proceed to the modern men and manuscripts.

Is there evidence of manipulation or change in Scripture dating from early history? If there is, then a case could be made for this disease or infection of the Scripture (corruption or leaven) continuing into modern times.

SATAN CHANGED GOD'S WORDS

Examining the passages of Scripture related to the seduction of Adam and Eve in the Garden reveals that the "old serpent" removed, added to, and changed the words God had spoken to Adam and Eve. In other words, **Satan corrupted God's Words**. Clearly, this passage in Genesis is the explanation of the fall of man, and is also an example of how **easily** "man" can be led astray by the alteration of God's Words.

Genesis 2:16-17:

And the LORD God commanded the man, saying, Of every tree of the garden thou mayest freely eat: [17] But of the tree of the knowledge of good and evil, thou shalt not eat of it: for in the day that thou eatest thereof **thou shalt surely die**.

These two verses are very clear. There is no question about what Adam and Eve were commanded to do. The consequence of disobedience was also clear. However, along came the cleverest serpent and he said,

Genesis 3:1:

Now the serpent was more **subtil** than any beast of the field which the LORD God had made. And he said unto the woman, Yea, hath God said, Ye shall not eat of every tree of the garden?

Satan was **taunting** Eve because she could not eat of every tree. He was tempting her to claim she could eat of every tree. He was appealing to her pride. And in addition, Satan **changed** God's Words and said in

Genesis 3:4:

And the serpent said unto the woman, **Ye shall not surely die**:

Remember what God said, "thou shalt surely die."

Genesis 2:17:

But of the tree of the knowledge of good and evil, thou shalt not eat of it: for in the day that thou eatest thereof **thou shalt surely die**.

One reason God gave us this account was as an example of His enemy corrupting or "infecting" His Words. Remember, this event occurred at the very beginning of Scripture and mankind. He seems to have placed the model in the Scriptures to alert us that this would be a constant problem throughout the existence of man on earth. His Words would be changed at the beckoning of our common enemy, that "old serpent", the Devil.

Man is so gullible. Man believed the "change" in the Words of God by Satan in the Garden of Eden. The changing of God's Words brought about the fall of man with all the consequences. If God's words have continued to be corrupted, what damage might be happening? If Satan lied about God's Words, could he still be "lying" and causing havoc? Who is the father of lies? [Jn. 8:44]

The Devil pulled the same kind of "tricks" again during Jesus' wilderness experience. He manipulated the Words of God. Isn't it interesting that God's Words place this manipulation at the transition into the "Church Age" about 2000 years ago? He was indicating this would continue to be a problem during this phase of man's existence. The phase that began with the appearance of the God-man, the Lord Jesus Christ, His death by the shedding of His blood on the Cross, and His resurrection.

Matthew 4:2-10

And when he had fasted forty days and forty nights, he was afterward an hungered. [3] And when the tempter came to him, he said, If thou be the Son of God, command that these stones be made bread. [4] But he answered and said, **It is written,** Man shall not live by bread alone, but by every word that proceedeth out of the mouth of God. [5] Then the devil taketh him up into the holy city, and setteth him on a pinnacle of the temple, [6] And saith unto him, If thou be the Son of God, cast thyself down: for it is written, He shall give his angels charge concerning thee: and in their hands they shall bear thee up, lest at any time thou dash thy foot against a stone. [7] Jesus said unto him, *It is written* again, Thou shalt not tempt the Lord thy God. [8] Again, the devil taketh him up into an exceeding high mountain, and sheweth him all the kingdoms of the world, and the glory of them; [9] And saith unto him, All these things will I give thee, if thou wilt fall down and worship me. [10] Then saith Jesus unto him, Get thee hence, Satan: for **it is written,** Thou shalt worship the Lord thy God, and him only shalt thou serve.

Satan conveniently left out of his quote in Matthew 4:6 "to keep thee in all thy ways" which is found in Psalm 91:11. The Psalm correctly stated says, "For he shall give his angels charge over thee, to keep thee in all thy ways"…. So we see there is evidence of Scriptural manipulation by Satan. Do you believe Satan could spiritually influence someone to change, add to, or remove God's Words today?

GOD'S WORDS STILL PRESENT

Dr. Waite points out that the verb tense of "It is written" (verse 4) is the perfect tense, meaning the action was begun in the past and is continuing to the present. Jesus was indicating that the Words of God were recorded in the past and those very Words written by Moses about 1500 years previously were still present and preserved when Jesus was in the wilderness.[1]

Almost every book of the Bible has been attacked in relation to its origin, author, and words. Some scholars believe that many writings were falsified or recorded at later dates than internal evidence in a book suggests. For example the JEDP theory is a hypothesis that the Pentateuch was written by four (4) different writers instead of Moses being the author. It is also called the Graf-Welhausin documentary hypothesis of the Pentateuch.[2]

Any prophecy in the Bible that is recognized as being given before the actual event occurring has always been attacked, and severely, because non-believers cannot accept an omniscient God. Therefore, in order to promote their disbelief and undermine the Words of God, they have proposed pseudo-authors that allegedly wrote **after** the events occurred. Over time all of these "theories" (or a better term for them would be heresies) have been debunked.

2 Peter 2:1-3 But there were false prophets also among the people, even as there shall be false teachers among you, who privily shall bring in damnable **heresies**, even denying the Lord that bought them, and bring upon themselves swift destruction.

---

[1] Waite, Th.D., Ph.D., D.A.; *Defending the King James Bible ;* The Bible For Today Press; Collingswood, NJ; ISBN 1-56848-000-8; 1995; pp. 9-11

[2] Hills, Th.D., Edward F; *The King James Version Defended;* The Christian Research Press, Des Moines, Iowa; ISBN 0-915923-00-9; Reprint 1993; p. 75

DEAD SEA SCROLL CONCERNS

Another concern for the Christian is the history of the Dead Sea scrolls. The Holman Bible Dictionary reports:

"Dead Sea Scrolls were discovered between 1947 and 1960 in a cave on the western Dead Sea shore near a ruin called *khirbet Qumran*. Eleven caves from the Qumran area have since yielded manuscripts, mostly in small fragments. About sixty percent of the scrolls have so far been published. These were composed or copied between 200 B.C. and A.D. 70, mostly around the lifetime of Jesus, by a small community living at Qumran. The contents comprise three main kinds of literature: (1) copies of Old Testament books, the oldest we now possess; (2) some non-biblical Jewish books known from elsewhere (such as 1 Enoch and Jubilees), probably written by the Essenes; (3) the community's own compositions, including: biblical commentaries (for example, on Habakkuk and Nahum), which interpret biblical prophecies as applying to the community and its times; rules of community conduct; and liturgical writings such as prayers and hymns.

The Qumran community belonged to the Essenes, one of four major Jewish religious movements described by the first century A.D. historian Josephus, but, strangely, unmentioned in the New Testament. The origins of the Essenes are uncertain: one major view is that they descended from the "Pious," who had fought for religious independence with the Maccabees; another view is that they originated in Exile in Babylonia, returning to Palestine sometime in the third or second century B.C. They opposed the cultic laws operating at the Temple, rejecting its priesthood, and following a different calendar. They lived apart from other Jews in strictly-disciplined groups. One such rather special group lived at Qumran. Unlike many Essene groups, they were celibates, and they traced their origin to a "Teacher of Righteousness," a messianic figure of whom little is known except that he was a priest, possibly a high priest. The Qumran biblical commentaries speak of his confrontation with a "Wicked Priest," possibly a Maccabean high priest of about 150 B.C.

The Scrolls show a surprising variety of beliefs, accounted for by two hundred years of community history, beginning with a belief in an eminent [sic] "end of days" which faded as the fulfilment did not materialize. Like other Essenes, they believed that by observing their own interpretation of the Jewish law and by frequent ritual bathing they preserved a faithful remnant. Thus they were ready for the restoration of the land by God, who would punish the wicked through two messiahs—one priestly, one lay. They had an interest in angels, astrology, and prophetic prediction. Peculiar to Qumran was a dualistic view of the world in which God had appointed an angel of light (one of his names being Melchizedek; see Genesis 14; Hebrews 7) and an angel of darkness to govern the world, all persons being assigned to the realm of one or the other. They also avoided the Temple and developed distinctive liturgical beliefs and practices based on a communion between earthly and angelic worship."[1]

Gail Riplinger reports that the Essenes who were responsible for the scrolls were essentially a cult.[2] They were opposed to the animal sacrificial system of the Old Testament commanded by God and they were opposed to a New Testament Messiah. She reports as a demonstration one passage in Leviticus 24:11 And *the Israelitish woman's son blasphemed the name of the LORD, and cursed. And they brought him unto Moses: (and his mother's name was Shelomith, the daughter of Dibri, of the tribe of Dan:)*, where they dropped the "name of the Lord" and substituted just the word, "Name".[3] As she rightly reports, the Luciferian movement uses "Name" as a code for their god and those in the future who will not take the "Name" should be killed. The Dead Sea scrolls reflect this same philosophy and some of the scrolls say that if the "Name" is not received over a 7-year period (? the time of Jacob's Trouble) they should be killed. The "Name" could be that deceiver referred to in the New Testament as the Antichrist. However, the Dead Sea scrolls were written before the New Testament. So the Essenes may have been heretics or a cult who were

---

[1] *Holman Bible Dictionary*; "Dead Sea Scrolls;" Holman Bible Publisher Database; © Navpress Software; 1997

[2] Some authors are trying to elevate the status of the Essene community to a sect like the Pharisees or Sadducees of Jesus' day instead of being a cult. The reason seems to be to elevate their corrupted Scripture to replace books of the Bible, claiming their materials are closer to the "real" Bible of Jesus day. See *The Canon Debate*; by McDonald and Sanders, Hendrickson Publishers, 2002; chapter 1

[3] Riplinger, Gail; *Which Bible Is God's Words;* Hearthstone Publishing, Oklahoma City, OK; ISBN 1-879366-81-9; 1994; p.27 This author is aware of the criticism in the 'literature' concerning Riplinger's work.

corrupting the Scripture. The Revelator, John, explained that those who do not worship the "beast" during the tribulation, which is also called the seventieth week of Daniel, would also be beheaded. It seems the Essenes may have had the same philosophical approach to life as the coming antichrist.

Rev. 20:4 And I saw thrones, and they sat upon them, and judgment was given unto them: and I saw the **souls of them that were beheaded for the witness of Jesus**, and for the word of God, and which had not worshipped the beast, neither his image, neither had received his mark upon their foreheads, or in their hands; and they lived and reigned with Christ a thousand years.

TWO PATHS

Now if there were very many instances of changing, adding to, or subtracting from (corrupting) Words in Scripture as the Essenes did, it would be very troubling. Before examining other passages in Scripture that may have been corrupted, however, let us review important men in history who have had an influence on the patient (the Bible) either directly or indirectly.

Isn't it interesting that there always seems to be two paths, two gates, two doors, two ways to choose? A patient can choose to live a life of debauchery and have significant medical problems or to live a healthy life with much less risk of significant disease. If the manuscripts the Bible is based upon were carried along one route by **the priesthood of believers,** it would be protected and preserved. If the manuscripts took another path and fell into the hands of heretics, it would be severely injured and scarred.

Two choices remind us of the Scripture, Matthew 7:13-14 Enter ye in at the strait gate: for wide is the gate, and broad is the way, that leadeth to destruction, and many there be which go in thereat: Because strait is the gate, and narrow is the way, which leadeth unto life, and few there be that find it.

The two choices presented are specific. One way is narrow, but not difficult or hidden; yet, few will find it. The other way is broad and wide; and, there will be many who will find it. And so it seems the men who have had an opportunity to preserve or corrupt the manuscripts the Bible is based upon have chosen either the strait gate or the wide gate.

If one looks at the accounts in the Bible, two paths can generally be identified. Cain chose the broad way before the flood, and after the flood Ham, Noah's son, continued along the same broad path. The descendants of Isaac's son, Esau, also chose the path of idolatry and apostasy. The problems associated with Esau's route are still being felt in Israel and Jerusalem, which has become known as "the cup of trembling" (ISA 51:17) by Christians. The Palestinian war with Israel is a direct result of the wrong path Esau took. That path leads through Edom to the Islamic nations of today.

In more recent times the "wide gate" has also caused many problems in America associated with humanism, philosophy, and the wisdom of the world. The Scriptures warn us about these problems. Col. 2:8 Beware lest any man spoil you through philosophy and vain deceit, after the tradition of men, after the rudiments of the world, and not after Christ. These problems will be explored extensively in this work because they are associated with the transmission of the original language manuscripts or texts and they are associated with dramatic changes in our society, churches, and individuals, particularly teenagers and young adults. These changes will be linked to the problem of "**Poly-Scripturae**" [many Scriptures]. They will be linked to the "two paths."

The next section examines the history of men associated with the symptoms, complaints, and alterations in the Scriptures.

The Wide Gate History: The Men

Matthew 7:13-14 *Enter ye in at the <u>strait</u> gate: for <u>wide</u> is the gate, and <u>broad</u> is the way, that leadeth to destruction, and <u>many</u> there be which go in thereat:* Because <u>strait</u> *is* the gate, and <u>narrow</u> *is* the way, which leadeth unto life, and <u>few</u> there be that find it.

Matthew 7:21-22 Not every one that saith unto me, Lord, Lord, shall enter into the kingdom of heaven; but he that doeth the will of my Father which is in heaven. Many will say to me in that day, Lord, Lord, have we not prophesied in thy name? and in thy name have cast out devils? and in thy name done many wonderful works?

(There are charts in the appendices which may prove helpful to the readers of this section.)

THE PHILOSOPHERS

Three Greek philosophers, Socrates (471-399 B.C.), Plato (427-347 B.C.), and Aristotle (384-322 B.C.) swayed some men who have had a great influence on the preservation of Scripture. The statements of these men reflect this influence. Those statements will be reported at the appropriate time.

First, let us examine the philosophy of Socrates' student, Plato (427 B.C.-347 B.C.), who taught Aristotle. Plato was a homosexual who taught the concept of "the ideal Republic". In his Republic he "prescribed among other things, socialism, selective breeding, contraception, infanticide, and the kidnaping of children from their parents for a 20-year period of state-controlled values clarification. (Sound familiar?) Throw in capital punishment for dissenters and you have the basics"[1] of his teaching.

The preceding gives one a sense of a few of their incredible ideas.

"Plato was a despiser of the God of Moses and tried to remake God in the image of Plato. He taught a counterfeit trinity: first the absolute pure being incomprehensible to man's mind; second, the Logos or Universal Reason or Divine Nous; and third, the Soul of the World which proceeded from the Logos."[2]

The trinity taught by Plato was not equal. The Logos was a created being. This form of thinking gave rise to *Arianism* that taught that Jesus Christ was a created being and he subsequently created the Holy Spirit. The heresies of *Socinianism* and *Unitarianism* were also children of this world philosophy. Alexandria of Egypt was the place where these heresies were incubated. Socinianism taught Christ was not God and Unitarianism pronounced there was no trinity, only God the father, a combination of Arianism and Socinianism.

---

[1] Grady, Th.D., Th.M., D.D., William P.; *Final Authority A Christian's Guide to the King James Bible;* Grady Publications, Inc., Schererville, Indiana; Sixth Printing, 1995; p. 82

[2] Sightler, M.D., James H.; *Tabernacle Essays on Bible Translation;* Sightler Publications; Greenville, SC; 1993; p6

PHILOSOPHERS' INFLUENCE

The infections (leaven) or corrupt ideas started by the unholy trinity of Socrates, Plato, and Aristotle, were carried over into the time of Christ by a Jew, Philo Judaeus (about 20 B.C. – A.D. 50). He was writing literature that amalgamated Jewish sacred Scripture (the Old Testament) and the writings of Plato. He was known for use of allegory. A member of a wealthy Jewish family in Alexandria, Egypt, he was well educated in Greek schools. Philo's writings—particularly his commentaries on the Scriptures—influenced the early church. He believed literal interpretation was sufficient for the average scholar, but for the enlightened ones such as himself, he advocated an allegorical interpretation. His harmonization of Judaism and Platonism gave rise to Neoplatonism. The essences of his teachings were: 1. the Logos or Reason created the universe, not God or the Absolute. 2. the Logos was assisted by a number of intermediate beings known as the Pleroma. 3. the account of the creation in Genesis was a myth, and only reflected how the creation was conceived in the mind of God.

Philo influenced Pantaenus (c. 181 A.D.) who founded and taught theologians at the infamous Catechetical School at Alexandria, Egypt. Pantaenus was noted for being one of the "deepest Gnostics". One of his students was Clement of Alexandria (A.D. 150-217), a "church father" who subsequently educated Origen (182-251 A.D.) and who felt honored to be called a Gnostic. Clement believed Plato was inspired because his writings contained the truth. His great mission was to show the bridge between the Gospel and wisdom of Gentiles and to show how a believer could rise to the position of a true Gnostic.[1]

THE WORST STUDENT

Origen, his student,

> "was probably the worst heretic and perverter of scripture in history and who sided with Arius in his teachings that Jesus

---

[1] Grady, William P.; *Final Authority;* p. 82

was a created being not eternally generated."[1]

He also denied a literal Hell and a physical resurrection. His mental faculties may have also been affected by his self-mutilation, the act of castrating himself out of a misinterpretation of Matthew 19:12 *For there are some eunuchs, which were so born from their mother's womb: and there are some eunuchs, which were made eunuchs of men: and there be eunuchs, which have made themselves eunuchs for the kingdom of heaven's sake. He that is able to receive it, let him receive it.* If he had only read Deuteronomy 23:1 *He that is wounded in the stones, or hath his privy member cut off, shall not enter into the congregation of the LORD,* he could have saved himself a lot of pain.[2]

Whether Origen actually changed the manuscripts of the Scriptures is not known for sure, but his prolific writings quote over 30,000 references to the Words that may have been quoted wrongly in order to "mesh" them with his scheme of belief. However, the manuscripts he used are impossible to establish, the same thing being true of his devoted follower, Eusebius (260-341 A.D.). Wilbur Pickering, quoting Zundz's *"The Text"*, says:

> "The insuperable difficulties opposing the establishment of "the" New Testament text of Origen and Eusebius are well known to all who have attempted it...Leaving aside the common difficulties imposed by the uncertainties of the transmission, the incompleteness of the material, and the **frequent freedom of quotation**, there is the incontestable fact that these two Fathers are frequently at variance; that each of them quotes the same passage differently in different writings; and that sometimes they do so even within the compass of one and the same work...Wherever one and the same passage is extant in more than one quotation by Origen or Eusebius, variation between them is the rule rather than the exception."[3]

Origen also believed in the preexistence of the human soul, regeneration by baptism, infant sprinkling, and transubstantiation. He alleged that Satan was paid a ransom by Christ's death, which allowed a "mystical kiss", whatever that means. He allegorically dismissed the Passover, Jesus' wilderness temptation, and the purging of Herod's temple. He accepted the Apocrypha and attributed the "Shepherd of Hermas" to inspiring his allegorical system. He had very little faith in the Scriptures. He said:

> "I do not condemn them (authors of Scripture) if they even

---

[1] Sightler, M.D., James H.; *Tabernacle Essays on Bible Translation;* p. 6-7

[2] Grady, Th.D., Th.M., D.D., William P.; *Final Authority;* p. 90

[3] Pickering, Wilbur N.; *The Identity Of The New Testament Text;* Publisher, Thomas Nelson, Nashville, TN; 1980; p. 64

sometimes dealt freely with things which to the eye of history happened differently, and changed them so as to subserve the mystical aims they had in view; so as to speak of a thing which happened in a certain place, as if it happened in another, or what took place at a certain time, as if it had taken place at another time, and to introduce into what was spoken in a certain way some changes of their own. They proposed to speak the truth where it was possible both materially and spiritually, and where this was not possible it was their intention to prefer the spiritual to the material. The spiritual truth was often preserved, as one might say, in the material falsehood."[1]

The preceding quote is from Origen, who has been so venerated by many scholars throughout history.

Origen was finally run out of Alexandria due to his heretical views and settled in Caesarea, a city on the edge of Judea and Syria. Here he established another school and library. After his death, Pamphilus (240-309 A.D.), his pupil, continued to catalog his extensive writings; and the library he established was the repository of Origen's famous book called the *Hexapla*. The *Hexapla* of Origen contained six versions of the Bible in Hebrew and Greek, side by side for comparison, and it is suspected of being the source of the very important manuscripts, Aleph (also called Sinaiticus) and B (also called Vaticanus), in the battle for the preserved Words of the Bible. The new head of Origen's Palestinian school after his death was his trusted student, Pamphilus, who became the mentor and teacher, amazingly, of Eusebius, the Bishop of Caesarea. Eusebius is closely connected with Emperor Constantine.

After the emperor of Rome, Constantine, was "converted" to Christianity on the battlefield in the early 4th century by a vision of a cross, he appointed Eusebius to produce the Bible for the empire. Incidentally, the same library Eusebius used to *produce* the Bible, became the source of Jerome's research that produced the Latin Vulgate. Eusebius produced the very important New Testament codices, Vaticanus, also known as B, and Sinaiticus, also known as Aleph.[2] When Constantine ordered 50 new "Bibles" made by Eusebius (now named Eusebius Pamphili after his mentor), he went to Pamphilus' Caesarean library and worked with numerous copyists to fill the order. Dean John William Burgon (1813-1888 A.D.), one of the world's great textual scholars, surmises,

"Constantine applied to Eusebius for fifty handsome copies amongst which it is not improbable that the manuscripts...B and Aleph were to be actually found."

And that such an opinion was not restricted to Majority advocates (this

---

[1] Grady, Th.D., Th.M., D.D., William P.; *Final Authority;* p. 94

[2] Sightler, M.D., James H.; *Tabernacle Essays on the Bible;* p. 7

will be explained later) is evidenced by Constantine Tischendorf's (1815-1874) (another textual scholar) euphoric speculation that

"Is it possible that this Bible (Aleph) could be one of the 50 copies which Emperor Constantine ordered Eusebius to place in Constantinople, his new capital?"[1]

The old saying comes to mind, "Where there is smoke, there is fire." There are many other reasons that Burgon and Tischendorf concluded Eusebius made the codices. We will deal with those facts later in the section on manuscripts.

PHILOSOPHERS' INFLUENCE ON ALLEGED "OLDEST AND BEST" MANUSCRIPTS

Following the above very important persons (VIPs), Plato, Origen, and Eusebius, in the history of the wide gate, we will skip to the 19th century and the alleged "*rediscovery*" of the Aleph and Sinaiticus codices (animal hides used for writing made into "books"). However, the influence of the VIPs has continued to be exerted as we will discover below.

The Aleph and B manuscripts or codices were considered lost by many significant "scholars" for about 1500 years until they were "found.". They were hailed as "the oldest and best" manuscripts. However, as we will see, the readings of the "lost" manuscripts were known, and had been rejected. The codices had remarkable defacement and corruption; and they had obviously been manipulated. These names of these two manuscripts should be known by every Bible believing saint because they have caused so many difficulties for us in the last 150 years. The production of the manuscripts were obviously influenced greatly by the Greek philosophers, Plato et al, the Jewish Neoplatonist, Philo, and the Gnostic and Arian, Origin.

Many authorities believe the manuscripts (codices) survived because of their rejection by the vulgate (common) church, (i.e. they were put in storage and not used) or perhaps, because of their lack of use by the new church of the empire, the Roman Catholic Church. Whatever the case, Jerome (A.D. 347-419) used them in the preparation of the Latin Vulgate (A.D. 405), the Bible of Roman Catholicism until the Vatican II council (1962-1965) . There will be an extensive discussion concerning the Latin Vulgate under the heading: *THE BROAD WAY: The Manuscripts.*

---

[1] Grady, Th.D., Th.M., D.D., William P; *Final Authority*; p. 110

HISTORY OF THE DEVELOPMENT OF TEXTUAL CRITICISM

Several men were enthusiastically involved in the alleged "rediscovery" of the B and Aleph codices in the 19th century. They idolized the manuscripts. The principal players were: 1. Brooke Foss Westcott (1828-1903) 2. Fenton John Anthony Hort (1828-1892) and 3. Constantine Tischendorf (1815-1874).

Tischendorf was a German textual scholar who had been influenced by the rationalistic thinking of his age. The development of rationalistic textual criticism is interesting. The invention of the printing press by Gutenberg in 1452 allowed men like Erasmus (1466-1536), Stephanus (1503-1559), Calvin (1509-1564) and Beza (1519-1605) in the early Reformation period to begin listing differences in manuscripts in the margins. However, they accepted the Greek Traditional and Hebrew Masoretic texts, which the majority of churches in Syria, Italy, France, Spain, and Germany used. **There were few differences in the texts.** What differences were present in the original language texts, they considered "accidental" differences. They (Erasmus et al) approached the texts in a more theological way; that is, God preserved the texts. They did not consider that emendations (additions) were in the text or added to the text on purpose by scribes. They only tried to establish the correct readings. They were not enthusiastic, to say the least, about the Latin Vulgate of Jerome and the Roman Church.

However, in the early age of rationalism, Hugo Grotius (1583-1645), a famous theologian and statesman from Holland, began making speculative changes in the text like one would with a secular book. Another Dutchman, Stephen Courelles, continued this trend that alarmed "the faithful" and drew new attention to the New Testament Text.

John Fell from Oxford in 1675 suggested ways the scribes may have changed the text and, so, Gerhard von Maestricht published a list of 43 rules in 1711 to deal with those alleged mistakes. Subsequently, attention was shifted away from the original Apostolic authors to uninspired scribes according to Edward F. Hills, one of history's finest textual critics.[1] Shortly thereafter searches began for the "oldest" manuscripts in order to establish a completely 'new' (altered) Greek text that would replace the traditional Greek text accepted by the dissenters from the Roman Catholic Church.

A Cambridge scholar by the name of Richard Bently (1662-1742) planned a "thoroughly naturalistic method" of textual criticism in the hope of

---

[1] Hills, Edward F.; *The King James Version Defended; pp. 62-63*

reproducing the N.T. Greek text supposedly available at the time of the Council of Nicea (325 A.D.) and supposedly subsequently lost.[1] Adding to the parameters of textual criticism was J. A. Bengal (1687-1752). He felt the hardest reading should be preferred over the easiest reading. This caused quite a stir in Germany amongst the orthodox Christians. I suppose orthodox churches were insulted by the implication that the Saints could not understand the more difficult readings; and so the scribes had chosen an easier reading and therefore corrupted the manuscripts.

THE ATTITUDE OF "SCHOLARS"

Incidentally, this same attitude persists today amongst "scholars". While preparing this work, the author encountered many disparaging remarks concerning Saints who have investigated the two paths that the texts of the New Testament had taken. Here is an example found on the "Advent.com" Internet site:

"One must be careful in assessing people who ….are *not* textual critics, and do not engage in textual criticism. Anyone...who claims providential preservation or some kind of divine sanction for a particular text, is not and cannot be a textual critic. It is unfortunate that these non-critics have infected the arguments about the... text, as their irrational, unreasonable, and uncritical arguments serve only to muddy what should be a reasonable and fruitful debate. It is even more unfortunate that some legitimate critics … have accepted their rhetoric. This argument, like all critical arguments, must be decided based on evidence and logic, not faith or claims of what "must" be so. The typical argument is "providential preservation" -- the claim that God *must* have preserved the original text in all its purity. But as Harry A. Sturz (who is about as sympathetic to the Byzantine text as anyone can be while not being a pure Byzantine-prioritist) notes, "Hills [the leading exponent of this sort of preservation] fails to show why the sovereign God *must* act in a particular way [Harry A. Sturz, *The Byzantine Text-Type & New Testament Textual Criticism* (1984), p. 42. Italics added.]"[2]

No one can show why God acts in a certain way. God says: "For my

---

[1] Ibid, p. 64

[2] Internet site: Advent.com

thoughts are not your thoughts, neither are your ways my ways, saith the LORD" (Isaiah 55:8)

If you read the quote above closely, you immediately realize Harry Sturz has no concept of **the priesthood of believers** and needs to be reminded of 1 Peter 2:9. *But ye are a chosen generation, a royal priesthood, an holy nation, a peculiar people; that ye should shew forth the praises of him who hath called you out of darkness into his marvellous light:* and Col. 2:8 *Beware lest any man spoil you through philosophy and vain deceit, after the tradition of men, after the rudiments of the world, and not after Christ.* Further along in this same article, the same author makes an equally confusing statement that the path of the text preferred by believers in the Textus Receptus "does **not** show the sort of massive inferiority" implied by others in the textual debate. Perhaps he is now trying to sooth roughed-up feathers. I wonder if there is anything ecumenical in his statement?

Surely the attitude of J. A. Bengal must have been as confusing and condescending to the orthodox Saints in Bengal's day as the above author is today. No wonder the German Saints rose up in disdain. The broad path continued, however, with the encouragement of a Prussian philosopher king, Frederick II who ruled 46 years (1740-1786). Cynicism toward the Biblical texts progressed and Johann Semler (1725-1795) maintained the concept that the Scriptures contained only "Jewish conceptions of merely local and temporal value which it was the task of scientific exegesis to point out."[1] He also believed the manuscripts had been corrupted by the scribes with their own additions, subtractions, and changes.

A student of Semler, J. J. Griesbach (1745-1812) was so infected with Semler's thinking that he believed the New Testament was contaminated by more glosses, interpolations and additions than any other manuscript. He further added the rule, that "The most suspicious reading of all is the one that yields a sense favorable to the nourishment of piety (especially monastic piety)"[2]. In other words if the reading seems "holy" or orthodox, disregard it.

"Griesbach's skepticism was shared by J. L. Hug (1765-1846), who in 1808 advanced the theory that in the 2nd century the New Testament text had become deeply degenerate and corrupt and that all extant New Testament tests were merely editorial revisions of the corrupted text. And Carl Lachmann (1793-1846) continued in this same skeptical vein. He believed that from the extant manuscripts it was not possible to construct a text which would reach any farther back than the 4th century. To bridge the gap between this reconstruction 4th

---

[1] Hills Th.D., Edward F.; *The King James Version Defended;* p. 65

[2] Ibid. p. 65

century text and the original text, Lachmann proposed to resort **to conjectural emendation.** [adding what he conjectured was right, my comment] In 1831 he published an edition of the Greek New Testament which reflected his views."[1]

WESTCOTT AND HORT

With the above background in mind we finally arrive at a pivotal point in *"The Wide Gate: The Men"*. Subtle influences had led "scholars" to reject the traditional New Testament text [Received Text] and they believed it was up to them to restore it. Prominent people involved in this type of thinking were Brooke Foss Westcott and Fenton John Anthony Hort in the nineteenth century. They were professors at Cambridge and, incidentally, were contemporaries of the great men of faith, Charles Haddon Spurgeon (the great preacher), William Booth (founder of the Salvation Army), George Mueller (the great supporter of orphanages and missionaries), and many others. While these men were laboring away in the work of the Kingdom, Westcott and Hort were busily preparing their (not God's) 'New' Greek Text. This Greek text would be prepared from the alleged "rediscovery" of Aleph and B manuscripts. The Vaticanus or B manuscript found in the Vatican would be their favorite. Why they favored these manuscripts, which had thousands of changes and thousands of differences between them and other manuscripts, cannot be understood until their lives and beliefs are examined.

Titus 1:15 but unto them that are defiled and unbelieving is nothing pure; but even their mind and conscience is defiled.

Interestingly, private letters to friends OFTEN reveal what one truly believes as opposed to the *public* professions of a leader, scholar, or teacher. Obviously, this is why elected officials were induced to enact the "Sunshine Law", the law that insures open government. Who could ever forget the revelations on tape of Richard Nixon's involvement in the Watergate scandal?

We have access to the private letters of Westcott and Hort. Their sons published their private communications. I have tried to obtain their books, but

---

[1] Ibid. p. 65

had been unable to achieve that goal until very recently. Therefore, writings and quotes from other authors have been utilized. Interestingly, I discovered Dr. Samuel C. Gipp's book, "An Understandable History of the Bible", and in chapter 8 he made this statement:

> "Brooke Foss Westcott (1825-1903) and Fenton John Anthony Hort (1828-1892) have been highly controversial figures in biblical history. On one side, their supporters have heralded them as great men of God, having greatly advanced the search for the original Greek text. On the other side, their opponents have leveled charges of heresy, infidelity, apostasy, and many others, claiming that they are guilty of wreaking great damage on the true text of Scripture. I have no desire to "sling mud" nor a desire to hide facts. I believe it is essential at this time that we examine what we know about these men and their theories concerning the text of the Bible. *I long sought for copies of the books about their lives*. These are *The Life and Letters of Brooke Foss Westcott*, by his son, Arthur, and *The Life and Letters of Fenton John Anthony Hort*, written by his son. **After literally months of trying**, I was able to acquire copies of them both for study. Most of the material in this section will be directly from these sources so as to prevent it from being secondhand. We cannot blindly accept the finding of any scholar without investigating what his beliefs are concerning the Bible and its doctrines. _Scholarship alone_ makes for an inadequate and dangerous authority, therefore we are forced to scrutinize these men's lives."[1] [my emphasis]

This author could not have said it better. I had also been looking for the same books for several months without success. Therefore I will have to rely on the quotes by other writers from those private, personal letters of the two men who did more to shape the "New Greek Text" than any other.

Hort stated that it was their intention to cast on the world a new text before they were branded as **heretics**. Listen to his words,

> "I have sort of a craving that our text should be cast upon the world before we deal with matters likely to brand us with suspicion. I mean, a text issued by men who are already known for what will undoubtedly be treated as dangerous heresy will have great difficulty in finding its way to regions which it might otherwise hope to reach and whence it would not be easily

[1]Gipp, Th.D., Samuel C. ; *An Understandable History of the Bible* ; Daystar Publishing, Northfield, Ohio; Second Edition; 2000 ISBN 1-890120-13-8; pp.195-196

banished by subsequent alarms."[1]

Westcott said,

"How certainly I should have been proclaimed a heretic."[2]

When speaking about someone else branded as a heretic, he said,

"If he be condemned, what will become of me?"[3]

By now you are wondering why these men were so alarmed at the possibility of being labeled heretics. The following proclamations will help you to understand.

Dr. Hort did not believe in the authority of the Bible. He states,

"Evangelicals seem to me perverted rather than untrue. There are, I fear, still more serious differences between us on the subject of authority, and especially the *authority* of the Bible."[4]

He also did not accept the infallibility of the Scripture, a fact which he mentioned in several places. One example is,

"But I am not able to go as far as you in asserting the absolute infallibility of a canonical writing."[5]

Inspiration was out of the question for these colleagues. He (Hort) refers to:

"the common orthodox heresy: inspiration"

when referring to the Scriptures.[6]

There are many other passages, quotes, and beliefs,[7] but one gets the idea that they didn't think much of the Bible they read. As a matter of fact "Dr. Hort says on the eve of his epoch-making project of the 'New' Greek Text:

"I had no idea till the last few weeks of the importance of texts, having read so little Greek Testament, and dragged on with the **villainous *Textus Receptus* ...think of that vile Textus Receptus leaning entirely on late MSS.;** it is a blessing there are such early ones."[8] [This is my comment for greater clarity: The Textus Receptus is the Greek New Testament

---

[1] Riplinger, Gail A.; *New Age Bible Versions*; AV Publications, Munroe, Ohio 1994; ISBN 0-9635845-0-2; p.622-623;

[2] Ibid. p. 620

[3] Ibid. p 618

[4] Gipp, Th.D., Samuel C.; *Gipp's Understandable History of the Bible;* p. 201

[5] Ibid. p 202

[6] Riplinger, Gail A.; *New Age Bible Versions; p. 32*

[7] Waite, Dr. D. A., Ph.D., Th.D. *Heresies of Westcott and Hort;* Bible For Today Press; Collingswood, NJ; This is an excellent little book that outlines most of their apostate and heretical beliefs.

[8] Grady, Th.D., Th.M., D.D.,William P.; *Final Authority;* p. 245

from which many translations were made including the KJB. Also, remember, as cited and explained previously, "older" manuscripts does not mean "uncorrupted or better".]

Dr. Gipp also reports Westcott and Hort had "strange bedfellows". They denied the inspiration and infallibility of the Scriptures but they had no trouble believing Charles Darwin, or the two homosexuals, Socrates and Plato, or the drug addicted Samuel Taylor Coleridge.

Dr. Hort wrote Mr. A. MacMillian saying:

"You seem to make (Greek) philosophy worthless for those who have received the Christian Revelation. To me, though in a hazy way, it seems full of precious truth, of which I find nothing, and should be very much astonished and perplexed to find anything in revelation."[1] [And I presume Dr. Hort meant revelation of Scripture implying there was more revelation in Greek philosophy (Plato et al)].

Dr. Hort joined "the 'Philosophical Society' and comments:

"Maurice urged me to give attention to Plato and Aristotle and to make them the **center point** of my reading."[2]

And to John Ellerton he writes:

"But the book which has most engaged me is Darwin. Whatever may be thought of it, it is a book that one is proud to be contemporary with...My feeling is strong that the theory is unanswerable. If so, it opens up a new period.' To his colleague, B.F. Westcott, he wrote excitedly... 'Have you read Darwin? How I should like to talk with you about it! In spite of difficulties, I am inclined to think it unanswerable. In any case it is a treat to read such a book."[3]

Anyone reading this book who favors Darwinism, may not realize that embracing evolution points to treating the Scriptures as mythology and as having no authority. As we will discover later in this manuscript, these two men were members of the Broad Church whose doctrine accepted evolution as truth, and believed the Scripture was not the final authority.

Another favorite bedtime story for Dr. Hort was the writings of Samuel T. Coleridge. Coleridge was addicted to heroin because of rheumatoid arthritis. However, I cannot grant this fact as an excuse for a man who traveled to various countries to study with Eastern gurus, who developed the harmony of Christianity and transcendental philosophy, and:

"who was responsible, more than any other single

---

[1] Gipp, Th.D, Samuel C.; *Gipp's Understandable History of the Bible; p 204*

[2] Riplinger, Gail A.; *New Age Bible Versions;* p. 618

[3] Gipp, Th.D., Samuel C.; *Gipp's Understandable History of the Bible;* p. 203

individual, for the diffusion of German neology through Cambridge University and thence through the Anglican church. His books, *Biographia Literia, Aids to Reflection, Confessions of an Enquiring Spirit* had a profound effect on Julius Hare, J.F.D. Maurice, and John Sterling. Coleridge and Maurice may be said to be the founders of that section of the church known as the Broad Church or Latitudinarian part, which by 1853 had gained the allegiance of 3500 Anglican priests."[1]

Coleridge wrote Kubla Khan and he thought his poems were as inspired as King David's Psalms. Maurice, who was Coleridge's chief disciple and a Unitarian, was also mentioned in the personal letters of Westcott and Hort. Drs. Westcott and Hort were also known as "lovers" of drinks made with alcohol. Their personal letters reflect this fact, and one book accused one of them of a hashish habit. Whether the latter is true cannot be confirmed but it would not be a surprise to learn that it was true.

Another interesting "investigation" and interest of Westcott and Hort was their involvement in paranormal occurrences. This is mentioned in their letters, but those who favor Westcott and Hort report it was just youthful interests. For example, James R. White in his book, *The King James Only Controversy*, says:

"Westcott's involvement in a club (The Ghostly Guild, my addition) was formed to *investigate* strange occurrences, not engage in devilish activity. Some of Westcott's friends called it the Cock and Bull Club."[2]

With this statement he proceeds to excuse their activities as being the possible activity of any sinful person.

Gail Riplinger in her book, *"New Age Versions"*, reports that James Webb, a researcher into the occult, reports the Ghostly Guild was an element in the occult underground. Riplinger reports Webb said,

"Ghost Society [was] founded by no less a person than Edward White Benson, the future Bishop of Canterbury. As A. C. Benson writes in his father's biography, the Archbishop was always more interested in psychic phenomena than he cared to admit. Two members of the Ghost Club became Bishops [Benson and Westcott] and one a Professor of Divinity [Hort]."[3]

Hort writes of his and Westcott's work to set this apparition association in motion.

"Westcott, Gorham, C. B. Scott, Benson, Bradshaw, Laud etc. and I have started a society for the investigation of ghosts and all supernatural appearances and effects, being disposed

---

[1] Sightler, James H.; *Tabernacle Essays on Bible Translation;* p. 12

[2] White, James R.; *The King James Controversy;* p. 245

[3] Riplinger, Gail A.; *New Age Versions;* p. 405

to believe that such things really exist...Westcott is drawing up a schedule of questions."[1]

In the very same letter Hort describes the Bible, extant in his day as the King James Bible from the Greek Textus Receptus, as "villainous".

Again we have only circumstantial evidence, but where there is smoke there is fire. Deut. 18:10-*11* *There shall not be found among you any one that maketh his son or his daughter to pass through the fire, or that useth divination, or an observer of times, or an enchanter, or a witch, Or a charmer, or a consulter with familiar spirits, or a wizard, or a necromancer.*

THE BROAD CHURCH

Westcott and Hort were members of the *Broad Church*. (I think it is important to pause at this point and remind the reader we are still taking the history that has influenced the subjective complaints. This is much like an epidemiological study. We must find the source of infection and trace the contacts. Having said that, let's move on.) The doctrines of the Broad church are astounding. Westcott and Hort are pivotal persons in the change in wording of the 'New' Greek text, which became the basis of the modern Bible versions. Now, these are the doctrines of the Broad Church to which Westcott and Hort belonged. This is a long quote from Dr. James Sightler's work, used with permission.

"First, the doctrine of original sin was denied and along with it the imputation of Adam's sin to his posterity. Sin was defined as selfishness rather than transgression of God's law or was seen as a negation or failure.

Second, the orthodox satisfaction theory of the atonement was denied and the moral influence theory substituted in its place, or atonement was ignored and incarnation stressed instead. By the satisfaction theory Jesus shed His blood on the cross to satisfy the debt of man's sin, as a propitiation, because God's righteousness is of such magnitude and man's sin so great that nothing else would suffice. But the moral influence theory says that Christ's death was merely the supreme example of God's love, serving only to move men's hearts toward repentance. Many even claimed that propitiation and vicarious sacrifice were barbaric or immoral. Broad Church theology saw salvation not in what Christ did but in what He was, therefore not in atonement at

---

[1] Ibid. p. 405

all but in incarnation. For some, salvation was appropriated by the individual through infant baptism and the Eucharist, so that salvation was a system of gradual reformation administered by the church. But for many other Broad churchmen, for Maurice in particular, the incarnation effected a mystical union of Christ with all men, so that all are saved, and the mission of the church is then simply to tell them so.

Before leaving points one and two we should state that the Platonic system of the Logos as a created being, with all souls that will ever be preexisting in the Logos, is driven by the idea of incarnation; that is, Transcendentalism, the Broad Church, and the Catholic Church, all of which incorporated Platonic ideas to greater or lesser degree, have always stressed incarnation and downplayed atonement. On the other hand the Biblical view of man as a fallen, sinful creature, alien from God, is driven by the idea of redemption, and so in this system propitiatory atonement is the primary doctrine and incarnation is correctly limited to Jesus alone for the purpose of atonement.

It is significant that Westcott again in his essay on Origen notes that Origen's writings have no teaching on justification and no theory of atonement. Westcott in this essay clearly sides with Origen as against Augustine, who did believe in the Fall and in the need for atonement. And as one would expect the word atonement in Romans 5:11 is translated reconciliation in the ERV (English Revised Version) of 1881 and in all its descendants down to this day. Westcott and his fellow translators were not orthodox enough to believe that the examples of atonement in the Old Testament foreshadowed Christ's work, or indeed that the entire Old Testament pointed toward Him.

Third, in Christology the Broad Church teaching varied from rarely held orthodoxy, to denial of the eternal Sonship, to subordinationism and Sabellianism, and on over to outright Arianism and Socinianism.

Fourth, the virgin birth was denied.

Fifth, eternal life was defined as the knowledge of God here and now on earth and did not refer to any supposed life after death. Eternal death or punishment was defined as separation from God.

Sixth, Heaven and Hell were not believed to be real places.

Seventh, the Resurrection of the Lord and His Ascension were spiritualized and made figurative. The resurrection of believers was also denied. The body was held to be only an earthly manifestation of the soul; and though the soul was immortal, there would be no resurrection of the body for either the righteous or unrighteous dead.

Eighth, the Second Coming of the Lord was taught as having happened in 70 A.D. at the fall of Jerusalem or as occurring at the death of the believer.

Ninth, verbal inspiration of the Scripture was denied, and its authority was restricted to matters of faith and practice and then only upon authentication by the reason or mind of the individual.

Tenth, the Church was taught to be the literal and only body of Christ. Christianity was said to be Christ, His Theanthropic life, continued in the Church on earth, and not any proposition or doctrine about Christ. Doctrines were consciously de-emphasized in favor of a mystical sense of union with Christ which is also to say union with the Church.

Eleventh, the incarnation was taught not as the miraculous appearance of God on earth in human flesh in the person of Jesus Christ alone, but as the union of God with all men in the unfolding of human history. The union of God with human flesh in Christ was often said to be only a type of the union of God with all men, thus universal redemption in the incarnation.

Twelfth, Darwin's theory of evolution was accepted, and the Genesis account of creation either denied or mutilated to harmonize with Darwin's ideas."[1]

MORE OF WESTCOTT AND HORT'S HERESIES

What heresy! And to think that Westcott and Hort (W/H) who believed the above 12 heresies, "developed" the Greek Text that the New Versions are based upon. But we will continue to look at their lives and try to root out all possible sources of infection (leaven). The source of infection is almost as important as the infection itself. After finishing with them (W/H) we will look at the lives of others involved in this whole process before moving on to the passage of the manuscripts through the ages via two routes. We will examine where the manuscripts pick up leaven (infection) in cities and schools; and, finally, examine the Scripture and versions of the texts to see if this leaven spilled over into the 'new' Greek text and subsequently into the 'new' versions.

Returning to the actual quotes from Westcott and Hort, we will shortly see that they believed and supported the heresies of the Broad Church. William R. Inge (1860), a contemporary of W/H, identified Westcott as a Broad churchman, Christian mystic, and Platonist.[2]

Westcott did not believe in miracles. He states:

"I never read an account of a miracle but I seem

---

[1] Sightler, M.D., James H.; *A Testimony Founded For Ever, The King James Bible Defended in Faith and History;* 2nd Edition; Sightler Publications, Greenville, SC; 2001; pp. 70-72

[2] Ibid. p. 42

instinctively to feel its improbability, and discover somewhat of evidence in the account of it."[1]

He did not believe in the literal second coming of Jesus. He wrote:

"As far as I can remember, I said very shortly what I hold to be the 'Lord's coming' in my little book on the Historic Faith. I hold very strongly that the Fall of Jerusalem was the coming which first fulfilled the Lord's Words; and, as there have been other comings, I cannot doubt that He is 'coming' to us now,"[2]

He went all over Europe to the 'appearances of Mary' and believed the appearances were:

"that of God revealing Himself, now, not in one form, but in many."[3]

His idea of heaven was, to say the least, interesting. He did not believe in a place, but like his second coming belief, spiritualized heaven. He wrote:

"heaven is a state and not a place", "Yet the unseen is the largest part of life. Heaven lies about us now in infancy alone; and by swift, silent pauses for thought, for recollection, for aspiration, we cannot only keep fresh the influence of that diviner atmosphere, but breathe it more habitually," and "We may reasonably hope, by patient, resolute, faithful, united endeavor to find heaven about us here, the glory of our earthly life." [4]

He allegorized much of Scripture. He considered "Moses" and "David" as poetic characters:

"No one now, I suppose, holds that the first three chapters of Genesis, for example, give a literal history – I could never understand how anyone reading them with open eyes could think they did – yet they disclose to us a Gospel. So it is probably elsewhere. Are we not going through a trial in regard to the use of popular language on literary subjects like that through which we went, not without sad losses in regard to the use of popular language on physical subjects? If you feel now that it was, to speak humanly, necessary that the Lord should speak of the 'sun rising,' it was no less necessary that he would use the names 'Moses" and 'David' as His contemporaries used them. There was no critical question at issue."[5]

We could go on with multiple other quotes. One author reviewed 1800 pages of letters and other writings by Westcott and Hort and found this kind of

---

[1] Gipp, Th.D., Samuel C.; *Gipp's Understandable History of the Bible;* p. 217

[2] Ibid. p. 218

[3] Riplinger, Gail A.; *New Age Versions;* p. 623

[4] Gipp, Th.D., Samuel C.; *Gipp's Understandable History of the* Bible; p. 218-219

[5] Ibid. p. 216-217

thinking pervasive throughout their literature. Dr. Sightler pointed out some additional weird thoughts these men had such as: 1. They would rather believe in Plato's City of Atlantis than the resurrection or the ascension. 2. They were Universalists and had abandoned the doctrine of atonement. 3. They demonstrated subordination beliefs (Jesus was subordinate to the Father) in their quotes. 4. Westcott thought eternal life was the knowledge of God here and now.[1]

THE LIBERAL MOVEMENT

William P. Grady said in his book, *Final Authority,* that liberal professors who took part in the Oxford movement nurtured Westcott and Hort. The Oxford movement was established to Romanize the Anglican Church of England. Westcott idolized the founder of the movement, an apostate poet, John Keble (1792-1866).[2]

Most of the views of Westcott and Hort can be found in the thinking of the men at the German Tubingen School, Tubingen, Germany before and after these men.[3] The School was apparently a cesspool of naturalistic and rational thought, which was followed by an even worse ideology known as mysticism or Transcendentalism.[4] They infected many men who studied there including many Americans. Their unbelief was carried back to England and across the ocean to the hallowed shores of America. How sad to see such intelligent, bright men subtly overcome by the spiritual warfare that rages about all mankind second by second.

F. C. Baur (1792 – 1860), a Tubingen professor, who established the Tubingen School of New Testament Interpretation taught the mythological approach to the Scriptures. This approach is that the concept of doctrinal truth is realized through collective myth and the message is hidden in the myth.[5] This development followed the earlier German Rationalism and *higher criticism*

---

[1] Sightler, James H.; *Tabernacle Essays on Bible Translation;* pp. 21-22

[2] Grady, Th.D., Th.M., D.D., William P.; *Final Authority;* pp. 219-220

[3] Tubingen School of Theology, established by Ferdinand Christian Baur (1792-1860), applied the Hegelian principle to the history of early Christianity. That is: Primitive Jewish (Petrine) Christianity, represented by the Gospel of St. Matthew, was the original force or thesis; Pauline Christianity was the antitheses of reaction against Peter, Matthew, and early Catholic Christianity according to Frederick A Norwood.

[4] Sightler, James H.; *Tabernacle Essays on Bible Translation; p. 7*

[5] Ibid. pp 7-8

(dealing with 'thoughts' and the original text whereas *lower criticism* dealt with restoring the text) that viewed miracles as impossible because nature could not be suspended. A demonstration of their apparatus for approaching what they considered a theological 'problem' would be this: "In the transcendental scheme of things the **inspiration** of Scripture is itself a myth, **an idea slowly evolving in the mind of the early church.**"[1] Many of the ideas of the theologians in the 19th century can be traced all the way back to Origen and subsequently to Plato. Therefore, when Philip Schaff went to Germany to study under Baur's tutelage, he was infected by many of these ideas. The Church to P. Schaff was **the literal body** of Christ on earth and the repository of higher truth, and so, authoritative. (Does this sound like Catholicism?)

The question becomes: "What is this higher truth?" Hegel, Schelling, and Strauss further developed this idea of higher truth in the early part of the 19th century. The basic concept is that of universalism, the doctrine that the incarnation is God in every man and that Jesus, a myth, was a type of this incarnation. These beliefs were transmitted to Joseph Priestly, the discoverer of oxygen and a Unitarian, who took the principles to England. Priestly's assistant, William Hazlett (1784) visited William Bently in America who was a Harvard graduate and pastor and who subsequently led his church into Unitarianism. Hazlitt also visited a classmate of Bently, James Freeman. Freeman was pastor of the first Anglican Church in America and also became a Unitarian.

Can you see the infection (leaven) spreading? To top all the above off, Samuel T. Coleridge, was a friend and associate of Priestly. It was Coleridge, a professor at Oxford, who helped Keble form and develop the Oxford movement, which infected that University with mythology, transcendentalism and Unitarianism.

In America Philip Schaff was to be chosen by Westcott and Hort for the American Revision Committee. There is much more that could be said about the interrelationship of all these men, and many others thanks to the labors of Dr. Sightler.

However, let us look for a brief time at Charles Hodge, Princeton professor, who went to Germany (oh my!) to study. He accepted the textual approach of Griesbach, who openly denied the divinity of Christ. In addition, he accepted the short form of the Lord's prayer used in new versions.[2] [Incidentally, the short form of the Lord's prayer is used in the Satanic Church's Bible.] Hodge was the teacher of B.B. Warfield who was the first of the Princeton theologians who began to draw away from the Biblical concept of inspiration and preservation of the Scriptures. Instead, he advocated providential restoration by textual critics and original autograph inspiration

---

[1] Ibid. p. 8
[2] Ibid. p. 41-43

only. Warfield was the grandson of Robert J. Breckenridge who trained at Princeton under Hodge. Breckenridge was a leader in the Presbyterian split away from liberal New Haven Theology, a harbinger of Broad Church theology. After Breckenridge's death and his restraint of Hodge, Hodge went on to be appointed to the American Revision Committee and, in spite of objections to its course, acquiesced to a sifting of Scripture in America. **The seed of infection (leaven) begun in the Garden of Eden has continued to spread. The subtle changing of God's Words would become an epidemic.**

The following is a complete chapter taken from Dr. Gipp's book, *"Understandable History of the Bible,"* and it is used with permission. The chapter demonstrates the spiritual battle and ugly infection (leaven) that was spread in the name of "religion" through the years shortly before, and during Westcott and Hort's time. Reading this chapter, that Dr. Gipp researched and wrote, will begin to remove the innocence of some who are poorly informed about this battle for the minds of "scholars" by the Roman Catholic Church. This section will also demonstrate the diabolical influence of "Romanism" on Westcott and Hort and many others. This is a warning to the reader. This chapter will be physically nauseating and revolting, but Dr. Gipp's rendition is easy reading and comprehensive. Dr. Gipp uses the words "Universal Text" for the "Received Text".

CONFUSION IN THE ROMAN CATHOLIC CAMP

"It is necessary to salvation that every man should submit to the Pope." (Boniface VIII Unum Sanctum, 1303.)

"For by grace are ye saved through faith; and that not of yourselves: it is the gift of God: Not of works, lest any man should boast." Ephesians 2:8, 9.

Here lie two totally contradictory statements. They cannot both be correct. The one that you believe will depend on which authority you accept. The Roman Catholic Church has long been antagonistic to the doctrine of salvation by grace. If salvation is by grace, who needs "mass?" If salvation is by grace, who needs to fear purgatory? If Jesus Christ is our mediator, who needs the Pope? If the Pope cannot intimidate people into obeying him, how can he force a nation to obey him?

The true Bible is the arch-enemy of the Roman Catholic Church. Rome can only rule over ignorant, fear-filled people. The true Bible turns "unlearned and ignorant" men into gospel preachers and casts out "all fear." Rome must find a way to supplant the true gospel with "another gospel." The only way to do this is to eliminate our faith in the Words of God.

Rome received the corrupted Local Text of Alexandria, Egypt and further revised it to suit her own needs. Some scholars call this revision the "Western" text. This, of course, makes it part of the already corrupted text and, therefore, still contains the Local Text readings. This text suited the Roman Catholic Church well, since it attacked the doctrines of the Bible. Rome is wise. To attack salvation by grace directly would expose her plot to all. So instead she used subtlety. The Roman Catholic Church strips Jesus Christ of His deity, separates the divine title "Lord" and "Christ" from the human name Jesus, having the thief on the cross address Him as "Jesus" instead of "Lord" (Luke 23:42). It also removes the testimony to His deity in Acts 8:37, and it eliminates the Trinity in I John 5:7.

You may ask, "Would not a weakening of the place of Jesus Christ weaken the Roman Catholic Church's reason for even existing?" The answer is "No." The Roman Catholic Church does not even claim to represent the gospel of Jesus Christ. Romanist Karl Adam admits this: "We Catholics acknowledge readily, without any shame - nay with pride - that Catholicism cannot be identified simply and wholly with primitive Christianity, **nor even with the Gospel of Christ**. (my emphasis)"

The vacancy left by the removal of Christ would be easily filled by Mary and other "saints" along with a chain of ritualism so rigid that no practitioner would have time to really "think" about the true gospel.

INVASION

The true gospel was fast spreading all over Europe due to the Old Latin translation of the Universal Text (same as the Textus Receptus, my addition) into the "vulgar" or "common" language. This Bible became known as the "Vulgate" since it was used so commonly all over Europe.

Rome enlisted the help of a loyal subject by the name of Jerome. He quickly translated the corrupt Local Text into Latin. This version included the Apocryphal books, fourteen books which no Bible-believing Christian accepts as authentic. To insure its success over the Old Latin, the Roman Catholic Church gave it the name "Vulgate," meaning "common." There was one problem which the Roman Catholic Church did not anticipate, the *same* problem which the businessmen publishing new versions cannot seem to avoid. *The common people recognized the true Words of God because the Holy Spirit bears witness to it!* They *refuse* to accept other versions!

True, many versions have been sold in the past and are being sold now. Yet, this is primarily due to the media "blitz" by which EVERY new Bible has been introduced since 1881. This is the same tactic used by Satan in Genesis chapter 3. Notice his first recorded words. Do you believe that Satan just walked up to Eve and asked, "Yea, hath God said?" No! In Genesis 3:1 we are picking up in the *middle* of a conversation, possibly one of many. Satan paved the way for his attack on God's Words by a little "softening up" publicity. Christians today do not realize that they "need a better translation" until they are told so by the Bible salesman a few times. *Suddenly*, they "realize their need" for a translation which is "closer to the originals." (*Most* of these Christians have never even read the one they have.) The next thing they know, they have eaten the fruit, and *God's blessing is gone.* To get God's blessing back, obviously, they need the next "thoroughly reliable" translation.

This is not an overstatement. An example of the "Bible business" is revealed by Dr. Edward Hills. He speaks in reference to the committee of the American Standard Version *promising* not to publish their translation at the same time as the English Revised Version. He points out, "They promised not to publish their own revised edition of the Bible until 14 years after the publication of the English Revised Version (R.V.), and in exchange for this concession were given the privilege of publishing in an appendix to this version a list of the readings which they favored but which the British revisers declined to adopt." It was obvious to these "contenders for the faith" that *two* new Bibles hitting the market at the same time just would not be conducive to *good profits.* These men are obviously "led by the spirit" but I am not entirely sure it is "Holy." It is a sad thing when men make merchandise of the Words of God.

The name "Vulgate" on the flyleaf of Jerome's unreliable translation did little to help sales. The Old Latin Bible, or "Italic" as it is sometimes called, was held fast by all true Christians who upheld the authority of the Bible over the authority of education.

Dr. Wilkinson informs us in reference to the Old Latin, "Not only were such translations in existence long before the Vulgate was adopted by the Papacy, and well established, but the people for centuries refused to supplant their old Latin Bibles by the Vulgate." He records Jacobus' Words, "The old Latin versions were used longest by the western Christians who would not bow to the authority of Rome - e.g. the Donatists; the Irish in Ireland, Britain, and the Continent; the Albigenses: etc;"

Dr. Wilkinson also records the words from the "Forum" of June 1887, "The old Italic version, into rude Low Latin of the second century, held its own as long as Latin continued to be the language of the people.

The critical version of Jerome never displaced it, and only replaced it when the Latin ceased to be a living language, and became the language *of the learned.* The Gothic version of Ulfilas, in the same way, held its own until the tongues in which it was written ceased to exist."

So we see that the Vulgate of Jerome was unused and unwanted by the true Christians for over nine hundred years. This caused the Roman Church much grief. There was only one remedy to the situation, eliminate the "other" old, archaic Bible. If it was necessary to violently *eliminate* the people who used this faithful translation, then they *did* it.

THE PLOT

The Roman Catholic Church has long been known for its persecution of true New Testament Christians. Beginning in about 600 A.D.(I have found through additional research, persecution started much earlier), persecution hounded these Christ-honoring, Bible-loving people. Pope Gregory I went so far as to systematically destroy and alter historical records pertaining to these Christians. Concerning one group, the Waldenses (or Waldensians), Dr. Gilly reports, "It is a singular thing, that the destruction or rapine, which has been so fatal to Waldensian documents, would have pursued them even to the place of security, to which all, that remained, were consigned by Morland, in 1658, the library of the University of Cambridge. The most ancient of these relics were ticketed in seven packets, distinguished by letters of the alphabet, from A to G. The whole of these were missing when I made inquiry for them in 1823."

Gilly also enlightens us with this report of the actions of Rome: "The agents of the Papacy have done their utmost to calumniate their character, to destroy the records of their noble past and to leave no trace of the cruel persecution they underwent. They went even further - they made use of words written against ancient heresies to strike out the name of heretics and fill the blank space by inserting the name of the Waldenses. Just as if, in a book written to record the lawless deeds of some bandit, like Jesse James, his name should be stricken out and the name of Abraham Lincoln substituted. The Jesuit Gretserin a book written against the heretics of the twelfth and thirteenth centuries, put the name Waldenses at the point where he struck out the name of these heretics." We find that Rome's wicked persecutions of the Waldenses culminated in a devastating massacre of their number in 1655. They were hounded as "heretics" until the mid 1800's when their persistence paid off and the vile actions against them ceased.

COUNTERATTACK

A major blow to the authority of Rome came in 1517, when a young Catholic priest by the name of Martin Luther nailed his historic 95 theses on the church door in Wittenburg. The nail drove deep into the hearts of truly born-again Christians who had for centuries been laboring under the tyranny of the Roman Catholic Church. The people flocked to their new, brave leader. From this, Lutheranism was established, but even more important, the fires of the Reformation were kindled.

The tide of the Reformation soon came sweeping across all of Europe until it washed the very shores of England. The already weakened authority of Rome was devastated by the onslaught of truth. Two-thirds of Europe was swallowed up in what can probably be referred to as the greatest spiritual awakening of all time. The Reformation was vital to the then future translation of the King James Bible. England, too, had been shackled to the hierarchy of Rome. It was the removal of these superstitious bonds that created the spirit in England of the supremacy of the Scripture which was prevalent at the time of the translation of the King James Bible. This would not have been the case had Luther not sparked the Reformation.

The most vital and immovable weapon in Luther's arsenal came in the form of his German translation of the New Testament of 1522. This put the pure Words of the Universal Text back into the hands of "Bible-starved" Christians. The Reformation ran wild across the continent, fueled by this faithful translation. Rome at this point was totally helpless to stop it. The Papacy needed something with which to fight this dreaded scourge of truth. It turned in desperation to two different sources.

In 1545 the Roman Catholic Church formed the Council of Trent. The Council of Trent systematically denied the teachings of the Reformation. The Council decreed that "tradition" was of equal authority with the Bible. It decreed also that justification was not by faith alone in the shed blood of Jesus Christ. In fact, it stated that anyone believing in this vital Bible doctrine was cursed. The Council's exact words are: "If anyone saith that justifying faith is nothing else but confidence in the divine mercy which remits sins for Christ's sake or that this confidence alone is that whereby we are justified, *let him be anathema.*" (Emphasis mine.)

We now see that the Roman Catholic Church is guilty of *officially* cursing Jesus Christ! Would God use *this* church to preserve His Words? The Council of Trent was viewed by the Protestants as somewhat of a "paper tiger." It certainly did not hold any authority over them. The barn door appeared securely locked, but the horse was triumphantly roaming all over the countryside! Yet there was to be an enemy much more feared than the boisterous Council of Trent - the Jesuits!

DIABOLICAL JESUITS

The Society of Jesus was founded in 1534 by a Spaniard by the name of Ignatius Loyola. Loyola was born don Inigo Lopez de Racalde, in the castle of Loyola in the province of Guipuzcoa in 1491. He was known as a youth to be treacherous, brutal and vindictive. He was referred to as an unruly and conceited soldier. Loyola was wounded at the siege of Pampeluna in 1521. Crippled by a broken leg and plagued by a limp the rest of his life, he sought "spiritual" conquests.

Loyola produced an elite force of men, extremely loyal to the Pope, who would set about to undermine Protestantism and "heresy" throughout the world. Their training would require fourteen years of testing and trials designed to leave them with no will at all. They were to learn to be obedient. Loyola taught that their only desire would be to serve the Pope.

The head of the Jesuits is called the "Black Pope" and holds the title of General, just as in the military. That they were to be unquestionably loyal to this man and their church is reflected in Loyola's own words, "Let us be convinced that all is well and right when the superior commands it," also, "...even if God gave you an animal without sense for master, you will not hesitate to obey him, as master and guide, because God ordained it to be so." He further elaborates, "We must see black as white, if the Church says so."

THE DEVIL'S PLAINCLOTHESMEN

What would be the method used by the Jesuits to achieve their goals? Would it be military might? Would it be acts of daring? Would it be a violent revolution to install a Roman sympathizer as ruler? No, these actions would all have their day of usefulness, later.

The Jesuits were to be the Vatican's "plainclothesmen." They were founded to be a secret society, a society that was to slide in behind the scenes and capture the positions of *leadership.* The Jesuits knew that to capture the leaders of any particular country or organization is to conquer the entire body.

Edmund Paris, the noted French author and leading authority on the Roman Catholic Church, has written many books exposing the *true* spirit and goals of the Vatican. He points out, "Politics are their main field of action, as all the efforts of these 'directors' concentrate on one aim: *the submission of the world to the papacy,* and to attain this the 'heads' must be conquered first."

The Jesuit priests were not required to dress in the traditional garb of the Roman Catholic priests. In fact, their dress was a major part of their disguise. They presented themselves to the world in a variety of manners. They passed themselves off in a number of ways. Paris asserts that this is still true today, "It is the same today: the 33,000 official members of the Society operate all over the world in the capacity of her personnel, officers of a truly secret army containing in its ranks heads of political parties, high ranking officials, generals, magistrates, physicians, faculty professors, etc., all of them striving to bring about, in their own sphere, 'Opus Dei,' God's work, in reality the plans of the papacy."

They have often been known to join the religious persuasion which they wish to destroy. Having done this, they would manifest all of the destructive force at their hands to weaken and tear down their sworn enemy of "Protestantism." Paris again reports just such an event which took place in Scandinavia in the late 16th Century, "In 1574 Father Nicolai and other Jesuits were brought to the recently established school of technology where they became fervent Roman proselytizers, while officially assuming Lutheranism." Dr. Desanctis points out, "Despite all the persecution they (the Jesuits) have met with, they have not abandoned England, where there are a greater number of Jesuits than in Italy; there are Jesuits in all classes of society; in Parliament; among the English clergy; among the Protestant laity, even in the higher stations. I could not comprehend how a Jesuit could be a Protestant priest, or how a Protestant priest could be a Jesuit; but my Confessor silenced my scruples by telling me, omnia munda mundis, and that St. Paul became a Jew that he might save the Jews; it is no wonder therefore, if a Jesuit should feign himself a Protestant, for the conversion of Protestants."

HOLY MURDER

Murder is not above the "means" which might be necessary to reach the desired "end." The General of the Jesuits will forgive any sins which are committed by the members of this Satanic order. In reference to the Jesuit General it is stated, "He also absolves the irregularity issuing, from bigamy, injuries done to others, murder, assassination ... as long as these wicked deeds were not publicly known and this cause of a scandal."

That the Jesuit priests have such liberties as murder is reflected in the following lengthy quote from Paris' book *The Secret History of the Jesuits.*

"Amongst the most criminal Jesuistic maxims, there is one which roused public indignation to the highest point and deserves to be examined; it is: 'A monk or priest is allowed to kill those who are ready to slander him or his community.'

So the order gives itself the right to eliminate its adversaries and even those of its members who, having come out of it, are too talkative. This pearl is found in the *Theology of Father L'Amy.*

There is another case where this principle finds its application. For this same Jesuit was cynical enough to write: 'If a Father, yielding to temptation, abuses a woman and she publicizes what has happened, and because of it, dishonours him, this same Father can kill her to avoid disgrace!'"

In 1572, the Jesuits, with the help of Prince Henry III were responsible for the St. Bartholomew's Day Massacre. At this infamous event, which took place on August 15, 1572, the Jesuits murdered the Huguenot (Protestant) leaders gathered in Paris for the wedding of Princess Margaret, a Roman Catholic, and Henry of Navarre, a Huguenot. The murders inspired Roman Catholics to slaughter thousands of Huguenot men, women, and children. Henry of Navarre was not killed but was forced to renounce Protestantism, although his renunciation was insincere, and he remained a Protestant until 1593. The number of victims in this Jesuit conspiracy is estimated to be at least 10,000. In 1589, when Henry III was no longer useful to the Roman Catholic Church, he was assassinated by a monk by the name of Jacques Clement. Clement was called an "angel" by the Jesuit priest, Camelet. Another Jesuit priest by the name of Guigard, who was eventually hanged, taught his students that Clement did nothing wrong.

In fact, he voiced his regrets that Henry III had not been murdered earlier at the St. Bartholomew's Day Massacre. He instructed them with lessons such as this: "Jacques Clement has done a meritorious act inspired by the Holy Spirit. If we can make war against the king, then let us do it; if we cannot make war against him, then let us put him to death ... we made a big mistake at the St. Bartholomew; we should have bled the royal vein."

The Jesuits' murderous ways were not yet completed in the history of French Protestants! When Henry III was murdered, Henry of Navarre a Huguenot, came to power. A hope for Catholic rebellion never materialized, and Henry IV was allowed to reign. In 1592, an attempt was made to assassinate the Protestant king by a man named Barriere. Barriere admitted that he had been instructed to do so by a Father Varade, a *Jesuit* priest. In 1594, *another* attempt was made by Jean Chatel who had been *taught* by Jesuit teachers and had confessed to the Jesuits what he was about to do. It was at this time that Father Guigard, the Jesuit teacher previously mentioned, was seized and hanged for his connection with this plot.

In 1598, King Henry IV issued the Edict of Nantes, granting religious freedom to the Huguenots. They were allowed full civil rights and the right to hold public worship services in towns where they had congregations.

This was the last straw! Henry IV had to be eliminated! This time the Jesuits would allow for more careful planning. Edmund Paris details the assassination of King Henry IV:

"On the 16th of May, 1610, on the eve of his campaign against Austria, he was murdered by Ravaillac who confessed having been inspired by the writing of Fathers Mariana and Suarez. These two sanctioned the murders of heretic "tyrants" or those insufficiently devoted to the Papacy's interests. The Duke of Epemon, who made the king read a letter while the assassin was lying in wait, was a notorious friend of the Jesuits, and Michelet proved that they knew of this attempt. In fact, Ravaillac had confessed to the Jesuit Father d'Aubigny just before and, when the judges interrogated the priest, he merely replied that God had given him the gift to forget immediately what he heard in the confessional."

THIS is the spirit of our enemy! THIS is the ruthlessness of the Roman Catholic Church against those who will not bow their knee to Rome! Would God use this church to preserve His Words?

Wherever there is a conspiracy against God's people or God's Words, there seems always to be the shadow of a Jesuit priest near. Often they present themselves as seemingly innocent to the proceedings around them when, in fact, they are the driving force behind such plots against God's work.

It is often said that you can tell a lot about a man by taking a close look at his enemies. If a man is disliked by Communists, then that shows that he is a non-Communist and considered dangerous to their cause. If a man is disliked by the Roman Catholic Church, then this shows that he is not useful in spreading the Roman Catholic dogma.

This same thing is true of the Bible. What did the Jesuits, the sworn enemy of truth, think of the Authorized Version?

THE GUNPOWDER PLOT

To show the hatred of the Roman Catholic Church against King James for initiating a translation which would not use the corrupt Latin Vulgate or the Jesuit Bible of 1582, we must quote from Gustavus Paine's book, *The Men Behind the King James Version.* The account recorded took place in 1605-1606.

"The story is too involved to give detail here, but on October 26, the Lord Chamberlain, Monteagle, received an unsigned letter begging him to stay away from Parliament on the day it opened. He took the letter to Robert Cecil, who on November 1 showed it to the king at a midnight meeting. The King shrewdly surmised a good deal of what it meant.

Monday, November 4, an agent of the royal party found in a cellar beneath the House of Lords a man named Guy Fawkes, disguised as a servant, beside piles of faggots, billets of wood, and masses of coal. The agent went away. Shortly Monteagle and one other came and talked, but gave no heed to Fawkes, who was still on guard until they were about to go. He told them he was a servant of Thomas Percy, a well-known papist. Still later, at midnight, soldiers found Fawkes booted and spurred and with a lantern outside the cellar door. He had taken few pains to conceal his actions. They dragged him into an alley, searched him, and found on him a tinderbox and a length of slow match. In a fury now, they moved the faggots, billets and coal and came upon barrel after barrel of powder, thirty-six barrels in all. Fawkes then confessed that he meant to blow up the House of Lords and the king.

On November 6, Percy, with others, rushed into an inn at Dunchurch, Warwickshire, with the news that the court was aware of their plan. By the 8th the whole attempt had dearly failed. When Parliament met a week after the stated day, the King, calm, gracious, and splendid told what had happened and then adjourned the meeting. At first Fawkes refused to name any except Percy who, with others, was killed in the course of a chase. In time he gave the names of all, who would have blown up the House of Lords 'at a clap.'

Guy Fawkes was baptized at St. Michael le Belfrey, York, April 16, 1570, son of Edward Fawkes, a proctor and advocate in the church courts of York. The father died and the mother married a Papist. In 1603 Guy Fawkes went to Madrid to urge that Philip III invade England. Thus he was a confirmed traitor, though egged on and used by more astute plotters.

Some of these men had been involved in the rising of the Earl of Esses. A number were former members of the Church of England. Most of them had some land and wealth. They were all highly disturbed beings, throwbacks, who meant to subvert the state and get rid of King James. Church and state, they were sure, must be at one, with fealty to the Pope.

For nearly a year, the plotters had been digging a tunnel from a distance, but had found the wall under the House of Lords nine feet thick. They had then got access to the cellar by renting a building. They had planned to kill the King, seize his children, stir up an open revolt with the aid from Spaniards in Flanders, put Princess Elizabeth on the throne, and marry her to a Papist. Though all but one, Sir Everard Digby, pleaded not guilty, the court, such as it was, condemned them all to death. That same week they were all hanged, four in St. Paul's churchyard where John Overall, the translator, could have looked on and four in the yard of the old palace.

Three months later came the trial of Henry Garnet, a Jesuit, thought to be head of the Jesuits in England. Brought up a Protestant, he knew of the plot but had shrunk in horror from it, though he left the chosen victims to their fate. The court condemned him also to die.

All this concerned the men at work on the Bible. At Garnet's hanging, May 3, in St. Paul's churchyard, John Overall, Dean of St. Paul's took time off from his translating to be present. Very gravely and Christianity he and the Dean of Winchester urged upon Garnet 'a true and lively faith to God-ward,' a free and plain statement to the world of his offense; and if any further treason lay in his knowledge, he was begged to unburden his conscience and show a sorrow and destination of it. Garnet, firm in his beliefs, desired them not to trouble him. So after the men assigned to the gruesome duty had hanged, drawn, and quartered the victim Dean Overall returned to St. Paul's and his Bible task."

Thus the "Gunpowder Plot" failed. As usual, where there was treachery there was a Jesuit.

Did the failure of this plan stop the Jesuits? Of course not. Garnet had allowed this drastic plan to be carried out too soon. He had forgotten the Jesuit rule to act a little at a time "surtout, pas trop de zele" (above all, not too much zeal).

A NEW PLAN

Let it be remembered, *Jesuits do not give up.* They would have to bide their time. They would once again resort to undercover activities as they had so many times before. Their task would be a difficult one, yet for the unfaltering Jesuits, not impossible. They would have to discredit the Reformation. They would have to dislodge the Universal Greek Text from the firm position it held in the minds and hearts of English scholarship. They would have to "wean" Protestantism back into the fold of Rome. To do this they would use the same plan as they had in similar situations: captivate the minds of scholarship. Men have long been worshippers of education. If an educator makes a claim, the "common" people will follow, because they have convinced themselves that anyone with that much education can't be wrong.

Evolution has been accepted as a fact by the average American because educators claim that it is true. The fact that they can produce no evidence to substantiate their theory is incidental. Education says it is so!

The Jesuits' task was to entice Protestant scholarship back to Rome. They knew that they could not wean the leaders of Protestantism back into Rome as long as the stubborn "heretics" clung to the pure text of the Reformers. This Bible would have to be replaced with one which contained the pro-Roman Catholic readings of Jerome's Vulgate and the Jesuit translation of 1582. It would be necessary to "educate" the Protestant scholars to believe that their Reformation Text was unreliable and that their Authorized Version was "not scholarly." Once thus programmed, the egotistical scholars would spontaneously attack their own Bible and believe that they were helping God.

The most important objective to be realized would be to replace the Bible as the final authority.

The Authorized Version had become a mightier foe than Rome had anticipated as Dr. McClure points out: "The printing of the English Bible has proved to be by far the mightiest barrier ever reared to repel the advance of Popery, and to damage all the resources of the Papacy. Originally intended for the five or six millions who dwelt within the narrow limits of the British Islands, it at once formed and fixed their language, till then unsettled; and has since gone with that language to the isles and shores of every sea."

THE DREADED HAPPENING

What the Roman Catholics had always dreaded had come to pass. The Word of God was translated from the true text into the clearest form of the common language, English. Protestants had long refuted and neutralized Roman Catholicism by the phrase, "The Bible says so." The Roman Catholic Church had been built on about 10% twisted Scripture and 90% superstition. Where men were ignorant, it could rule by playing on their fears. But, when the "ignorant and unlearned" people received Christ as personal Saviour and clung faithfully to the King James Bible, they were not only immovable but could easily refute any heresy, be it Catholic or otherwise.

AIDING THE ENEMY

The job of the Jesuits would be aided by the natural process of time. Every major religious persuasion follows a natural pattern which is nearly impossible to avoid. They begin in the form of a revival, not a week long revival meeting, but a spiritual awakening which leads its followers away from the world system and into Bible literalism. The Reformation is a good example. People drew nearer to the Bible, believed it literally, and the end result was a revival which swept Europe and drew people out of the Roman Catholic system.

The next step is education. The infant Reformation had nowhere to send its converts to learn the Bible. It certainly could not allow them to return to the Roman school of philosophy for their education. So the second step is to build your own schools and train your own preachers and teachers.

The third step is culture. Once a movement has established itself, it forms its own culture. This process takes from 50 to 100 years. After this period of time, the movement has proved to the world that it is not a "fly by night" outfit but is a force to be reckoned with. This was true of Lutheranism, as it is now true of Fundamentalism.

Fifty years ago, a Fundamentalist preacher was considered a backwoods "hick" with no education and was able to preach nothing more than "hell, fire, and damnation." Today, the world has awakened to the fact that Fundamentalism is a powerful force. Fundamental churches are found to be the largest and fastest growing in the country. Television and magazines are producing special stories concerning the Fundamental movement. The election of 1980 showed the amount of influence that Fundamentalism could have. Fundamentalism has proven that it is here to stay. This acceptance produces a kind of "home-grown" arrogance. This is not a derogatory comment, but is true.

When the preachers of the Reformation graduated from basements and dungeons to the pulpits of the largest, fastest growing churches in Europe, they realized that they had fought their way to victory. As they saw their colleges grow and multiply, they prided themselves in the job they had done. But the new-found ease of life began to make a subtle change. They found themselves beginning to appreciate the "finer" things of life. A pastor who had been satisfied in the early days of the Reformation with a basement and one candle for light to preach by, twenty-five years later found himself in a fine, clean, functional building. As his congregation grew and space was needed, the church built bigger buildings, but the new buildings passed from functional simplicity to a "touch of elegance." The chandeliers became more ornate. The ceiling became higher. The pews were more comfortable. The windows saw the use of stained glass, a Roman Catholic custom. The pastor found social acceptance in the community. Each succeeding building was "bigger and better" with more elaborate masonry. The preachers and people began to find time to "appreciate" the arts and sciences. The Christians soon had a culture which was separate from but parallel to that of the world. This left the door open for the next and final step, apostasy.

The preachers became "clergy." Their separated lives and Biblical education led to Phariseeism. Their colleges expanded from just training ministers to covering a wider spectrum of occupations. Basic Bible courses were supplemented by a study of "the arts."

Revival is from God. Education is necessary to the training of God's ministers, but culture is a product that appeals to the flesh. Once the flesh is allowed to offer its preferences, apostasy sets in. Standards become a little more lax. College professors are hired according to their academic abilities first and the spiritual convictions second. Statements like "We must have the best" and "I want to be first-class" are used to comfort the fears of anyone who feels that the churches and schools seem a little worldly. Of course, a school administrator might find himself thinking, "The average Christian doesn't understand our minute changes. They aren't educated like we are."

There suddenly appears a Christian with an open Bible, who points out Scripture which may condemn the newfound "culture" of a church or school. The school amazingly finds itself in the same position as the

Roman Catholic Church, refuted by an ignorant Christian who believes the Bible. Which is to be the final authority, the school or the Bible? Time after time, education has found that it has come too far to turn back. "We are!" came the answer from Oxford, Cambridge, and Westminister in England. "We are!" came the answer from Harvard, Princeton, and Yale in America. Education has conceived culture and given birth to apostasy!

RIPE FOR CONQUEST

England in the early 1800's was ripe for apostasy. The Reformation had come a long way since Luther nailed his theses on the door of Wittenberg. It had traversed Europe with the truth, leaving in its wake churches and schools that represented the pure text of Scripture. The educational foundation had been laid, upon which culture was built. Gone were the attempts to blow up Parliament. Gone was the fear of ending up like Tyndale for believing "the Book." Gone was the reign of terror inflicted by "bloody" Mary. The churches built around the Authorized Version were rich and prosperous. The colleges, from their meager beginnings, had become great universities, pressing on with higher education. There were a few "common" people who still feared Rome, but the "educators" knew that their fears were "unfounded." England was ripe for a transfer of authority from the Bible to education, and Rome was willing to supply the education. The absolute reign of the Authorized Version would soon end.

OPERATION "UNDERMINE"

The Authorized Version had withstood countless attacks, but it would now be subject to a systematic campaign to exalt several authorities to a position equal to it. These perverted "authorities" would then join forces to portray the Authorized Version as weak, unreliable, inaccurate, outmoded, and generally untrustworthy. Once the Authorized Version had been successfully dethroned, education would be free to exalt whatever authority it desired to. The Roman Catholic Church, of course, would be close at hand to see to it that the authority which was to be exalted would be in agreement with its own corrupt Latin Vulgate. The authorities to be exalted as equal with the Authorized Version came from several different quarters, but all with the same intent. Replace the Universal Text of the Authorized Version with the Local Text of Alexandria, Egypt.

SCIENCE "FALSELY SO-CALLED"

One of the authorities which would be used to discredit the Authorized Version was "textual criticism." Textual criticism is known as a "science." By being called a science, it will be accepted by the educated mind. It is a process which looks at the Bible as it would look at the uninspired writings of any secular writer. This one fact alone means that the power of God to preserve His Words is ignored in favor of the naturalistic method of evaluating the "chance" of God's Words being preserved. Textual criticism allows God to "inspire" His originals, but seeks to replace God as the active agent in preserving His Words. Earlier we established that the Bible was a spiritual book, that God was active in its conception, and that it would be reasonable to assume that God could be just as active in its preservation. One might ask at this point if textual criticism could not be the method which God used to preserve His Words? The answer is unequivocally, "No." Here are the reasons why: Textual critics look at the Bible today through the same eyes as the Egyptian scribes did who perverted the Universal Text to construct the Local Text centuries ago. Those well-educated scribes thought that the Bible was subject to them instead of them being subject to the Bible. This outlook allowed them to eliminate the power of God from their minds and make whatever changes they deemed necessary to reach a conclusion which seemed logical to them. They were the Holy Spirit in their minds!

Today textual critics do the same, in that, before they ever start their work, they are convinced that God cannot preserve His Words without their assistance. Scholars today believe that God inspired Words but preserved thoughts. Another reason why textual criticism could not be the method God used to preserve His Words is that it comes from Rome.

The Catholic Encyclopedia states, "A **French priest**, Richard Simon (1638-1712), was the first who subjected the general questions concerning the Bible to a treatment which was at once comprehensive in scope and scientific in method. Simon is the forerunner of modern Biblical criticism ... The use of internal evidence by which Simon arrived at it entitles him to be called the father of Biblical criticism"

The same source also mentions the Catholic scholar Jean Astruc:

"In 1753 Jean Astruc, a French Catholic physician of considerable note published a little book, Conjectures sur les memoires originaux dont il parait que Moise s'est servi pour composer le livre de la Genese, in which he conjectured, from the alternating use of two names of God in the Hebrew Genesis, that Moses had incorporated therein two pre-existing documents, one of which employed Elohim and the other Jehovah. The idea attracted little attention till it was taken up by a German scholar, who, however, claims to have made the discovery independently. This was Johann Gottfried Eichhorn ... Eichhorn greatly developed Astruc's hypothesis."

The same source also speaks of yet another Roman Catholic infidel:

"Yet, it was a Catholic priest of Scottish origin, Alexander Geddes (1737-1802), who broached a theory of the origin of the Five Books (to which he attached Joshua) exceeding in boldness either Simon's or Eichhorn's. This was the well-known 'Fragment' hypothesis, which reduced the Pentateuch to a collection of fragmentary sections partly of Mosaic origin, but put together in the reign of Solomon. Geddes' opinion was introduced into Germany in 1805 by Vater."

Dr. Benjamin Wilkinson records how the naturalistic, unsaved Roman Catholic scholars judged in favor of the perverted Egyptian manuscripts: "Some of the earliest critics in the field of collecting variant readings of the New Testament Greek were Mill and Bengel. We have Dr. Kenrick, Catholic Bishop of Philadelphia in 1849, as authority that they and others had examined these manuscripts recently exalted as superior, such as the Vaticanus, Alexandrinus, Bezae, and Ephraem, and had pronounced in favor of the Vulgate, the Catholic Bible."

Stop and think! Naturalistic as opposed to spiritual. Unsaved as opposed to saved. Roman Catholic as opposed to Biblical. These men conceived and developed theories which attacked the reliability of Scripture and judged in favor of the perverted Egyptian manuscripts.

Are these men and methods worthy of fellowship? Would a perfect and righteous God use such a hodgepodge of infidelity to preserve His hallowed Words? Some may say that textual criticism is good if carried on by good, godly Christian men. This cannot be true. The "mass" is a Roman Catholic invention contrived to prevent people from knowing the truth. Would the mass be "good" if performed by good, Bible-believing scholars? Of course not! Elisha took poison and made it fit to eat, (II Kings 4:38-41). We cannot! Neither can we take a method instigated by the Roman Catholic Church in order to overthrow the Bible and filled with the poison of Romanism and miraculously make it fit to use! Textual criticism is a "science" (falsely so-called - I Timothy 6:20) whose authority we cannot accept in place of the Bible.

THE GREEK GAME

Another authority by which to judge and down-grade ...the Authorized Version is to change the meaning of the translation and the Words used in Scripture. First the student is taught that he must not accept a word as it is in the Authorized Version. He is told to study the Greek or Hebrew words to see if there is another way the words could be translated. The student, with the purest of motives, proceeds to a lexicon or a Greek or Hebrew dictionary [see below, HDW] and discovers to His horror that the translators of the Authorized Version have translated the words improperly! In truth, the exact opposite has happened. The lexicon and/or dictionary have defined the words improperly! The poor, naive, well-meaning student does not know it, but he has been "headed off at the pass."

Years before this poor student ever turned the first page of his lexicon, Roman Catholics provided the pages he would turn! Let me explain. If the student can be taught to doubt the accuracy of the translation of any given Word in the Bible, then we will turn to a lexicon or dictionary to find the '"true" meaning. He does not realize it, but in doing this, he removes the Bible from its position as final authority and bestows that honor upon an uninspired lexicon or dictionary. All this leaves Satan to do, is to provide that student with a lexicon or dictionary which reads the way he (Satan) wants it to! This is a subtle and dangerous precedent. Most often, it is taught in complete, innocent sincerity.

This is much like the phrase used to explain the Communist's takeover of many countries which were once thriving with many missionaries: "The missionaries taught us to read, but the Communists gave us the books." (The Communists do not argue about the proper translation of Marx.)

Many unsuspecting colleges teach their students to accept the lexicon or dictionary as an authority above the Bible, but the lexicons and dictionaries are provided by the infidels. John R. Rice points out the result of such "authority switching" while discussing Isaiah 7:14 in the Revised Standard Version: "The most active opposition to the Revised Standard Version has been about changing the translation of Isaiah 7:14 from, 'Behold, a virgin shall conceive,' to 'Behold, a young woman shall conceive and bear a son.' Dr. Luther Weigle, chairman of the translators, said that in the Hebrew English lexicon the word 'alma' means simply 'young woman,' not necessarily 'virgin' and he said that the word for 'virgin' in the Hebrew is 'bethulah.'" He did not tell you, however, that the lexicon he uses was prepared by unbelieving critics.

Gesenius, the German orientalist and biblical critic, is described in the Encyclopedia Britannica in these words:

"To Gesenius, who was an exceptionally popular teacher, belongs in a large measure the credit of having freed Semitic philosophy from theological and religious prepossession, and of inaugurating the strictly scientific (and comparative) method.

His chief work, Hebraisches u. Chaldais- ches Handworterbuch (1810-1812), has passed through several editions (Eng. ed.: Francis Brown, S. R. Driver and Charles A. Briggs, A Hebrew and English Lexicon of the Old Testament, 1907).

Gesenius, a notorious liberal, specialized in changing the theological terminology of the Bible into that of liberals. Brown, Driver, and Briggs, translators of the lexicon in English were, all three of them, radical liberals, and two of them were tried in the Presbyterian church for outrageous infidelity."[76]

Wilkinson reports that two of the infamous Roman Catholic scholars previously mentioned also entered into the practice of providing definitive works. "Simon and Eichhorn were co-authors of a Hebrew Dictionary."

Such infidelic works are accepted because they are produced by "great scholars." They are then used by good, godly men who do not realize the price of bowing to unbelieving scholarship.

GRIESBACH

Another important step in subtlety removing the authority of the Authorized Version is to exalt the unreliable MSS of the Local Text of Egypt. This will be commented on later. Let it suffice for now to reveal the man who laid the groundwork for just such a move. His name was J.J. Griesbach (1745-1812).

Griesbach divided the extant MSS into three groups. One was called the "Constantinopolitan" family which is our Universal Text. The other two were known as "Western" and "Alexandrian."

As can be expected, Griesbach was not a Bible believer. In fact, he stated, "The New Testament abounds in more glosses, additions, and interpolations purposely introduced than any other book." He was also antagonistic to any verse which taught the fundamental doctrines of the

Christian faith. Whenever possible he devised means to cast doubt on such passages. He said, "the most suspicious reading of all, is the one that yields a sense favorable to the nourishment of piety (especially monastic piety). When there are many variant readings in one place, that reading which more than the others manifestly favors the dogmas of the orthodox is deservedly regarded as suspicious."

It is strange indeed that Dr. Griesbach should expect orthodox Christians to manipulate the book which they truly believe to be from God, in order to teach Christianity more fervently. He never mentioned any apprehension that heretics might delete and alter doctrinal passages. What kind of scholarship is it that naturally suspects born-again Christians of an act bordering on sacrilege, but never doubts the integrity of infidels? Is this God's method?

Whatever it was that possessed Griesbach to suspect Christians of such criminal acts also possessed two of his followers. Hills explains:

"Westcott and Hort professed to 'venerate' the name of Griesbach above that of every other textual critic of the New Testament. Like Griesbach they believed that the orthodox Christian scribes had altered the New Testament manuscripts in the interest of orthodoxy. Hence like Griesbach, they ruled out in advance any possibility of the providential preservation of the New Testament text through the usage of believers. But at the same time they were very zealous to deny that heretics had made any intentional changes in the New Testament text. 'It will not be out of place,' they wrote, 'to add here a distinct expression of our belief that even among the numerous unquestionably spurious readings of the New Testament, there are no signs of deliberate falsification of the text for dogmatic purposes.' The effect of this one-sided theory was to condemn the text found in the majority of the New Testament manuscripts and exonerate that of B and Aleph."

Thus the Local Text, supported by the Roman Catholic Church, became an authority equal to or higher than the Universal Text of the Authorized Version in spite of the many doctrinal changes. After all, Griesbach, Westcott, and Hort had already established that heretics never falsify Scripture--only Christians do!

As the infidelity of men such as this is accepted as authoritative, Christians begin to look to their Bible with more and more skepticism. What more could Satan desire?

Are these men to be blamed for their failure to accept the Bible as infallible, or have they been unsuspecting dupes of a plan much bigger and far more serious than they could have ever suspected? Let us see.

THE PUPPETEER

One man who became greatly responsible for the fall of England to a sympathetic acceptance of Roman Catholic ideas was Cardinal Wiseman (1802-1865). Wiseman was the prime mover in installing the Roman Catholic Church back on the shore of England. He was born and raised in England. He went to Rome to study under Cardinal Mai, the editor of the Vatican Manuscript. Wiseman had a desire to see England return to the fold at Rome. One of the major obstacles to this was the supremacy which the Authorized Version held there. Where the Authorized Version prevails, Rome cannot.

THE PUPPETS

While in Rome, he was visited by several Neo-Protestants. He was instrumental in "weaning" these men back into subjection to the Pope. One of his visitors was William Gladstone (1809-1898), who was to become prime minister of England. He was a man known for his change from being a Conservative to a Liberal. Another visitor was Anglican Archbishop Trench, who returned to England to promote a revision of the Authorized Version and even joined the Revision Committee of 1871.

Still another was John Henry Newman. Newman was the brilliant English churchman who was a leader of Oxford University and the English clergy. Newman was a close friend with Herrell Froude. Froude, Wilkinson tells us, was the son of a High Churchman, "who loathed Protestantism, denounced the Evangelicals, and brought up his sons to do the same."

These two, Newman and Froude, joined affinity with John Keble. Keble, like Froude, was of High Church background. He was strongly anti-Protestant and anti-Evangelical. Newman and Froude visited Wiseman in Rome in 1833. Having been taken in by the beautiful architecture of Rome's cathedrals and the solemn grandeur of the high masses, the two Oxford professors inquired of Wiseman as to what terms the Roman Catholic Church would require to accept the Church of England back into the Roman Church. Wiseman's reply was cold and clear: The Church of England must accept the Council of Trent. At this, Newman left Rome stating, "I have a work to do in England," a work indeed, in which he, Froude, Keble, and Edward Pusey joined forces to swing England back to Rome and to remove their primary adversary, the hated King James Bible. Newman, brilliant man that he was, provided the strong intellectual leadership needed. Pusey was the moralist, and Keble spoke through the delicate words of the poet and captivated the hearts and minds of many an unsuspecting young scholar. Any who lacked a strong stand on Bible principles would be easy prey for these apostates.

Newman, in fact, was so taken in by the spell of Rome that he, in 1845, left the Church of England and formally joined the Roman Catholic Church, following a similar apostate, named Ward, who had written a book teaching the worship of Mary and "mental reservation." Mental reservation is the act, condoned by the Roman Catholic Church, of lying to keep from revealing your ties to Rome.

Wilkinson records Newman's betrayal:

"Public sentiment was again aroused to intensity in 1845 when Ward, an outstanding Tractarian, published His book which taught the most offensive Roman views, Mariolatry, and mental reservation in subscribing to the Thirty-nine Articles. When Oxford degraded him from his university rights, he went over in September to the Church of Rome. It became very evident that Newman soon would follow. On the night of October 8 Father Dominic, of the Italian Passionists, arrived at Newman's quarters in a down pouring rain. After being received, he was standing before the fire drying his wet garments. He turned around to see Newman prostrate at his feet, begging his blessing, and asking him to hear his confession. Thus the author of Lead Kindly Light passed over to Rome, and within one year 150 clergyman and eminent laymen also had joined the Catholic Church."

Where was Wiseman through all of this? He was naturally close at hand. In 1836, three years following Newman and Froude's visit, he had moved to Ireland to supervise the Oxford Movement through his paper, the "Dublin Review." Wiseman was described as, "a textual critic of the first rank, and assisted by the information seemingly passed on to him from the Jesuits, he was able to finish the facts well calculated to combat confidence in the Protestant Bible."

England had graduated from "revival" to "education," and her "education" had developed into her own unique "culture." From there, the Roman Catholic Church was willing to supply the apostasy.

WHERE WE STAND

Today in colleges and churches across America and around the world, truly good, godly men who love the Lord Jesus and sincerely desire to serve Him, are unsuspectingly propagating the Roman Catholic method of textual criticism. The result is that Christian soldiers...go out to fight Rome...with...an unreliable translation of the Rome-supported Local Text, which is worthy of all suspicion.

Education in America has come to the place of either having to swallow its pride, admit it has been wrong, and return to the true Bible; or else make another more vehement attack on the Authorized Bible in hopes of finally silencing it and its supporters... Christians be warned! The Revised [Standard] Version did not ring the death note for the King James Bible. It rang the death note for England!

All of the translations before and after 1881 which were going to replace the Authorized Version lie silently in the "grave" right now. Those which do not, shall soon join their ranks in the halls of the "improved," "thoroughly reliable," "truly accurate," and "starters of a new tradition," dead. They have failed to start one revival. They have failed to induce Christians back to reading their Bibles, and have only succeeded in casting **doubt on the true Words of God.**[1] [My emphasis, and deletions. HDW]

This concludes Dr. Gipp's chapter, which is used with permission. Some information was repeated in this section, but rightfully so. The student of the Scripture must be aware of the devices of the enemy; and his tactics so often elude us that repeating and emphasizing information is good for anyone. This section brings to a close a look at *"The Wide Gate History: The Men"* and their interrelationships. We will touch on more men in this category in other sections as we proceed. If the reader has paid close attention, the connections are clear. Before moving on to the men and women who have preserved the Scripture, examine this verse.

1 Cor. 15:33 Be not deceived: evil communications corrupt good manners.

Having read the preceding material, this verse should come alive! In addition, it should be clear that the infection started in the Garden of Eden continues to spread among men.

---

[1] Gipp, Th.D., Samuel C., *Gipps Understandable History of the Bible,* Chapter 7, pp. 130-194

I would like to remind the reader that we are still collecting the history of the complaints and the history of the leaven (infection). We are still in the "Subjective" portion of the SOAP anachronism. We have not arrived at "*the lie that changed the modern world*", although we have seen a number of nauseating, detestable deceits by men who were supposed to be protecting and preserving the Words of God. Instead they were protecting and preserving their positions of power just as the leaders of Israel were doing when they crucified our Lord. What man does in the name of religion! Incidentally, this same spirit is found in the Islamic "jihad" movement of the modern age. This "spirit" justifies "whatever means" is necessary to arrive at the end they desire, which includes the killing of women and children.

We have not arrived anywhere near the "Objective" portion of the acronym, SOAP. In the objective section we apply the preceding information to explain all the changes in the Hebrew and Greek texts and all the changes in the "new" versions everyone recognizes, but very few people understand. Now, our next step in the history of the patient is to examine the history of the men of the "strait" gate who are members of the **priesthood of believers.**

THE STRAIT GATE HISTORY: THE MEN

(There are charts in the appendices, which may assist the reader.)

Matthew 7:13-14 Enter ye in at the strait gate: for wide *is* the gate, and broad *is* the way, that leadeth to destruction, and many there be which go in thereat: Because strait *is* the gate, and narrow *is* the way, which leadeth unto life, and few there be that find it.

Matthew 7:21-22 Not every one that saith unto me, Lord, Lord, shall enter into the kingdom of heaven; but he that doeth the will of my Father which is in heaven. Many will say to me in that day, Lord, Lord, have we not prophesied in thy name? and in thy name have cast out devils? and in thy name done many wonderful works?

WORDS ARE TO BE KEPT

Since the beginning of the history of the Bible, God has commanded that His Words were to be recorded and kept in a special place.

Ex 40:20a And he took and put the testimony into the ark

In addition, it was to be read periodically to the "people" and the Lord assured them that "the book" would be available for ever..

Exodus 17:14a *And the LORD said unto Moses,* **Write this for a memorial in a book,** and rehearse it in the ears of Joshua:. Isaiah 30:8 Now go, **write it** before them in a table, and note it in a book, that it may be for the time to come **for ever and ever**: Deut. 17:18-19 And it shall be, when he sitteth upon the throne of his kingdom, that he shall **write him a copy** of this law in a book out of that which is before the priests the Levites: And it shall be with him, and **he shall read** therein all the days of his life: that he may learn to fear the LORD his God, to keep all the words of this law and these statutes, to do them: Deut. 31:24-26 And it came to pass, when Moses had made an end of writing the words of this law in a book, until they were finished, That Moses commanded the Levites, which bare the ark of the covenant of the LORD, saying, **Take this book of the law, and put it in the side of the ark of the covenant** of the LORD your God, that it may be there for a witness against thee. [my emphasis]

OLD TESTAMENT MEN WHO INITIALLY KEPT "THE WORDS"

There are many other places in Scripture where God commands that His Words are to be handled in a specific way and by specific people. Before Jesus Christ's first advent, and in Old Testament times, a special group of men among the Priests, called scribes, arose who were responsible for copying the Writings. Judges 5:14 Out of Ephraim was there a root of them against Amalek; after thee, Benjamin, among thy people; out of Machir came down governors, and out of Zebulun **they that handle the pen of the writer.** 2 Samuel 8:17 And Zadok the son of Ahitub, and Ahimelech the son of Abiathar, were the priests; and Seraiah was **the scribe**; 2 Samuel 20:25

And Sheva was **scribe**: and Zadok and Abiathar were the priests: Ezra 7:6 This Ezra went up from Babylon; and he was a ready **scribe** in the law of Moses, which the LORD God of Israel had given: and the king granted him all his request, according to the hand of the LORD his God upon him. Jeremiah 36:4 Then Jeremiah called Baruch the son of Neriah: and Baruch wrote from the mouth of Jeremiah all the words of the LORD, which he had spoken unto him, upon a roll of a book. [my emphasis]

"According to G. F. Moore (1927), the earliest of these scribes were called Tannaim (teachers). These not only copied the text of the OT with great accuracy, but also committed to writing their oral tradition, called Mishna, a work of six main sections, dealing with agricultural laws, feasts, laws regarding women, fines, sacrifices, and purifications. The Tannaim were followed by a group of scribes called Amoraim (Expositors). These were the scholars who in addition to their work as copyists of the OT also produced the Talmud, which is a commentary on the Mishna. The Amoraim were followed in the sixth century by the Masoretic to whom the Masoretic (meaning traditional) Old Testament text is due. These Masoretic took extraordinary pains to transmit without error the OT text. Many complicated safeguards against scribal slips were devised. W. J. Martin states the number of letters in a book was counted and its middle letter was given. Similarly with the Words and again the middle Words of the book were noted. They collected any peculiarities in spelling. They recorded the number of times a particular Word or phrase occurred. It is generally believed that the Masoretic introduced vowel points and other written signs to aid in pronunciation into the text. God, working through Jewish scribes to preserve the purity of the text, can be summed up in the words of Rabbi Akiba (died about AD 135), "The accurate transmission is a fence for the Torah. He also stressed the importance of preserving even the smallest letter. Thus the promise of Christ in Matthew 5:18 was fulfilled."[1]

Matthew 5:18 For verily I say unto you, Till heaven and earth pass, one jot or one tittle shall in no wise pass from the law, till all be fulfilled.

"Not only the Law of Moses, but also the Psalms were preserved in the Temple by the priests, and it was probably the priests who divided the Hebrew Psalter into five books corresponding to the five books of Moses. It was David who

---

[1] Moorman, Jack; *Forever Settled;* The Bible for Today, Collingswood, N.J.; BFT 1428; 1985; pp. 5-6

taught the priests to sing Psalms as part of their public worship service. We are told when David brought the ark to Jerusalem: I Chronicles 15:16-17 And David spake to the chief of the Levites, to appoint their brethren to be singers with instruments of music .... So the Levites appointed Heman ... Asaph ... Ethan.

Like David, Heman, Asaph and Ethan were not only singers but also inspired authors, and some of the Psalms were written by them. It is likely that the books of Solomon were collected together and carefully kept at Jerusalem. Some of Solomon's proverbs, we are told, were copied out by the men of Hezekiah King of Judah (Proverbs 25:1). During the period of the kings also private and partial collections of the books of the Prophets had already been formed and were in possession of individuals. This is apparent from the frequent references made by the prophets, such as Jeremiah and Ezekiel to the language of their predecessors or to the former history of the nation, from the explicit mention of a prediction of Micah, delivered a century before, by the elders in addressing the people (Jeremiah 26:17-19), and from "the books" of which Daniel (9:2) speaks at the close of the captivity, and in which the prophecies of Jeremiah must have been included. Except for periodic revivals under Godly rulers, such as Asa, Jehoshaphat, Hezekiah and Josiah, the days of the kings were times of spiritual darkness in which the priests neglected their God-given task of guarding and teaching God's holy Law. Note for example the years which preceded the reign of good king Asa. II Chronicles 15:3 *Now for a long season Israel hath been without the true God, and without a teaching priest, and without law.* During the reign of Manasseh, the original copy of the Law had been mislaid and was not found again until Josiah's time (2 Kings 22:8). Because the priests were thus unfaithful in their office, Jerusalem was finally destroyed and the Jews were carried away captive to Babylon (Micah. 3:11,12). But in spite of everything, God was still watching over His holy Words and preserving it by His special providence. Thus when Daniel and Ezekiel and other true believers were led away to Babylon, they took with them copies of all the Old Testament Scriptures which had been written up to that time. After the Jews returned from the Babylonian exile, there was a great revival among the priesthood through the power of the Holy Spirit. Zechariah. 4:6 Not by might, nor by power, but by My Spirit, saith the LORD of hosts. The Law was again taught in Jerusalem by Ezra the priest, who: Ezra 7:10 Prepared his heart to seek the law of the LORD, and to do it, and to teach in Israel statutes and judgments. By Ezra and his successors, under the guidance of the Holy Spirit, all the Old Testament books were gathered together into one Old Testament canon and preserved until the days of our Lord's earthly ministry. By that time, the Old Testament text was so firmly established that even the Jews rejection of Christ could not disturb it. Unbelieving Jewish scribes transmitted this traditional Hebrew OT text, blindly but faithfully, until the dawn of the Protestant Reformation, at which time it again passed into the possession of Christian Church."[1]

SPECIFIC WAYS DEVELOPED TO PRESERVE AND KEEP THE WORDS

Dr. D. A. Waite reports that:

"**The Old Testament Hebrew Text Was Accumulated by the Jews**. Let us take a look at the Old Testament of the KING JAMES BIBLE and why it has a superior text. First, it was **accumulated** by the Jews, and secondly, it was **authorized** by Jesus.

a. Romans 3:1-2--The Jews Were Named by God to Be the Guardians of the Old Testament. A Scripture text we ought to use to prove that the Jews were the **God-appointed custodians** of the Old Testament is Romans 3:1-2. No Gentile was to put his unclean hands upon God's Old Testament. Even the New Testament (with the possible exception of one book) was written by Jews, God's ancient earthly people Israel, who one day will be restored to faith when they see their Messiah and they will look upon Him "Whom they have pierced." (Zechariah 12:10).

Rom. 3:1-2: *What advantage then hath the Jew? or what profit is there of circumcision? (2) Much every way: chiefly, because that **UNTO THEM WERE COMMITTED THE ORACLES OF GOD**.*

Strong gives this information about the word, "oracles":

"3051. logion {log'-ee-on}; neuter of 3052; an utterance (of God): -oracle. The *"oracles of God"* are the very "utterances" or Words of God. Unto them (the Jews) "were committed the

---

[1] Ibid. pp3-4

oracles of God." This is why we place so much confidence in the traditional Masoretic Hebrew Old Testament text that those Jews guarded and kept for us. That is why the KING JAMES translators used this text as the basis for their Bible rather than the Latin Vulgate (which was not Hebrew at all) or the Septuagint Greek (which is not Hebrew), or Symmachus, or Theodotion (all these are Greek), or an ancient tribal tradition, or any other source which is not the Masoretic Hebrew text. None of these other things should ever have a say in how the text should read, nor should any of them be used to contradict the traditional Masoretic Hebrew text that underlies the KING JAMES BIBLE.

b. The Methods of the Old Testament Guardians. Let us take a look at how the Jews fulfilled this Biblical promise by their strict rules in copying the Hebrew Old Testament. This is from *General Biblical Introduction* by H. S. Miller written in 1960, pages 184-185. He lists eight rules the Jews used in the copying of the Synagogue Rolls of the Old Testament Scriptures. These rules are mentioned in the Talmud:

1. The parchment must be made from the skin of clean animals; must be prepared by a Jew only, and the skins must be fastened together by strings taken from clean animals.

2. Each column must have no less than 48 nor more than 60 lines. The entire copy must be first lined. . . .

3. The ink must be of no other color than black, and it must be prepared according to a special recipe.

4. No words nor letter could be written from memory; the scribe must have an authentic copy before him, and he must read and pronounce aloud each word before writing it. [For instance "In the beginning God created the heaven and the earth" You would have to pronounce the word "in the beginning" in Hebrew, (*b'reshith*); "God," (*Elohim*); "created," (*bara*); "the heavens" (*eth hashamaim*); "and the earth" (*wa eth ha arets*). He had to pronounce every word before he wrote it down, with an authentic copy before him. He had to pronounce it aloud, not just see it in his mind. This was to avoid any errors, duplications, omissions, etc.].

5. He must reverently wipe his pen each time before writing the word for "God" [which is Elohim] *and he must wash his whole body before writing the name "Jehovah"* [which is translated "LORD" in our KING JAMES BIBLE] *lest the Holy Name be contaminated.*

6. Strict rules were given concerning forms of the letters, spaces between letters, words, and sections, the use of the pen, the color of the parchment, etc.

7. The revision of a roll must be made within 30 days after the work was finished; otherwise it was worthless. One mistake on a sheet condemned the sheet; if three mistakes were found on any page, the entire manuscript was condemned. [What if the man got from Genesis all the way through to Malachi and found three mistakes? He would have to start from Genesis and go all the way to Malachi again. You see the meticulousness with which the Jews were ordered to guard the Words of God? Those men believed that the words they were copying were God's holy Words. Because of this, they guarded them, unlike men today who add, subtract, and change at will such as has been done in the NKJV, NASV, NIV, and in other new versions. To that extent, they are perversions of truth and Scriptures.]

8. Every word and every letter was counted, [Notice that. The words and letters were counted. Think of counting all the letters on every page of the Hebrew Old Testament. Talk about exactness. Yet that was the method God used to preserve the Old Testament.] *and if a letter were omitted, an extra letter inserted, or if one letter touched another, the manuscript was condemned and destroyed at once." [Miller, op. cit., pp. 184-185]* [My comments in brackets.]

These are historic rules the Jews used. Miller also added these words which we should bear in mind:

"Some of these rules may appear extreme and absurd, yet they show how sacred the Holy Words of the Old Testament was to its custodians, the Jews (Rom. 3:2), and they give us strong encouragement to believe that **WE HAVE THE REAL OLD TESTAMENT, THE SAME ONE WHICH OUR LORD HAD AND WHICH WAS ORIGINALLY GIVEN BY INSPIRATION OF GOD.** *" [Miller, op. cit., p. 185]*

c. A Brief History of the Traditional Hebrew Masoretic Old Testament Text. Let us take a brief look at the history of the Hebrew Old Testament text. The word, *"Masoretic,"* is from the Hebrew *masar* ("to hand down"). It means to hand down from person to person. The Masoretes were "traditionalists" who guarded the Old Testament Hebrew text. There were families of Hebrew scholars in Babylon, in Palestine, and in Tiberius. According to most students of these matters, these Masoretes safeguarded the consonantal text. [According to some fundamentalist writers, the vowels were present in the Hebrew language right from the start. All the Masoretes had to do was to guard both consonants and vowels. They may very well be correct in this.] I say "consonantal text" because, as one school of thinking understands it, originally the Hebrew was written only in consonants, there were no vowels. For instance, in our English language, if we use the word "*WATER*" the vowels are "*a*" and "*e.*" By analogy, if it were a Hebrew word, all they would have had would have been "*WTR.*" They knew what the word meant. We would have recognized it, but with other vowels, it might have been "*WAITER.*" So, to safeguard the Words, to be sure what the Word of God was saying and teaching, they put in the vowel markings. Underneath the consonants, for example, you might find a small "*t*" which is the sound "*ah*"; you might find three dots which is the sound "*eh*"; or you might find two dots which is the sound "*ay*"; one dot is "*ee.*" These are called *matres lectiones*, ("mothers of reading") which enabled Gentiles (and other Jews who were not as familiar with the text) to read those Hebrew words with the vowels in there and know exactly what word it would be. So it would be, for instance "*WATER*" instead of "*WAITER.*" These Masoretes guarded the consonantal text and later put in these vowels. They wanted to make sure we knew what those Words were, especially for the benefit of those of us who are not Jews, and who would not understand the history of it. The Masoretes flourished from about 500 to 1000 A.D. They were supposed to have standardized the Hebrew Old Testament in about 600-700 A.D. by putting in the vowel pointings to aid in the pronunciation of the consonantal text. Their text is called the Masoretic Text or "M.T." if you want to abbreviate it. Some people spell the word "Massoretic," some "Masoretic." I prefer "Masoretic" with only one "s.".["1]

NEW TESTAMENT WORDS RECEIVED; AND THE COMMAND TO KEEP THEM

So we see the diligence of the men who preserved the Old Testament text, a special group of scribes appointed out of the priests of Israel. We will examine the Old Testament manuscripts that they preserved into the early Reformation in

[1] Waite, Th.D., Ph.D., D.A.; *Defending the King James Bible: A Four Fold Superiority"*; The Bible For Today, Collingswood, N.J.; ISBN 1-56848-000-8; 1994; pp. 23-27

the following sections of this book. Next we will examine the New Testament era and concepts concerning preservation of the Words.

Joh 17:8 For I have given unto them the words which thou gavest me; and they have **received** them, and have known surely that I came out from thee, and they have believed that thou didst send me. [my emphasis]

There is evidence in the New Testament that many priests were added very early to the Christian faith. Acts 6:7 *And the word of God increased; and the number of the disciples multiplied in Jerusalem greatly; and a great company of the priests were obedient to the faith.* In John 12:42 it is mentioned that many of the chief rulers believed on Him. There can be little doubt that among some of these priests and chief rulers that there were scribes who joined the priesthood of believers. In the years to come these men undoubtedly taught those in the church how to copy with proficiency and accuracy. This helped the church in the first few centuries to spread rapidly with their copies; especially, in light of the persecutions from the Sanhedrin and Roman emperors. The Christians extended into Europe and beyond, carrying with them their precious copies of Scripture.

The New Testament was written between the A.D. 40's and 90's by men who were "moved by" the Spirit of God [2 Pe 1:21]. Paul said to Timothy: "*All scripture is given by inspiration of God, and is profitable for doctrine, for reproof, for correction, for instruction in righteousness."* [2TIM 3:16] Peter reported that Paul's epistles were already considered Scripture while Peter and possibly Paul were still alive: "And account that the longsuffering of our Lord is salvation; even as our beloved brother Paul also according to the wisdom given unto him hath written unto you; As also **in all his epistles,** speaking in them of these things; in which are some things hard to be understood, which they that are unlearned and unstable wrest, as they do also the **other scriptures,** unto their own destruction." [2PE 3:15-16] Jesus told His Apostles in John 14:25-26: "*These things have I spoken unto you, being yet present with you. But the Comforter, which is the Holy Ghost, whom the Father will send in my name, he shall teach you all things, and bring all things to your remembrance, whatsoever I have said unto you.*"

Dr. Jack Moorman says of the preceding verse:

"Here Jesus answers beforehand a question which Bible scholars have been asking down through the ages. Why is it that the first three Gospels, Matthew, Mark, and Luke, agree together so closely, and why is it that the Gospel of John differs from these first three Gospels so widely? Both these agreements and these differences are due to the inspiration which the Apostles received from the Holy Spirit and the control which He exercised over their minds and memories. It was not due to a theorized common source. Read verse 26 above again. [Do you believe what Jesus said? Do you wrest with Scriptures as Peter said?] In the Gospels, therefore, Jesus reveals Himself through the account of His earthly ministry. The rest of the New Testament books are His divine commentary on the meaning of that ministry. These remaining books were written in accordance with His promise to His Apostles: John 16:12-13 **I have yet many things to say unto you, but ye cannot bear them now. Howbeit, when he, the Spirit of truth, is come, he will guide you into all truth: for he shall not speak of himself; but whatsoever he shall hear, that shall he speak: and he will show you things to come.** It was in fulfillment of this promise that the Holy Spirit descended upon the Apostles at Pentecost, filled their minds and hearts with the message of the risen, exalted Lord, and sent them out to preach this message, first to the Jews at Jerusalem and then to all the world. Then followed the conversion of the Apostle Paul and the Epistles which he wrote under the inspiration of the Holy Spirit. Then James, Peter, John, and Jude were inspired to write their Epistles, and Luke to tell the story of the Acts of the Apostles. Finally, the Revelation proceeded from the inspired pen of John on Patmos, announcing those things that were yet to come. Volumes, of course, could be filled with a discussion of these sacred developments, but here a bare statement of the essential facts must suffice."[1]

Jesus commanded *the priesthood of believers* to keep His Words. The word, keep, means to guard, protect and preserve in the following verses.[2]

Joh 14:15 If ye love me, **keep** my commandments.

Joh 14:21 He that hath my commandments, and **keepeth** them, he it is that loveth me: and he that loveth me shall be loved of my Father, and I will love him, and will manifest myself to him.

---

[1] Moorman, Jack; *Forever Settled;* p. 44
[2]

The word "keep" comes from the Greek word, tereo, which is defined by Strong's Dictionary as Greek 5083. tereo... (a watch; perhaps akin to 2334); **to guard** (from loss or injury, properly, **by keeping the eye upon**; and thus differing from 5442, which is properly to prevent escaping; and from 2892, which implies a fortress or full military lines of apparatus), i.e. to note (a prophecy; figuratively, to fulfil a command); by implication, to detain (in custody; figuratively, to maintain); by extension, to withhold (for personal ends; figuratively, to keep unmarried); by extension, to withhold (for personal ends; figuratively, to keep unmarried):--hold fast, keep(- er), **(pre-, re-)serve**, watch.

Joh 14:23 Jesus answered and said unto him, If a man love me, he will **keep** my words: and my Father will love him, and we will come unto him, and make our abode with him.

Joh 14:24 He that loveth me not **keepeth** not my sayings: and the word which ye hear is not mine, but the Father's which sent me.

Joh 15:10 If ye **keep** my commandments, ye shall abide in my love; even as I have kept my Father's commandments, and abide in his love.

NEW TESTAMENT WORDS PRESERVED

Following the INSPIRED writing of the New Testament books by Holy Ghost guided men, the question must arise as to how they were selected, preserved, and maintained.

"The first **New Testament** books to be assembled together were the Epistles of Paul. The Apostle Peter, shortly before he died, referred to Paul's Epistles as Scripture and in such a way as to indicate that at least the beginning of such a collection had already been made (II Peter 3:15-16). Even radical scholars, such as L. J. Goodspeed (1926), agree that a collection of Paul's Epistles was in circulation at the beginning of the second century and that Ignatius (117) referred to it. [Even Paul considered his epistles authoritative. See 1Co 14:37, 2Co 10:1-16, Gal 1:6-12, 2Thess. 3:6-14. Paul places Luke's gospel equivalent to Deuteronomy—See 1Tim 5:18; my addition] When the Four Gospels were collected together is unknown, but it is generally agreed that this must have taken place before 170 AD because at that time Tatian made his harmony of the Gospels (Diatessaron), which included all four of the canonical Gospels and only these four. Before 200 AD Paul [his epistles], the Gospels, Acts, I Peter and I John were recognized as Scripture by Christians everywhere (as the writings of Irenaeus, Clement of Alexandria, and Tertullian prove) and accorded an authority equal to that of the Old **Testament** Scriptures. It was Tertullian (160-221 A. D.), moreover, who first applied the name **New Testament** to this collection of apostolic writings. The seven remaining books, 2 and 3 John, 2 Peter, Hebrews, James, Jude and Revelation, were not yet unanimously accepted as Scripture. By the time the fourth century had arrived, however, few Christians seem to have questioned the right of these disputed books to a place in the **New Testament** canon. Eminent Church Fathers of that era, such as Athanasius, Augustine, and Jerome, include them in their lists of the **New Testament** books. Thus through the Holy Spirit's guidance of individual believers, silently and gradually - but nevertheless surely, the Church as a whole was led to a recognition of the fact that the twenty-seven books of the **New Testament**, and only these books, form the canon which God gave to be placed beside the Old **Testament** Scriptures as the authoritative and final revelation of His will. This guidance of the Holy Spirit was negative as well as positive. It involved not only the selection of canonical **New Testament** books but also the rejection of all non-canonical books, which were mistakenly regarded as canonical by some of the early Christians. Thus Irenaeus and Clement of Alexandria used the Shepherd of Hermas as Holy Scripture, [I question Iranaeus using it! HDW] and Clement and Origen wrongly gave the same status to the Teaching of the Twelve Apostles. Clement likewise commented on the Apocalypse of Peter and the Epistle of Barnabas, to which Origen also accorded the title "catholic." And in addition, there were many false Gospels in circulation, as well as numerous false Acts ascribed to various Apostles. But although some of those non-canonical writings gained temporary acceptance in certain quarters, this state of affairs lasted for but a short time. Soon all Christians everywhere were led by the Holy Spirit to repudiate these spurious works and to receive only the canonical books as their **New Testament** Scriptures. Having said all this, it must also be acknowledged that there is a deep and sacred mystery in the formation of the Written Word on Earth just as there had been in the incarnation and development of the Living Word"[1]

THE PRIESTHOOD OF BELIEVERS SPREADS

The famous church historian, Andrew Miller said:
"In less than a hundred years from the day of Pentecost the gospel had penetrated into most of the provinces of the Roman empire, and was widely diffused in many of them.... In large central cities, such as Antioch in Syria, Ephesus in Asia,

---

[1] Ibid. pp. 44-45

and Corinth in Greece, we have seen Christianity well established, and spreading its rich blessings among the surrounding towns and villages. We also learn from ecclesiastical antiquity, that what these cities were to Syria, Asia, and Greece, as Carthage was to Africa. When Scapula, the president of Carthage, threatened the Christians with severe and cruel treatment, Tertullian (160-221 A.D.), in one of his pointed appeals, bids him bethink himself. "What wilt thou do," he says, "with so many thousands of men and women of every age and dignity as will freely offer themselves? What fires, what swords, wilt thou stand in need of! What is Carthage itself likely to suffer if decimated by thee: when every one there shall find his near kindred and neighbors, and shall see there matrons, and men perhaps of thine own rank and order, and the most principal persons, and either the kindred or friends of those who are thy nearest friends? Spare then, therefore, for thy sake, if not for ours."[1]

However, Tertullian's typical appeal was not to be honored at that time. Numerous appeals by Christian leaders to the Emperors in Rome, prior to the development of a state religion and after the Roman Catholic church was established, would be ignored.

PERSECUTIONS INTENSIFY

In spite of Christianity being a peaceful and non-combative religion, the slaughter of Christians by the thousands commenced under the reigns of Emperors Nero (60-68 A.D.),Domitian (81-97 A.D.), Trajan (98-117 A.D.), Hadrian (117-138 A.D.), Pius (138-161 A.D.), Marcus Aurelieus (161-180 A.D.), Septimus Severus (193-211), Maximum (235-238), Decius (249-251 A.D.), Valerian (253-260 A.D.), and Diocletian (284-305 A.D.). The last Emperor of this period, Diocletian, was the worst.

It is at this point that there is a need to introduce to you a little known or taught concept. In order to justify the massacre of so so many Christians, all kinds of false charges had to be trumped up. For example, Christians were accused of boiling and eating their babies, of having orgies, of attempting to usurp the authority in Rome, of cannibalism because of the Lord' supper, of

---

[1] Miller, Andrew; *Church History;* London; c 1860; Fundamental Baptist CD Rom; Way of Life Literature; Port Huron, MI; p. The Rapid Progress of Christianity

causing disruptions of pagan worship and other just as ridiculous charges.

Peter Allix, writing in 1690, tells us

> "that the Roman President having caused some slaves to be apprehended that belonged to Christians, made them confess, at the sight of tortures prepared for them, that the Christians did eat children in their assemblies, and that they there promiscuously polluted themselves by abominable incests; which was afterwards confirmed by weak Christians, who for fear of torments abjured their religion."[1]

Of course, this was just following the precedent set by the Sanhedrin who, "true to form," leveled false charges against Jesus in order to justify capital punishment; and likewise, punishment of His followers occurred because of false witnesses. Is it any wonder that God considers false witnesses an abomination? In spite of torture the Scriptures were copied and passed to the various developing churches. Certain men of stature in those churches rose up (see below). Antioch of Syria had become the center of Christianity as opposed to Jerusalem. It was here where the saints were first called Christians. There were many reasons for this development and change of venue, but among the major reasons were: 1) Paul, Barnabus, Silas, and Mark were missionary leaders there. 2) The persecutions in Jerusalem were too great for the Christians, and so the dispersion of Christians began. 3) Antioch was a crossroads for culture and trade from the East and West.

As Emperor Trajan, who ascended to the throne in 98 A.D. and lasted to 117 A.D., was passing through Antioch on his way to fight the Parthian war (107), he encountered a great earthquake. He was severely injured, and he sought an object for his frustration. In this case it was Ignatius (35-116 A.D.), one of the pastors there and a man of outstanding Christian character and piety. Tarjan had been primed by Pliny the Younger's (governor of Bithynia and Pontus) letters to him concerning the Christians, and so charged the pious Ignatius and sent him to Rome "where he was exposed to the fury of wild beasts in the theater, and by them devoured."[2]

Paul and others established churches in the surrounding territories. One of these churches was the church at Ephesus. The Apostle John is said to have fled the destruction of Jerusalem in 70 A.D. and moved to Ephesus where he was

---

[1] Allix, Peter; *Some Remarks Upon the Ecclesiastical History of the Ancient Churches of the Albigenses;* 1690; Oxford: At the Clarendon Press; Chapter 2, p. 1; Fundamental Baptist CD ROM; There is also confirmation of this kind of thinking in the letters of Pliny the Younger to Emperor Trajan.

[2] Jones, William; *The History of the Christian Church, from the Birth of Christ to the 18th Century,* 5th edition, 1826, Printed by W. Myers, Castles Street, Holbor, London; p. 6, section 1

apparently boiled in oil and when he did not die was banished to the island of Patmos where he wrote the Apokalypsis in 90-95 A.D.[1]

VENERABLE POLYCARP

In the nearby city of Smyrna, which was near Ephesus where the Apostle John lived, Polycarp (69-166 A.D.), who was a disciple of John, was pastor. He held the position for many years:

"and which he had filled up with honor to himself, to the edification of his Christian brethren, and the glory of his divine Master. It only remained for him now to seal his testimony with his blood. The eminence of his station marked him out as the victim of popular fury. The cry of the multitude against Polycarp was, "This is the doctor of Asia, the father of the Christians, the subverter of our gods, who teaches many that they must not perform the sacred rites, nor worship our deities. Away with these Atheists." [The crowds believed Christians were atheists because they did not worship the many gods of the people. My comment] The philosophy of the emperor could not teach him that this pretended atheism [Christianity] was a real virtue, which deserved to be encouraged and propagated amongst mankind. Here reason and philosophy faded [failed] him; and his blind attachment to the gods of his country caused him to shed much blood, and to become the destroyer of the saints of the living God! ... The friends of Polycarp, anxious for his safety, prevailed on him to withdraw himself from public view, and to retire to a neighboring village, which he did, continuing with a few of his brethren, day and night, in prayer to God, for the tranquility of all the churches. The most diligent search was, in the mean time, made for him without effect. But when his enemies proceeded to put some of his brethren to the torture, with the view of compelling them to betray him, he could no longer be prevailed on to remain concealed. "The will of the Lord be done," was his pious ejaculation; on uttering which, he made a voluntary surrender of himself to his persecutors, saluted them with a cheerful countenance, and invited them to refresh themselves at his table, only soliciting from them on his

---

[1] van Braght, Thieleman J.; *Martyrs Mirror*; Herald Press, Scottdale, PA; First published in 1660; p. 96

own behalf one hour for prayer. They granted his request, and his devotions were prolonged to double the period, with such sweetness and savour, that all who heard him were struck with admiration, several of the soldiers repenting that they were employed against so venerable an old man. His prayer being ended, they set him on an ass, and conveyed him towards the city, being met on the road by Herod the Irenarch (a kind of justice of the peace) and his father Niceres, who were chief agents in this persecution. [Cave's *Life of* Polycarp, p. 53.] Many efforts were tried to shake his constancy, and induce him to abjure his profession; at one time he was threatened by the proconsul with the fury of wild beasts. "Call for them," said Polycarp, "it does not become us to turn from good to evil." "Seeing you make so light of wild beasts," rejoined the magistrate, "I will tame you with the more terrible punishment of fire." But Polycarp bravely replied, "You threaten me with a fire that is quickly extinguished, but are ignorant of the eternal fire of God's judgment, reserved for the wicked in the other world. But why do you delay? Order what punishment you please." Thus, finding him impenetrable both to the arts of seduction and the dread of punishment, the fire was commanded to be lighted, and the body of this venerable father burnt to ashes, in the year 166."[1]

Polycarp is a prime example of *the priesthood of believers* who would be responsible for transmitting the text from one church to another by carefully made copies. Can you imagine this venerable old man doing anything other than the best job humanly possible for the pure propagation and preservation of the Scriptures?

THE APOSTLE JOHN DISCIPLED POLYCARP WHO DISCIPLED IRENAEUS

It was Polycarp who discipled Irenaeus (130-200 A.D.) and sent him into Gaul (France). He became the pastor at Lyons, France. A heretical group called the Gnostics was continuing to cause turmoil among all the churches including the church in France. Men such as Polycarp and Irenaeus were aware of the

---

[1] Jones, William; *The History of the Christian Church, from the Birth of Christ to the 18th Century;* the section of "The State of the Christian Profession under the Reigns of Adrian and the Antonines, pp. 3-4

Gnostic heresy and would be aware of changes to the Scripture that would support the Gnostic position. As a matter of fact, Marcion was evicted from the Church at Rome because of his corruption of Scripture and the Gnostic heresy. The philosophy of the Gnostics was introduced into the church by the Alexandrian school from Greek philosophy, and the Apostles Paul and John dealt with the Gnostic heresies in 2nd Timothy and 1st John.

"In his Second Epistle to Timothy, Paul cites two **Gnostics** by name, Hymenaeus and Philetus, who were undermining the teaching of the doctrine of the resurrection (II Tim. 2:18). Presumably, they were allegorizing the teaching, and possibly paving the way for a reincarnation teaching. John's Epistles bristle with refutation for the **Gnostics**. The Apostle John was a great defender of orthodox Christology, as his Gospel suggests, and he exposed heretical Christology in his Epistles. In the First Epistle, he condemned as anti-Christian the teaching that Jesus was not the Christ or the Messiah (I Jn. 2:22). This heresy was later known as Adoptionism; it taught that Jesus of Nazareth was adopted by the 'Christ Spirit' at his baptism and this Spirit left Him at His death. The other Christological heresy denounced by John was the Gnostic teaching that Jesus Christ (as God) was manifest in the incarnation (I Jn. 4:3) [not in the flesh, my clarification]. This heresy was later known as Docetism, that is, Christ only "seemed" to be in the flesh, but really He was a phantom. Because of the intensity of the Christological battle John was waging with the **Gnostics**, he gives the strongest revelatory statement on orthodox Christology, stating, "For there are three that bear record in heaven, the Father, the Word, and the Holy Ghost, and these three are one" (I Jn. 5:7)."[1]

Irenaeus continued to fight this heresy and his statements lend support to the preservation of Scripture because his statements reflect the **searching of Scripture** handed down through Polycarp and John to refute the Gnostics.

"Irenaeus gives us this for one character of the Gnostics, that they embraced doctrines which were not to be found in the writings of the Prophets or the Apostles."[2]

There is an account of the beliefs of Irenaeus as reported by Eusebius (265-340 A.D.), the architect of Bible codices for Emperor Constantine. Remember

---

[1] Strouse, Thomas M.; *The New Age Movement: Ancient Gnosticism;* The Baptist Theological Journal, Vol. 1, Issue 1, Tabernacle Baptist Seminary, Virginia Beach, VA

[2] Allix, Peter, *Some Remarks upon the Ecclesiastical History of the Ancient Churches of the Albegenses,* Gnostic Reference, Chapter 2, p2 of 4

Irenaeus came from Smyrna and was discipled by Polycarp who in turn was taught by the Apostle John. In Peter Allix's book, *Ecclesiastical History*, the account of Irenaeus' beliefs is parallel to the Apostle's Creed. How fortunate for us that we have a report that goes so far back to the early post-Apostolic period when Irenaeus lived. These statements clearly demonstrate a solid foundation. Surely, Irenaeus had copies of the same manuscripts preserved and used by Polycarp. The following brief quotations came from Peter Allix's book.

Irenaeus upheld that the Scriptures were:

"both clear and perfect". [from Peter Allix]

He rejected the doctrines which heretics grounded upon the interpretation of some parables, maintaining that:

"nothing ought to be established *but* upon clear and evident places of Scripture." [from Peter Allix]

The Gnostics used extensive allegorical interpretation of Scripture. Irenaeus didn't like allegorical interpretation. He was opposed to public penance or punishment. He did not proclaim or support celibacy. Celibacy was not known in Asia where Polycarp instructed Irenaeus demonstrating that these first Christians of the Gauls, the Lyons' area of France, had derived their original doctrine by direct Apostolic descent from the East. Remember the linkage of Irenaeus back to the Apostle John in Ephesus and Polycarp in Smyrna. He rejected the custom of the Marcosians, a Gnostic sect, of anointing those they received into their communion with balm, opobalsamo, and the anointing of persons at the point of death with oil and water, "last rights". "Last rights" by Gnostics is not the calling together of the elders to anoint and pray for someone sick as James reports (James 5:14). It is rather a mystical anointing at the time of death similar to what a Catholic Priest does that is called Extreme Unction, which can even be "for the remission of sins".

Irenaeus rejected the use of images by the heathens and Gnostics:

"which makes it evident that the Christians had no images, much less that they gave to them any religious worship." [from Peter Allix]

He rejected the idea of transubstantiation. Many authors attribute to him the belief in this heretical doctrine, but it appears they did not understand Irenaeus' statements:

"that he knew nothing of the separability of accidents". [from Peter Allix]

This thought, the separability of accidents [accidents is a Gnostic term], preceded from the Gnostics and simply means that material substances can become something else such as the blood and flesh of Jesus Christ. Irenaeus proclaimed that our bodies are nourished by the food from God, and that the bread and wine of the Lord's Supper was food and was **symbolic**. The wine was simply a product of the fruit of the vine. He also maintained that the Lord's

Supper was wholly different in meaning from the sacrifices of the Old Testament.

He plainly rejected the invocation of angels, instead recommending that of our Savior Jesus Christ be petitioned. He asserts that the Virgin Mary was a sinner which he describes in Latin as "intempestivam festinationem" which is based on John 2:3. This simply means that she was infested with many temptations, "so far was he from believing her wholly free from sin".

This demonstrates that when he said in Latin:

"Quod alligavit Virgo Eva per incredulitatem, hoc Virgo Maria solvit per fidem; What the Virgin Eve bound up by her unbelief, that the Virgin Mary set free by her faith;" [from Peter Allix]

that he did not believe the Virgin is the person that saved men, but his meaning is:

"like that of Hesychius, who said, speaking of the women to whom Jesus Christ appeared after his resurrection; Invenere enim, saith he, mulieres, quod olim amisere per Evam; lucrum invenit ea, quae damni occasionem praebuerat. For the women found what formerly they lost by Eve; she found the gain, who had been an occasion of the loss." [from Peter Allix]

There are many passages in Irenaeus' writings that confirm this same doctrine; that is, Mary does not save, but rather she needs a Savior.

He did not believe that:

"we ought to have recourse to the intercession of saints and this doctrine of Irenaeus was so emphatic that he plainly asserts that the **apostolical succession is of no consideration without the truth of doctrine.**" [from Peter Allix]

He maintained that Jesus had come in the flesh and that after His resurrection He was in the flesh, although it was glorified. He clearly stated that the custom of observing:

"a fast before Easter was very great, and that there was no law of the Apostles or of Jesus Christ enjoining it, every one using it according to his own free will and devotion." [from Peter Allix]

We find also, that whatsoever respect Irenaeus had:

"for **the Church of Rome, he was no more inclined to be led by her sole authority, than Polycarp was**, whom he much commends; and if he considered her as an Apostolic Church, yet he never attributed to her any authority over the other flocks of the Lord." [from Peter Allix]

From the preceding "we may however perceive what was the state of the Christian religion in Gaul," a little after the middle of the second century and on into the third century which is the time when **Irenaeus** lived and flourished.[1]

Having read this is there any doubt that Irenaeus used the same Scriptures handed down to him through the Apostle John to Polycarp to him, and that he was already using them to establish the correct doctrine as churches were established in Europe? It was during this same period that the Scriptures were already being corrupted by Marcion at Rome and by neoplatonists in Alexandria at the Catechetical School and by others around the empire. Irenaeus was another member of *the priesthood of believers* who helped establish the churches in the Piedmont and valleys of the Gaul area, which were so persecuted from their beginnings. As we will see, their doctrine was pure and their life was simple. After the Roman Church became apostate, the position of members of the churches in the Piedmont was that of "dissenters" from Rome. Irenaeus did not help establish the Catholic Church and was not the first Catholic father as is so often claimed. The claim is probably by those who have an agenda. He did quote from Scriptures, which were similar to those found in the Alexandrian texts, but he was a defender *against* the Gnostics. Perhaps his quotes from the Alexandrian text were part of his apologetics. Having said that, additional information from Jack Moorman's, *The Early Church Fathers and the AV version,* shows Irenaeus used 20 discernable quotes in his writings. Only 5 quotes were *possibly* linked to the Alexandrian text. Most likely, the quotes were made from memory so that Irenaeus did not have to get out his codices and look up a Scripture. I suspect that the quotes of Irenaeus do not match other supposedly "Alexandrian" quotes because as we will see, the entire Alexandrian question is a mess.

Wilbur Pickering in his book, *The Identity of the New Testament Text,* says on page 105 that writings of Irenaeus :

"are about equal in volume to those of all preceding Fathers together...and... "from the time of Irenaeus on there can be no doubt concerning the attitude of the church's New Testament writings—they are Scripture."[2]

Finally, the following is a quote, which will substantiate Irenaeus, and other early post-Apostolic church leaders, dependence on the Words handed down from the Apostles.

"This fervor of the Apostolic age was passed into the second century through men like Polycarp, bishop in Smyrna (A.D. 69-155). Revered as a personal disciple of John, he perpetuated his mentor's fiery denunciation for any who would

---

[1] Ibid. p. 2-4 The preceding information in this work concerning Irenaeus was all obtained from Peter Allix's book. Most modern writers have glossed over or hidden the real work of this member of the priesthood of believers, Irenaeus.

[2] Pickering, Wilbur; *The Identity of the New Testament Text;* The Bible For Today; Collingswood, NJ; B.F.T. #556; 1980, p105-106

distort the Divine record. **"Whosoever perverts the oracles of the Lord...he is the first-born of Satan."** An impressive insight into the expectations of such men for the conscientious scribes and transcriptional accuracy can be gleaned from the ambitions they affixed to their own writings. Irenaeus concluded his work *On the Ogdoad* with the following charges:

I adjure you who shall copy out this book, by our Lord Jesus Christ and by his glorious advent when he comes to judge the living and the dead, that you compare what you transcribe, and correct it carefully against this manuscript from which you copy; and also that you transcribe this adjuration and insert it in the copy.

However the most significant factor which accounts for the early domination of our traditional text is in its convenient recourse to the extant original. As the patriarch trio of Adam, Methuselah, and Noah preserved the entire pre-flood oral tradition, the church's accessibility to New Testament autographs offered a similar security for the written record. This providential arrangement provided a fail-safe deterrent against fabrications which insured a steady transmission of faithfully executed copies. That the originals were utilized in this very manner is confirmed by the written testimony of Tertullian as late as the year 208 A.D. In his defensive work entitled *On Persecution Against Heretics*, he rebukes the skeptics of his age with the challenge:

Come now, you who would indulge a better curiosity, if you would apply it to the business of your salvation, run over the apostolic churches, in which the very thrones of the apostles are still pre-eminent in their places, **in which their own authentic writings are read,** *uttering the voice and representing the face of each of them severally. Achaia is very near you, [in which] you find Corinth. Since you are not far from Macedonia, you have Philippi; (and there too) you have Thessalonians. Since you are able to cross to Asia, you get Ephesus. Since, moreover, you are close upon Italy, you have Rome, from which there comes even into our own hands the very authority (of apostles themselves).*

How happy is its church, on which apostles poured forth **all their own doctrine** *along with their blood!"*[1]

I cannot over-emphasize the importance of the preceding quotes and thoughts. This material refutes in no uncertain terms the opinion of so many

---

[1] Grady, PhD., Th.M., D.D., William P.; *Final Authority*; p. 30

modern textual critics that the "Scripture had been lost" in the first and second centuries and that by the third and forth centuries it had to be "reconstructed" by a church council "which added pious statements to the traditional text."[1]

CLEMENT OF ROME

In Rome a similar pattern was in progress that had occurred in other major metropolitan centers. Initially, the doctrine passed down by the Apostles was followed. Then things would begin to fall apart and dispersion into the countryside and remote valleys would occur. Clement of Rome (97-140 A.D.) was a pastor in Rome and was a man known for his administrative abilities. His epistle to the Corinthian church has been preserved and reflects his concern for a Church he considered being equal in stature to the Church at Rome. They were having managerial problems and he told them,

"Ye knew full well the Holy Scriptures, *and have thoroughly searched the Oracle of God.*"[2]

This is a clear and preserved reference to the Scriptures handed down from the Apostles. The church at Rome was not "lording it over" the Corinthian Church at this time. Clement of Rome sounds like another member of the **priesthood of believers.**

---

[1] There is a separate booklet published by Bible For Today Press that goes with this work which critiques, *The Textual Criticism of the New Testament*, by K. W. Clark. Clark's paper was given to me by an Alexandrian (those who except manuscripts from Egypt as "the oldest and best MSS) in defense of the Alexandrian position after the preceding information was written. It confirms this continuing modern (wrong!) belief by neutral textual critics that *all* the texts of Scripture were lost, corrupted and not available for use by the *early priesthood of believers*. This false concept will be discussed in detail in the section dealing with manuscripts.

[2] Armitage, Thomas; *A History of the Baptists;* 1890; Way of Life Literature, Port Huron, MI; p. Post-Apostolic time, p. Christianity in the 2nd Century.

PAPIAS

The following is said of Papias (80-155 A.D.):

"In the third book of his *Ecclesiastical History* Eusebius quotes a statement of an older writer, namely, Papias (d. 160), bishop of Hierapolis.[1] "If anyone ever came," Papias relates, "who had followed the elders, I inquired into the words of the elders, what Andrew or Peter or Philip or Thomas or James or John or Matthew, or any other of the Lord's disciples, had said, and what Aristion and the elder John, the Lord's disciples, were saying".[2]

Perhaps we have found yet another member of the priesthood of believers, who are not like the corrupters of Scripture without any remorse. The priesthood of believers cared nothing about the traditions or pronouncements by Nicolaitans, who seek power [Rev. 2:6,15], or their corrupted manuscripts. They care only for the pure preserved words of Scripture.

TERTULLIAN

In Northern Africa Tertullian (160-221 A.D.), a contemporary of Irenaeus who was in Lyons of France (Gaul), was also fighting corruption in the local church and the persecutions from the emperors of Rome.

"TERTULLIAN was a lawyer at Carthage (in North Africa). He became a Christian, and joined the church in that city. His views on baptism we have already mentioned. (He was not a pedobaptizer, or in other words he did not believe in baptism of infants, but 'believer's baptism'. my clarification.) He was elected an elder, and wrote ably in defense of the Christian religion. It was reputed in 215, that the tenth part of the inhabitants [of Carthage, my clarification] were Christians, and there were many congregations in other parts. Tertullian thought they had increased too fast, and lost in the crowd the

---

[1] Eusebius, *Eusebius' Ecclesiastical History;* Hendrickson Publishers; Peabody Mass.; Translated by C.F. Cruse; ISBN 1-56563-371-7; 2000; p.104

[2] Hills, Edward F.; *The King James Defended;* p70

simplicity of the Christian religion. Awhile he had endeavored to stem the torrent, by a strict scrutiny at the admission of members, and as several came to join the church, who had been, or pretended they had been baptized elsewhere, he insisted on re-examining and rebaptizing them, unless they could make it appear that they had been baptized by churches in communion with that of Carthage. [Rob. Hist. Bap. c. 22, p. 183]"[1]

Rebaptism [believer's baptism] of new believers became a hallmark of the early Puritans (See the chart in the appendices, *Dissenters*) because of their disregard for apostate churches.

The following quote makes very clear the doctrinal stance of Tertullian in regards to his approach to the Scriptures, his approach to baptism, and his certainty as to **faith alone saves**. Obviously, he had copies of the original autographs. Jack Moorman testifies that 82 % of his extant quotes of Scripture in his writings are from the Received Text.[2] He was very respected in the East and West, as the following story will show, because the lady asking the question is from Phrygia (Turkey). Remember Tertullian is in North Africa. This also brings up another point. Travel between the major cities in those days was not as difficult as one might expect. There are several reasons for this fact: 1) The Romans had built numerous roads for their military to have rapid access to uprisings in the land they controlled. 2) Sailing vessels were plentiful for transporting goods between Egypt (Africa), the Middle East (Israel and Syria), present-day Turkey, Greece, Italy, and Spain across the Mediterranean. Therefore, contact between Carthage, Antioch, Ephesus, Rome, Lyons, Byzantium (Constantinople), Smyrna, and other important Biblical cities was not as complicated as suspected. Tertullian was probably in contact with the important 'Christian' leaders of his day such as Irenaeus, and even those who were spewing heresies in places like Alexandria, Egypt and others. Many through the ages attest to the fact that he was discipled well. Some authors have complained of his asceticism, but I can find no information as to the extent of that practice. Perhaps he simply rejected the opulent lifestyle of Bishop Cyprian of Carthage who sat on a throne surrounded by his 12 deacons on a lower level. He probably lived an austere life, as many denominations such as the German Baptists recommend even in this modern age. And now the quote mentioned above for you to make your own judgment.

---

[1] Orchard, G. H.; *A Concise History of the Baptist;* Bedfordshire, England; 1855; Way of Life Literature, Fundamental Baptist Electronic Disc, p. Chapter 2 Section II: African Churches; p 3 of 7

[2] Moorman, Jack; *Early Church Fathers and the Authorized Version: A Demonstration;* The Bible For Today; Collingswood, NJ; B.F.T. # 2136; p. 31

"Tertullian was inquired of, by a rich lady named Quintilla, who lived at Pepuza, a town in Phrygia, whether infants might be baptized on condition, they ask to be baptized and produce sponsors? In reply to Quintilla, Tertullian observes, "That baptism ought not to be administered rashly, the administrators of it know. Give to him that asketh? every one hath a right, as if it were a matter of alms? yea, rather say, Give not that which is holy to dogs, cast not your pearls before swine, lay hands suddenly on no man, be not partakers of other men's sins. If Philip baptized the eunuch on the spot, let us remember that it was done under the immediate direction of the Lord.... the eunuch was a believer of Scripture, the instruction given by Philip was seasonable; the one preached, the other perceived the Lord Jesus, and believed on him; water was at hand, and the apostle having finished the affair was caught away. But Paul, you say, was baptized instantly: true; because Judas, in whose house he was, instantly knew he was a vessel of mercy. The condescension of God may confer his favors as he pleases; but our wishes may mislead ourselves and others. It is therefore most expedient to defer baptism, and to regulate the administration of it according to the condition, the disposition, and the age of the person to be baptized; and especially in the case of little ones. What necessity is there to expose sponsors to danger? Death may incapacitate them for fulfilling their engagements, or bad dispositions may defeat all their endeavors. Jesus Christ said indeed, hinder them not, &c., but that they should come to him as soon as they are advanced in years, as soon as they have learnt their religion, when they may be taught whither they are going, when they are become Christians, when they begin to know Jesus Christ. What is there that should compel this innocent age to receive baptism? and since they are not allowed the disposal of temporal goods, is it reasonable that they should be entrusted with the concerns of heaven? They just know how to ask for salvation, that you may seem to give to him that asketh. Such as understand the importance of baptism, are more afraid of presumption than procrastination, **and faith alone saves the soul.**"[1] [my emphasis]

---

[1] Orchard, G. H.; *A Concise History of the Baptists;* p. Chapter 2, Section II: African Churches; 3 of 7

TERTULLIAN HAD THE PRESERVED MANUSCRIPTS

Tertullian also said:
"I hold sure title-deeds from the original owners themselves...I am the heir of the Apostles just as they carefully prepared their will and testament, and committed it to a trust...**even so I hold it**."[1] [my emphasis]

INFECTION PURIFIED AND REFINED IN THE FIRES

Such was the doctrinal status of the believers who could stand against the wiles of Satan during the post-Apostolic days. They were fighting infection (leaven) from paganism, heresy, and Rome. The following statement by G. H. Orchard exemplifies those views of leaven expressed earlier by this author:

"**All historians speak of the Christian church sustaining, to an eminent degree, the character of a pure virgin, for above one hundred years**. The severity of the times would check insincere persons making a profession; the examples of the apostles and their successors were still kept in view; besides, the churches were composed of obscure persons in the estimation of the world; nor did learning adorn her ministers, so as to awaken any fears of rivalship among the philosophers or literati of the day. Yet their obscurity, with their "excess of virtue," [Gibbon's Hist. c. 15] was no guard to their lives or property. It was a maxim with the Romans, to tolerate the religions of those nations they conquered: but this indulgence they extended not to the professors of the gospel. Various reasons and motives combined to occasion an alteration in their wonted policy, though the true grounds are assigned by Paul Rom. 8:7. Gal. 4:29. The **first Christians were poor; and their benevolence towards each other was calculated to keep them free of worldly encumbrances**, yet it is equally evident they were numerous, and the success of the gospel enraged the pagan priests, who reported to the governor the vilest accusations against them. [Some causes

---

[1] Pickering, Wilbur; *Identity of the New Testament Church;* p. 108

assigned for these calumnies by Mr. Robert Turner, are supported neither by reason nor evidence, particularly on Christians eating their own offspring, c. 4.] Those vile reports were ably refuted by apologists, whose works were presented to the emperor. [W. Reeve's *Apologies of the Fathers*] The insinuations of the enemy were but too credulously regarded, and often regulated the policy of the presiding governor. The priests lived by the altars. In the public games, merchants, tradesmen, mechanics, servants, and the rustic who sold the sacrifices, were all interested in maintaining the pagan worship. Hence that popular ridicule, contempt, and persecution, which governments sometimes durst not, or could not, control. Whenever religion influenced the heart, whether of parent or child, it proved a kind of restless **leaven**, which attempted, by every silent and lawful means, to impregnate the whole body with which it stood connected, so that, Christianity was often accused of disturbing the previous harmony of families, and of infusing sectarian principles into the inhabitants of towns and provinces. Nor did Christianity feel in her proper station, in standing at a distance, and surveying the region of misery with philosophic apathy; but its advocates boldly advanced into the very centre of **infection**, and endeavored to apply the only remedy provided for its cure; yet such was the nature and desperate state of the **disease**, that it urged the **infected** to aim the destruction of every benefactor. "Beside, all other people professed a national religion, and the multitude looked on each other's idols with indifference; but Christianity formed a sect of distinct and separate character." [Gibbon's Hist. c. 15] "It did not confine itself to the denial or rejection of every other system: it carried on its forehead all the offensive character of a monopoly, which, when understood, spread an alarm over the Roman empire for the security of its establishments." [Chalmers's *Evid. Christianity*, c. 4, p. 105] Every awakening providence, as earthquake, famine, drought, plague, &c., was by pagans attributed to the anger of their gods against the followers of the Cross; this view of things being impressed on the minds of the multitude, often occasioned the rabble to demand the blood and lives of valuable men."[1] [my emphasis]

---

[1] Orchard, G. H.; *A Concise History of the Baptists;* p. Chapter I, Churches in Italy, Section II: 2 of 4

NOVATIANS, MEMBERS OF THE PRIESTHOOD OF BELIEVERS, KEEP THINGS "PURE"

By the 3rd century all the above problems were beginning to drive Christians out of the visible churches and into smaller groups. They moved to the country away from cultural centers, met in their homes, and remained "pure". Tertullian separated from the large church in Carthage because of apostasy in that church and joined a smaller group of individuals who would later become known as the Novatians. The name is derived from Novatian (c 250 A.D.) who was a presbyter (elder) in the church at Rome. Novatus of Carthage, Tertullian's city, joined him. Together they fought the readmission to the church at Rome those who became apostate during the persecutions. He was not successful, however, and a man known as Cornelius was chosen pastor. Novatian subsequently left the church (as had Tertullian in Carthage) and formed a group which was the first to become known as the Puritans. These early Puritans were also the 'dissenters' who fought pedobaptism, the act of baptizing infants. The doctrine of infant baptism proclaimed by Rome was to become the rallying cry by her and their "ecclesiastical authority" to slaughter many thousands of the "faithful". Rome proclaimed the heresy that baptism regenerates and, therefore, it was necessary to baptize babies to 'save' them in case they died. G.H. Orchard, Jean Paul Perrin, Peter Allix and other noted historians report this travesty.

This is what the noted historian William Jones says about Novatian: "He was," says he, "an elder in the church of Rome, a man of extensive learning, holding the same doctrine as the church did, and published several treatises in defense of what he believed. His address was eloquent and insinuating, and his morals irreproachable. He saw with extreme pain the intolerable depravity of the church. Christians within the space of a very few years were caressed by one emperor, and persecuted by another. In seasons of prosperity many persons rushed into the church for base purposes. In times of adversity, they denied the faith, and reverted again to idolatry. When the squall was over, away they came again to the church, with all their vices, to deprave others by their examples. The bishops, fond of proselytes, encouraged all this; and transferred the attention of Christians from the old confederacy for virtue, to vain shows at Easter, and other Jewish ceremonies, adulterated too with Paganism. On the death of bishop Fabian,

Cornelius, a brother elder, and a violent partisan for taking in the multitude, was put in nomination. Novatian opposed him; but as Cornelius carried his election, and he saw no prospect of reformation, but on the contrary, a tide of immorality pouring into the church, he withdrew and a great many with him. Cornelius, irritated by Cyprian, who was just in the same condition, through the remonstrance of virtuous men at Carthage, and who was exasperated beyond measure with one of his own elders, named Novatus, who had quitted Carthage, and gone to Rome to espouse the cause of Novatian, called a council and got a sentence of excommunication passed against Novatian. **In the end, Novatian formed a church, and was elected bishop. Great numbers followed his example, and all over the empire Puritan churches were constituted and flourished through the succeeding two hundred years. Afterwards, when penal laws obliged them to lurk in corners, and worship God in private, they were distinguished by a variety of names, and a *succession of them continued till the Reformation.*"**[1] [my emphasis]

There was no significant difference between Novatian churches and other Bible believing Christian churches as to doctrine. They were accused of many atrocities and sins during the years, but it is accepted by many that they were false accusations to justify their slaughter by the Roman Church.[2] As we have noticed, the false witness problem has been as serious a problem for Christians as it was for our Saviour and for Steven (Acts 6:11,13). The persecutions from these false charges caused the 'pure' and 'poor' Christians to be scattered to the far reaches of the Empire. As the close of the 3rd century and the early part of the 4th century arrived we find "The Faith" as strong as ever and the churches growing in spite of persecutions. The Novatians were being scattered all over the empire and were beginning to be called by the names of their leaders or by the locations in which they lived. "So as early as 254, these Dissenters are complained of, as having infected France with their doctrines."[3]

They are the oldest of churches **for which there is a record and a succession of them has continued into the modern age.** The doctrine of the

---

[1] Jones, William; *The History of the Christian Church, from the Birth of Christ to the 18th Century;* Way of Life Fundamental Baptist Electronic Library; Port Huron, MI; p. 4-5 in the section "From the Death of Constantine, to the close of the 4th Century"; AD 337--400

[2] Orchard, G. H.; *A Concise History of the Baptists*; Chapter 2; Section 1; "Churches of Italy", p.2 of 5

[3] Ibid. p. 2 of 5

early *dissenters* from apostasy was above reproach, and has been investigated by many "learned" men over the years who have rewarded the *"Dissenters"* with the highest of honors. The *Dissenters*, which began with the Novatians and continued with the Donatists, Waldenses and etc. were the men and women of **the priesthood of believers**.

By the time Constantine came to power in 306 A.D., these churches were flourishing all over the empire. The leaders of these churches were offered inclusion in the newly formed Roman church, but they refused. They desired religious liberty to practice the simple faith they espoused.

"In the year 331 Constantine changed his [tolerant] policy towards the Novatians, and they were involved, with other denominations, in distress and sufferings. Their books were sought, they were forbidden to assemble together, and many lost their places of worship. The orthodoxy of the Novatian party, with the influence of some of their ministers, is supposed to have procured some mitigation of the law. Constantine's oppressive measures prompted many to leave the scene of sufferings, and retire into more sequestered spots. Claudius Seyssel, the **popish archbishop**, traces the rise of the Waldensian **heresy** to a pastor named Leo, leaving Rome at this period, for the Valleys."[1] [emphasis mine]

Please note that the Roman church considered these Saints heretics and they remonstrate that they refused to come under the authority of the state church. They were slandered, murdered, and tortured during the next few centuries as **Rome tried to rewrite history and stamp out their memory.**

While the Churches of the Novationists were developing throughout other regions of the West (Italy, Spain, France) and East (Greece, Asia Minor, Syria), most of the churches in Africa were becoming apostate and were known as the Valentinians, Sabellians, Monarchians, Ophites, Bardesanes, Basilides, Manicheans, and others. There were only a few Churches of the Novatianists [Puritans] in Africa.

The Novationists were persecuted for other reasons.

"This party arose while the Catholics had much trouble in their church with apostates in the Decian persecution, this might have had an influence in the adoption of their severe discipline. Both the Donatists and the Novatians rebaptized those who came to them from the Catholics. They were also equally reproached as Puritans, because it was said they pretended they were more religious than their neighbors. And, different from the established church, they held that the visible church of Jesus Christ does not, and ought not to, consist of

---

[1] Ibid. p. 3 of 5

any but sound members, who were not contaminated with spots and falls."[1]

The noted historian William Jones says this of the Novatians:

"The doctrinal sentiments of the Novatians appear to have been very scriptural, and the discipline of their churches rigid in the extreme. **They were the first class of Christians who obtained the name of (CATHARI) Puritans, an appellation which doth not appear to have been chosen by themselves, but applied to them by their adversaries**; from which we may reasonably conclude that their manners were simple and irreproachable. Some of them are said to have disapproved of second marriages, regarding them as sinful; but in this they were in common with Tertullian and many other eminent persons. A third charge against them was, that they did not pay due reverence to the martyrs, nor allow that there was any virtue in their relics! -- A plain proof of their good sense."[2] [In other words, they did not pray to the Saints.]

The root of the Roman church, which has caused so much havoc, began in the following way. In the 2nd century the Apostolic churches grew and generally a council of the congregation made up of pastor, deacons, and members, settled problems amongst themselves. As the churches continued to grow and meetings between churches occurred, it was deemed necessary to form ecclesiastical bodies. By the 4th century these hierarchical bodies had grown, and districts with 'bishops' were formed. The bishops developed considerable authority. In addition the rules governing the churches had been relaxed to accommodate more members and the church bodies began to exhibit vile persons and doctrines not compatible with the Scriptures and distinctly different from the Novatian churches. The Metropolitan bishop position became the seat of the papal monster which raised its head from the sea of people.

"As the old disciples retired to their graves, their children, along with the new converts, both Jews and Gentiles, under new **ministers from the Alexandrian school**, came forward and new-modeled the cause. Having now traced the features of the churches generally, and finding their assumption of

---

[1] Benedict, David; *A History of the Donatist;* Nickerson, Pawtucket, RI, 1875; p. Chapter 9, "Comparison of the Novatians and the Donatists"

[2] Jones, William; *The History of the Christian Church, from the Birth of Christ to the 18th Century: including the very interesting account of the Waldenses and Albigenses;* 5th edition, 1826; printed by W. Myers; Holborn, London, Way of Life Electronic Disc, Port Huron, MI; "From the Death of Christ to the Fourth Century"; p. 5 of 12

power, with their aspect and composition, of an antichristian character, we must dissent from these, and leave them; directing our investigation to other claimants, until we can trace some honorable and scriptural distinction."[1]

LOCAL INDEPENDENT PURITAN CHURCHES

The developing Roman churches were in opposition to the Puritan churches. The bishops gradually increased their opposition to the Puritans (Novatians or Cathari), and as the churches they controlled develop into the state church under Constantine, capital punishment began by request of the "bishops". These Christians were scattered from the early 4th century to the reformation into remote parts where they were called: 1) the Paterines or Sufferers, 2) the Messalians (Hebrew) or Euchites (Greek) in Greece 3) Paulicians in Asia Minor 4) The Albigensians from the town of Albi, France 5) The Waldensians (meaning valley) from the valleys and Piedmont area of Spain, France, and Italy (This name did not come from Peter Waldo, one of their outstanding pastors) 6) The Gazari in Germany 7) The Arnoldists from Arnold of Brescia, Italy, and Barbe from beard 8) Vaudois and Berengarians from the valleys and Piedmont in Northern Italy, Spain and France [see the map in the appendix] 9) The Petrobrussians from Peter de Bruys and Gundulphus in France and the Netherlands. 10) These aggressive evangelizers even carried their beliefs into England where they were called Lollards, and into Bohemia [Czechoslovakia] as they sought to escape the fury of the Catholic Church. For simplification the remainder of this work will combine all these groups and use the familiar name, the Waldensians.

The accounts recorded in multiple history books of their persecutions and slaughters, and of the destruction of their homes, books, and records for their simple beliefs defy one's imagination. They were killed by the hundreds of thousands! What were those simple beliefs? They were derived from the preservation of copies of Scripture handed down from church to church through *the priesthood of believers.* Some of their writings were secretly hidden away and protected by their lives.

"They said a Christian church ought to consist of only good people: a church had no power to frame any constitutions, i.e., make laws; it was not right to take oaths; it was not lawful to kill mankind, nor should he be delivered up to the officers of justice

---

[1] Orchard, G. H.; *A Concise History of the Baptists;* Chapter 2; "Oriental Churches"; Section 6 and 7, p. 307

to be converted; faith alone could save a man; the benefit of society belonged to all its members; the church ought not to persecute; the law of Moses was no rule for Christians. The Catholics of those times baptized by immersion; the Paterines, therefore, in all their branches, made no complaint of the action of baptism; but when they were examined, they objected vehemently against the baptism of infants, and condemned it as an error."[1]

They were also called **Trinitarians**.

You will recall that the Paterines [the Sufferers] were descendants of the early *priesthood of believers*. The Roman church "hated" these saints because they would not adopt the beliefs of the Catholic Church and would not come under their authority. Peter Allix in his book, *"Some Remarks upon the Ecclesiastical History of the Ancient Churches of Piedmont"*, said that:

"The Bishop of Meaux highly chargeth (Theodore) Beza for saying, that the Waldenses, time out of mind, had stiffly opposed the abuses of the Romish Church, and that they held their doctrine from father to son, **ever since the year 120**, as they had heard and received it from their elders and ancestors."[2] [my emphasis)]

This Bishop of the Roman church, as well as many others, tried to stamp out their memory. Their ancestry cannot be determined for certain and it cannot be determined primarily because of their slaughter and the destruction of their records. One thing is for certain; they did **not** get their name from Peter Waldo (1160) as the Catholics try to say they did in order to date the origin of the Waldensians from a later date. The reason the Roman church tries to date them later is: 1) to be able to accuse them of apostasy from the Church at Rome in order to have some justification for killing them and 2) to make it seem that the Catholic Church was more successful early on. Allix says:

"I own, that sometimes the Churches of the Valleys have been denominated from Waldo, because he had a great number of disciples, who joined themselves with those who were already separated from the Romish Church; but **I utterly deny** once more, that ever they were absolutely called by the name of Waldenses, because he was the first founder of their sect. This is that which I undertake to make out beyond all

---

[1] Ibid. p. 2 of 7

[2] Allix, Peter; *Some Remarks upon the Ecclesiastical History of the Ancient Churches of Piedmont;* Oxford, Claredon Press, 1690, 1821; p. Chapter 19, Way of Life Electronic Disc; Port Huron, MI

possible contradiction."[1]

William Jones writes,

"Reinerius Saccho, an inquisitor, and one of their most implacable enemies, who lived only eighty years after Waldo, admits that the Waldenses flourished **five hundred years before that preacher.**"[2] And historian David Benedict says, "Cranz, in his history of the **United Brethren**, as quoted by Ivimey, has the following statement respecting the origin of the Waldenses. "These ancient Christians, (who, besides the several names of reproach given them, were at length denominated Waldenses, from one of the most eminent teachers, Peter Waldus, who is said to have emigrated with the rest from France into Bohemia, and there to have died) date their origin *from the beginning of the fourth century*; when one Leo, at the great revolution in religion under Constantine the great, opposed the innovations of Sylvester, bishop of Rome," etc. [Ivimey, p. 57.][3]

EXAMPLES OF INDEPENDENT BAPTISTS BELIEFS

My deepest conviction from reviewing the literature and G. H. Orchard's book, "A Concise History of the Baptists", is that these saints probably originated in the immediate post-Apostolic times from Polycarp in Smyrna, Irenaeus' ministry in Lyons, and Novatian's ministry in Rome. They subsequently migrated East and West into Phyrgia, Macedonia, Greece and North into the Piedmont, Bohemia, France, Spain, and England. Many men of renown from these regions are mentioned in the books that are referenced for this work. Let it suffice for now to list their beliefs in detail; the same beliefs that are also found in other languages such as French and Latin, and to then relate a sermon by one of *the priesthood of believers* among the Waldenses. This material was extracted from the book by Jean Paul Perrin in 1847, *History of the*

---

[1] Ibid. Chapter 19

[2] Jones, William; *The History of the Christian Church;* p. Chapter V, Section 1, Way of Life Electronic Disc, Port Huron, Mi.

[3] Benedict, David; *A General History of the Baptist Denomination in America, and other Parts of the World;* London, Printed by Lincoln and Edmonds, 1813, p. "A General Account of the Baptists, in Foreign Countries and Ancient Cities"

Waldenses.

"Confessions of the Faith of the Waldenses"

"The confessions of faith of the Waldenses show clearly how pure their doctrines have been, and how far they have kept themselves from the errors and heresies which were imputed to them; and therefore that they were unjustly persecuted.

The following confession is extracted from the work entitled "The Spiritual Almanac," and also from "The Memorials" of George Morell. It is found also in both the original Waldensian and in the French languages, in the "Histoire des Vaudois," by Brez; volume ii., p. 281--

1. We believe and do firmly hold all that which is contained in the twelve articles of the Symbol, called the Apostles' Creed; and account for heresies all that which is disagreeable to the said twelve articles.

2. We believe that there is one God, Father, Son, and Holy Ghost.

3. We acknowledge for Holy Canonical Scripture, the books of the Bible -- Genesis. -- Exodus. -- Leviticus. -- Numbers. -- Deuteronomy. -- Joshua -- Judges. -- Ruth. -- I. Samuel. -- II. Samuel. -- I. of Kings. -- II. of Kings. -- I. of Chronicles. -- II. of Chronicles. -- Ezra. -- Nehemiah. -- Esther. -- Job. -- Book of Psalms. -- Proverbs of Solomon. -- Ecclesiastes. -- Song of Solomon. -- Prophecy of Isaiah. -- Jeremiah. -- Lamentations of Jeremiah. -- Ezekiel. -- Daniel. -- Hosea. -- Joel. -- Amos. -- Obadiah. -- Jonas. -- Micah -- Nahum. -- Zephaniah. -- Habakkuk. -- Haggai. -- Zechariah. -- Malachi.

After which follow the Apocryphal books, which are not received by the Hebrews; but we read them as Jerom saith in his prologue to the Proverbs, for the instruction of the people, *not to confirm the authority of ecclesiastical doctrines*

Third Book of Esdras. -- Fourth of Esdras. -- Tobit. -- Judith. Wisdom. -- Ecclesiasticus. -- Baruch, with the epistle of Jeremiah. -- Esther, from chapter X. to the end. -- Song of the three children. -- History of Susanna. -- History of the Dragon. -- First of Machabees. -- Second of Machabees -- Third of Machabees.

After these follow the books of the New Testament

The Gospels of Matthew, -- Mark, -- Luke, -- and John. --

Acts of the Apostles. -- Epistle of Paul to the Romans. -- First epistle to the Corinthians. -- Second epistle to the Corinthians. -- Epistle to the Galatians. -- Epistle to the Ephesians. -- Epistle to the Philippians. -- Epistle to the Colossians. -- First epistle to the Thessalonians. -- Second epistle to the Thessalonians. -- First epistle to Timothy. -- Second epistle to Timothy. -- Epistle to Titus. -- Epistle to Philemon. -- Epistle to the Hebrews. -- Epistle of James. -- First epistle of Peter. -- Second epistle of Peter. -- First epistle of John. -- Second epistle of John. -- Third epistle of John. -- Epistle of Jude. -- Revelation of John.

4. The books above-mentioned teach us -- That there is one God Almighty, wise and good, who in his goodness made all things. For he created Adam after his own image and likeness. But through the malice of the devil, and the disobedience of Adam, sin entered into the world: and we became sinners in Adam, and by Adam.

5. That Christ was promised to the fathers, who received the law, to the end, that knowing their sin by the law, and their unrighteousness and insufficiency, they might desire the coming of Christ, that he might make satisfaction for their sins, and accomplish the law by himself.

6. That Christ was born at the time appointed by God his Father; at the time when all iniquity did abound, and not for the sake of our good works. For all were sinners: But that he might show us grace and mercy, as he was true.

7. That Christ is our life, and truth, and peace, and righteousness: our shepherd and advocate; our sacrifice and priest, who died for the salvation of all those who should believe, and rose again for our justification.

8. In like manner we firmly believe, that there is no other mediator and advocate with God the Father, besides Jesus Christ; as to the Virgin Mary, she was holy, humble, and full of grace. Thus do we believe concerning all the other saints; that they wait in heaven, for the resurrection of their bodies at the day of judgment.

9. We do likewise believe, that after this life, there are but two places, the one for those that are saved, the other for the damned, which we call paradise and hell; altogether denying that imaginary purgatory of antichrist, invented against the truth.

10. Moreover we have always looked upon all human inventions as an unspeakable abomination before God: as the feasts and vigils of saints; and the water called holy water; and the abstaining upon certain days from flesh, and such like

things, and chiefly the masses.

11. **We have in abomination all human inventions, as proceeding from antichrist**; which stir up trouble, and are prejudicial to the liberty of the spirit.

12. We believe that the sacraments are signs of a holy thing; or visible forms of an invisible grace; holding it good and necessary, that the faithful do sometimes make use of the said signs or visible forms, when it can be done. Notwithstanding, we do believe and hold that the said faithful may be saved, though they do not receive the aforesaid signs, when they have neither place nor opportunity of so doing.

13. **We do acknowledge no other sacraments, besides Baptism and the Lord's Supper**.

14. We honor the secular powers, with subjection, obedience, promptitude, and payment.

WALDENSIAN CONFESSION OF FAITH [continued]

The following confession is extracted from "Mendes Francois" by Charles du Moulin, p. 65--

1. We believe that there is but one God, who is a spirit, creator of all things, Father of all, who is above all, by all, and in us all, whom we must worship in spirit and truth; upon whom alone we wait, and to whom we give the glory of our life, food, raiment, health.

2. We believe that Jesus Christ is the Son and Image of the Father; that in him doth all fullness of the Godhead dwell, by whom we know the Father; who is our mediator and advocate, and there is no other name under heaven given unto men, whereby they may be saved: in whose name alone we invocate the Father, and use no other prayers than those contained in the holy scripture, or agreeable thereto in substance.

3. We believe that the Holy Ghost is our comforter, proceeding from the Father, and from the Son: by whose inspiration we make prayers, being renewed by him, who formeth all good works within us, and by him we have knowledge of all truth.

4. We believe that there is one Holy Church, which is the congregation of all the elect and faithful, which were from the

beginning of the world, and shall be to the end thereof -- of which our Lord Jesus Christ is the head, which is governed by His Words, and guided by the Holy Ghost: In which all good Christians ought to remain, for it prays for all incessantly, and the word thereof is agreeable to God, without which no one can be saved.

5. We hold that the ministers of the church ought to be unblameable, as well in life as doctrine. Else that they ought to be deposed from their function, and others substituted in their room; and that no person ought to presume to take that honor, but he who is called of God, as Aaron; feeding the flock of God, not for filthy lucre's sake, or as having superiority over the clergy; but as being an example to the flock, in word, in conversation, in charity, in faith, and in chastity.

6. We confess that kings, princes, and governors, are ordained and established ministers of God, whom we must obey. For they bear the sword for the defense of the innocent, and the punishment of evil-doers; for that reason we are bound to honor and pay them tribute.

From which power and authority no man can exempt himself, as may appear from the example of our Lord Jesus Christ, who refused not to pay tribute, not taking upon him any jurisdiction of temporal power.

7. We believe that in the sacrament of baptism, the water is the visible and external sign, which represents to us that which, by virtue of the invisible God so working, is within us: that is to say, the renovation of the spirit, and the mortification of our members in Jesus Christ; by which also we are received into the holy congregation of God's people, protesting and declaring before it our faith and change of life.

[Note from the publisher of this electronic edition of Perrin: It is obvious that at least many of the ancient Waldenses who lived prior to the Reformation did not practice infant baptism. They held to believer's baptism as practiced in the first churches during the days of the Apostles. According to this confession of faith, the Waldenses looked upon baptism (1) as symbolic of the believer's identification with Christ, (2) as the door to church membership, and (3) as pertaining only to those who could declare their faith and show the evidence of a changed life before the congregation. See the article "Were the Waldenses Baptists or Pedobaptists?" at the *Electronic Baptist History Library* at the Way of Life Literature web site -- **http://wayoflife.org/~dcloud**. It is also available on the

Fundamental Baptist CD-ROM Library which can be obtained from Way of Life, D. W. Cloud]

8. We hold that the sacrament of the table, or supper of the Lord Jesus Christ, is a holy commemoration and thanksgiving, for the benefits which we have received by his death and passion, which is to be received in faith and charity; examining ourselves, that so we may eat of that bread, and drink of that cup, as it is written in the holy scripture.

9. We confess that marriage is good and honorable, holy, and instituted of God, which ought to be forbidden to none, if there be no impediment by the word of God.

10. We acknowledge that those who fear God, seek to please him, and to do the good works which he hath prepared, that we may walk therein; which are charity, joy, peace, patience, benignity, goodness, mildness, sobriety, and other works contained in the holy scripture.

11. We confess we must beware of false teachers, whose end is to divert the people from the true worship of God, that they may rely upon creatures, putting their confidence in them; and also that they may desist from the good works which are contained in the holy scripture, to do those that are invented by men.

12. We hold the Old and New Testament for the rule of our life; and we agree to the general confession of faith, with the articles contained in the symbol of the Apostles."[1]

"Epistle of Pastor Bartholomew Tertian, to the Waldensian Churches of Pragela"

That the holy zeal and affection may be known, with which the Barbs or Pastors of the Waldenses endeavored to call the people to repentance, and to instruct them in the faith, we insert a pastoral letter of one of their ministers.

---

[1] Perrin, Jean Paul; *History of the Ancient Christians, History of the Waldenses ;* Griffith and Simon, Philadelphia, PA; 1847; p. 51-54; Way of Life, Fundamental Baptist Electronic Disc; Port Huron, MI.

Jesus be with you. To all our faithful and well-beloved Brethren, health and salvation be with you all. Amen.

"These are to advertise your brotherhood, and hereby acquit myself of the duty which I owe to you On God's part, principally touching the care of the salvation of your souls, according to that light of truth which the Most High hath bestowed upon you, that it would please every one of you, to maintain, increase, and cherish, to the utmost of your power, without diminution: those good beginnings and customs left unto us by our ancestors, of which we were not worthy. For it would be of little profit to us to be renewed by the fatherly kindness, and the light which God hath given us, if we addict ourselves to mundane, diabolical, and carnal conversation, abandoning the principal which is God, and the salvation of our souls, for this short temporal life. The Lord saith in the Gospel, What doth it profit a man to gain the whole world, and to lose his own soul? For it would have been better never to have known the way of righteousness, than having known it, to act contrary thereto. We shall be inexcusable, and our condemnation the greater, for there are greater torments prepared for those who have had the greatest knowledge. "Wherefore let me beseech you, by the love of God, not to diminish, but to increase the love, fear and obedience due to God, and to yourselves among yourselves; and to keep all the good customs which you have heard and understood from God by our means; and that you would remove from among you all defects and wants troubling your peace, love and concord; and everything which deprives you of the service of God, your salvation, and the administration of the truth; if you desire God to be propitious to you in your temporal and spiritual good things. For you can do nothing without him; and if you desire to be heirs of his glory, do that which he commandeth you. If you will enter into life, keep my commandments. Likewise be careful that there be not nourished among you any sports, gluttony, whoredom, dancing, or other debaucheries, nor questions, nor deceits, nor usury, nor discords. Neither support nor entertain among you any persons of a wicked life nor those who give a scandal or ill example amongst you; but let charity and fidelity reign amongst you, and every, good example; doing to one another as everyone would have done to himself. For otherwise it is not possible for any one to be saved, or have the favor either of God or men in this World, nor glory in the other. And it is necessary that the guides chiefly have a hand in this, and such who rule and govern: for when the head is sick, all the members are disordered thereby. Therefore if you hope and desire to enjoy eternal life, to live in esteem: and good repute, and to prosper in this world in your temporal and spiritual good things, cleanse yourselves from all disorderly ways, that God may be always with you, who never forsakes those that, put their trust in him. But know this for certain, that he doth neither hear nor dwell with sinners, nor in the soul that is addicted to wickedness, nor with the man who is subject to sin. Therefore let every one purify the ways of his heart, and fly from danger, if he will not perish therein. Put in practice these things; and the God of 'peace be with you. Accompany us in our true, devout and humble prayers, that he would be pleased to save all those his faithful, who put their trust in Christ Jesus. Amen.

BARTHOLOMEW TERTIAN

Ready to serve yea; in all things possible, according to the will of God."

This epistle of the pastor, Tertian, gives us a proof of the holy zeal that they had to lead the people to God"[1]

THE MEN OF THE REFORMATION AND THE CONNECTION TO THE INDEPENDENTS

These faithful people continued to copy their "Bible," and other materials such as what you have read; and, much of which has been documented in Perrin's book, "The History of the Ancient Christians" and Andrew Miller's book "Church History." Their history [**priesthood of believers**] extends into the Reformation and the time of the Reformers John Wycliff (1330-1384), John Huss (1369?-1415), Jerome of Prague (1370-1416), Desiderous Erasmus (1466-1537), Martin Luther (1483-1546), Philip Melancthon (1497-1560), Jacques Lefevre D'Etaples (1455-1560), William Farel (1489-1565), John Calvin(1509-1564), William Tyndale (1484-1536), and others. Waldensian churches were still present as the Reformation dawned. They were still adhering to the simple, pure doctrine handed down by the churches from the second and third centuries. The Roman Church was still trying to exterminate "the men" who opposed their system. These men were outside of the inner workings of the Catholic Church or

---

[1]Ibid. p. 49-50

had left it completely. Outside of the Roman Church, Wycliff and Tyndale, helped the Reformation explode. Many significant men on the inside of the Roman Church supported the protest of Romanism and the establishment of Protestantism, particularly Luther and Calvin. We will see that all these men *were linked* and were *associated with* the simple, pure *priesthood of believers*, the Waldensians.

WYCLIFF ASSOCIATED WITH INDEPENDENTS

Wycliff was to become known as the "Morning Star of the Reformation". He was born into an age, which followed the crusades of Rome (1147-1291), and just after the infamous children's crusade of 1212 during which 30,000 boys and girls were killed. In addition, Rome's papal offices had been moved to Avignon, France, where the hate of the English for the French and vice-versa caused the hundred-year war. Wycliff was born in Wycliff, England, and he trained at Oxford. He was so successful that he became the king's chaplain. He obtained his doctorate in 1374, and turned his ire and intellectual prowess against Rome. **He was greatly influenced by the Lollards, the independents** who were spiritual descendants of the Novatians and Waldensians and whom he helped train. Joseph Ivimey in his 1811 book, *A History of the English Baptists,* says, "In the reign of Henry III, archbishop Usher says, from Matthew Paris, "the orders of the Friars Minorites came into England to suppress this Waldensian heresy." And in the reign of Edward III, about the year 1315, Fuller informs us, in his ecclesiastical history, that:

> **"WALTER LOLLARD**, that German preacher, or, (as Perrin calls him in his history of the Waldenses,) one of their barbs, came into England, a man in great renown among them; and who was so eminent in England that, as in France they were called *Berengarians* from Berengarius, and *Petrobrusians* from Peter Bruis, and in Italy and Flanders, *Arnoldists*, from the famous Arnold of Brescia; so did the Waldensian Christians for many generations after bear the name of this worthy man, being called *Lollards*."[1]

---

[1] Ivimey, Joseph; *A History of the English Baptists, Including an Investigation of the History of Baptism in England from the earliest period to which it can be traced to the close of the seventeenth century. To which are prefixed, testimonies of ancient writers in favour of Adult Baptism: extracted from Dr. Gill's piece, entitled, "The Divine Right of Infant Baptism Examined and*

And, by this information, we see the connection to the *priesthood of believers* from the past.[1]

William Grady says:

> "In his condemnation of doctrinal abuse, Wycliff anticipated later reformers' attitude toward immoral prelates, excessive territorial holdings, religious extortion, heresies such as purgatory, transubstantiation, the priesthood and auricular confession. Wycliff despised these false teachings as leaving the masses beholden to Rome. The priests...and monks of his day were known for their taste for good food and bad women [and] their monasteries as dens of thieves, nests of serpents, houses of living devils."[2]

Wycliff saw the need to place the Scripture into the hands of the common man. He subsequently started the monumental task of translating the Latin into the English of his day. He was proficient only in Latin so he had to use the Latin manuscripts to translate into Anglo-Saxon. The Duke of Lancaster, John of Gaunt, protected him from Rome in those days. This man who was the favorite son of King Edward was obviously raised up by God to shelter Wycliff. His translation was based on Latin manuscripts because he did not know Greek or Hebrew. Importantly, his translation was **not** based on the Latin Vulgate as modern scholarship claims. It was based on old Latin manuscripts from various areas. After Wycliffe died it was altered by John Purvey to make it read like the Latin Vulgate, the Bible of Rome, produced by Jerome. Purvey later defected to Rome.[3] Was he a Jesuit?

Wycliff's translation was so revered that a whole wagon load of hay was traded for just one hour with the Book. The cost of production of the Book at that time was equivalent to "a clergyman's entire year's salary." The cost was so great because an experienced copyist had to spend about 10 months of solid work to produce one Book. The Bible was so prized that the hungry people of those days would spend the whole night studying it after a hard day's work. The dawn of the next morning would surprise them, and they would be off to another "weary day". After the invention of the printing press a dire caution concerning the Bible came true: that is, with a cheap price it would no longer be prized. You tell me if that is the case today in so many countries! This is not true in countries like China where people still cherish even a page out of the Book.

Disproved; 1811; p. Chapter 2, 1180-1540; Way of Life, Fundamental Baptist Electronic Disc, Port Huron, MI

[1] Grady, PhD., Th.M., D.D.,William P.; *Final Authority;* p. 124

[2] Ibid. p. 122

[3] Ibid. p. 123

JOHN HUSS

The year Wycliff died John Huss [aka John of Hassinetz] was an eleven year old in Hussinetz, Bohemia [Czechoslovakia]. His father died when he was young, and his mother assumed responsibility. They were poor but he managed to get into the University at Prague probably because of the earnest prayers of his mother. He was brilliant and soon earned his Master of Arts in 1396. At that time he was a 'firm' supporter of the Papacy. Queen Sophia of Bavaria soon chose him as her confessor. Because of his academic abilities he was already familiar with the philosophical work of Wycliff, but had not seen his theological effort. In 1402 John Huss was appointed preacher of the Chapel of Bethlehem in Prague. His preparation for sermons at the Chapel caused several changes in him and the people of the area. 1) Huss began preaching against the debauchery of the region 2) He preached in opposition to the ordinary clergy, prelates [hierarchy], and nobles. 3) A great clamor arose in the area. 4) John Huss' inner conscience was awakened. 4) The queen protected him. 5) He developed a Biblically based approach to life. 6) Dr. Wylie in his book, *The History of Protestantism,* said he restored "the Word of God to the knowledge of his countrymen." It was not long before God provided the theological works of Wycliff for Huss through two unusual events. One was the arrival of two of Wycliff's students, James and Conrad of Canterbury, graduates of Oxford, as missionaries to Bohemia and Bavaria. The other was the death of Queen Anne, wife of Richard II of England and sister of the King of Bohemia. Her Bohemian attendants consequently returned from England to Prague with the writings of the great Reformer, Wycliff. Wycliff had been Queen Anne's discipler. One can just imagine the 'books' brought to Bohemia by these ladies, and among them were probably copies of the Scriptures which were being preserved by *the priesthood of believers*.[1]

About the same time there was a great hoax perpetrated on the citizens of Bavaria, Bohemia, Poland and other far away places. An alleged relic of Christ's blood was causing many 'miracles' and people were traveling long distances to obtain some 'mercy'. A panel of three men including Huss was appointed to investigate the affair and, of course, it was proven false.

Huss continued to excel and was appointed rector of the University. Eventually the Pope learned of Huss' "heresies" and the "happenings" in Prague.

---

[1] Wylie L.L.D., J.A.; *The History of Protestantism;* London, Paris, New York & Melbourne: Cassell and Co., Limited, 1899; Way of Life, Fundamental Baptist Electronic edition, May 2000, Book 3, John Huss and the Hussite Wars.

Emissaries from the Pope came to Prague, confiscated Wycliff's books, and burned them in the street. All of these acts culminated in Huss leaving Prague and returning to his hometown. He continued to mature spiritually, however, and because of his great influence on the people of the area his respect and popularity grew. He became more and more recalcitrant to Rome and its false teachings.

Now enters a knight in shining armor, Jerome of Prague. He had trained at Oxford and came away with the opinions of Wycliff imbedded. Jerome had been arrested and thrown in prison because of his defense of the simple faith in Paris and Vienna. He escaped and arrived in Bohemia where he came alongside Huss. These two men set off a fire in Bohemia and surrounding countries.

While all this was going on in Bohemia, the Papacy had become a quagmire of ridiculous claims and infighting. Three separate Popes were appointed in Spain, Italy, and France. The rival Popes tried to defeat one another. Europe was thrust into anarchy. There was much blood shed in those years and the Reformers, Huss and Jerome opened the people's eyes. As the "three Pope" Papal situation resolved, the eyes of the 'antichrist' in Rome turned to these men. Huss was eventually lured to Italy where he was arrested. After an arduous experience he was martyred. Jerome of Prague who had come to assist him was also arrested and martyred. Their testimonies at the time of their arrest and martyrdom in the flames are moving and should be sought out to be read by all who love the Words of God.[1] The lesson to be gleaned from these two early Reformers is that the Lollards of England through Wycliff and eventually to Huss and Jerome of Prague spread the light [the Blessed Gospel Light]. The *priesthood of believers* continued to have an effect on the people who were exposed to their simple, pure doctrine based on the Words of God. The murder of these two believers would cause a reaction toward Rome, which was devastating. The ensuing years after their death led to the formation of cooperative groups of Waldensian believers in several regions. An outgrowth of one of these groups was **the United Brethren** who are still with us today as a viable denomination.

"They do not seem to have had any regular (i.e., separate class) minister... A portion of this people, called Waldenses, came down from the mountains to live in peace under the protection of Ziska. This state of civil discord lasted upwards of twelve years. The agitated state of the kingdom for so many years must have been very injurious to the cause of undefiled religion. The Council of Basil, in 1433, took great pains to bring

---

[1] Miller, Andrew; *Church History;* c 1860; Chapter 31; "The Reformation in Bohemia" An excellent presentation of the arrest and martyrdom of Huss and Jerome of Prague may be found in Chapter 31, "The Reformation in Bohemia"]

the Protestant delegates to submit implicitly to the council; but they utterly refused. After many intrigues by the Catholics, a division was effected among the Protestants, consequently their importance became lessened. The affairs of the kingdom remained in a very unsettled state even to the middle of this century [15th century], about which time Rokyzan, archbishop of Prague; tired with contentions, advised the advocates of reform to retire to the lordship of Latitz, about twenty miles from Prague, a place desolated by war, where they might establish their own way of worship, choose their own ministers, introduce their own discipline and order, according to their own consciences and judgments. Numbers adopted the suggestion, and embraced the privilege, and in 1457 they formed themselves into a society. This body being made up of persons entertaining religious views wide of each other, they chose the name of UNITAS FRATRUM, OR **THE UNITED BRETHREN**, though they were generally called **PICARDS**. [They came from diverse backgrounds, but eventually organized themselves based upon the doctrine received from the Apostles. my addition]   These brethren bound themselves to a vigorous discipline in church affairs, and not to defend themselves with the sword, but suffer the loss of all for conscience sake... In 1459 these godly people, made up of all classes, obtained from their king, Pogiebracius, a place to worship in, where they established a society on the model of primitive simplicity... These brethren re-baptized all such as joined themselves to their congregation." [1]

ERASMUS

Of these nine men, Wycliff, Huss, Jerome, Erasmus, Luther, Melancthon, Lefevre, Farel, and Calvin, the most outstanding scholar was Erasmus. It was Erasmus who was responsible for **the first printed Greek text**, which was the foundation for the later editions of the printed Greek texts by Stephanus (1550), Beza (1598), and Elzevir (1633). The Beza edition became the basis for the 1611 King James Bible translation into English.

---

[1] Orchard, G.H., Baptist Minister, *A Concise History of the Baptist*, Bedfordshire, England, 1855, Chapter 2, Section X, "Baptists in Bohemia", Way of Life Electronic Edition 2000b

Erasmus was left an orphan by the age of 13. His guardians stole all his assets and to cover their deeds convinced him to enter a monastery. The year Columbus discovered America, Erasmus was ordained as an Augustinian priest at Stein. He never liked being a priest and left for the University of Paris at his earliest convenience where he became a first rate scholar in literature. Straightway, he became known as one of the world's greatest humanists. A humanist at that time in history did not have a bad connotation. A humanist was simply someone who had gained a great deal of human knowledge. It was not viewed as a form of "religion" as that which is called Humanism today. There are 'modern' writers who are not informed on this change in terminology. They have assailed Erasmus for being "a humanist"; not understanding the terminology refers to his great knowledge.

"By his travels he was brought into contact with all the intellectual currents of his time and stimulated to almost superhuman efforts. He became the most famous scholar and author of his day and one of the most prolific writers of all time, his collected works filling ten large volumes in the Leclerc edition of 1705 (phototyped by Olms in 1962). As an editor also his productivity was tremendous. Ten columns of the catalogue of the library in the British Museum are taken up with the bare enumeration of the works translated, edited, or annotated by Erasmus, and their subsequent reprints."[1]

Erasmus at a young age was asked by Lord Mountjoy to come to England. He resided at Oxford and Cambridge from 1498 until 1515 on various return visits to England, and had many honors and recognitions bestowed upon him. He was a very learned scholar in the area of Greek and was head of that department at Cambridge.

He has been called a "deadbeat" by those opposed to the traditional text. If he were such, it would be hard to explain not only his qualifications, but the many requests and offers by the heads of states in many countries to entice Erasmus to come.

"He was offered and declined professorships at the University of Leipzig and Ingolstadt; Francis I invited him to his personal court in France; Pope Paul III attempted to entice him to Italy with a cardinals hat; and King Charles of the Netherlands offered him a position as a personal counselor. The man known as the "journalist of scholarship" received the following invitation from country number *five:*

"I propose therefore that you abandon all thought of settling elsewhere. Come to England, and assure yourself of a hearty welcome. You shall name your own terms; they shall be

---

[1] Hills Th.D., Edward F.; *The King James Version Defended*; p. 196

as liberal and honorable as you please...We shall regard your presence among us as the most precious possession that we have...We shall ask nothing of you save to make our realm your home...Come to me, therefore, my dear Erasmus, and let your presence be your answer to my invitation. (King Henry VIII, King of England)"[1]

Now, you tell me: "Was he a "deadbeat"?

Erasmus was influenced by three different views of his time in regard to the preservation of Scripture, according to Dr. Edward F. Hills. One view stressed the importance of the decline in Greek and Latin languages during the dark ages. Laurentius Valla (1405-1457) projected this view and latched onto some Greek manuscripts he had discovered. He compared the Greek text to the Latin Vulgate and found the Greek text was much different than the Vulgate, Rome's Bible.

"Also, there were omissions and additions in the Latin translation, and the Greek wording was generally better than that of the Latin."[2]

Martin Dorp (1514) who defended the Latin Vulgate represented the second view. He stated the Roman Church could not be wrong all these centuries. He implied the heretical Greek church had corrupted the text and that the Vulgate was right. Dorp begged Erasmus not to print his Greek text. After Erasmus' text was published in 1516, a Spanish scholar, Stunica, openly condemned it. Peter Sutor of this same view said that if:

"the Vulgate were in error, the entire authority of Holy Scripture would collapse."[3]

Incidentally, Dorp later changed his view and agreed with the 'common faith' view, which was the third influence on Erasmus. This view supported the Scriptural certainty of *preservation* of God's Word; that is, the Greek Church had been:

"the providentially appointed guardian of the New Testament text."[4]

Pope Leo X (1513-1521) and other high officials of the Roman Church held the 'common faith' view, although Pope Leo X had many moral deficiencies. All of these men, including Erasmus, tried to reform the Church of Rome from within to accept the common view. It was not to be, however, because by the time of the Council of Trent in 1546 the tide had shifted back to Rome.

---

[1] Grady, Ph.D., Th.M., D.D., William P.; *Final Authority;* p. 130

[2] Hills, Th.D., Edward F.; *The King James Version Defended*; p. 196

[3] Ibid. p. 197

[4] Ibid. p. 197

Erasmus' views were determined by the influences above. He had long grown tired of Rome's exploitation, and spoke out against the Catholic Church and its abuses. In opposition to one of Rome's greatest fears, the Scripture in the hands of the populace, Erasmus had been instilled with the intense desire to place the Words of God into the hands of the common people. In this famous quote he said,

"I would have those Words translated into all languages, so that not only Scots and Irishmen, but Turks and Saracens might read them, I long for the plowboy to sing them to himself as he follows the plow, the weaver to hum them to the tune of his shuttle, the traveler to beguile with them the dullness of his journey."[1] [my emphasis]

"To conclude, there was no man in all Europe better prepared than Erasmus for the work of editing the first printed Greek N.T. text, and this is why, we may well believe, God chose him and directed him providentially in the accomplishment of this task."[2] [my emphasis]

MARTIN LUTHER

Martin Luther, a contemporary of Erasmus, was born into a very poor family in Germany. His father chopped wood and his mother carried it "on her back" in order to supply food for the family. However, his pious father desired to make his eldest son a scholar; and at the age of fourteen Luther left home for the Franciscan school at Magdeburg, Germany where he almost starved to death. With his parents permission he went to his relatives in Eisenach where there was a good school. His circumstances were no better though and he had to go from house to house singing for food. One day while singing before a home he encountered Ursula, the wife of Conrad Cotta. She and her husband had compassion on Luther and, subsequently, gave him shelter, food, and an education. With the tutelage of his adopted family he learned to play several instruments such as the flute and lute, and he added music to his studies.

With the stress of surviving removed, Luther's brilliance emerged and he developed into a fine student. He went on at the age of 18 to the University in Erfurt. By 1505 he had secured his doctorate in philosophy and had begun to form his own ideas, generally opposing the establishment.

---

[1] Grady, PhD., Th.M., D.D., William P.; *Final Authority;* p. 131

[2] Hills, Th.D., Edward F.; *The King James Version Defended;* p. 196

"In a state of trembling anxiety about the salvation of his soul, he was one day searching the library at Erfurt for something new, when the hand of God directed him to a Bible. He read the title page — it is indeed the Holy Bible! He was greatly excited and interested as he rapidly turned over its leaves. He was then twenty years of age, and had not so much as seen the precious volume before. Let the Protestant reader note this — he had been brought up by pious parents, lived four years in a Christian family, and had not even seen a Bible! The same ignorance of the Words of God prevails in Roman Catholic communities to this hour. The Bible forms no part of a Catholic priest's education, and the people are forbidden to read it. Tens of millions are now in circulation, but in a strictly Roman Catholic district it would be difficult to find a single copy. Some extracts are used in the church service, and even pious Catholics are ready to believe that these extracts contain the substance of the whole Bible. Such is the narrow and precarious foundation on which their faith is built, and such the blinding, ruinous power of that fearful system of darkness and idolatry"[1]

Shortly after obtaining his degree in 1505 he entered the Augustinian monastery in Erfurt, and therefore, the monkhood. He was never happy as a monk and he states 16 years later:

"I was never in heart a monk, nor was it to mortify the lust of my fleshly appetites, but, tormented with horror and the fear of death, I took a forced and constrained vow."[2]

Luther was by the grace of God allowed encounters with two men. They were known as Staupitz and the other 'an aged monk' who gently led him to the understanding of personal forgiveness of sins and of grace rather than works for salvation. He embraced the concepts and was finally released from the shackles of Satan and saved. He said that until he met these two men he was ("to use his own words"), "in the swaddling-bands of *popery*, and had not seen its evils"[3] Following his conversion Luther was a changed man and he became a fiery defender of the faith based on the Scriptures. He could never completely divest himself of all the 'teachings' of Rome, but he came "a million miles" from where he had been spiritually. As a matter of fact, one could say he was a new creature.

"The schism which took place in the Roman community, through the public preaching and writing of

---

[1] Miller, Andrew; *Church History;* London, c 1860, Way of Life Literature Electronic Edition; May 2000; Chapter 33, The Reformation of Germany
[2] Ibid.
[3] Ibid.

Luther and his associates, must have been a source of infinite satisfaction to the persecuted Waldenses. When the barbs, or pastors of the valleys, became acquainted with the reformation in Germany, they deputed, in 1526, persons to visit and inquire into its truth. The deputation returned with some printed books to the brethren. "The Vaudois took encouragement," says Mezeray, "to preach openly from Luther's appearing in the character of a reformer, but these zealous advocates for religion were punished by a decree made by Anthony Chassaue, and massacred." [Fr. Hist., p. 615] It was found by the Waldenses in their communications and conferences with Luther, that their views were not in unison with his on the ordinances, but that they were more conformable to the sacramentarians, or those who **deny** the real presence. [Id., p. 948] Other brethren made a like visit into Germany, and conferred with Ecolampadius, Bucer, and others, who from the statement given, exhorted them to remedy certain evils which they perceived to exist among them; viz.--First, In certain points of doctrine; Secondly, In church order; and Thirdly, In irregular conduct of members, who mingled with Catholics in worship. After these preliminaries, the Waldenses appear, during 1530, to have been employed in paving the way for a more unreserved intercourse between themselves and the reformers."[1]

Again we discover *the intimate relationship and contact* between the Waldensians and the Reformers, especially Wycliff and Luther. The Waldensian contact was probably George Morell. [See the index of this work for links to Morell.]

Luther was assigned to the University at Wittenberg and "the rest is history". He continued to grow in understanding and knowledge and in the fateful year of 1517 nailed to the door of the chapel, Schloss Kirk of Wittenberg, on October 31st, 1517 the 95 theses. Over the following years the spark of protest started by Wycliff and brought to a raging fire by Erasmus and Luther, continued to spread through schools, universities, churches, and even the domains of rulers and government, as the full blown fire of the Reformation.

The following quote is about Luther who hated the Waldensians before he got saved. One can see the work of the Holy Ghost in his life as he "rejoiced" that the "suspicion" toward these poor, plain people had been removed.

"**LUTHER**, in the year 1588, published the *Confessions of the Waldenses*, to which he wrote a preface. In that preface he

---

[1] Orchard, G.H.; *A Concise History of the Baptists;* p. Chapter 2, Section XI, 24; Way of Life Literature Electronic Disc, May 2000

candidly acknowledges that, in the days of his popery he had hated the Waldenses, as persons who were consigned over to perdition. But having understood from their confessions and writings the piety of their faith, he perceived that those good men had been greatly wronged whom the Pope had condemned as heretics; for that, on the contrary, they were rather entitled to the praise due to holy martyrs. He adds, that among them he had found one thing worthy of admiration, a thing unheard of in the Popish church, that, laying aside the doctrines of men, they meditated in the law of God, day and night; and that they were expert, and even well versed in the knowledge of the Scriptures; whereas, in the papacy, those who are called masters wholly neglected the Scriptures, and some of them had not so much as seen the Bible at any time. Moreover, having read the Waldensian Confessions, he said he returned thanks to God for the great light which it had pleased him to bestow upon that people; rejoicing that all cause of suspicion being removed which had existed between them and the reformed, they were now brought together into one sheepfold under the Chief Shepherd and Bishop of souls."[1]

Before Luther and Calvin became prominent, there were hidden in almost all the countries of Europe, particularly in Bohemia, Moravia, Switzerland, and Germany, many Waldensians, Wickliffites, and Hussites, who adhered to the following doctrine, reported by G.H. Orchard:

"The kingdom of Christ or the visible church he had established on earth was an assembly of true and real saints, and therefore should not be assessable to the wicked and unrighteous, and should be exempt from all those institutions, which human prudence suggests, to oppose the progress of iniquity, or to correct and rearm transgressors."[2]

The *priesthood of believers* was still present in spite of the harsh opposition. Some met in secret and others were more open. This severe resistance can best be exemplified by a description of "a violent outrage" against the Waldensians living in the valley of Pragela in the Piedmont about 1400. Catholics perpetrated this attack ostensibly for "religious" reasons, but in reality, probably for loot.

"The attack, which seems to have been of the most furious

---

[1] Jones, William; *A History of the Christian Church; p. Chapter 5, Section 4*; "Luther"

[2] Orchard, G.H.; *Concise History of the Baptist,* Chapter 2, Section XI, #12, "The German and Dutch Baptist"

kind, was made towards the end of December, when the mountains were covered with snow, and thereby rendered so difficult of access that the peaceable inhabitants of these valleys were wholly unapprised that any such attempt was meditated; and the persecutors were in actual possession of their caves ere the owners seem to have been apprised of any hostile design against them. In this pitiable strait they had recourse to the only alternative which remained for saving their lives--they fled, though at that inauspicious season of the year, to one of the highest mountains of the Alps, with their wives and children; the unhappy mothers carrying the cradle in one hand, and in the other, leading such of the offspring as were able to walk. Their inhuman invaders pursued them in their flight, until darkness obscured the objects of their fury. Many were slain before they could reach the mountains. Overtaken by the shades of night, these afflicted outcasts wandered up and down the mountains covered with snow; destitute of the means of shelter from the inclemency of the weather, or of supporting themselves under it, by any of the comforts which Providence has destined for that purpose; benumbed with cold, some fell asleep, and became an easy prey to the severity of the climate; and when the night had passed away, them were found in their cradles, or lying upon the snow, fourscore of their infants, deprived of life; many of their mothers were dead by their side, and others just on the point of expiring. During the night their enemies had plundered their abodes of everything that was valuable. This seems to have been the first general attack made by the Catholic peasantry on the Waldenses. They had been hitherto sheltered from the pontiff's measures, by the Dukes of Savoy, so that the rage of their enemies had been restrained to a few solitary cases of arrested heresy; but this kind of assault, planned, no doubt, by the clergy, was of a novel character; and so deeply impressed were the minds of these people with the circumstances of the Sufferers, as to speak of it for a century after, with feelings of apparent horror. We have rather minutely detailed this affair, in order to show its influence on the minds of the Waldenses, and to account, in some measure, for the change which took place soon after, in their views and conduct."[1]

Along with the turmoil surrounding Martin Luther came a man sent by God

---

[1] Orchard, G.H.; *A Concise History of the Baptists;* Chapter 2, Section XI, 18, "About the year 1400"

to assist and comfort him. Philip Melancthon arrived shortly before Luther was to leave Wittenberg for an appearance before authorities. The famous linguist and Hebrew scholar, Reuchlin, had recommended him, and he was assuming the Greek chair at the University.[1] Initially Melancthon was not well received because of his youth and sickly appearance. After his first address to the University, all that changed and he was received as a "treasure". He became a great assistant to Luther. Melancthon had distinguished himself by obtaining a bachelors degree at age 14 from the University of Heidelberg. It was Reuchlin, a family relation that had presented him with a Greek Bible and grammar, which would become "the study of his life."

"All the leading Reformers, without exception, were of lowly birth. Luther first saw the light in a miner's cottage; Calvin was the grandson of a cooper in Picardy; Knox was the son of a plain burgess of a Scottish provincial town; Zwingle was born in a shepherd's hut in the Alps; and Melancthon was reared in the workshop of an armourer. Such is God's method. It is a law of the Divine working to accomplish mighty results by weak instruments. In this way God glorifies himself, and afterwards glorifies his servants."[2]

When Luther left for the Diet [assembly of leaders] at Worms to face heresy charges, Melancthon wanted to go with him. Luther denied his request explaining that if he was treated as Huss was when he was betrayed in Italy, then his dear friend Melancthon would have to carry on the work. It is note-worthy to mention that at each appearance before the court of the empire or Roman church, Luther would always appeal to Scripture when asked to defend himself. Of course, the Roman clergy had not read the Bible for years. At Worms when he was demanded to retract his 20 volumes of writings, the Reformer gave his famous reply:

"Since your most Serene Majesty, and your High Mightiness, require from me a direct and precise answer, I will give you one, and it is this. I cannot submit my faith either to the Pope or to the Councils, because it is clear as day they have frequently erred and contradicted each other. **Unless, therefore, I am convinced by the testimony of Scripture**, or on plain and clear grounds of reason, so that conscience shall bind me to make acknowledgment of error, I can and will not retract, for it is neither safe nor wise to do anything contrary to conscience." And then, looking round on the assembly, he

---

[1] Wylie, J.A.; *The History of Protestantism;* Cassell and Company, London; 1899; Way of Life, Fundamental Baptist CD ROM; p. Book 5, Chapter 11, "Luther's Journey to Augsberg

[2] Ibid.

said—and the words are among the sublimest in history—"
*HERE I STAND. I CAN DO NO OTHER. MAY GOD HELP ME.
AMEN.*"[1]

After Luther's excommunication, his enemies continued to fight out of allegiance to Rome. The wear and tear of the battles consummated in his death that was most likely caused by the plague and a myocardial infarction [heart attack] on Feb 17, 1546.

One should note that those churches, which did **not** embrace **all** of Luther's doctrine, became known as the Reformed Denomination as opposed to Lutheranism. The name, Reformed, was first given to the French Protestants, who were called Huguenots because they met near a gate called Hugon at midnight. They adopted Calvin's doctrine. An account of their slaughter at a wedding is as bad if not worse than the winter massacre of the Waldensians. The Reformed Church later split into a multitude of sects and parties out of which came the Armenians and Quakers. One final comment; the Mennonites claim direct ancestor-ship from the Waldensians, and the Amish are a branch of the Mennonites.

JACQUES LEFEVRE D'ETAPLES

In France a similar figure to Wycliff was emerging. His name was Jacques Lefevre D'Etaples. In 1512 this elderly priest after studying the epistles of Paul wrote:

"It is God who gives us, by faith, that righteousness which by grace alone justifies to eternal life".[2] This Reformer had gotten his hands on Scripture and actually read it. He is another who could be described as a member of the "Dawn of the Reformation" group. He quickly caused a stir among the students and faculty at Sorbonne, or Theological Hall of the great Paris University where he was soon to be appointed head of the department because of his great intellect. He just as quickly pointed out "that it [saved by grace through faith] had been taught by Irenaeus in early times long before the scholastic theology was heard of; and especially that this doctrine was not his, not Irenaeus', but God's, who had

---

[1] Ibid. "Luther before the Diet at Worms"; p. Book 6; Chapter 6

[2] Wylie, J.A.; *History of Protestantism;* "The Rise of Protestantism in France, 1510-1536; Chapter 1

revealed it to men in his Word.."[1]

Did you catch the link between Lefevre and Irenaeus? All of this was happening in France five years before Luther was noted in France.

At his feet sat a student, William Farel, born among the Alps of Dauphine near Grenoble in 1489. This district was one of the Waldensian areas although he was raised a catholic and defended the hierarchy at this stage of his life with vehemence. Having heard of the Sorbonne, he left the Alps for Paris in 1510 and wound up a student of Lefevre. As Lefevre grew in knowledge and wisdom from studying the Bible, he would tell his students:

"Salvation is of grace".[2]

Just as Luther had struggled, the young Farel at Lefevre's feet began to despair until he heard the words:

"of grace, without money and without price,"

that the gates of heaven are opened by the Cross of Christ. Farel came back to Lefevre and joined his master in his recent admission to sainthood with these words:

"All things appear to me under a new light. Instead of the murderous heart of a ravening wolf, he came back, he tells us, quietly like a meek and harmless lamb, having his heart entirely withdrawn from the Pope and given to Jesus Christ."[3]

OLIVETAN, FAREL, CALVIN, AND LEFEVRE

As usual, the young man, Farel, developed a vigorous witnessing program in France. His activity and others, such as Olivetan who also studied under Lefevre and who translated the Bible into French, drew persecution. It is no small coincidence that another man who was to become noted as one of the great Reformers sat at the feet of Lefevre. That man was John Calvin. Farel fled to Switzerland before Calvin arrived in Paris, and there Farel drew large crowds and introduced the Reformation into his native country. He became the pioneer for Calvin.

Calvin encountered Farel in Geneva in August of 1536. Because of the war in France with the Roman Empire Calvin had come to Switzerland. Farel was pleased that God had sent to him a helper, but Calvin had ideas of returning to Basel or Strasbourg for further education. Calvin, the author of the *Christian*

---

[1] Ibid.

[2] Ibid. Book 13, Chapter 2

[3] Ibid

Institutes was challenged by Farel to quit fleeing God and to cease thinking only of himself. Calvin acquiesced and was immediately appointed professor of theology. He labored in Geneva for 28 years and became the celebrated French Reformer. The "seed" that may have lead to his "reported" salvation was "planted" in Paris with the help of his relative, Olivetan, a Waldensian, who told Calvin:

> "True religion is not that mass of ceremonies and observances which the church imposes upon its followers, and which separates souls from Christ. O my dear cousin, leave off shouting with the papists, The fathers! The doctors! The church! and listen to the prophets and apostles. Study the scriptures." "I will have none of your new doctrines," answered Calvin, "their novelty offends me. I cannot listen to you. Do you imagine that I have been trained all my life in error? No! I will strenuously resist your attacks." Olivetan put the Bible into his hands, entreating him to study the Words of God. The Reformation at that time was agitating all the schools of learning. Masters and students occupied themselves with nothing else — some, no doubt, from mere curiosity, or to throw discredit upon the Reformers and their new doctrines; but there was a general awakening of conscience, and a readiness to believe the true gospel of the grace of God. Happily for Calvin he was among the latter class. The Holy Scriptures, by the blessing of God, separated him from Roman Catholicism, as they had done his cousin Olivetan. It is supposed that Calvin was under deep exercise of soul for more than three years — from 1523 to 1527. D'Aubigne, who is the best authority on this point, says, "Yet Calvin, whose mind was essentially one of observation, could not be present in the midst of the great movement going on in the world, without reflecting on truth, on error, and on himself. Oftentimes, when alone, and when the voices of men had ceased to be heard, a more powerful voice spoke to his soul, and his chamber became the theater of struggles, as fierce as those in the cell at Erfurt. Through the same tempests, both these great Reformers reached the haven of rest." But the conversion of Calvin lacks the thrilling interest which all have found in the conversion of Luther, and chiefly from the absence of details. The letters which he wrote to his father at this time, and also those of Olivetan to his friends, have not been found. Theodore Beza, his most intimate friend, says, "Calvin having been taught the true religion by one of his relations named Peter Olivetan, and having carefully read the holy books, began to hold the teaching of the Roman church in

horror, and had the intention of renouncing its communion." Here, it is only the intention of leaving Rome; but his own words in after life [after Calvin died] are positive: "When I was the obstinate slave of the superstitions of popery," he says, "and it seemed impossible to drag me out of the deep mire, God by a sudden conversion subdued me, and made my heart more obedient to His word." Thus we see the various spiritual links between the Sorbonne and the first and greatest Reformers. "Farel," says D'Aubigne, "is the pioneer of the Reformation in France and Switzerland. He rushes into the wood, hews down the giants of the forest with his axe. Calvin came after, like Melancthon, from whom he differs indeed in character, but whom he resembles in his part as theologian and organizer. These two men built up, settled, and gave laws to the territory conquered by the first two Reformers." And Beza speaks of Lefevre as the man who "boldly began the revival of the pure religion of Jesus Christ; and that from his lecture room issued many of the best men of the age and of the church."[1]

GOD, THE REFORMATION, AND TYNDALE

This same progress of reformation was taking place in Spain and other regions. The reason the reader was taken through the Reformation was to bring one to these understandings: (1) The OOO God was preparing an atmosphere for men spiritually and academically in England to develop the best scholars the world has ever known; and the situation will probably never be matched again. In the second part of the 16th century in England, men had developed spiritual and linguistic skills that overcome anyone with amazement. For example, Erasmus, the great scholar, prepared the groundwork for the *first* printed Greek New Testament text. Could this have been coincidence? Could this have been providentially controlled by the OOO God since the first printed text was about to become a reality? The men who followed his work, Stephanus, Beza, and Elzevir, added only a few changes. However, the great work of translating the Words of Scripture into the "classical" English, the language which would

---

[1] Miller, Andrew; *Church History; c 1860;* London; "The Reformation in French Switzerland, Chapter 49; p. Calvin's Conversation; Way of Life, Fundamental Baptist Electronic Disc, May 2000. An interesting fact is that George Morrell, a well known Waldensian Bard, visited Ecolampadius, Calvin's forerunner in Basel, Switzerland, in 1530

subsequently become the universal language by the 20th century, fell into the hands of some of the most spiritual and academically qualified men in history. (See below) (2) The second reason the Reformation was reviewed was to present the influence of the **priesthood of believers** on the Reformers through the "Waldensian" channel who were representative of independent Baptist churches.

The first individual in England to note is the reformer William Tyndale (1484-1536). He was born about 100 years after the death of Wycliff whose theology continued to seep through the common faith. Rome had done all it could do to destroy his memory (and other Reformers and their books) with threats, persecutions, murders, and burnings. There was great spiritual and moral decline emanating from Rome.

"It is saying but little, that at this era evangelical religion was low. Effects never exist apart from causes; and as the ministry was a mass of ignorance and superstition, no one has a right to expect grapes from thorns, or figs from thistles. The people never rise in moral excellence and social virtues higher than their teachers. ... The people relied 'on the merit of their own works toward their justification, such as pilgrimages to images, kneeling, kissing, and cursing of them, as well as many other hypocritical works in their store of religion; there being marts or markets of merits, full of holy relics, images, shrines, and works of superstition, ready to be sold; and all things they had were called holy: holy cowls, holy girdles, holy pardons, holy beads, holy shoes, holy rules. 'They were greatly seduced by certain famous and notorious images, as by our Lady of Walsingham, our Lady of Ipswich, St. Thomas of Canterbury, St. Anne of Buxton, the Rood of Grace [an image at Boxley in Kent which was cleverly rigged to bow its head, roll its eyes, smile and frown] ... To these they made vows and pilgrimages, thinking that God would hear their prayers in that place rather than in another place. They kissed their feet devoutly, and to these they offered candles, and images of wax, rings, beads, gold, and silver abundantly.' The moral and intellectual condition of the clergy can scarcely be described. Their power over the masses was complete. The destiny of the people for both worlds was in their hands. With their influence they encircled them from the cradle to the grave. Claiming to be the viceregents or the representatives of the Holy One, their lives were a perpetual exposition of the hypocrisy which marked them. Decency was thrown aside, and morality unknown. Brothels were kept in London for the especial use of the priesthood. The confessional was abused, and profligacy was all but universal. ... The moral state of the people under such teaching was almost beyond conception. Ignorance, vice, and immorality of the worst kind, reigned all but universally" (Evans, *Early English Baptists*, I, 1862, pp. 28,29,33)."[1]

Tyndale was born near the village of North Nibly. He was ordained into the priesthood in 1502. He trained at Oxford and earned his MA in 1515. Remember this: that just three years before Tyndale was born the Spanish Inquisition was begun and in 15 years 8,800 had been burned to death and 90,000 imprisoned under the popes Inquisitor General in Spain, Thomas de Torquemada. A monthly magazine, *Christ for the Nations,* in February of 2002 reported that:

"The notorious, medieval Supreme Council of the Inquisition followed...with the full approval of the crown. The secret proceedings, use of torture, absence of counsel for the accused, lack of right to confront hostile witnesses, confiscation of property, and finally death by fire, resulted in the demise of thousands of terrified Jews."

In 1492, 500,000 Jews had been driven out of Spain and their possessions confiscated. This was also the time of the terrible persecutions of the Waldensians in Bohemia and Moravia.

"The popes of Tyndale's day were very powerful and very wicked. Sixtus IV (1471-1484) established houses of prostitution in Rome. Innocent VIII (1484-1492) had seven illegitimate children, whom he enriched with church treasures. Alexander VI (1492-1503) lived with a Spanish lady and her daughter, and reveled in the grossest forms of debauchery. "The accounts of some of the indecent orgies that took place in the presence of the pope and [his daughter] Lucrezia are too bestial for repetition" (Kerr, pp. 228,29). He had five children, and his favorite son, Caesar Borgia, murdered his brother and his brother-in-law."[2]

---

[1] Cloud, David; *William Tyndale: The Father of our English Bible*, p. 2 of 20, *Nov.30, 1999;* Way of life Electronic Edition, May 2000; file://D:\fundamentalBaptistLibrary2000\qadocl.htm

[2] Ibid. p. 2 of 20

THE CONNECTIONS: BAPTISTS, REFORMERS, AND TYNDALE

After Oxford Tyndale moved to Cambridge where he probably studied under Erasmus who was there between 1509-1514. At Cambridge he developed a strong fellowship with two other students, John Fryth and Thomas Bilney. They shared, studied together and preached the gospel to others. Research shows that Tyndale may well have been an Anabaptist as shown in some Welsh manuscripts that are extant and by fact that he associated with some independent Baptists in London.

"Davis (*History of the Welsh Baptists*, 21) claims that William Tyndale (A.D. 1484-1536) was a Baptist. He was born near the line between England and Wales, but lived most of the time in Gloustershire. 'Llewellyn Tyndale and Hezekiah Tyndale were members of the Baptist church at Abergaverney, South Wales.' There is much mystery around the life of Tyndale. Bale calls him 'the apostle of the English.' 'He was learned, a godly, and a good- natured man' (Fuller, *Church History of Britain*, 1191). It is certain he shared many views held by the Baptists; but that he was a member of a Baptist church is nowhere proved. He always translated the word ecclesia by the word congregation, and held to a local congregation of a church (Tyndale, *Works II*, 13, London, 1831). There were only two offices in the church, pastor and deacons (1400). The elders or bishops should be married men (I, 265). Upon the subject of baptism he is very full. He is confident that baptism does not wash away sin. 'It is impossible,' say he, 'that the waters of the river should wash our hearts' (Ibid. 30). Baptism was a plunging into the water (Ibid., 25). Baptism to avail must include repentance, faith and confession (III, 179). The church must, therefore, consist of believers (Ibid., 25). His book in a wonderful manner states accurately the position of the Baptists"[1].

---

[1] Christian, A.M.,D.D.,LL.D., John T.; *A History of the Baptists, Together with Some Account of Their Principles and Practices;* Baptist Sunday School of the American Baptist Association; Texarkana, Ark.-Tex; 1922 p. 187-188

TYNDALE'S DESIRE

In 1530 he was arrested with a friend and they were fined 100 pounds each for distributing Scriptures. After leaving Cambridge he tutored the children of Sir John Walsh, a knight of Henry VIII, at Soderbury. It was here, while debating a "fanatical" priest who could not reason with Scripture as could Tyndale, he uttered the famous Words:

"I defy the pope, and all his laws; and if God spare my life many years, *I will cause a boy that driveth the plough to know more of the Scripture than you."* [1]

While at Soderbury he had translated one of the works of Erasmus, *The Christian Soldier's Manual.* Tyndale admired Erasmus but:

"saw through the defects in his character". [2]

His great goal was to translate the original language texts of Hebrew and Greek into English for the reasons sited above. He knew it would be a battle. The following reasons he placed in his *Introduction to the Five Books of Moses:*

"A thousand books had they rather to be put forth against their abominable doings and doctrine, than that the Scripture should come to light. For as long as they may keep that down, they will so darken the right way with the mist of their sophistry, and so tangle them that either rebuke or despise their abominations, with arguments of philosophy, and with worldly similitude's, and apparent reasons of natural wisdom; and with wresting the Scriptures unto their own purpose, clean contrary unto the process, order, and meaning of the text; and so delude them in descanting upon it with allegories . . . that though thou feel in thine heart, and art sure, how that all is false that they say, yet couldst thou not solve their subtle riddles. *Which thing only moved me to translate the New Testament. Because I had perceived by experience, how that it was impossible to establish the lay people in any truth, except the Scripture were plainly laid before their eyes in their mother tongue, that they might see the process, order, and meaning of the text:* for else, whatsoever truth is taught them, these enemies of all truth quench it again . . . **that is with apparent reasons of sophistry, and traditions of their own making; and partly in**

---

[1] Grady, PhD. Th.M., D.D., William P.; *Final Authority;* p. 132

[2] Cloud, David; *William Tyndale: The Father of Our English Bible;* p. 4 of 20; Way of Life Literature Electronic Edition, May 2000, Port Huron, MI;

juggling with the text, expounding it in such a sense as is impossible to gather of the text itself" (Tyndale, Introduction to *Five Books of Moses*)."[1] [my emphasis]

On his return to London he tried to obtain a place to stay from the local Bishop, Cuthbert Tonsel, but was turned away. A sympathetic local merchant was provided by God who gave him a place of rest and money for simply:

"praying for his father and mother, their souls, and all Christian souls."[2]

As usual God's providential care is far more than one could expect.

During this time King Henry VIII desired an annulment of his marriage to Queen Catherine because she was childless. He therefore did everything he could to appease the Pope. The atmosphere in England turned more ominous for the pious Tyndale. He was brought before the Chancellor who had been appointed by Cardinal Thomas Wolsey for heresy and treated "like a dog". The following quote is a description of the men and those trying times for Christians.

"In 1522, Tyndale was brought before the authorities to answer for his "heretical" opinions. "When I came before the Chancellor, he threatened me grievously, and reviled me, and rated me as though I had been a dog; and laid to my charge whereof there could be none accuser brought forth, as their manner is not to bring forth the accuser; and yet, all the Priests of the country were there the same day." ROME WAS REACHING OUT ITS LONG ARM AND DIRECTLY FINGERING THE MAN WHO YEARNED TO TRANSLATE THE ENGLISH SCRIPTURES. The Cardinal who had appointed this Chancellor was none other than Thomas Wolsey, who had been appointed Cardinal by Pope Leo X, and who would continue to persecute God's people throughout his life. Wolsey himself aspired to the papacy and pursued this object zealously, though unsuccessfully. Later Wolsey lamented to the pope that the printing press had made it possible for "ordinary men to read the Scriptures." The pope at the time of this early persecution against Tyndale was Adrian VI (1522-1523), who had only recently made Wolsey his legate or personal representative in England. The Bishop of Worcester (the area in which Tyndale was first persecuted) was Julio di Medici, who later became Pope Clement VII (1523-1534). The Chancellor who berated the 38-year-old Tyndale in 1522 was Thomas Parker, who later displayed his unreasonable fury against the truth by digging up the bones of

---

[1] Ibid. p. 4 of 20

[2] Grady, PhD., Th.M., D.D., William P.; *Final Authority; p. 132*

William Tracy and burning them to ashes. This was done in 1531, during the persecutions that were being poured out upon Bible believers throughout England. Tracy had been condemned after his decease "because in his last will he had committed his departing Spirit to God, through Jesus Christ alone, and left no part of his property to the priests, to pray for his soul" (Anderson, *Annals of the English Bible*, I, pp. 296,97)."[1]

TYNDALE AND LUTHER

Tyndale sensed the changing gloomy mood, realized he would not be able to accomplish the translation of the Bible into English, and fled England, not realizing he would never return. He went to Germany where he lodged in Hamburg. He immediately went to Wittenberg where the formidable Martin Luther was residing. Luther said:

" I have been born to war and fight with factions and devils"[2]

William P. Grady found this quote by Dr. J. R. Green that epitomizes the situation with the great Reformer, Luther.

"We find him [Tyndale] on his way to the little town which had suddenly become the sacred city of the Reformation. Students of all nations were flocking there with an enthusiasm which resembled that of the crusades. "As they came in sight of the town," a contemporary tells us, "they returned thanks to God with clasped hands, for from Wittenberg as heretofore from Jerusalem the light of evangelical truth had spread to the utmost parts of the earth." It was at Luther's instance that Tyndale translated there the gospels and epistles."[3]

TYNDALE'S GREAT ACHIEVEMENT

Tyndale completed his translation by 1525 and had it ready for the printer in

---

[1] Cloud, David; *William Tyndale: The Father of our English Bible;* p. 4-5 of 20;

[2] Grady, Ph.D., Th.M., DD., William P.; *Final Authority;* p. 132

[3] Ibid. p. 133

Cologne. However, a bitter spy for the Romans, John (Cochlaeus) Dobneck uncovered Tyndale's plan for printing and shipping English New Testaments back to England. He exposed Tyndale's preparation by getting several printers drunk and "loosening" their tongues. Cochlaeus' plan was fouled, however. William Roye, another man who came alongside, discovered the plot and assisted Tyndale with getting the sheets already printed to Worms, Germany where the publication was completed. The final form was hidden in barrels and containers headed for England and successfully smuggled into Tyndale's native land. There were approximately 1500 English New Testaments smuggled into England.

"But notwithstanding the impending dangers, five Hanseatic merchants took the precious books into their ships, and sailed for London. They expected to find the enemy on guard, but instead, the way was open and the books were landed and safely conveyed to the Merchants' warehouse in Thames Street. If the enemy slept, the friends of the Bible were awake and expectant. Not only in London, but in Oxford and Cambridge, they anxiously awaited the coming of the newly printed English Testaments. The soil was prepared for the seed. For almost a hundred and fifty years this preparation had been going forward: so intimately allied was the close of the fourteenth with the beginning of the sixteenth century. The name of John Wycliffe was still fresh in the minds and hearts of his friends; neither was it forgotten by his enemies, for they still kept alive the fires of persecution so early kindled against his followers. Then these Lollards, or Broders in Christ, still preserved and read the old brown manuscripts of Wycliffe's New Testament. They were familiar also with religious tracts of his writing. Besides all this there was a more recent preparation which began with the revival of learning, and the publishing of Erasmus' Greek and Latin Testament. A movement which influenced the educated, not excepting those of the Universities. Finally, by way of preparation, the influence of Luther must not be forgotten, which was beginning to sweep like a great wave over England. Thus the way was fully prepared, and from the first the people received these newly printed Testaments joyfully, but, from necessity, secretly" (Condit, *The History of the English Bible*, pp. 103,104)."[1]

Catholic authorities despised Tyndale's translation and every means of confiscating them was made. A search of young men at Oxford and Cambridge was made and Tyndale's long time friend, John Fryth, and others were caught

---

[1] Cloud, David; *William Tyndale: The Father of Our English Bible;* p. 6 of 20

with the "forbidden Book". They were marched down the street and made to toss their Books on a fire and then imprisoned in a foul dungeon for months. During the imprisonment four young men died and one of them was Fryth. He was burned alive at the stake.

"Being both bound to the stake, "there was present," says Foxe, "one Dr. Cooke, that was parson of the Church called All-hallows, in Honey-lane, situate in the midst of Cheapside. The said Cooke made open exclamation, and admonished the people, that they should in no wise pray for them, any more than they would for a dog." At these words, Fryth, smiling, prayed the Lord to forgive him! The Doctor's words, however, "did not a little move the people to anger, and not without cause. The wind made his death somewhat longer, as it bore away the flame from him to his fellow; but Fryth's mind was established with such patience, that, as though he had felt no pain, he seemed rather to rejoice for his fellow than to be careful for himself!" This painful event was felt and lamented far and near; and in fact it marks an era, which will be noticed afterwards more particularly."[1]

The sorry person overseeing this entire travesty was none other than the aspiring pope, Cardinal Wolsey. The historian, J.A. Wylie, in his book, *The History of Protestantism,* makes this comment concerning Tyndale's New Testament and Cardinal Wolsey.

"The printing...was completed in the end of 1525, and soon thereafter 1,500 copies were dispatched to England. "Give diligence" — so ran the solemn charge that accompanied them, to the nation to which the waves were wafting the precious pages — "unto the words of eternal life, by the which, if we repent and believe them, we are born anew, created afresh, and enjoy the fruits of the blood of Christ." Tyndale had done his great work. While Wolsey, seated in the splendid halls of his palace at Westminster, had been intriguing for the tiara, that he might conserve the darkness that covered England, Tyndale, in obscure lodgings in the German and Flemish towns, had been toiling night and day, in cold and hunger, to kindle a torch that might illuminate it."[2]

During this time King Henry VIII and the Pope forbade the reading of

---

[1] Anderson, Christopher; *Annals of the English Bible;* 1861; Section "England Reign of Henry VIII, 1533, Way of Life Literature Electronic Edition, May 2000

[2] Wylie, J.A.; *History of Protestantism;* Book 23, Chapter 3, "William Tyndale and the English New Testament"

Scriptures. House to house searches were made and many arrests occurred. One noted person was a Lollard and Bible teacher and reader, Father Hacker, in 1527. He was tortured to reveal a number of his friends and the prisons were filled to capacity with persons whose only crime was reading the Words of God.

Tyndale's Bible continued to be printed and smuggled into England and some estimates are as high as 18,000 made it into his motherland. However, so thorough was the destruction that today only one copy remains and a few fragments.[1] Tyndale also wrote many books and sermons such as, *The Revelation of Antichrist, The Supplication of Beggars, The Parable of the Unrighteous Mammon, The Obedience of a Christian Man,* and *How Christian Rulers ought to Govern.* In his book, *The Practice of Prelates,* Tyndale says,

"Even so the Bishop of Rome, at the beginning, crope along upon the earth, and every man trod upon him in this world. But as soon as there came a Christian Emperor, he joined himself unto his feet, and kissed them, and crope up a little with begging,—now this privilege, now that,—now this city, now that ... St. Peter's patrimony,—St. Peter's rents,—St. Peter's lands,—St. Peter's right; to cast a vain fear and superstitiousness into the hearts of men ... And thus, with flattering and feigning, and vain superstition, under the name of St. Peter, he crept up and fastened his roots in the heart of the Emperor; and with his sword climbed up above all his fellows; and brought them under his feet. And as he subdued them with the Emperor's sword, even so, by subtlety and help of them, after that they were sworn faithful, he climbed above the Emperor and subdued him also; and made him stoop unto his feet, and kiss them another while. Yea, Celestinus crowned the Emperor Henry the Fifth, holding the crown between his feet. And when he had put the crown on, he smote it off with his feet again, saying—that he had might to make emperors and put them down again. ... And as the pope played with the Emperor, so did his branches and his members, the bishops, play in every kingdom, dukedom, and lordship ... And thus, —the Ivy tree hath under his roots, throughout all Christendom, in every village, holes for foxes, and nests for unclean birds, in all his branches,—and promiseth unto his disciples all the promotions of the world" (Tyndale, "The Practice of Prelates").["][2]

Tyndale continued his translation work in Germany. John Fryth's wife and children had also come and stayed in mainland Europe to avoid the evil in

---

[1] Cloud, David; *William Tyndale: The Father of Our English New Testament;* p. 7 of 20

[2] Ibid. p 10 of 20

England. Tyndale wrote John Fyrth in England and encouraged him with these words from his wife. She "is well content with the will of God, and would not, for her sake, have the glory of God hindered."[1] [I placed this quote here lest anyone think the wives of these men were opposed to their activity.]

One of the books Tyndale translated was Jonah and he placed this statement in the preface. David Cloud says this about the quote of Tyndale to follow Dr. Cloud's comment:

"An excerpt from this Prologue illustrates Tyndale's keen spiritual discernment, and particularly his understanding of biblical repentance. Such discernment is absolutely necessary in an effective translator of the Holy Scriptures, yet it is so sadly lacking in most modern translators. **To have great textual knowledge and linguistic skills is utterly insufficient if not accompanied by at least an equal degree of spiritual life and discernment.** There is no doubt in this proclamation of Tyndale's as to his deep spiritual understanding.

Tyndale said:

"As the envious Philistines stopped the wells of Abraham, and filled them up with earth, to put the memorial out of mind, to the intent that they might challenge the ground; even so the fleshly-minded hypocrites stop up the veins of life, which are in the Scripture, with the earth of their traditions, false similitudes, and lying allegories; and that, of like zeal, to make the Scripture their own possession and merchandise, and so shut up the kingdom which is in God's Word; neither entering in themselves, nor suffering them that would. ...

Since the world began, wheresoever repentance was offered, and not received, there God took cruel vengeance immediately. As ye see in the flood of Noah, in the overwhelming of Sodom and Gomorrah, and all the country about; and as ye see of Egypt, of the Amorites, Canaanites, and afterwards of the very Israelites; and then at the last of the Jews too, the Assyrians, and Babylonians, and so throughout all the empires of the world.

Gildas preached repentance to the old Britons that inhabited England: they repented not; and therefore God sent in their enemies upon them on every side, and destroyed them up, and gave their land to other nations; and great vengeance hath been taken in that land for sin, since that time. Wickliffe preached repentance unto our fathers not long since: they repented not, for their hearts were indurate; but what followed?

---

[1] Ibid. p 13 of 20

They slew their true and right king, and set up three wrong kings in a row, under which all the noble blood was slain up, and half the commons too; what in France, and what with their own sword, in fighting among themselves, for the crown; so the cities and towns decayed, and the land was brought half into a wilderness, in respect of that it was before.

And now Christ, to preach repentance, is risen yet once again out of his sepulcher, in which the pope had buried him, and kept him down with his pillars and pole-axes, and all disguisings of hypocrisy—with guile, wiles, and falsehood, and with the sword of all princes, which he had blended with his false merchandise. And as I doubt not of the ensamples that are past, so I am sure that great wrath will follow, except repentance turn it back again and cease it (Tyndale, Prologue to Jonah)."[1]

TYNDALE BETRAYED AND MARTYRED

Tyndale was soon to be betrayed by a gambler, Henry [sometimes called Harry] Philips, who had been entrusted with a large sum of money to be taken to a person in London. He lost all his money and needed cash. A scheme was concocted with a local Catholic monk to apprehend Tyndale. All the details of the conspiracy are not known, but it was successful and Tyndale was arrested and burned at the stake on October 6, 1536 at Vilvorde. He was heard crying in a loud voice this famous prayer, a prayer that would soon be answered:

"Lord, open the eyes of the King of England"

as the flames snuffed out the life of another member of the *priesthood of believers.*[2]

I stated in the preface, my prayer is that this work would help create a firm foundation to help members withstand the persecutions to come. Are you sensing the courage it takes by men such as Polycarp and Tyndale, to continue to praise God through the extreme of Christian trials? As Tyndale pleaded, are your eyes opened and are you a true member of the **priesthood of believers?** The gate is strait [narrow] and "few there be that find it." That narrow, strait "Gate" **is** Jesus Christ. He is not hard to find. The gate is accessible **to all,** "For God so loved the world, that he gave his only begotten Son, that whosoever believeth

[1] Ibid. p. 13 of 20

[2] Grady, PhD. Th.M., D.D., William P.; *Final Authority;* p. 137

in him should not perish, but have everlasting life." [John 3:16]. God is not a liar. If you are not saved, please see appendix one (1)!

As is so often the case, during Tyndale's life God providentially provided shelter and money for him, and as Tyndale had so aptly described God's retribution in his prologue to Jonah, Cardinal Wolsey and Henry Philips were charged with treason. Wolsey was burned at the stake and Philips was pursued relentlessly.

"Some have claimed that Tyndale's translation was condemned only because it contained controversial notes which were opposed to Romanism, but Marion Simms, author of *The Bible from the Beginning*, discerningly comments, "The [Catholic] church, however, was opposed to any Bible for the common people, and doubtless would have sought to destroy it in any event" (Simms, p. 168)."[1]

The persecutions did not cease immediately in England. Men and women were slaughtered and tortured. One woman, Anne Askew, in 1546 was tortured on a rack to the point her joints were dislocated and she could not walk to her execution. Her Roman Catholic husband and son had betrayed her. Yet, she would not reveal her friends who loved the Word, and went to her grave proclaiming the following expressions:

"I believe all those Scriptures to be true, which He hath confirmed with his most precious blood. Yea, and as St. Paul saith, those Scriptures are sufficient for our learning and salvation, that Christ hath left here with us; so that I believe we need no unwritten verities to rule his Church with" (Anderson, II, p. 198). Her sole authority was the Bible, and for this she must die. In June she was condemned to be burned, with two other Bible believers. In July she was carried to the Tower prison and tortured on the rack repeatedly in an effort to force her to identify other believers. She said, "Then they did put me on the rack, because I confessed no ladies or gentlemen to be of my opinion, and thereon they kept me a long time; and because I lay still and did not cry, my Lord Chancellor and Master Rich took pains to rack me with their own hands till I was nigh dead" (Anderson, II, p. 196)."[2]

Tyndale's work could not be completed by the time of his death. He was working on the translation of the Old Testament. Miles Coverdale and John Rogers continued his work and the Coverdale Bible appeared in Europe in 1535. John Roger's pen name to avoid arrest was Thomas Matthew, and his Bible was called, The Matthew Bible. He followed Tyndale into the flames and this entry

[1] Cloud, David; *William Tyndale: The Father of Our English Bible;* p.18 of 20
[2] Ibid. p. 18 of 20

into official registers records the martyrdom and his pseudonym:

"The sentence pronounced on him before his martyrdom contains, four times, the expression, 'Johannes Rogers alias Matthew.' The Council Register of Mary's reign says, 'John Rogers alias Matthew, is ordered to keep his house at Paul's; and we know that he was for some time a prisoner in his own house" (Simms, *Bible from the Beginning*, p. 176)."[1]

TYNDALE'S WORK SPAWNS OTHER WORKS

Shortly after Tyndale's death, King Henry "divorced" himself from the Pope, but Romanism continued in England for some time. He did authorize the Coverdale Bible because it contained a picture of him seated on the throne with the title, Defender of the Faith; and Coverdale removed any disparaging remarks toward the King and his rule in the side margins. After the obese King Henry's death, which he may have believed to be near since he allowed the Coverdale Bible and authorized [licensed] the Matthew Bible, King Edward VI came to power who was a definite Protestant. He remained in power for only a short time but approved many editions of the New Testament (35) and the complete Bible (14). After his death, his half-sister Queen Mary came to power who was a staunch Roman Catholic. She became known as Bloody Mary because of her relentless pursuit of Bible loving Protestant preachers and readers.

Some notable men anticipated her bloody reign and escaped to Geneva, Switzerland, where they put together the Geneva Bible. Geneva was known at that time as the Holy City. Among those who were on the first committee to "translate" the Bible were Theodore Beza, John Knox, William Whittingham and Miles Coverdale. They labored 6 years to produce their work, and it would be the Bible brought to the 'new' world by the pilgrims.

KING JAMES MAKES HIS APPEARANCE

The Geneva Bible would remain the Bible of the "priesthood" people until the King James Bible (KJB) of 1611. Momentous events in history would build until the KJB was printed. Bloody Mary was found dead in her bed on

---

[1] Ibid. p. 19 of 20

November 15, 1558. The reaction to her reign was to forever seal England as a Protestant nation. In the wake of her time in power, Queen Elizabeth ruled 45 years and allowed 150 editions of the Bible and the New Testament to be printed. She tried to break all ties with Rome, but had to appease her constituents, three-quarters who remained Catholics. She walked a tightrope trying to please a large contingent of Puritans and the Catholics. Catholics were regrouping at the Council of Trent and some of the Calvinists and Lutherans who were aware of these events mistreated the Puritans. They were afraid the Puritans would "rock the boat" and cause a reversion to oppression. Queen Elizabeth died without an heir and would be followed by the King of Scotland, King James VI, crowned King James I of England. James was the son of Mary, the Queen of Scots (1542-1587), and a notorious Catholic of Scotland. Mary was imprisoned and beheaded by her half sister, Queen Elizabeth.

Much has been written about King James I who would authorize the KJB. Some writings would be seditious and some would be written with an agenda. The truth is that he was a good man who suffered much from gouty arthritis and various physical deformities. A patient, with the problems the King had, can become one of two kinds of persons: the first is a surly human, the second is a kind compassionate, and understanding person. King James became the latter.

This man was attacked satanically and was castigated because of his appearance, difficulties, and spiritual inclinations. He was called a slouch, but had mastered the languages of Latin, French, and Greek by the age of eight, in addition to being taught Italian and Spanish.[1] He continued to master languages including Hebrew.

He was hated by the Roman Catholic Church as is evident in the **"Gun Powder Plot"** of the Jesuits and by this comment of the Spanish Ambassador to England in 1607.

"He is a Protestant...The king tries to extend his Protestant religion to the whole island. The King is a bitter enemy of our religion [Roman Catholicism] he frequently speaks of it in terms of contempt. He is all the harsher because of this last conspiracy [the Gun Powder Plot] against his life...He understood that the Jesuits had a hand in it."[2]

---

[1] Grady, PhD, Th.M., D.D., William P.; *Final Authority;* p. 146

[2] Gipp Th.D., Samuel C.; *Gipp's Understandable History of the Bible;* p. 384

FALSE ACCUSATIONS AGAINST KING JAMES

In order to try to destroy this devout Christian's reputation and place in history, he has been called through the years and even into modern times a homosexual, dumb, unlearned, pervert, and other unflattering terms. All the accusations are without proof. All accusers have been identified as false witnesses. [sound familiar] Listen to the truth next:

"King James was regarded by those of his own time as 'the British Solomon'. He was wise not only in politics and academics, but in Theology. He was devotedly interested in the Word of God. He made it clear that he wanted the Holy Word of God to be in the hands of people and not chained to pulpits or hoarded in cellars **to be read only by Greek scholars.**" [my emphasis] King James said, "Keep your body clean and unpolluted while you give it to your wife whom only it belongs for how can you justly crave to be joined to a Virgin if your body be polluted? Why should the one half be clean, and the other defiled? And suppose I know, fornication is thought but a venial sin by most of the world, yet remember well what I said in my first book regarding conscience, and count every sin and breach of God's law, not according as the vain world esteems of it, but as God judge and maker of the law accounts of the same:" ...and "God gives not kings the style of gods in vain, for on his throne his scepter do the sway...So kings should fear and serve their God again. If they would enjoy a happy reign, observe the statues of your heavenly king; and from his law make all your laws to spring...and so ye (shall in princely virtues shine). Resembling right your might king divine." ...And "Now faith ...is the free gift of God (as Paul sayeth). It must be nourished by prayer, which is nothing else but a friendly talking to God. Use oft to pray when ye are quiet, especially on your bed."[1]

---

[1] Ibid. p. 369-372

THE INCOMPARABLE KING JAMES

King James could quote many texts of Scripture. His wife, family, and subjects worshiped him. He desired the Scripture to be placed into the hands of the people. And lastly, Dr Gipp has outlined the accomplishments of this great king as compared to other famous people. He calls King James, the INCOMPARABLE. Examine what this humble man did compared to Columbus, Wright brothers, Henry Ford, or Thomas Edison who Dr. Gipp called geniuses because they changed history by their inventions and achievements:

"1.   He united the nations of England, Ireland, and Scotland to form the foundation of the British Empire. In fact, he was the first to use the term "Great Britain". This would be the power base that would be used to influence the world in the "ways" of Britain.

2. He commissioned the translation of the Authorized Version. This single volume was to affect each Briton that came into contact with it in such a way as to fully exploit his individual potential for good (a feat it still achieves today on anyone who will read it!). This effect brought a strain of civilization to England that was lacking in other colonial powers. As a rule, England was more benevolent to its colonies than its contemporaries were to theirs. To this day, independent nations that were at one time British colonies profit from their earlier association with Great Britain. In too many cases these nations' best years were those when they were being "exploited" by this "horrible" colonial power!

3. He established the first Christian colony in the New World. This was the foundation upon which the United States was built. Remember, France and Spain both had colonies here before England did. But their Roman Catholicism forced God to withhold His blessing from their endeavors and then to supplant them with the Bible-exalting British.

4. King James insistence on jury trials...has been carried around the globe by Western civilization in sharp contrast to the tyrannical kangaroo courts of Muslim and Communist nations.

5. King James exalted womanhood and the sanctity of marriage. He held the institution so highly that he himself spent **fifteen days** in prayer and meditation before entering into that sacred bond with Anne of Denmark. James own words confirm

his high regard for this godly institution. In speaking to his heir, he said concerning marriage: "But the principle blessing that you can get of good company will stand, in your marrying of a godly and virtuous wife...being flesh of your flesh and bone of your bone...Marriage is the greatest earthly felicity...without the blessing of God you cannot look for a happy marriage."[1]

We can only surmise what a blessing it would be for America to return to these principles!

The fabrication by those who rewrite history promotes the idea that America was founded for 'free enterprise and multi-culturalism'. This could not be further from the truth. Patrick Henry says:

"It cannot be emphasized too strongly or too often that this great nation was founded, not by religionists, but by Christians, not on religions, but on the gospel of Jesus Christ"[2]

This writer was told the 'first' pilgrims came to America to "escape the tyranny of religious persecution". That is not true either. King James sent them with the gospel in hand. They called their settlement in 1609, Jamestown, in honor of their great King! Separatists (not persecuted for their religion) from England did come over on the Mayflower to Plymouth in 1620. The great historian, Thomas Armitage, said:

"Before Plymouth Rock was known, and nearly a quarter of a century before Massachusetts Bay Colony was organized, the soil of Virginia [at Jamestown] was hallowed by praise to God in public worship."[3]

Did you get how subtly the rewriters of history have been changing the truth? They started with (1) the settlers "came to escape religious persecution", and they have now changed it to (2) "the practice of free enterprise and multi-culturalism". Is there any hope that the truth will ever be told in our history books?[4]

---

[1] Ibid. p. 378

[2] Ibid. p. 379

[3] Armitage, Thomas, *A History of the Baptist,* Originally published 1890 by Bryan, Taylor, and Co. NY, NY, Reprinted by the Baptist Standard Bearer, Inc. Paris, Arkansas, p. 619 and 724

[4] Grady, PhD., Th.M, D.D. William P.; *What Hath God Wrought, A Biblical Interpretation of American History;* Grady Publications, Inc.; Knoxville, TN; ISBN 0-9628809-2-2; Seventh Printing; 2001; p. 27- 30; This reference supports the opposite view to Dr. Gipp's position. Dr. Grady does shed 'grace' on Jamestown in *Final Authority*, page 152, however. This whole area will require further research for this author. This comment is not intended to cast disparaging remarks, just confusion on my part.

Now, because of the **priesthood of believers'** correlation, the great achievement by King James I that needs to be closely examined is the authorization of the King James Version and the appointment of the translators. King James was quite dissatisfied with the Geneva Bible because of its seditious and Calvinistic marginal notes which clashed with his concept of the divine right of kings. The King gave several examples such as: 1) The marginal note on Exodus 1:19 said the midwives who were disobedient to Pharaoh were "lawful". 2) The note on II Chronicles 15:16 said:

"Herein [Asa] showed that he lacked zeal: for she [his mother] sought to have died...but he gave place to foolish pity."[1]

William Grady goes on to say:

"this could hardly be acceptable to a son whose first order of business as England's newest monarch had included the honorable interment of his own mother's body in Westminster Abbey".[2]

King James also recognized that the Bible translated on English soil would add esteem to his maligned régime. James felt "no man could serve two masters" and the desire to "unite the kingdom behind a single Bible" encouraged him to **authorize the translation** with the following statement:

"That a translation be made of the whole Bible, as consonant as can be to the original Hebrew and Greek; and this to be set out and printed, without any marginal notes, and only to be used in all churches of England, in time of Divine service."[3]

"In response to the pharisaical, nit-picking of the 20th-century Nicolaitanes who would challenge the extent of James' actual endorsement ("Strictly speaking, the Authorized Version was never authorized." [Geisler and Nix]), we submit the contemporary testimony of Bishop Bancroft, [who initially was resistant to the project]. He states to an aide,

"I move you in his majesty's name that, agreeably to the charge and trust committed unto you, no time may be overstepped by you for the better furtherance of this holy work...**You will scarcely conceive how earnest his majesty is to have this work begun!**"[4]

Tyndale's prayer "to open the eyes of the king" was hardly three-quarters

---

[1] Grady, PhD., Th.M. D.D., *Final Authority*, p. 152
[2] Ibid. p. 152
[3] Ibid. 153
[4] Ibid. 153

of a century old! King James requested the best scholars of the land be assembled to do the work. They were divided into six teams and assigned to three locations; Cambridge, Oxford, and Westminster. There were initially fifty-four men chosen, but by the time the translation had begun the team had lost seven. The following information concerning these men was obtained from Dr. Gipp's book, *Understandable History of the Bible,* Dr. D.A. Waite's book, *Defending the King James Bible,* and William P. Grady's book, *Final Authority.*

SOME TRANSLATORS OF THE KING JAMES BIBLE

<u>1</u>. The first man to receive our attention is **Dr Lancelot Andrews**, Dean of Westminster, and Chairman of the Westminster group of ten men. They met in the famous Jerusalem Chambers and their responsibility was Genesis through II Kings. Dr Andrews was conversant in 15 languages and had prepared his own devotional in Greek. He acquired most of his language studies at Cambridge in the Oriental languages. He would go on vacation once a year and spend a month with his parents. He would find a "master" in a foreign language while on vacation to whom he was unknown and spend his vacation learning a new language. He was known as a great man of prayer and preaching. He did not have just head knowledge, but was "a man of great practical preaching ability and an ardent opponent of Rome. His abilities were recognized by Henry, Earl of Huntington, who took him into the north of England, "where he was the means of converting many Papists by his preaching and disputations,"[1] He was such an outstanding preacher he was called the "Star of Preachers"[2] He was said to spend many hours a day in prayer and in family devotions. He abounded in joy and cheer and was a gracious host. But that's not all. Listen to what was said about his ability as a translator:

> "But we are chiefly concerned to know what were his qualifications as a translator of the Bible. He ever bore the character of a 'right godly man,' and a 'prodigious student.' One competent judge speaks of him as 'that great gulf of learning'! It is also said, that 'the world wanted learning to know how learned this man was.' A brave, old chronicler remarks, that such was his skill in all languages, especially the Oriental, that had he been present at the confusion of tongues at Babel, he might have served as the Interpreter-General! In his funeral sermon by Dr Buckridge, Bishop of Rochester, it is said that Dr.

---

[1] Gipp Th.D., Samuel C., *Gipp's Understandable History of the Bible;* p. 288
[2] Ibid. p. 289

Andrews was conversant with fifteen languages.`[1]

2. John Bois was reading Hebrew at the age of five. His father taught him and by the ripe old age of six he was writing Hebrew "in a fair and elegant character".[2] He was renowned for conversing with his professors at St. John's College, Cambridge, in Greek. His age was fifteen. In the offices of Dr Downe, the chief of Greek languages, Bois chose the twelve hardest Greek authors in prose available that could be read with Dr. Downe. He was frequently found at four AM studying and would stay until eight PM. These books were in Classical Greek that is found in 3 different dialects, Ionic, Doric, and Attic. I have it on good word that doing what he did is a most difficult challenge. His Greek library was the most extensive and expensive Greek library ever made. And now the kicker, he was just as skilled in Hebrew. When the groups ran into difficulty with translation, he was one of the twelve chosen for the final review. He was so skilled in the Greek New Testament that he could turn to "any word, at any time", that it contained. He acted as secretary of the committee. He was a voluminous writer and left over 30,000 pages. Yet he had a tender side demonstrated by the care he gave his mother. He would walk 20 miles just to have breakfast with her and he read all the way.

3. Dr. John Overall was another noted scholar in the area of the church fathers. This was the knowledge necessary to confirm the authenticity of certain passages such as 1John 5:7, known among scholars as the Johannine Comma. He was known for his opposition to Rome and their "scriptural perversions", his translation ability, and his defense of the faith. He was present at the hanging of Jesuit Henry Garnet, of the "Gun Powder Plot", and tried to get him to make a profession of faith. Garnet died in his sins. He had spoken Latin so much that it was hard for "him to speak English in a continued oration".[3]

4. William Bedwell was another scholar in Oriental languages. He developed a Persian dictionary that is still available in the Bodelian Library at Oxford. He published a book, *A Discovery of the Impostures of Mahomet and of the Koran.* This was attached to his book, *Arabian Trudgeman.*

"He published in quarto an edition of the epistles of St. John in Arabic, with a Latin version, printed at the press of Raphelengius, at Antwerp, in 1612. He also left many Arabic manuscripts to the University of Cambridge, with numerous notes upon them, and a font of types of printing them. His fame for Arabic learning was so great, that when Erpenius, a most renowned Orientalist, resided in England in 1606, he was much indebted to Bedwell for direction in his studies. To Bedwell,

---

[1] Ibid. p. 290

[2] Grady, PhD., Th.M., DD., William P., *Final Authority,* p. 156

[3] Waite, Th.D., PhD., D.A.; *Defending the King James Version;* p. 77

rather than to Erpenius, who commonly enjoys it, belongs the honor of being the first who considerably promoted and revived the study of the Arabic language and literature in Europe. He was also tutor to another Orientalist of renown, Dr. Pococke."[1]

He also invented a ruler for geometric purposes like the Gunther's scale that was called the 'Bedwell's Ruler'. He had a fondness for mathematic. Some scholars today think we have an advantage in modern times over the KJV translators:

"by reason of the greater attention which is supposed to be paid at present to what are called the 'cognate' and 'Shemitic' languages, and especially the Arabic by which much light is thought to be reflected upon Hebrew words and phrases. It is evident, however, that Mr. Bedwell and others, among his fellow-laborers, were thoroughly conversant in this part of the broad field of sacred criticism."[2]

He also had his own lexicon and after his death "the voluminous manuscripts of his lexicon were loaned" to Cambridge to aid others.

5. **Dr. Hadrian Savaria** was educated in several languages, especially Hebrew. He published several manuscripts in Latin against Beza, Danaeus, and other Presbyterians.

6. **Dr. Robert Tighe** was noted to be "an excellent textuary and profound linguist".[3]

7. **Miles Smith** was called "the walking library".[4] He was asked to write the preface to the 'new' Bible.

8. **John Laifield** was unique because of his ability in the area of architecture and lent his talents in the area of the tabernacle and temple.

9. **Dr. John Reynolds** [or Rainolds] is the one who was known as "the living library, a third university"[5] He was already a fellow at Corpus Christi College at age seventeen. William Grady reports Anthony Wood said of Dr. Reynolds:

"that he was 'most prodigiously seen in all kinds of learning; most excellent in all tongues,"...a prodigy in reading, famous in doctrine, and the very treasure of erudition."[6]

He was raised a Roman Catholic, but he was born again and became a Puritan. He was a passionate and vigorous anti-Papist against his former Church.

---

[1] Gipp, Th.D., Samuel C.; *Gipp's Understandable History of the Bible; p. 293*

[2] Ibid. p. 294

[3] Ibid. p. 293

[4] Grady, Ph.D., Th.M., D.D., William P.; *Final Authority;* p. 157

[5] Ibid. p. 157

[6] Ibid. p. 157

Dr. Gipp records this quote concerning this outstanding man and scholar:

> "About the year 1578, John Hart, a popish zealot, challenged all the learned men in the nation to a public debate. At the solicitation of one of Queen Elizabeth's privy counselors, Mr. Reynolds encountered him. After several combats, the Romish champion owned himself driven from the field. At that time, the celebrated Cardinal Bellarmine, the Goliath of the Philistines at Rome, was professor of theology in the English Seminary at that city. As fast as he delivered his popish doctrine, it was taken down in writing, and regularly sent to Dr. Reynolds; who from time to time, publicly confuted it at Oxford. Thus Bellarmine's books were answered, even before they were printed."[1]

One of the great customary fabrications the Catholics regularly proclaim is that an outstanding person recants his opposition to the Church on his deathbed. They tried this with Dr. Reynolds, but

> "he was not dead enough and received word of the rumor; and set his name to the following declaration: 'These are to testify to all the world, that I die in the possession of that faith which I have taught all my life, both in my preachings and in my writings, with an assured hope of my salvation, only by the merits of Christ my Savior."[2]

10. **Dr John Harding** was Royal Professor of Hebrew in the University for thirteen years. When he was appointed to the translation committee he was regarded as one of the greatest scholars.

11. **Dr. Edward Lively** was regarded at the time of his appointment as:

> "one of the best linguists in the world…Much dependence was placed on his surpassing skill in Oriental languages."[3]

12. **Dr. Francis Dillingham** was able to debate using the Greek language. He was another scholar in the original languages. He had no respect for popish doctrine. He was antagonistic to Romanism and he published a book, *Manual of Christian Faith,* taken from the Church Fathers. He wrote many papers on various points associated with the catholic controversy.

13. **Thomas Harrison** was the chief examiner **for** Greek and Hebrew professors. No one taught the languages at the University without going through him. He was also Vice-Master of Trinity College in Cambridge.

14. **Lawrence Chaderton** was also raised a Roman Catholic. He was in London studying to become a lawyer and got saved. Subsequently, he joined a Puritan Congregation in London. He diligently studied the Latin, Greek, and

---

[1] Gipp, Th.D., Samuel C.; *Gipp's Understandable History of the Bible;* p. 299

[2] Ibid. p. 300

[3] Ibid. p. 295

Hebrew tongues and became very skilled in them. He thoroughly reviewed the writings of the Rabbis, so far as they contributed to the understanding of the Word.

Although there are many others on the committee, the stories of their lives and qualifications continue along the same lines as the preceding 14 men concerning character, scholarship and abilities. The book that reveals the most about these translators is Alexander McClure's, *Translators Revived.* However, there is one final story about a translator that epitomizes the "state of the art" in the modern age amongst teachers, professors, and the like as opposed to these **priesthood of believers** translators.

15. **Dr. Richard Kelby** had an incident occur in his life immediately after the KJB translation was finished. The episode exemplifies "what many are trying to tell" the 'intellectuals' today who think that, because of their computers and superior research, they have an edge. They believe they can change any word in the KJB translation because of self-esteem or rather their unsurpassed knowledge, but let this story act as a parable in their lives. I pray they can hear.

"I must here stop my reader, and tell him that this Dr. Kilby was a man so great in learning and wisdom, and so excellent a critic in the Hebrew tongue, that he was made professor of it in this University; and as also so perfect a Grecian, that he was by King James appointed to be one of the translators of the Bible, and that this Doctor and Mr. Sanderson had frequent discourses, and loved as father and son. The Doctor was to ride a journey into Derbyshire, and took Mr. Sanderson to bear him company; and they resting on a Sunday with the Doctor's friend, and going together to that parish church where they were, found the young preacher to have no more discretion than to waste a great part of the hour allotted for his sermon in exceptions against the late translation of several words, (not expecting such a hearer as Dr. Kilby) and showed three reasons why a particular word should have been otherwise translated. When evening prayer was ended, the preacher was invited to the Doctor's friend's house, where after some other confidence, the Doctor told him, he might have preached more useful doctrine, and not filled his auditor's ears with needless exceptions against the translation; and for that word for which he offered to that poor congregation three reasons why it ought to have been translated **as he and others had considered all of them, and found thirteen more considerable reasons why it was translated as now printed.**"[1] [my emphasis]

It is time to remind the reader that we are still taking a history of facts

---

[1] Ibid. pp. 300-301

relating to our patient. We are still in the Subjective portion of the SOAP acronym. We will continue to gather all the pertinent facts we can that may have a bearing on reaching the proper Assessment of the patient, the Word. Next, we will turn our attention to the manuscript history, and following that to the Objective, which will examine the patient [Bible] to see what damage, if any, has been done by the infection [leaven]. A proper history and physical assists a physician immensely to arrive at the correct diagnosis. It cannot be done superficially, and previous exams are of limited help.

The Wide Gate:
The Manuscripts

Matthew 7:13-14 *Enter ye in at the strait gate: for wide is the gate, and broad is the way, that leadeth to destruction, and many there be which go in thereat: Because strait is the gate, and narrow is the way, which leadeth unto life, and few there be that find it.*

Matthew 7:20-21 *Not every one that saith unto me, Lord, Lord, shall enter into the kingdom of heaven; but he that doeth the will of my Father which is in heaven. Many will say to me in that day, Lord, Lord, have we not prophesied in thy name? and in thy name have cast out devils? and in thy name done many wonderful works?*

CONFLICTING APPROACHES TO MANUSCRIPT RESEARCH

There are two opposing views in regard to manuscript research and appraisal. When I first started examining textual criticism and its relation to manuscript evaluation, the concept of two views was surprising. I thought everyone who was interested in the Bible, and the research related to it, would be working together in a combined effort. Why would unsaved persons waste their time reviewing the manuscripts concerning the Bible? Of course this position was naïve for two reasons. 1) The unsaved 'world' would like nothing better than to show that the scripture is baseless, or poorly documented, or a myth. 2) Many in this field of endeavor are probably hedging their 'bets'. This means they don't really believe the Scripture and would like to show it is like any other book, but, just in case the Bible is "real", and more than just a book, they try to act positive toward it. Additionally, there is the thought that just studying the Bible will get them a "ticket to heaven" if it turns out to be true.

The first approach to textual criticism belongs to the Wide Gate crowd. Most scholars are in this group because it is alleged to be "scientific". Those two facts alone should make anyone who is a believer cautious. I will state the two facts again, 1) There is a crowd. 2) It's scientific. I guess they called it scientific because they proposed a "theory". Anyone can propose a theory about anything. What makes a study scientific is the ability to study the hypothesis by testing. Otherwise it is psuedo-science and winds up being resolved by personal opinions. **I cannot** come up with a way to scientifically test whether a manuscript found in garbage cans, closets, garbage dumps, monasteries, or the Vatican is the Words of God.

Having done some research earlier in my life on the effects of drowning and near-drowning on the lungs, I have a great deal of difficulty understanding how a textual critics can call looking at a lot of manuscripts and placing them in "families" as "scientific".

In Bruce Metzger's work, *The Text of the New Testament,* he spends a number of pages on the development of the modern critical period. He lauds the accomplishments of men such as Griesbach and Lachmann who began the:

"overthrow of the Textus Receptus".[1]

---

[1] Metzger, Bruce M.; *The Text of the New Testament; Its Transmission, Corruption, and Restoration;* Oxford University Press, New York & Oxford; 3rd Edition; 1992; p. 124

He reports Lachmann replied to his critics by saying they had a:
"blind preference for the familiar but corrupt later text to the earlier, purer form."[1]

Metzger goes on to say:

"the judgment of most later scholars has agreed with Hort's [remember Westcott and Hort, see below, HDW] evaluation of Lachman and his work: [The following is Hort's evaluation of Lachman, HDW]

'A new period began in 1831 when for the first time a text was **constructed** directly from the ancient documents without the intervention of any printed edition, and when the first systematic attempt was made to substitute **scientific method for arbitrary choice** in the discrimination of various readings. In both respects the editor, Lachmann, rejoiced to declare that he was carrying out the principles and unfilled intentions of Bently, as set forth in 1716 and 1720."[2][my emphasis, and comments]

Oh my!! The preceding quote by Metzger taken from Hort's writings sounds so foolish. You should not continue until you understand that these two men are in the "modernistic" camp, which exalts the reasoning of humans called humanistic rationalism.

Please be aware that there is no way to test either method alluded to by Hort in his comment above. A retired, research and registered pharmacist, friend of mine, Thomas Eller, concurs on the scientific method. The scientific method is this: a theory or hypothesis must be able to be tested. All other methods are constructed on personal opinions as to the evidence.

All other methods are similar to what a jury is asked to do: to arrive at a decision based on witnesses and evidence. The jury in a legal trial depends on the **veracity** or believability of witnesses and the evidence. Having observed the opinions of the two sides as to their beliefs, that is the Hort/Westcott textual critic group verses the Received Text group, the people of the jury, you, can make your own decision. The evidence (history and actual manuscripts) shows that the preponderance of facts about the two routes favors the path leading to the Received Text as the preserved Words of God. A much more in depth look at all of these factors will follow. Some of the factors are involved in *"The Lie,"* which is yet to be presented.

However, it should not be assumed that every person investigating the manuscripts from the 'alleged' scientific point of view is an "unbeliever," but this point of view gives too much credence to 'the scientific method' and too

---

[1] Ibid. p. 125
[2] Ibid. pp. 125-126

much power to man. This way of evaluating the manuscripts is called the **natural approach** to textual criticism. This method allegedly evaluates all material associated with the research **neutrally**. That is: one needs to investigate the Bible like the secular world would. The natural approach to the study of the manuscripts of the Bible is like the approach to **any other book**. Therefore, a secular book or the Bible handed down through the centuries could be corrupted by many means; and a conflation or amalgamation of **all** copies is necessary to arrive at the original wording of the book. The neutral approach cannot accept that a special divine route or handling of the Book or copies of the original autographs is possible. The belief that there is an OOO God who could preserve and protect His Words is either 1) far from their 'belief scheme'; or 2) they have been innocently taken down the rabbit trail of humanistic rationalism and don't know how to get back. Is it possible they truly believe **they** have been assigned the job of restoring the Words? They object to the opposing view on the grounds that nowhere in Scripture does it say God will preserve His Words in any **particular way**, which is not true.[1]

THE DOCTRINE OF PRESERVATION: OLD OR NEW?

The following are typical comments that one finds in the literature. W. Edward Glenny, former professor at Central Baptist Seminary, says:

"The doctrine of the preservation of Scripture was first introduced in a church creed in 1647. As we have argued above IT IS NOT A DOCTRINE THAT IS EXPLICITLY TAUGHT IN SCRIPTURE, nor is it the belief that God has perfectly and miraculously preserved every word of the original autographs in one manuscript or text-type. It is a belief that God has providentially preserved His Word in and through all the extant manuscripts, versions and other copies of Scripture...not only does no verse in Scripture explain how God will preserve His Word, but THERE IS NO STATEMENT IN SCRIPTURE FROM WHICH ONE CAN ESTABLISH THE DOCTRINE OF THE PRESERVATION OF THE TEXT OF SCRIPTURE....it is also obvious from the evidence of history that GOD HAS NOT MIRACULOUSLY AND PERFECTLY PRESERVED HIS WORD IN ANY ONE MANUSCRIPT OR GROUP OF MANUSCRIPTS, OR IN ALL THE

---

[1] For information about "how" or the "means" God commanded His Words to be preserved, see <u>Thou Shalt Keep Them;</u> Kent Brandenburg, Editor; Pillar and Ground Publishing, El Sobrante, CA.

MANUSCRIPTS."[1] [my emphasis]

Glenny goes on to "**proclaim**" and **deny** from his *seat* **of authority** [see the preface to this work] that the Bible does not proclaim preservation of Scripture and boldly explains away the following passages:

Psalm 12:7 Thou shalt keep them, O LORD, thou shalt preserve them from this generation for ever.

Psalm 105:8 He hath remembered his covenant for ever, the Word which he commanded to a thousand generations.

Psalm 119:89 For ever, O LORD, thy Word is settled in heaven.

Psalm 119:152 Concerning thy testimonies, I have known of old that thou hast founded them for ever.

Psalm 119:160 Thy Word is true from the beginning: and every one of thy righteous judgments endureth for ever.

Isaiah 40:8 The grass withereth, the flower fadeth: but the Word of our God shall stand for ever.

Matthew 5:18 For verily I say unto you, Till heaven and earth pass, one jot or one tittle shall in no wise pass from the law, till all be fulfilled.

Matthew 24:35 Heaven and earth shall pass away, but my words shall not pass away.

PROFESSORS WHO SOUND LIKE BREAKING GLASS

One would suppose a young student listening to his professor audaciously denying the preceding verses would have his faith in the written Words shaken to the core. Let me assure every student of God's Words that many men in history in seats of authority have tried refuting God's Words. They wind up sounding like the breaking of glass or the tinkling of bells, instead of the triumphant cry of a martyr [as you have seen] who died willingly for the mighty preserved, inerrant, verbally and plenarily inspired Words of the Almighty Living God.

This is another comment by James Price of Tennessee Temple University:

"One may infer the doctrine of preservation from the statements in the Bible, but the explicit term 'preserve' (or its derivatives) is

---

[1] Glenny, W. Edward; *The Bible Version Debate; pp. 93, 95, 99;* Way of Life Literature, Port Huron, MI; Electronic Disc, 2000; Reported at file://D:\FundamentalBaptistLibrary2000\www\fbns\preservation. p. 2 of 6

never used in the KJV of the written word of God"[1]

David Cloud responds to this statement in an article he wrote, *"Fundamentalists following Textual Critics in Denying/Questioning Biblical Preservation"*, this way.

"When he [James Price] was understandably challenged for stating that God did not promise to preserve the Scriptures, Dr. Price replied, "I know the passages that infer preservation, and I believe the doctrine. I just don't think that the Bible explicitly states how God preserved His Word." He is therefore not as bold as Glenny, but he does most definitely cast doubt upon preservation by his claim that the Bible NOWHERE explicitly states or promises preservation. [read the statement above again, HDW] If that is the case, how can he believe in such a thing! He says there are inferences. Are those inferences authoritative so that a doctrine can be built on them? If so, what is he getting at? Either God has promised to preserve the Scripture, or He has not. What is this strange, muddled, middle-of-the-road position? Dr. Price wants to have his cake and eat it, too, but it won't work. I predict that many of his seminary students will be more consistent and will reject the doctrine of preservation altogether, as have most of the authors of modern textual criticism."[2]

SACRED REVIEW

The **second** approach to manuscript review, which is called by the author of this work **sacred review**, is the belief that the OOO God has **providentially** preserved His Words through fallen man, **and** through **the priesthood of believers** of the Old and New Testament eras. What a sacred reviewer does is: **A.** simply review what a holy God has done providentially by observing God at work in the preservation of His Words and, **B.** observes the enemy spiritual forces at work corrupting His Words by addition, subtraction, or change. This author believes sacred wisdom is required to differentiate between the two methods.

All of the preceding information should immediately cause one to consider

---

[1] Cloud, David; *Fundamentalist Following Textual Critics;* Way of Life Literature, Port Huron, MI; Electronic Disc, 2000; Reported at file://D:\FundamentalBaptistLibrary2000\www\fbns\preservation.htm ; p. 2 of 6

[2] Ibid. p. 2 of 6

as a result of the two views, there are two routes by which the manuscripts were received by the two groups. This is the case. You have glimpsed the men of the two routes under the sections, The Broad Gate: The Men, and The Strait Gate: The Men. There are two routes and two views.

In addition, the neutral approach has many many theories as to how 'restoration' of the Words should be accomplished. Those theories have been in a constant state of flux since they were proposed starting with Hugo Grotius (1583-1645), Richard Simon (1638-1712), Richard Bently (1662-1742), Jean Astruc (1753), Johann Semler (1725-1795), Alexander Geddes (1737-1802), J. J. Griesbach (1745-1812), Westcott and Hort in the late 1800's, and continuing into the 'modern' age with Erwin Nestle, Kurt Aland, F. F. Bruce, Bruce M. Metzger, E. C. Colwell, F. G. Kenyon, Kirsopp Lake, and others.

PROVIDENTIAL PRESERVATION

Next we move to the concept of **Biblical preservation**. So many people have failed to grasp this easily understood principle. Therefore, two examples will be given to highlight the concept. Before beginning this discussion, let's remember: God can work supernaturally outside of the rules of nature as demonstrated by the miracles of Jesus, and he can work within the natural world using the laws of nature. The work He does using the laws He established to control and run His universe is described as **providential care**. Both types of intervention by God can be found in the Bible. We will examine only Biblical providential care.

The first example of His providential care is the story of Moses in Exodus 2:1-10. Moses providentially was born into a priestly family descended from Levi as he needed to be a priest for the nation Israel. Remember a priest intercedes for the people of God. His mother placed him at three months of age in a bulrush basket that she covered with slime and pitch, and then placed it into the Nile River. He floated down the Nile and got stuck in the bulrushes, providentially, at the place where and the time when Pharaoh's daughter "just happened" to be bathing in the Nile. Although Pharaoh was killing Hebrew children, the daughter was providentially moved to keep the baby. To top it all off, the daughter's maid "just happened" [providentially] to call Moses' real mother to nurse him. His mother had placed him in the basket, hoping to save his life, and now she was in essence his mother again. He just happened to grow up in the courts of Pharaoh so that in God's timing he could stand before the Pharaoh and represent the people of Israel. In this story God did not work outside the laws of nature, so far as we know them, but he certainly worked providentially.

The second story comes from the New Testament. Starting at Acts 23:11 and going through the remainder of the book, there is a story as incredible as the story of Moses. Paul was told by Jesus in Acts 23:11 that he was to cheer up; that he was going to be a witness for the Lord in Rome. Who would believe that after beatings, court trials, murder plots, shipwrecks, snake bites, and prisons that Paul would wind up in Rome, as God had said, in his own rented house testifying to rulers, guards, Jews, and Gentiles? An amazing story, but done through the providential care of God.

Jack Moorman sums up the situation concerning the preservation of Scripture in the New Testament era in a way that only the Holy Spirit could prompt:

> "Just as the divine glories of the New Testament are brighter far than the glories of the Old Testament, so the manner in which God has preserved the New Testament Text is far more wonderful than the manner in which He preserved the Old Testament text. God preserved the Old Testament text by means of something physical and external, namely, the Aaronic priesthood. God has preserved the New Testament text by means of something inward and spiritual namely, **the universal priesthood of believers.**"[1] [my emphasis]

Now, do I believe God can providentially care for the preservation of His written Words? You bet I do! The caveat is that there is absolutely no way to prove that this approach or that the textual critic's approach is correct. One has to accept whichever position is chosen by faith, just as one has to choose by faith between evolution and creation. But to convince the nay-sayers that there are more facts to support preservation, just as there are more facts that support creation as opposed to evolution, we will need to look at the question of manuscripts in detail. This approach requires much time and patience. However, it is rewarding when the job is finished because one becomes more convinced than ever before that God has providentially cared for His Words. And so, we return to the task of history taking and the gathering of facts in the SOAP work-up of our "patient," the Word.

---

[1] Moorman, Jack; *Forever Settled;* The Bible For Today, Collingswood, N.J. #1428; 1985; pp. 46-47

ARE THERE MANUSCRIPT FAMILIES?

The world of textual criticism has divided the ancient New Testament manuscripts into classes or families of texts. There is disagreement among them as to the proper classification, as one would expect, but here are the most popular 'families'. If someone wants to be a "classifier", an extensive knowledge of the original languages and dialects is needed. However, do not be led to believe that if you do not have linguistic talents, you cannot understand the concepts. James White, a textual critic, lists the types.

"They are:

The Alexandrian text-type, found in most papyri, and in the great uncial codices Aleph and B. [Please note that his designation for the codices Aleph and B is apropos. We will have much more to say on the Alexandrian text-type later.]

The Western text-type, found both in Greek manuscripts and in translations into other languages, especially Latin.

The Byzantine text-type, found in the vast majority of later uncial and minuscule manuscripts.

The Caesarean text-type, disputed by some, found in P45 and "family 1" (abbreviated f)"[1]

The question naturally arises as to how these text types developed. There were two reasons.

1. During the first two centuries immediately after the writing of the New Testament books, there was a tremendous "attack" on the written Words. Satan was not successful discrediting the Living Word so he turned his attention to the inspired Words. [see the Preface to this work, p. V] This was accomplished by using men who did not have respect toward the Words of God the way the Old Testament scribes did. They had no problem with changing the wording so that it better fit their philosophy.

2. Copyist errors occurred. These type errors have always been a problem when copying anything. However, the tremendous demand for copies of the epistles and gospels while the church was under horrendous persecution caused more than the usual scribal errors.

To summarize: There were intentional and unintentional errors. Many have denied the intentional errors because there was no proof. Westcott and Hort were

---

[1] White, James; *The King James Only Controversy;* Bethany House Publishers, Minneapolis, Minn.; ISBN 1-55661-575-2; p. 43

among those who claimed "no intentional errors". However, among intentional errors that were made in 'good faith' and those that were made to satisfy a requirement of someone's belief system.

Bruce Metzger describes an example of a "good faith" error. He relates that in the margin of codex Vaticanus at Hebrews 1:3 there is a rather:

> "indignant note by a recent scribe who restored the original reading of the codex...for which a corrector had substituted the usual reading...[which said] "Fool and knave, can't you leave the old reading alone and not alter it!"[1]

Alterations in the text made because of doctrinal considerations are difficult to judge but they were made. Irenaeus, Tertullian, Eusebius, and many other church Fathers complained about the corrupting of Scripture by the heretics:

> "In the mid-second century Marcion expunged his copies of the Gospel according to Luke of all references to the Jewish background of Jesus. Tatian's *Harmony of the Gospels* contains several textual alterations which lent support to ascetic or encratite [sic] views."[2]

According to Metzger, eliminating what was considered unacceptable doctrinally or inserting what was necessary to "prove" a tenet was not unusual. He then goes on to give several examples, not only in manuscripts related to Scripture, but in lay literature such as *The Pilgrim's Progress.*[3]

Unintentional errors are not unusual either and were the most common, especially in scriptoriums. A scriptorium was a facility established to copy manuscripts by reading aloud a text that was then recorded by numerous scribes at their desks. The types of unintentional errors are:

1. Haplography: writing once what should have been written twice.
2. Dittography: writing twice what should have been written once.
3. Metathesis: an inadvertent exchange in the proper order of letters or words.
4. Fusion: the combining of the last letter of the first word with the first letter of the following word, or else of combining two separate words into a single compound word.
5. Fission: refers to the improper separation of one word into two.
6. Homophony: words of entirely different meaning may sound alike and substituted.
7. Misreading similar-appearing letters: dated in history because at various stages of the alphabet development some letters, which later were written quite differently, resembled one another in shape.

---

[1] Metzger, Bruce; *The Text of the New Testament;* pp. 195- 196
[2] Ibid. p. 201
[3] Ibid. pp. 195-207

8. Homoeoteleuton: a Greek term meaning, "having the same ending", and identifies the loss of text that can result when the eye of the copyist inadvertently passes over all the words preceding a final phrase that is identical with that which closes the sentence immediately preceding, or immediately following.

9. Homoeoarkton: means, "that which has a similar beginning" and involves a similar loss of intervening words, as the eye of the scribe jumps from one beginning to another.

10. Variants based on vowel points only: Hebrew was consonants only until the seventh or eighth century when vowel indicators were added by the Masoretes to keep the meaning from being lost.[1]

So it is easy to see how variants would occur. The question arises as to the classification of those variants into *different* families. We will give a brief discussion of those "families" and then look at the origin of the concept.

The Western text family is alleged to have arisen "in the better educated Christian circles."[2] It is reasoned that these persons were better able to write, and subsequently, made comments in the margins of their text. When these annotated manuscripts were copied the comments were incorporated into the text.

The Alexandrian family characteristics are said to have developed for different reasons:

"Among the Christian scribes of Alexandria developments took another turn. According to Streeter (1924), these learned Christians followed the tradition of Alexandrian classical scholarship, which was always to prefer the shortest reading in places in which the manuscripts differed. The Alexandrians were always ready to suspect and reject New Testament readings which seemed to them to present difficulties. John Burgon (1896), one of England's greatest believing Bible scholars, proved this long ago by pointing out a relevant passage in Origen's Commentary on Matthew.

In this Commentary, Origen, the leading Christian critic of antiquity, gives us an insight into the arbitrary and highly subjective manner in which New Testament textual criticism was carried on at Alexandria about 230 A.D. In his comment on Matt. 19: 17-21 (Jesus' reply to the rich young man) Origen reasons that Jesus could not have concluded his list of God's commandment with the comprehensive requirement, Thou shalt love thy neighbour as thyself. For the reply of the young man was, All these things have I kept from my youth up, and Jesus evidently accepted this statement as true. But if the

[1] Ibid. pp. 33-42
[2] Moorman, Jack; *Forever Settled;* p. 53

young man had loved his neighbor as himself, he would have been perfect, for Paul says that the whole law is summed up in this saying, Thou shalt love thy neighbour as thyself. But Jesus answered, If thou wilt be perfect etc., implying that the young man was not yet perfect. Therefore, Origen argued, the commandment, Thou shalt love thy neighbour as thyself, could not have been spoken by Jesus on this occasion and was not part of the original text of Matthew. The clause had been added, Origen concluded, by some tasteless scribe."[1]

Bruce Metzger points out that Westcott and Hort developed the naturalist neutral approach to classifying the texts of the New Testament into families. Metzger, like most modern textual critics, has blindly accepted the "theories" of Westcott and Hort because they think like calculators, or computers, or cold fish. He is also a heretic.

"In the introductions to the books of the *Reader's Digest Bible*, Metzger questions the authorship, traditional date, and supernatural inspiration of books penned by Moses, Daniel, and Peter, and in many other ways reveals his liberal, unbelieving heart...He piously claims on one hand that the Bible is the inspired Words of God; but out of the other side of the mouth he claims the Bible is filled with myth and error. He denies the Bible's history, its miracles, and its authorship, while, in true liberal style, declaring that this denial does not do injustice to the Words of God, because, he says, the Bible is not "written for history but for religion" and is not to be read "with a dull prosaic and literalistic mind!"[2]

ONLY ONE FAMILY OF MANUSCRIPTS

The truth is there is really only one family. I took you through the preceding concepts to show how following the logic of the naturalist's textual criticism can easily mislead you. By now you were probably thinking all the above sounds good, correct, and true. THE TRUTH IS THERE IS BUT ONE FAMILY OF TEXTS, THE RECEIVED TEXT. All the other texts are very confusing and **differ from one another** to a great extent. This fact can be

---

[1] Ibid. p. 53

[2] Cloud, David; *Unholy Hands on God's Holy Book, A Report on the United Bible Society;* 1985; Part I of II; Way of Life Literature, Electronic Edition, May 2000

illustrated by Herman Hoskier's research which showed there were over 3000 differences between Codex Vaticanus and Codex Alexandrus **in the gospels alone.** To claim that they can be placed into families is fabricated and arbitrary. In other words, the classification of manuscripts by textual critics is an area which produces great dissension even among the textual critics and turns out to be based on purely ***personal opinion.*** The concept also provides a critic with many hours of idle conjecture. That there are a few similarities between a few corrupted texts because of recopying cannot be refuted, but a 'family' it does not make:

> "Though there is [some] truth in the above commonly presented position and we have quoted Dr. Hills at length, yet the basic idea of textual types or families has its source in the naturalistic viewpoint and we do not believe that it represents the facts concerning the distribution of MSS [manuscript**s**] in the early centuries. With some 85% or more of the 5000 extant MSS falling into the category of the Received Text, **there is in fact only one textual family – the Received**. All that remains is so contradictory, so confused, so mixed, that not by the furthest stretch of imagination can they be considered several families of MSS."[1] [my emphasis]

DEAN BURGON AND HIS ATTACK ON THE PSEUDO-PRINCIPLES OF MODERNISTIC TEXTUAL CRITICISM

There is a strong suspicion on my part that Westcott and Hort devised the "family" approach in order to confuse the ordinary person by disguising the fact that there are so few MSS to support their position. Even the word "family" connotes the sense of 'numbers', suggesting to a person there are a lot of MSS in this or that category.

When you read a naturalist textual critic's comments, it is like reading a government IRS document. It is confusing and may be misleading. Wilbur Pickering comments that he read all 314 "boring" pages of the preface to a new version written by Hort. This is not the case with a contemporary of Westcott and Hort, John William Burgon, one of history's greatest defenders of the Received Text and a first rate textual critic:

> "The author of *The Revision Revised*, John William

---

[1] Moorman, Jack; *Forever Settled;* p. 205

Burgon (1813-1888), was one of the greatest British Bible scholars of the 19th century. He was Gresham Professor of Divinity at Oxford, Fellow of Oriel College, vicar of St. Mary's (the university church), and during the last 12 years of his life, he was Dean of Chichester. In the latter half of the 1800s, Burgon defended the Bible as the infallible and inerrant Words of God, inspired to its very jots and tittles, and he fought a manly battle against the encroachment of theological modernism. The series of messages on biblical inspiration that Burgon preached at Oxford University in 1860 are apologetic masterpieces. Burgon observed: "At the root of the whole mischief of these last days lies disbelief in the Bible as the Word of God. This is the fundamental error." Burgon defended the historicity and Mosaic authorship of Genesis and rejected any scientific theory which is contrary to Divine Revelation. He wisely stated, "Destroy my confidence in the Bible as an historical record, and you destroy my confidence in it altogether; for by far the largest part of the Bible is an historical record." His position was: "Either, with the best and wisest of all ages, you must believe the whole of Holy Scripture; or, with the narrow-minded infidel, you must disbelieve the whole. There is no middle course open to you. . . . He who surrenders the first page of his Bible, surrenders all. . . . No, Sirs! The Bible (be persuaded) is the very utterance of the Eternal; as much God's Word, as if high heaven were open, and we heard God speaking to us with human voice. . . . The Bible is none other than the voice of Him that sitteth upon the throne! Every book of it,--every chapter of it,--every verse of it,--every word of it,--every syllable of it,--(where are we to stop?),--every letter of it,--is the direct utterance of the most High! . . . The Bible is none other than the Word of God: not some part of it, more, some part of it, less; but all alike, the utterance of Him who sitteth upon the Throne; absolute,--faultless,--unerring,--supreme!" We say to that, Amen and Amen and Amen! It is certain that such an unhesitating and glorious defense of the Bible has not been heard at Oxford University in the last one hundred years!"[1]

Burgon single handedly collected over **86,489** church father citations from the New Testament text **before** the Council of Nicea in 325 A.D.,[2] and was noted

---

[1] Cloud, David; *Revision Revised;* Fundamental Baptist Information Service, Port Huron, MI; Electronic Disc, May 2000; p. 1-2

[2] Pickering, Th.D., Wilbur; *The Identity of the New Testament Text,* The Bible For Today, Collingswood, NJ; B.F.T. #556; p. 66

for spending 13 hours "running down **one** disputed letter" in a text.[1] One does not get that "empty" feeling when one reads the works of distinguished scholars such as Dean Burgon, Edward Hills, or D.A. Waite. For this reason, shortly, I am going to let you read for yourself Dean Burgon's comments concerning the "scientific theories" and deceit of Westcott and Hort. His comments will also address the "family" of the Traditional Text.

Several comments concerning issues we have not covered in this paper before you begin Dean Burgon's testimony will make his remarks more understandable.

FACTS TO HELP UNDERSTAND

Fact One: Dr. Scrivener, a contemporary of Burgon, Westcott, and Hort, was on the committee that developed the "New" Greek Text in the late 1800's. He was a believer and first-rate scholar who almost resigned from the committee, but stayed on in hopes he might "save something". It is understood by many that he fought with Westcott and Hort many long hours:

"The minority in the Committee was represented principally by Dr. Scrivener, probably the foremost scholar of the day in the manuscripts of the Greek New Testament and the history of the Text. If we may believe the word of Chairman Ellicott, the countless divisions in the Committee over the Greek Text "was often a kind of critical duel between Dr. Hort and Dr. Scrivener." Dr. Scrivener was continuously and systematically outvoted.

"Nor is it difficult to understand," says Dr. Hemphill, "that many of their less resolute and decided colleagues must often have been completely carried off their feet by the persuasiveness and resourcefulness, and zeal of Hort, backed by the great prestige of Lightfoot, the popular Canon of St. Paul's and the quiet determination of Westcott, who set his face as a flint. In fact, it can hardly be doubted that Hort's was the strongest will of the whole Company, and his adroitness in debate was only equaled by his pertinacity."

The conflict was intense and ofttimes the result seemed

---

[1] Green, Jay P.; *Unholy Hands on the Bible, An Introduction to Textual Criticism; Vol. 1;* Sovereign Grace Trust Fund, Lafayette, Indiana; ISBN 1-878442-63-5; 1990; p. XIX

dubious. Scrivener and his little band did their best to save the day. He might have resigned; but like Bishop Wilberforce, he neither wished to wreck the product of revision by a crushing public blow, nor did he wish to let it run wild by absenting himself. Dr. Hort was being pricked by Dr. Scrivener and he wrote his wife confirming the battle as follows: "July 15, 1871. We have had some stiff battles today in Revision, though without any ill feeling, and usually with good success. But I, more than ever, felt how impossible it would be for me to absent myself."

Concerning the battles within the Committee, Dr. Westcott writes: "May 24, 1871. We have had hard fighting during these last two days, and a battle-royal is announced for tomorrow."[1]

Fact Two: A recension is a complete revision.

Fact Three: *"The Convocation of the Southern Province"* is like *"The Southern Baptist Convention"*. It was the organization of the Anglican Church whose jurisdiction was the southern part of England

Fact Four: The Codex B or Vaticanus is the manuscript "worshipped" by Westcott and Hort that has been maintained in the Vatican. The Codex Aleph or Sinaiticus is the manuscript found at St. Catherine's Monastery in the Sinai by Tischendorf and "worshipped" by him and Westcott and Hort, also.

Fact Five:.   There will be several early witnesses mentioned we have not covered such as the Peschitto (Syrian name, meaning simple), a Syrian text of the Hebrew Scriptures, or the Armenian Peshitta, meaning straight, which is the New Testament in Armenian language. The Sahidic manuscripts are those MSS that came from Egypt called Coptic manuscripts. When this section is finished, we will examine the history of the early witnesses to the texts, which are the Church Fathers writings, Peschito, Peshitta, Sahidic and others. You will see for yourself that Drs. Westcoot [sic] and Hoot [sic] intentionally did not consider most **known** important witnesses to the true text, which is the Received Greek Text. [Ninety-nine percent (99%) of all MSS support the Received Text]

Fact Six: Prior to revealing *"The Lie"* and quoting Dean Burgon's comments, a brief discussion of the salient features of Westcott and Hort's "theory" will be presented. Their theory was responsible for leading many who participate in textual criticism astray, and as you will see, is no longer considered viable by most textual critics today, but the consequences of their theory, the 'new' Greek Text, was not abandoned. Why? There seems to be an agenda.

Many of these comments were obtained from Wilbur Pickering's *The Identity of the New Testament Text.*

---

[1] Moorman, Jack; *Forever Settled;* p. 205

THE "THEORY" OF MODERNISTIC TEXTUAL CRITICISM

I.   **The Basic Approach:**
The basic approach that Westcott/Hort took in evaluating the manuscripts of the New Testament was: to treat them like any other book, and they believed no new principle "whatever" was "needed or legitimate" in the approach to manuscripts. In other words, the Scripture was not "special" or received by supernatural means. The words could be treated like any secular book.

II. **Genealogy:**
Genealogy was: to recover the texts of successive ancestors by using analysis and comparison of the most recent texts with prior texts. They reported that by working backwards the common ancestor could be recovered. The many manuscripts could then be reduced to one or perhaps two. As we will see, this was never done although they said the method had been applied. They proposed this hypothetical, never tried system in order to reduce the overwhelming majority of manuscripts that favor the Received Text (TR). Therefore, one old manuscript without any recent copies would be on the same level, or equivalent to, or as good as, or better than any recent plentiful copies of the Received Text. Now all they had to claim was that the recently recovered 'old' Codices B and Aleph were as good as or better than any recent manuscript. This is a very convenient way for a textual critic to get rid of many documents favoring the TR. Now all the families they dreamed up, the Western, the Antiochian (the Syrian), the Alexandrian, and Neutral texts, were considered equivalent because they allegedly had traced them back by genealogy to early dates. THEY HAD NOT. All that was left for them to do was to find a way to get rid of the "villainous" TR family and exalt the Codex B which they preferred. So, along came their next proposal.

III. **Conflation:**
Conflation was: to combine older text readings into one new text reading to make it a fuller text and 'more pious'. Westcott and Hort alleged that they demonstrated eight conflated readings in the TR, but never demonstrated any in the other alleged text types. Upon the acceptance of conflation and therefore a complete [Lucian] recension in 350 A.D, (see below) many modern textual critics such as Kirsopp Lake, and Vincent Taylor have 'staked their souls'.[1] Westcott and Hort went on to state that prior to the Church Father, Chrysostom, who died in 407, no TR (Syrian or Antiochian) reading could be found. This was the cornerstone to their theory which many textual scholars still "buy into." They

---

[1] Pickering, Th.D., Wilbur; *The Identity of the New Testament Text;* p. 37, 72

even carried this further by claiming the 'conflation' of the TR was done two different times. One 'conflation' of the TR occurred early in the post-Apostolic period at Antioch and the second between 250 and 350 AD. They even went so far to suggest Lucian (d. 311) as the leader, called the Lucian Recension. There is not one shred of evidence for these recensions, but the concept has gained wide acceptance among textual critics like F. C. Burkitt and H. C. Thiessen.[1] If a doctor set out to treat a patient, on as 'little or no evidence' as Westcott and Hort put forth, he or she would be 'sued until the cows come home'. [A thorough discussion of all this and more can be found in Wilbur Pickering's work, *The Identity of the New Testament Text*]. In addition, Dean Burgon and others have shown in extensive detail the TR readings existed prior to Lucian in many church father quotations, reaching back to the second and third centuries.[2]

IV. **Textual Readings Based on Internal Evidence:**

The obvious *simplicity* of the readings in the TR caused Westcoot [sic] and Hoot [sic] to face one last problem in order to deal their attempted death blow to the text received from the **priesthood of believers.** Therefore, they invented one final significant prerequisite in their secret plan for textual scholars of the Westcott and Hort school to use. The prerequisite dealt with the readings within a manuscript and it had two aspects: 1. brevior lectio potior, the shorter reading is to be preferred over longer readings, and 2. proclivi lectioni praestat ardua, the harder reading is to be preferred. They allegedly made these conditions up based on two assumptions: 1. the tendency of scribes to add material to the text, and 2. the tendency of scribes to simplify the text when confronted with a difficult reading. The real reason the prerequisites were "developed" and, incidentally, they were only **a theory which could not be established by testing or research,** was to get rid of the TR. So what do you imagine they said about the readings in the TR? That's right. They were too simple and they were too long. They were a "full text", meaning the text had been added to, and they exhibited "harmonistic assimilation", meaning they had been simplified. Now the readings in the TR could be thrown out in favor of the reading in Westcott and Hort's 'new' Greek text.

---

[1] Ibid. p. 38

[2] Moorman, Jack; *Early Church Fathers and the Authorized Version: A Demonstration!, Companion Volume to Early Manuscripts and the Authorized Version;* Moorman's works support the early quotes of the RT Text

THE LIE

As one will see, there are numerous fabrications or lies associated with this whole process of textual criticism. Most modern textual critics have abandoned the theories of Westcott and Hort because of their obvious fabrication of data and "assumptions. Does this remind you of the modern day pharmaceutical companies who have lied about their research that is alleged to support their applications for drug approval by the FDA; or of companies like Enron, Tyco, Worldcom, etc. who lied for "mammon" [money], or Presidents of the United States of America who lied to retain power? Here are the lies of Westcott and Hort. One can only speculate about all the reasons, "Why?" **"Here is the revelation of *The Lie(s) That Changed The Modern World"* broken into <u>eight</u> interrelated parts.

<u>Fact Seven:</u>   FIRST PART OF THE LIE: Westcott and Hort had been preparing, *in secret,* a Greek text for over 30 years to replace the Greek Received Text. In addition, they were developing a new critical apparatus to be used by textual critics to accomplish this feat. The Convocation of the Southern Province of Great Britain specifically instructed them to change *only:*

"the plain and clear errors" [in the Greek Text]. "To construct a 'new' Greek Text *formed no part of the Instructions* which the Revisionists received at the hands of the Convocation of the Southern Province."[1]

Westcott and Hort directly disobeyed and rebelled against authority and fraudulently paraded before the committee, piece-by-piece their scheme that was hatched over thirty years to "cast on the world" a 'new' Greek text because of their revulsion for the Received Text. Their coercion and intimidation of those on the committee was made possible because of their positions at institutions of higher learning, which in and of itself is revolting. The effects of this spirit of rebellion, which the Scriptures says is as witchcraft, [1Sam 15:23] has led to long term effects which will be discussed later. Westcott and Hort had agreed to the terms of the Convocation, but intentionally hid their plans in order to get the meetings started.

          THE SECOND PART OF THE LIE: The second part of the lie has

[1] Fuller, David Otis; *True or False;* Grand Rapids International Publications; 1990 Institute for Biblical Textual Studies, ISBN 0-944355-12-9, 1995; p.129

just been uncovered in the last few years. The critical apparatus which Westcott and Hort developed was primarily established on a concept called "Genealogy". They reported the transmission of the New Testament text through families based on their research. The deceit is this: THEY NEVER APPLIED THEIR 'THEORY' TO THE MANUSCRIPTS *AS THEY HAD CLAIMED TO HAVE DONE.* Wilbur Pickering in his thesis for Dallas Theological Seminary reports the following:

"M.M. Parvis answers: "Westcott and Hort never applied the genealogical method to the NT MSS..." Colwell agrees. [He says:]

"That Westcott and Hort did *not* apply this method to the manuscripts of the New Testament is obvious. Where are the charts which start with the majority of late manuscripts and climb back through diminishing generations of ancestors to the Neutral and Western texts? The answer is that they are nowhere. Look again at the first diagram, and you will see that ....[they] are not actual manuscripts of the New Testament, but hypothetical manuscripts. The demonstrations or illustrations of the genealogical method as applied to New Testament manuscripts by the followers of Hort,...use hypothetical manuscripts, not actual codices. ...All the manuscripts referred to are *imaginary* manuscripts, and the later of these charts was printed sixty years after Hort."

How then could Hort speak of only "occasional ambiguities in the evidence for the genealogical relation," or say—[Pickering now quotes Hort]

"So far as genealogical relations are discovered with perfect certainty, the textual results which follow from them are perfectly certain, too, being directly involved in historical facts; and any apparent presumptions against them suggested by other methods are mere guesses against knowledge."

[then Pickering says] when he had *not* demonstrated the existence of any such relations, much less with "perfect certainty"? [1]

[Because he lied][my emphasis]

THE THIRD PART OF THE LIE: The third part of the lie is that Westcott and Hort declared the absence of readings of the traditional text from the writings of the Ante-Nicene Fathers. Wilbur Pickering said, "Dr. Hort draws largely from his imagination and wishes" concerning absent readings.[2] Even recent textual critics deny the evidence of patristic quotes and slant their

---

[1] Pickering, Th.D., Wilbur; *The Identity of the New Testament Text;* Revised Edition; Thomas Nelson Publishers; Nashville, TN; Available through The Bible for Today, #556, Collingswood, NJ

[2] Ibid. p. 66

reporting, although *many* researchers have shown church fathers quotes support the TR.[1] Dean Burgon, Westcott and Hort's contemporary, destroyed all their arguments, but his information was disregarded by the well known modern technique of "spin". ["Spin" will be demonstrated in Dean Burgon's quotes below]

THE FOURTH PART OF THE LIE: The fourth part of the lie is the myth asserted by Westcott and Hort and his followers "that the true New Testament text was lost for more than 1500 years and then restored by Westcott and Hort."[2] Do you think God would allow His Words to be lost for 1500 years and then found? Do you remember the verses that proclaim that He would preserve them? Please just look up and read a few verses IN THE KJB, which affirm God's intention: Psa 12:6-7, Mat. 4:4, Mat. 24:35, Mat. 5:17-18, Psa 105:8, Psa 119.

THE FIFTH PART OF THE LIE: The fifth part of the lie concerns the committee Drs. Hoot (sic) and Westcoot (sic) controlled because of their positions of authority. They caused the committee of the Southern Convocation to produce a "new" English version called the *Revised Version* [sometimes known as the ERV, the English Revised Version]. This "new" version was translated from *their* "new" Greek text that was prepared in secret over thirty years. This was in clear rebellion against the authority and rules established to govern the committee by the Southern Convocation.

THE SIXTH PART OF THE LIE: The sixth part of the lie concerns their false statement in the front of the "new" version of the Bible they *produced*. I have in my possession a copy of the *Revised Version* of 1885, which is a family Bible, passed down through the generations. [sometimes known as the ERV, the English Revised Version] The wording in the preface to this old book, which is Westcott and Hort's version, leads one to believe that it is just an updating of the King James Bible (KJB) of 1611. It is not "just" an updating of the KJB as a result of discovery of 'older' manuscripts, but it is a completely 'new' version. I personally consider this another subtle deceit.

THE SEVENTH PART OF THE LIE: The seventh part of the lie concerns conflation. Conflation is the intentional embellishing or combing of the text of Scripture to make it sound more 'pious' and as a result 'fuller.' An example would be the addition of Lord or Christ to the name of Jesus to make it read–the Lord Jesus Christ. Westcott and Hort alleged they found eight examples, but intimated many more were left to be uncovered. Textual critics to this day have not found any more, and as a matter of fac, Dean Burgon eliminated all but two of the eight W/H had supposedly found.[3] Westcott and

---

[1] Ibid. pp. 69-70

[2] Hills, Th.D., Edward F.; *The King James Version Defended*; p. 194

[3] Pickering, Th.D., Wilbur, *The Identity of the New Testament Text;* p. 61

Hort would have you believe that at least 20% of the Received Text has been conflated. This is not true. There is no proof of this speculation.

THE EIGHTH PART OF THE LIE: The eighth part of the lie concerns the fabrication of "recensions" of the MSS. Drs. Westcoot [sic] and Hoot [sic] invented two meetings of early church authorities, which constructed a 'new' text for the Scriptures. They allege one occurred in the early Christian era in Antioch, and the other one about 250 to 350 A. D., which conflated the text from several "families" of texts. **There is absolutely no history of such meetings, much less a 'new' Greek text being "put together" during this time.** Dean Burgon was incensed by their attempt to fabricate the two meetings as you will see in his comments to follow this section. Westcott and Hort tried everything and anything to explain away the huge number of manuscripts with only minor scribal errors that supported the Received Text. Drs. Westcott and Hort called the Received Text the Syrian or Antiochian Text.

We will examine the effects these lies have had on the modern world under the heading of the plan, part of the SOAP acronym. First, however, we will continue to list information that is important for understanding Dr. Burgon's comments which will follow shortly.

FACT EIGHT: A lectionary in the early church was a grouping of Scriptures to be read in the church service, usually on certain days.

FACT NINE: The committee chairman of the Anglican Convocation of the Southern Province, Bishop Charles Ellicott did not believe there was enough 'knowledge' among the committee members to change the Greek text. Bishop Ellicott said in 1861:

> "It is my honest conviction that for any authoritative REVISION, we are not yet mature; *either in Biblical learning or Hellenistic scholarship.* There is good scholarship in this country,...*but it has certainly not yet been sufficiently directed to study of the New Testament...*to render any national attempt at REVISION either hopefully or lastingly profitable."[1]

FACT TEN: Uncials (or majuscules) are manuscripts written in something like capital letters and the word comes from the Latin, uncia, meaning 'a twelfth part'. Classical books were generally written in this fashion until about the sixth century. Overlapping this time period were the manuscripts written in minuscules (or cursives), which was a script of smaller letters in a running hand. Minuscule comes from the Latin, minuscules, meaning 'rather small'. Otherwise, manuscripts were written in cursive or 'running' hand and were used for rapid writing and non-literary documents.[2]

The following quotes of Dean Burgon were found in David Otis Fuller's

---

[1]Grady, Ph.D., Th.M., D.D., William P.; *Final Authority*; *p. 252*

[2] Metzger, Bruce; *The Text of the New Testament;* p. 9

book, *True or False?*, and *Unholy Hands on the Bible,* by Jay P. Green. Dean Burgon's comments have been made available in a book published by the Dean Burgon Society, *Revision Revised.*

I have placed emphasis on the areas that should be particularly noted. *Also,* this is some of the material that greatly influenced D. A. Waite, Th.D., Ph.D., President of the Dean Burgon Society to reconsider the Received Text. The author of this work highlighted words, enlarged the font, and underlined the points. The italicized points are Dean Burgon's notations and emphasis. Please note:

1. These comments made by Dean Burgon were written without the benefit of hindsight since he was a contemporary.

2. He did not have the published personal letters of Westcott and Hort that were available after their deaths. They were published by their sons.

This makes Dean Burgon's comments even more insightful. After the published personal letters of Westcott and Hort and the revelations of investigative authors like Dr. D. A. Waite, most Bible believers understand and realize just how apostate they were.[I have chosen to place only the preface and certain quotations in this work. You would benefit from reading *Revision Revised* in its entirety. It may be obtained from The Dean Burgon Society. It is **DBS #611 @ $25.00 + $5.00 S&H]**

Comments by Dean Burgon *were selected* from the three sections of Dean Burgon's work:

1. *The Preface*
2. *The New Greek Text*
3. *Westcott and Hort's 'New' Textual Theory*

REVISION REVISED
By John William Burgon

[*The Revision Revised*, London: John Murray, 1885. Portions taken from the Preface, The New Greek Text, and Westcott and Hort's 'New' Textual Theory.]

Preface

"A systematic treatise is the indispensable condition for securing cordial assent to the view for which I mainly contend. It requires to be demonstrated by induction from a large collection of particular instances, as well as by the complex exhibition of many converging lines of evidence, that **the testimony of one small group of documents, or rather, of one particular manuscript, (namely the Vatican Codex B, which, for some unexplained reason, it is just now the fashion to regard with superstitious deference,) is the reverse of trustworthy.** Nothing in fact but a considerable Treatise will ever effectually break the yoke of that iron tyranny to which the excellent Bishop of Gloucester and Bristol [Bishop Ellicott] and his colleagues have recently bowed their necks; and are now for imposing on all English-speaking men.

In brief, if I were not, on the one hand, thoroughly convinced of the strength of my position, (and I know it to be absolutely impregnable) and if on the other hand, I did not cherish entire confidence in the practical good sense and fairness of the English mind, I could not have brought myself to come before the public in the unsystematic way which alone is possible in the pages of a Review. I must have waited, at all hazards, till I had finished 'my Book.'

In the end, when partisanship had cooled down, and passion had evaporated, and prejudice had ceased to find an auditory, **the 'Revision' of 1881 must come to be universally regarded as what it most certainly is, the most astonishing, as well as the most calamitous literary blunder of the Age.**

I pointed out that **'the New Greek Text'** which, in defiance of their instructions, the Revisionists of 'the Authorized English Version' had been so ill-advised as to spend ten years in elaborating, **was a wholly untrustworthy performance, was full of the gravest errors from beginning to end,** had been constructed throughout on an entirely mistaken theory. Availing myself of the published confession of one of the Revisionists, I explained the nature of the calamity which had befallen the Revision. **I traced the mischief home to its true authors, Drs. Westcott and Hort, a copy of whose unpublished Text of the N.T. (the most vicious in existence) had been confidentially, and under** pledges of *the strictest secrecy*, placed in the hands of every member of the revising Body. I called attention to the fact that, unacquainted with the difficult and delicate science of Textual Criticism, the Revisionists had in an evil hour surrendered themselves to Dr. Hort's guidance, had preferred his counsels to those of Prebendary Scrivener, (an infinitely more trustworthy guide) and that the work before the public was the piteous (but inevitable) result. All this I explained in the October number of the *Quarterly Review* for 1881.

In thus demonstrating the worthlessness of the 'New Greek Text' of the Revisionists, I considered that I had destroyed the key of their position. And so perforce I had. For if the underlying Greek Text be mistaken, what else but incorrect must the English [Revised] Translation be? But on examining the so-called 'Revision of the Authorized Version,' I speedily made the *further discovery* that the Revised English would have been in itself intolerable. even had the Greek been let alone. In the first place, to my surprise and annoyance, it proved to be a new translation (rather than a revision of the old) which had been attempted.

Painfully apparent were the tokens which met me on every side that the Revisionists had been supremely eager not so much to correct none but "plain and clear errors", as to introduce as many changes into the English of the New Testament Scriptures as they conveniently could.

A skittish impatience of the admirable work before them, and a strange inability to appreciate its manifold excellences, a singular imagination on the part of the promiscuous Company which met in the Jerusalem Chamber that they were competent to improve the Authorized Version in every part, and an unaccountable forgetfulness that the fundamental condition under which the task of Revision had been by themselves undertaken, was. that they should abstain from all but "necessary" changes–this proved to be only *part* of the offence which the Revisionists had committed

It was found that they had erred through defective scholarship to an extent and with a frequency which to me is simply inexplicable. I accordingly made it my business to demonstrate all this in a second Article which appeared in the next (the January) number of the *Quarterly Review*, and was entitled "The New English Translation."

Thereupon, a pretense [known in modern times as spin, HDW] was set up in many quarters, (but only by the Revisionists and their friends) that all my labour hitherto had been thrown away, because I had omitted to disprove the principles on which this 'New Greek Text' is founded. I flattered myself indeed that quite enough had been said to make it logically certain that the underlying 'Textual Theory' must be worthless. But I was not suffered to cherish this conviction in quiet. It was again and again cast in my teeth that I had not yet grappled with Drs. Westcott and Hort's "arguments". "Instead of condemning their Text, why do you not disprove their theory?" It was tauntingly insinuated that I knew better than to cross swords with the two Cambridge Professors. [The modern era calls this "spin" by 'spin doctors,' HDW]

This reduced me to the necessity of either leaving it to be inferred from my silence that I had found Drs. Westcott and Hort's arguments unanswerable, or else of coming forward with their book in my hand, and **demonstrating that in their solemn pages** an attentive reader finds himself encountered *by nothing but a series of unsupported assumptions,* that their so called theory is in reality nothing else but a weak effort of the imagination, **that the tissue which these accomplished scholars have been thirty years in elaborating, proves on inspection to be a flimsy and as worthless as any spider's web.**

A yet stranger phenomenon is, **that those who have once committed themselves to an erroneous theory, seem to be incapable of opening their eyes to the untrustworthiness of the fabric they have erected,** even when it comes down in their sight like a child's house built with playing cards, and presents to every eye but their own the appearance of a shapeless ruin. [This is called "PRIDE," HDW]

A pamphlet by the Bishop of Gloucester and Bristol (Bishop Ellicott) which appeared in April 1882, remains to be considered. Written expressly in defense of the Revisers and their New Greek Text, this composition displays a slenderness of acquaintance with the subject now under discussion, for which I was little prepared. Since it is the production of the Chairman of the Revisionist body, and professes to be a reply to my first two articles, I have bestowed upon it an elaborate and particular rejoinder extending to an hundred-and-fifty pages. I shall in consequence be very brief concerning it in this place.

The respected writer does nothing else but reproduce Westcott and Hort's theory in Westcott and Hort's words. He contributes nothing of his own. The singular infelicity which attended his complaint that the 'Quarterly Reviewer' "censures their (Westcott and Hort's) Text" but "has not attempted a serious examination of the arguments which they allege in its support", [This is the second aspect of 'spin': to get several people saying the same thing.] I have sufficiently dwelt upon elsewhere. The rest of the Bishop's contention may be summed up in two propositions; the first, **that if the Revisionists are wrong in their 'New Greek Text' then not only Westcott and Hort, but Lachmann, Tischendorf and Tregelles must be wrong also, a statement which I hold to be incontrovertible.** [true] The Bishop's other position is also undeniable, viz. That in order to pass an equitable judgment on ancient documents, they are to be carefully studied, closely compared, and tested by a more scientific process than rough comparison with the Textus Receptus. Thus, on both points, I find myself entirely at one with Bp. Ellicott.

When, however, such an one as Tischendorf or Tregelles, Hort or Ellicott, would put me down by reminding. me that half-a-dozen of the oldest Versions are against me,—"that argument" (I reply) **"is not allowable'**

on your lips. For if the united testimony of five of the Versions really be, in your account, decisive, why do you deny the genuineness of the last twelve verses of St. Mark's Gospel, which are recognized by every one of the Versions? Those verses are besides attested by every known copy, except two of bad character, by a mighty chorus of Fathers, by the unfaltering Tradition of the Church universal. First remove from St. Mark 16:20 your brand of suspicion, and then come back to me in order that we may discuss together how 1 Tim. 3:16 is to be read.

It was said just now that I cordially concur with Bp. Ellicott in the second of his two proposition, viz., that "no equitable judgment can be passed on ancient documents until they are carefully studied, and closely compared with each other, and tested by a more scientific process than rough comparison with" the Textus Receptus. I wish to add a few words on this subject, because what I am about to say will be found as applicable to my Reviewer in the Church Quarterly as to the Bishop. Both have misapprehended this matter, and in exactly the same way. **Where such accomplished Scholars have erred, what wonder if ordinary readers should find themselves all a-field?**

In this department of sacred Science, men have been going on too long *inventing their facts* and delivering themselves of oracular decrees, *on the sole responsibility of their own inner consciousness.* There is great convenience in such a method certainly, a charming simplicity which is in a high degree attractive to flesh and blood. It dispenses with proof. It furnishes no evidence. It asserts when it ought to argue. It reiterates when it is called upon to explain. "I am Sir Oracle."

This, which I venture to style the *unscientific method*, reached its culminating point when Professors Westcott and Hort recently put forth their Recension of the Greek Text. Their work is indeed quite a psychological curiosity. Incomprehensible to me it is how two able men of disciplined understandings can have seriously put forth the volume which they call "introduction-appendix." **It is the very *reductio ad absurdum*** [reduction to the absurd, HDW] of the *uncritical* method of the last fifty years. And it is especially in opposition to this new method of theirs that I so strenuously insist that the consentient voice of Catholic Antiquity [not Catholic Church but universal, my addition] is to be diligently inquired after and submissively listened to. For this, in the end, will prove our only safe guide.

I find myself in the meantime, met by the scoffs, jeers and misrepresentations of the disciples of this new school, who instead of producing historical facts and intelligible arguments, **appeal to the decrees of their teachers; which I disallow, and which they are unable to substantiate. They delight in announcing that Textual Criticism made "a fresh departure"** with the edition of Drs. Westcott and Hort, that the work of those scholars "marks an era", and is spoken of in Germany as "epoch-making."

My own belief is, that the Edition in question, if it be epoch-making at all, marks that epoch at which the current of critical thought, reversing its wayward course, began once more to flow in its ancient healthy channel. 'Cloudland' [dreamland] having been duly sighted on the 14th September 1881, "a fresh departure" was insisted upon by public opinion, and a deliberate return was made to *terra firma*, and *terra cognita*, and common sense. So far from "its paramount claim to the respect of future generations" being "the restitution of a more ancient and a purer Text", I venture to predict that the edition of the two Cambridge Professors will be hereafter remembered as indicating the furthest point ever reached by the self-evolved imaginations of English disciples of the school of Lachmann, Tischendorf and Tregelles. The recoil promises to be complete. English good sense is ever observed to prevail in the long run, although for a few years a foreign fashion may acquire the ascendant, and beguile a few unstable wits. [How sad Dean Burgon would be today if he were able to know how wrong he would be. How upset he would be to know that the hand of scholarship by Nicolatians, who 'lord' it over others, has suppressed the truth.]

But instead of all this, **a Revision of the English Authorized Version having been sanctioned by the convocation of the Southern Province in 1871, the opportunity was eagerly snatched at by two irresponsible scholars of the University of Cambridge for obtaining the general sanction [by deceit] of the Revising body, and thus indirectly of Convocation, for a private venture of their own,–their own privately devised Revision of the Greek Text.** On that Greek Text of theirs, (which I hold to be the most depraved which has ever appeared in print), with some slight modifications, our Authorized English Version has been silently revised; silently, I say, for in the margin of the English no record is preserved of the underlying Textual changes which have been introduced by the Revisionists. On the contrary, use has been made of that margin to insinuate suspicion and distrust in countless particulars as to the authenticity of the Text which has been suffered to remain unaltered. In the meantime, the country has been flooded with two editions of the New Greek Text; and thus **the door has been set wide open for universal mistrust of the Truth of Scripture to enter."[1]**

[Only portions of the following text are submitted here. The remainder is in the appendix. Please remember we are still taking the history of the patient. HDW]

---

[1] Fuller, DD., David Otis; *True or False?;* p. 123-129

"The New Greek Text"

(By Dean John William Burgon)

A revision of the Authorized Version of the New Testament, purporting to have been executed by authority of the Convocation of the Southern Province, and declaring itself the exclusive property of our two ancient Universities, has recently (17th May, 1881) **appeared,** of which the essential feature proves to be that it is rounded on an entirely New Recension of the Greek Text. **A claim is at the same time set up on behalf of the last-named production that it exhibits a closer approximation to the inspired Autographs than the world has hitherto seen.** Not unreasonably the 'New English Version' rounded on this 'New Greek Text' is destined to supersede the 'Authorized Version' of 1611. It is clearly high time that every faithful man among us should bestir himself and in particular, that such as have made Greek Textual Criticism in any degree their study should address themselves to the investigation of the claims of this, the latest product of the combined Biblical learning of the Church and of the sects.

...The provision, then, which the Divine Author of Scripture is found to have made for **the preservation in its integrity of His written Word,** is of peculiarly varied and highly complex description. First, by causing that a vast multiplication of copies should be required. All down the ages beginning at the earliest period, and continuing in an ever-increasing ratio until the actual invention of printing, He provided the most effectual security imaginable against fraud. True, that millions of the copies so produced have long since perished, but it is nevertheless a plain fact that there survive of the Gospels alone upwards of one thousand copies to the present day... **In truth, the security which the Text of the New Testament enjoys is altogether unique and extraordinary.** To specify one single consideration, which has never yet attracted the amount of attention it deserves, **'Lectionaries' abound, which establish the Text which has been publicly read in the churches of the East, from at least A.D. 400 until the time of the invention of printing.**

...And to come to the point, we refuse to throw in our lot with those who, disregarding the witness of every other known Codex, every other Version, every other available Ecclesiastical Writer, insist on following the dictates of a little group of authorities, of which nothing whatever is known with so much certainty as that often, when they concur exclusively, it is to mislead.

.... But it has only to be stated, that Tregelles **effactually persuaded himself that eighty-nine ninetieths of our extant manuscripts and other authorities may safely be rejected** and lost sight of when we come to amend the text and try to restore it to its primitive purity, to make it plain that in Textual Criticism he must needs be regarded as an untrustworthy teacher.

...**"The case of Dr. Tischendorf"** (proceeds Bp. Ellicott) **"is still more** easily disposed of. Which of this most inconstant Critic's texts are we to select? Surely not the last, in which an exaggerated preference for a single manuscript which he has had the good fortune to discover, has betrayed him into an almost child-like infirmity of critical judgment. Surely also not his seventh edition, which ... exhibits all the instability which a comparatively recent recognition of the authority of cursive manuscripts might be supposed likely to introduce." ... Tischendorf one of the worst of guides to the true text of Scripture.... And after assuring us that "the study of Grouping is the foundation of all enduring Criticism", they produce their secret, viz. that in "every one of our witnesses" except codex B, the "corruptions are innumerable".

...May we be permitted without offence to point out that the "idiosyncrasies" of an "individual mind" to which we learn with astonishment that we "are obliged to come at last" are probably the very worst foundation possible on which to build the recension of an inspired writing? With regret we record our conviction, that these accomplished scholars have succeeded in producing a Text vastly more remote from the inspired autographs of the Evangelists than any which has appeared since the invention of printing.

... And thus the men who were appointed to improve the English Translation are exhibited to us remodeling the original Greek. At a moment's notice, as if by intuition, (by an act which can only be described as the exercise of instinct) these eminent Divines undertake to decide which shall be deemed the genuine utterances of the HOLY GHOST, and which not. Each is called upon to give his vote, and he gives it. [This sounds just like the recently conducted "Jesus Seminars" held in California, HDW]

... Next in importance after the preceding, comes the Prayer which the Savior of the world breathed from the Cross on behalf of His murderers (St. Luke 23:34). These twelve precious words, "Then said Jesus, Father, forgive them; for they know not what they do", like those twenty-six words in St. Luke 22:43,44 which we have been considering already, Drs. Westcott and Hort enclose within double brackets in token of the **"moral certainty"** they entertain that the words are spurious. And yet these words are found in every known uncial and in every known cursive Copy, except four; besides being found in every ancient Version.

What does astonish us, however, is to find learned men in the year of grace 1881, freely resuscitating these long-since-forgotten betises of long-since-forgotten Critics, and seeking to palm them off upon a busy and a careless age, as so many new revelations.

... But we respectfully submit that "Syrian", "Western", "Western and Syrian", as critical expressions, are absolutely without meaning,... Progress is impossible while this method is permitted to prevail. If these distinguished Professors have enjoyed a Revelation as to what the Evangelists actually wrote, they would do well to acquaint the world with the fact at the earliest possible moment. If, on the contrary, they are merely relying on their own inner consciousness for the power of divining the truth of Scripture at a glance, they must be prepared to find their decrees treated with the contumely which is due to imposture, of whatever kind.

"Westcott and Hort's New Textual Theory"

[By Dean John William Burgon]

"Who is this that darkeneth counsel by words without knowledge?" Job 38:2

"Can the blind lead the blind? shall they not both fall into the ditch?" St. Luke 6:39

The correction of known textual errors of course we eagerly expected. And on every occasion when the Traditional Text was altered, we as confidently depended on finding a record of the circumstance inserted with religious fidelity into the margin, as agreed upon by the Revisionists at the outset.

In both of these expectations, however, we found ourselves sadly disappointed. The Revisionists have not corrected the "known Textual errors." On the other hand, besides silently adopting most of those wretched fabrications which are just now in favor with the German School,

... A hazy mistrust of all Scripture has been insinuated into the hearts and minds of countless millions, who in this way have been forced to become doubters–yes, doubters in the Truth of Revelation itself.

... For ourselves, shocked and offended at the unfaithfulness which could so deal with the sacred Deposit, we made it our business to expose, somewhat in detail, what had been the method of our Revisionists.

... We willingly accept the assurance that it is only because Dr. Westcott and Hort are virtually responsible for the Revisers' Greek Text that it is so imperiously demanded by the Revisers and their partisans that the "Theory" of the two Cambridge professors may be critically examined.

...We can sympathize also with the secret distress of certain of the body, who now, when it is all too late to remedy the mischief, begin to suspect that they have been led astray by the hardihood of self-assertion; overpowered by the *facundia praeceps* of one who is at least a thorough believer in his own self-evolved opinions; imposed upon by the seemingly consentient pages of Tischendorf and Tregelles, Westcott and Hort. Without further preface we begin.

... Lachmann's ruling principle then, was exclusive reliance on a very few ancient authorities, because they are "ancient" lies constructed his Text on three or four, not infrequently on one or two, Greek Codices. Of the Greek Fathers, he relied on Origen. Of the oldest Versions, he cared only for the Latin. To the Syriac he paid no attention. We venture to think his method irrational. But this is really a point on which the thoughtful reader is competent to judge himself. Tregelles adopted the same strange method.

... **Tischendorf,** the last and by far the ablest Critic of the three, knew better than to reject "eighty-nine ninetieths" of the extant witnesses. He had recourse to the ingenious expedient of adducing all the available evidence, but adopting just as little of it as he chose. And he chose to adopt those readings only, which are vouched for by the same little band of authorities whose partial testimony had already proved fatal to the decrees of Lachmann and Tregelles.

Happy in having discovered (in 1859) an uncial codex (Aleph) second in antiquity only to the oldest before known (B), and strongly resembling the famous 4th century codex in the character of its contents, he permitted his judgment to be overpowered by the circumstances. He at once (1865-72) remodeled his seventh edition (1856-9) in 3505 places, "to the scandal of the science of Comparative Criticism, as well as to his own grave discredit for discernment and consistency." **And yet he knew concerning Codex Aleph that at least *ten different Revis*ers from the 5th century downwards had labored to remedy the scandalously corrupt condition of a text which, "as it proceeded from the first scribe," even Tregelles describes as "very rough."**

But in fact the infatuation which prevails to this hour in this department of sacred science can only be spoken of as incredible. Enough has been said to show (the only point we are bent on establishing) that **the one distinctive tenet of the three most famous Critics since 1831 has been a *superstitious reverence* for whatever is found in the same little handful of early, but not the earliest, nor yet of necessity the purest documents.** ... *we absolutely refuse to bow down before the particular specimens of Antiquity which you have arbitrarily selected as the objects of your superstition.*

...You are illogical enough to propose to include within your list of "ancient Authorities", codices 1, 33, and 69, which are severally MSS. of the 5th, 6th, and 14th centuries. And why? Only because the Text of those three copies is observed to bear a sinister resemblance to that of codex B. But then why, in the name of common sense, do you not show corresponding favor to the remaining 997 cursive Copies of the N.T., seeing that these are observed to bear the same general resemblance to codex A? You are forever talking about "old readings." Have you not yet discovered that *all* "readings" are "*old*"?

Some remarks follow, on what is strangely styled "Transmission by printed Editions," in the course of which Dr. Hort informs us that Lachmann's Text of 1831 was "the first rounded on documentary authority." On what then, pray, does the learned professor imagine that the Texts of Erasmus (1516) and of Stunica (1522) were rounded?

... **Is it gravely pretended that readings become "morally certain," because they are "strongly preferred"?** Are we, (in other words) seriously invited to admit that the "strong preference" of "the individual mind" is to be the ultimate standard of appeal? If so, even though you (Dr. Hort) may "have no doubt" as to which is the purer manuscript, do you not plainly see that a person of different "idiosyncrasy" from yourself may just as reasonably claim to "have no doubt" that you are mistaken?

... *Dr. Hort is for setting up what his own inner consciousness "pronounces to be right," against "documentary evidence," however multitudinous.* He claims that his own verifying faculty shall be supreme; shall settle every question. Can he be in earnest?

We are next introduced to the subject of "genealogical evidence.".... *But as usual, Dr. Hort produces no instance. He merely proceeds to suppose* a case which he confesses does not exist. So that we are moving in a land of shadows....

Not so thinks Dr. Hort. "This presumption," (he seems to have persuaded himself), may be disposed of *by his mere assertion* that it "is too minute to weigh against the smallest tangible evidence of other kinds." As usual, however, he furnishes us with no "evidence of other kinds." Indeed, he furnishes us with no evidence at all, either "tangible" or "intangible." Can he wonder if we smile at his unsupported dictum, and pass on? ... But does the learned Critic really require to be told that we want no diagram of an imaginary case to convince us of that? [yes!]

The one thing here which moves our astonishment is that Dr. Hort does not seem to reflect that therefore (indeed by his own showing) codices B and Aleph, having been demonstrably "executed from one and the same common original," are not to be reckoned as two independent witnesses to the Text of the New Testament, but as little more than one.

High time, however, is it to declare that, in strictness, *all this talk about genealogical evidence, when applied to manuscripts is moonshine.* [Dean Burgon had highlighted this sentence. I just enlarged the font.] The expression is metaphorical, and assumes that it has fared with MSS. as it fares with the successive generations of a family; and so, to a remarkable extent, no doubt, it has. But then, it happens, unfortunately, *that we are unacquainted with one single instance of a known ms. copied from another known ms. And perforce all talk about genealogical evidence, where no single step in the descent can be produced, in other words, where no genealogical evidence exists, is absurd.*

... *The one great fact, which especially troubles him and his joint editor, (as well it may) is The traditional Greek Text of the New Testament Scriptures.* Call this Text Erasmian or Complutensian, the Text of Stephens, or of Beza, or of the Elzevirs; call it the "Received," or the "Traditional Greek Text," or whatever other name you please. *The fact remains that a text has come down to us which is attested by a general consensus of ancient copies, ancient Fathers, and ancient versions.* This, at all events, is a point on which, (happily) there exists entire conformity of opinion between Dr. Hort and ourselves. *Our readers cannot have yet forgotten his virtual admission that, beyond all question the Textus Receptus is the dominant Graeco-Syrian Text of A.D. 350 to A.D. 400.*

Obtained from a variety of sources, this Text proves to be essentially the same in all. *That it requires Revision with respect to many of its lesser details is undeniable.* But it is at least as certain that it is an excellent text as it stands, and that the use of it will never lead critical students of Scripture seriously astray, which is what no one will venture to predicate concerning any single critical edition of the N.T. which has been published since the days of Griesbach, by the disciples of Griesbach's school.

... *Their absolute contempt for the Traditional Text, their superstitious veneration of a few ancient documents,* (which **documents, however, they freely confess are *not* more ancient than the 'Traditional Text' which they despise**) *knows no bounds.*

... Their expedient has been as follows. **Aware that the Received or Traditional Greek Text (to quote their own words) "is virtually identical with that used by Chrysostom and other Antiochian Fathers in the latter part of the 4th century." and fully alive to the fact that it "must, therefore, have been represented by manuscripts as old as any which are now surviving," they have invented an extraordinary hypothesis in order to account for its existence.**

They assume that the writings of Origen "establish the prior existence of at least three types of text." The most clearly marked of which, they call the "*Western*," **another, less prominent, they designate as** "*Alexandrian,*" **the third holds (they say) a middle or** "*Neutral*" **position.** (*That all this is mere moonshine, a day-dream and no more, we shall insist, until some proofs have been produced that the respected authors are moving amid material forms; not discoursing with the creations of their own brain.*)

... **Dr. Hort favors us with the assurance that, "The Syrian Text, to which the order of time now bring us, is the chief monument of a new period of Textual history. Now, the three great lines were brought together, and made to contribute to the formation of a new Text different from all." "The 'Syrian Text' must in fact be the result of a 'Recension,' performed deliberately by editors, and not merely by scribes."**

But why "must" it? Instead of "must in fact," we are disposed to read "may–in fiction."

... But then, since *not a shadow of proof* is forthcoming that any such recension as Dr. Hort imagines ever took place at all, what else but a purely gratuitous exercise of the imaginative faculty is it, that Dr. Hort should proceed further to invent the method which *might*, or *could*, or *would*, or *should* have been pursued, if it had taken place?

Having, however, in this way, (1) assumed a "Syrian Recension," (2) invented the cause of it, and (3) dreamed the process by which it was carried into execution, the Critic hastens, *more suo,* to characterize the historical result...

So then, in brief, the "theory" of Dr. Westcott and Hort is this that, somewhere between A.D. 250 and A.D. 350, (1) "The growing diversity and confusion of Greek Texts led to an authoritative Revision at Antioch, which (2) was then taken as a standard for a similar authoritative Revision of the Syriac Text, and (3) was itself at a later time subjected to a second authoritative Revision." This "final process" having been "apparently completed by (A.D.) 350 or thereabouts."

... It is plain, therefore, that Dr. Hort is in direct antagonism with the collective mind of patristic antiquity. Why, when it suits him, he should appeal to the same ancients for support, we fail to understand.

... **To speak with entire accuracy, Drs. Westcott and Hort require us to believe that the authors of the (imaginary) Syrian Revisions of A.D. 250 and A.D. 350, interpolated the genuine text of the Gospels with between 2877 (B) and 3455 (Aleph) spurious words; mutilated the genuine text in respect of between 536 (B) and 839 (Aleph) words, substituted for as many genuine Words, between 935 (B) and 1114 (Aleph) uninspired words, licentiously transposed between 2098 (B) and 2299 (Aleph); and in respect to number, case, mood, tense, person, etc. altered without authority between 1132 (b) and 1265 (Aleph) words.**

... With perfect truth has the latter remarked on the practical "identity of the text, more especially in the Gospels and Pauline Epistles, in all the known cursive mss., except a few." We fully admit the truth of his statement that "Before the close of the 4th century, a Greek Text not materially differing from the almost universal text of the 9th (and why not the 6th? or the 7th? or the 8th? or again, of the 10th? of the 11th? of the 12th?) century was dominant at Antioch." And why not throughout the whole of Eastern Christendom? Why this continual mention of "Antioch". this perpetual introduction of the epithet "Syrian"? Neither designation applies to Irenaeus or to Hippolytus, to Athanasius or to Didymus, or Gregory of Nazianzum or to his namesake of Nyssa, to Basil or to Epiphanius, to Nonnus or to Macarius, to Proclus or to Theodorus Mops., to the earlier or to the later Cyril. In brief, "The fundamental text of the late extant Greek mss. generally is, beyond all question, identical with (what Dr. Hort chooses to call) the dominant Antiochian or Graeco-Syrian text of the second half of the 4th century. The Antiochian (and other) Fathers, and the bulk of extant mss. written from about three or four, to ten or eleven centuries later, must have had, in the greater number of extant variations, a common original either contemporary with, or older than, our oldest extant mss..

So far then, happily, we are entirely agreed. The only question is, how is this resemblance to be accounted for? Not, we answer, not, certainly, by putting forward so violent and improbable, so irrational a conjecture as that, first, about

A.D. 250, and then again about A.D. 350 an authoritative standard text was fabricated at Antioch, of which all other known mss. (except a very little handful) are nothing else but transcripts. **But rather, by loyally recognizing, in the practical identity of the Text exhibited by ninety-nine out of one hundred of our extant mss., the probable general fidelity of those many transcripts to the inspired exemplars themselves from which remotely they are confessedly descended.**

...Equally impossible is it to overlook its practical identity with the Text of Chrysostom, who lived and taught at Antioch until A.D. 398, when he became Abp. [Bishop] of Constantinople.

... Of our two primitive versions, "the Syriac and the old Latin," the second is grossly corrupt, owing (says Dr. Hort) to a perilous confusion between transcription and reproduction; the preservation of a record and its supposed improvement. Further acquaintance with it only increases our distrust." In plainer English, "the earliest readings which can be fixed chronologically" belong to a version which is licentious and corrupt to an incredible extent. And although "there is no reason to doubt that the Peschitto (or ancient Syriac) is at least as old as the Latin Version," yet, according to Dr. Hort, it is "impossible" (he is nowhere so good as to explain to us wherein this supposed "impossibility" consists) to regard "the present form of the version as a true representation of the original Syriac text." The date of it, (according to him) may be as late as A.D. 350.

... Washed overboard! Put completely out of sight! Athanasius and Didymus, the two Basil and the two Gregories, the two Cyrils and the two Theodores, Epiphanius and Macarius and Ephraem, Chrysostom and Severianus and Proclus, Nilus and Nonnus, Isidore of Pelusium and Theodoret, not to mention at least as many more who have left scanty, yet most precious, remains behind them: all these are pronounced inferior in authority to as many 9th or 10th century copies!

... **That the testimony of the Fathers, as a whole, must perforce in some such way either be ignored or else flouted, if the text of Drs. Westcott and Hort is to stand we were perfectly well aware. It is simply fatal to them, and they know it**

... Thus then, at last, at the end of exactly 150 weary pages, **the secret comes out!** The one point which the respected editors are found to have been all along driving at: the one aim of those many hazy disquisitions of theirs about intrinsic and transcriptional probability, genealogical evidence, simple and divergent, and the study of Groups, the one reason for all their vague terminology, and of their Baseless theory of "Conflation," and of their disparagement of the Fathers: the one *raison d'etre* of their fiction of a "Syrian" and a "Pre-Syrian" and a "Neutral" text; the secret of it all comes out at last! A delightful, a truly Newtonian simplicity characterizes the final announcement. *All* *is summed up in the curt formula–Codex B!* ...[Hort says] "B very far exceeds all other documents in neutrality of text."

... What! Again? Why, we "have found" nothing as yet but reiteration. Up to this point we have not been favored with *one particle of evidence!* In the meantime, the convictions of these accomplished Critics, (but not, unfortunately, those of their readers) are observed to strengthen as they proceed. On reading p. 224, we are assured that, "The independence (of B and Aleph) can be carried back so far" (*not a hint is given how*) "that their concordant testimony may be treated as equivalent to that of a ms. older than Aleph and B themselves by at least two centuries, probably by a generation or two more."

How that "independence" was established, and how this "probability" has been arrived at, we cannot even imagine. The point to be attended to, however, is, that by the process indicated, some such early epoch as A.D. 100 has been reached. So that now we are not surprised to hear that, "The respective ancestries of Aleph and B must have diverged from a common parent extremely near the Apostolic autographs"

... *And thus, by an unscrupulous use of the process of reiteration,* [now called 'spin'] *accompanied by a boundless exercise of the imaginative faculty,* [creative spin] *we have reached the goal to which all that went before has been steadily tending: that is, the absolute supremacy of codices B and Aleph above-all other codices, and when they differ, then of Codex B.*

... The only indication we anywhere meet with of the actual ground of Dr. Hort's certainty, and reason of his preference, is contained in his claim that, "Every binary group (of mss.) containing B is found to offer a large proportion of readings, which, on the closest scrutiny, have the ring of genuineness, while it is difficult to find any readings so attested which look suspicious after full consideration." And thus we have, at last, an honest confession of the ultimate principle which has determined the text of the present edition of the N.T. "The ring of genuineness"!

... And thus, behold, "at last" we have reached the goal! ... *individual idiosyncrasy, not external evidence. Readings strongly preferred, not readings strongly attested.* "Personal discernment" (self! still self!) conscientiously exercising itself upon Codex B. This is a true account of the Critical method pursued by these accomplished scholars. *They deliberately claim "personal discernment" as "the surest ground for confidence."* Accordingly, they judge readings by their looks and by their sound. When, in their opinion, words "look suspicious," words are to be rejected. If a word has "the ring of genuineness," (i.e. if it seems *to them* to have it) they claim that the word shall pass unchallenged.

...But enough of this. We really have at last, (be it observed) reached the end of our enquiry. Nothing comes after Dr. Hort's extravagant and unsupported estimate of Codices B and Aleph. On the contrary. **Those two documents are caused to cast their somber shadows a long way ahead, and to darken all our future.** [If Dean Burgon had only known how prophetic these words were when he wrote them in the 1880's]

... So Dr. Hort hastens to frown it down: "It would be an illusion to anticipate important changes of text (i.e. of the text advocated by Drs. Westcott and Hort) from any acquisition of new evidence."

(1) The impurity of the texts exhibited by Codices B and Aleph is not a matter of opinion, but a matter of fact. These are two of the least trustworthy documents in existence. So far from allowing Dr. Hort's position that "A text formed" by "taking Codex B as the sole authority, would be incomparably nearer the truth than a text similarly taken from any other Greek or other single document." We venture to assert that it would be, on the contrary, by far the foulest text that had ever seen the light. Worse, that is to say, even than the text of Drs. Westcott and Hort. And that is saying a great deal. In the brave and faithful words of Prebendary Scrivener (*Introduction*, p. 453), words which deserve to become famous, "It is no less true to fact than paradoxical in sound, that the worse corruptions to which the New Testament has ever been subjected, originated within a hundred years after it was composed: that Irenaeus (A.D. 150), and the African Fathers, and the whole Western, with a portion of the Syrian Church, used far inferior manuscripts to those employed by Stunica, or Erasmus, or Stephens thirteen centuries later, when moulding the Textus Receptus." And Codices B and Aleph, are, demonstrably, nothing else but specimens of the depraved class thus characterized.

(2) Next, We assert that, so manifest are the disfigurements jointly and exclusively exhibited by codices B and Aleph that instead of accepting these codices as two "independent" witnesses to the inspired original, **we are constrained to regard them as little more than** *a single reproduction of one and the same scandalously corrupt and (comparatively) late cop*y. By consequence, we consider their joint and exclusive attestation of any particular reading, "an unique criterion" of its worthlessness; a sufficient reason, not for adopting, but for unceremoniously rejecting it.

(3) Then as for the origin of these two curiosities, it can perforce only be divined from their contents. That they exhibit fabricated texts is demonstrable. No amount of honest copying, preserved in for any number of centuries, could by possibility have resulted in two such documents. Separated from one another in actual date by 50, perhaps by 100 years, they must needs have branched off from a common corrupt ancestor, and straightway become exposed continuously to fresh depraving influences. The result is, that codex Aleph, (which evidently has gone through more adventures and fallen into worse company than its rival) has been corrupted to a far greater extent than codex B, and is *even more untrustworthy.* **Thus, whereas (in the Gospels alone) B has 589 readings quite**

peculiar to itself, affecting 858 words, Aleph has 1460 such readings, affecting 2640 words.

One solid fact like the preceding, (let it be pointed out in passing) is more helpful by far to one who would form a correct estimate of the value of a Codex, than any number of such "reckless and unverified assertions," not to say preemptory and Baseless decrees, as abound in the highly imaginative pages of Drs. Westcott and Hort.

(4) Lastly, we suspect that these two manuscripts are indebted for their preservation, solely to their ascertained evil character, which has occasioned that the one eventually found its way, four centuries ago, to a forgotten shelf in the Vatican library, while the other, after exercising the ingenuity of several generations of critical correctors, eventually (viz. in A.D. 1844) got deposited in the waste paper basket of the convent at the foot of Mount Sinai. [This statement refers to the manuscript found in a waste paper basket by Tischendorf called Vaticanus or Codex B]

Had B and Aleph been copies of average purity, they must long since have shared the inevitable fate of books which are freely used and highly prized. Namely, they would have fallen into decadence and disappeared from sight. But in the meantime, behold, their very antiquity has come to be reckoned to their advantage. And, strange to relate, is even considered to constitute a sufficient reason why they should enjoy not merely extraordinary consideration, but the actual surrender of the critical judgment.

… Vanquished by the Word incarnate, Satan next directed his subtle malice against the Word written. Hence, as I think, the extraordinary fate which befell certain early transcripts of the Gospel. First, heretical assailants of Christianity, then, orthodox defenders of the Truth, lastly and above all, self-constituted Critics, who (like Dr. Hort) imagined themselves at liberty to resort to "instinctive processes" of Criticism; and who, at first as well as "at last," freely made their appeal "to the individual mind." Such were the corrupting influences which were actively at work throughout the first hundred and fifty years after the death of St. John the divine.

Profane literature has never known anything approaching it, and can show nothing at all like it. Satan's arts were defeated indeed through the church's faithfulness because, (the good providence of God had so willed it) the perpetual multiplication, in every quarter, of copies required for ecclesiastical use, not to say the solicitude of faithful men in diverse regions of ancient Christendom to retain for themselves unadulterated specimens of the inspired text, proved a sufficient safeguard against the grosser forms of corruption. But this was not all.

"The church, remember, has been from the beginning the 'witness and keeper of Holy Writ.'. Did not her divine Author pour out upon her, in largest measure, "the Spirit of Truth,' and pledge Himself that it should be that Spirit's special function to "guide" her children "into all the Truth"? That by a perpetual miracle, sacred manuscripts would be protected all down the ages against depraving influences of whatever sort, was not to have been expected: certainly, was never promised.

But the church, in her collective capacity, hath nevertheless–as a matter of fact–been perpetually purging herself of those shamefully depraved copies which once everywhere abounded within her pale: retaining only such an amount of discrepancy in her Text as might serve to remind her children that they carry their "treasure in earthen vessels." as well as to stimulate them to perpetual watchfulness and solicitude for the purity and integrity of the deposit.

Never, however, up to the present hour, has there been any complete eradication of all traces of the attempted mischief, any absolute getting rid of every depraved copy extant. These are found to have lingered on anciently in many quarters. A few such copies linger on to the present day. The wounds were healed, but the scars remained, nay, the scars are discernible still.

What, in the meantime, is to be thought of those blind guides, those deluded ones, who would now, if they could, persuade us to go back to those same codices of which the church has already purged herself; To go back in quest of those very readings which fifteen or 1600 years ago, the church in all lands is found to have rejected with loathing?

... we [Dean Burgon] hold to be the method which, without prejudice or partiality, ascertains *which form of the text enjoys the earliest, the fullest, the widest, the most respectable and–above all things–the most varied attestation.* That a reading should be freely recognized alike by the earliest and by the latest available evidence, we hold to be a prime circumstance in its favor. The copies, versions, and Fathers, should all three concur in sanctioning it, we hold to be even more conclusive. If several Fathers, living in different parts of ancient Christendom, are all observed to recognize the words, or to quote them in the same way, we have met with all the additional confirmation we ordinarily require. Let it only be further discoverable how or why the rival reading came into existence, and our confidence becomes absolute.

... We deem this laborious method the only true method, in our present state of imperfect knowledge: the method, namely, of adopting that reading which has the fullest, the widest, and the most varied attestation. Antiquity and respectability of witnesses are thus secured. *How men can persuade themselves that nineteen copies out of every twenty may be safely disregarded, if they be but written in minuscule characters, we fail to understand.*"[1]

---

[1] Fuller, DD., David Otis; *True or False?*; p. 129-141

This concludes the amazing comments by one of the world's best sacred reviewers concerning the "constructed" false 'new' Greek text that underlies all the 'new' versions.

CONFUSION AMONG MODERNISTIC TEXTUAL CRITICS

Please do not think that Dean Burgon is the only person to defend the Received Text with such vigor. Many outstanding persons have taken a strong stand just like Dean Burgon, but their voices have almost been silenced by the attitudes reflected below.

"Those students who read works such as Miller's *General Biblical Introduction* or Metzger's *The Text of the New Testament* (said by many to be "the standard in the field") or Kenyon's *Our Bible and the Ancient Manuscripts* or Kurt Aland's *The Text of the New Testament* are left with the idea that there has been no serious scholarly rejection of the theories underlying the modern Greek text. This is plainly a deception. Metzger does mention Burgon and Salmon, but he tells us nothing of consequence of their work apart from shallow caricatures. The same can be said for Kenyon. Aland summarizes the defense of the Received Text as mere "clamorous rhetoric" (*The Text of the New Testament*, p. 19). This is an incredibly proud position."[1]

Yet, in spite of the preceding attitude of Kurt Aland, reportedly the "best" textual critic in the world today, Aland says,

"The age of Westcott and Hort...is definitely over!".[2]

How does one reconcile the two positions? They seem to be diametrically opposed. Who is the author of confusion? The truth is the field of textual criticism is in a quandary. Wilbur Pickering, quoting K.W. Clark, says:

"The textual history that the Westcott-Hort text represents is no longer tenable in the light of newer discoveries and fuller textual analysis. In the effort to construct a congruent history, our failure suggests that we have lost the way, that we have reached a dead end, and that only a new and different insight

---

[1] Cloud, David; *For Love of the Bible, The Battle for the King James Version and the Received Text from 1800 to Present;* Way of Life Literature, Oak Harbor, WA.; 2nd Edition; 1999; p. 78

[2] Gipp, Th.D., Samuel C.; *Gipp's Understandable History of the Bible*; p. 37

will enable us to break through."[1]

The truth is 'their way' never was reasonable! Burgon demonstrated that clearly as you have seen. However, even with the proof staring them in the eyes, the current textual scholar is unwilling to throw all the garbage in the waste paper basket and start with the Received Text where they should have been all along. Bruce Metzger, a supposedly 'great' critic, writing in his book, *The Text of the New Testament,* is one who typically throws ice water on Dean Burgon, claiming on pages 135 and 136 that he was "speculative," "unable to comprehend," and "a champion of lost causes." Well, Dr. Metzger, perhaps in light of recent revelations by the likes of Kurt Aland, Dr. E. Hills, Dr. D.A. Waite, and others, you should apologize? These men and Wilbur Pickering have decimated the theories of Westcott and Hort.

I seriously wonder if the influence of the Jesuits from the Reformation is still affecting the scholarship in seminaries, monasteries, universities, and colleges. The reason I wonder if Jesuits are still having influence is because of the actual facts relating to the MSS. They prefer MSS which are even worse, as you will see, than the comments that have been made relating to their corruption. Could the "love of money" be involved since their 'books' sell for oodles?

One interesting comment concerning codex Aleph is that a Scribe in the 19th century says he wrote the manuscript found by Tischendorf:

"...Constantine Simonides, a Greek of Syme, who had just edited a few papyrus fragments of the New Testament alleged to have been written in the first century of the Christian era, suddenly astonished the learned world in 1862 by claiming to be himself the scribe who had penned this manuscript in the monastery of Panteleemon on Mount Alto, as recently as the years 1839 and 1840."[2]

This reminds me of the story concerning the first manuscripts that were printed on the printing press. They were done as forgeries for money. They were supposed to look authentically old. And the plot was successful for a while, garnering lots of money until the forgers were caught. The forgers of the 'new' Greek text have been caught, but it appears the avalanche started by modernistic textual critics will continue. There are two factors involved: 1. Pride because "scholars" caught with their hands in the cookie jar will defend their "right," and 2. There is too much money to be made off the 'new' versions and books written about them.

The situation with the manuscripts preferred by textual critics from the days of J. J. Griesbach to the present is not any better than the printing press forgeries. The "ring of genuineness," or rather personal preference seems to be the way the

---

[1] Pickering, Th.D., Wilbur; *The Identity of the New Testament Text;* p. 97

[2] Gipp, Th.D., Samuel C.; *Gipp's Understandable History of the Bible;* p. 123

scholars selected the manuscripts to study. If you have beliefs like the Broad Church mentioned above, then manuscripts prepared and corrupted by heretics would be your preference. As we will see that seems to be the case. Here are some facts concerning a few of these documents they preferred from their preferred region, Egypt.

PAPYRUS MANUSCRIPTS

When one sees a P before a number it designates the document is a papyrus fragment. An example would be P75. Most of the fragments have been found in the sands of Egypt where the climate is good for preservation of papyrus material. The bad part is the fact that most of the corruption of texts occurred in the Alexandrian region of North Africa. Even Kurt Aland:

> "admits things were so bad in Egypt and Alexandria, that Aleph, B, and even the papyri must have had their origin somewhere else! Aland, in this bewildering turn around, is actually telling us that the "Alexandrian" Text did not really come from Alexandria!! Students of the debate have long known that Alexandria was the worst place on earth to get a Bible. Now, even Kurt Aland agrees, though it virtually leaves his favorite manuscripts as " appearing out of nowhere."[1]

Origen, head of the theological school at Alexandria (Catechetical: question and answer) was one of the principal "rewriters" of Scripture. His philosophy caused him to report:

> "The Scriptures are of little use to those who understand them as written."[2]

He devised the Hexapla, a 6 column work which:

> "was a colossal undertaking to revise the LXX text. It contained five columns in Greek. The first column consisted of the Hebrew. The second comprised the Hebrew Text Tendered in Greek letters, the third Aquila's version, the fourth Symmachus' version, the fifth the Septuagint revised by Origen and the sixth Theodotian's version."[3]

[1] Moorman, Jack; *Early Church Fathers and the Authorized Version;* B.F.T. #2136; The Bible For Today, Collinswood, NJ.; p. 10

[2] Gipp, Th.D., Samuel C.; *Gipp's Understandable History of the Bible;* p. 126

[3] Moorman, Jack; *Forever Settled;* p. 73

Eusebius was an admirer of Origen and his philosophy. He probably used Origen's fifth column to produce the 50 Bibles Emperor Constantine requested immediately. The suggestion by numerous critics is that codex Vaticanus is one of the 50 copies.[1]

In addition to Origen's heretical tendencies, other heresies came out of Egypt such as the Valentinian and Arian heresies. Origen has also been called the:

"father of Arianism"[2]

Can there be any doubt that out of the sands of Egypt would arise corrupted texts? Most textual critics now believe the Antiochian text was corrupted in Egypt. Is it any wonder that our God called his Son out of Egypt or brought the nation Israel out? Yet modern textual critics continue to use the texts from polluted schools, heretics, and corrupted denominations as their gold standard.

Most of the eight-eight extant [in existence] papyri pieces were discovered in Oxyrhincus in the Libyan Desert south of Cairo.[3] The textual critics would even have you believe that the corrupt papyri show no support for the Received Text. This simply is not true. Of the 88 pieces only 13 support the Alexandrian Text according to Stewart Custer and F.C. Kenyon.[4]

The most significant ones are the P45 (3rd Century), P46 (known as the Chester Beaty Papyri, c. 200), P66 (c. 200), and P75 (known as the "Bodmer Papyrus II", 3rd Century). Jack Moorman says these are the "favorite sons" of the modern textual critic. The result of analysis of these documents shows some interesting features, which is astounding in light of their source. The papyri show readings that favor the:

Sinaiticus	60 times
Vaticanus	124 times
Received Text	**139 times**[5]

With information like this how can anyone support the concept of a Lucian recension of the Received Text in the late 3rd and 4th century as Westcott and Hort proposed? [Remember, the recension was the "formation" or "construction" of the 'Syrian' (W/H name for the Received Text) text proposed by Westcott and Hort.] Scholars still do though! Be aware that the readings of the Received Text, or what W/H called the Syrian text, are more homogeneous, but the Alexandrian text (also called the *critical* text) readings are "all over the place". Even

---

[1] Fuller, DD., David Otis; *Which Bible?*; Grand Rapids International Publications, 1990 Institute for Biblical Textual Studies; ISBN 0-944355-24-2; p. 3

[2] Ibid. pp. 3, and 95

[3] Moorman, Jack; *Forever Settled;* p. 75

[4] Ibid. p. 77

[5] Ibid. p. 78

genealogical theories grow pale in the face of this information. In summary, there was an early text called the Received Text that was corrupted **rather than** a *critical* text which was used to "construct" the Received Text called a recension.

UNCIALS

Much of the following information was taken from Jack Moorman's work, *Forever Settled.* The uncials (manuscripts written in capital letters would look something like this:

BELIEVEONTHELORDJESUSCHRISTANDTHOUSHALTBESAVED,

but in a different language. There are about 267 extant uncial manuscripts which contain parts of the New Testament, but only 5 which are alleged to be "the oldest and best". Below is the list and where they are currently located.

"Though there are ...extant uncial MSS [manuscripts] containing substantial portions of the NT, and several hundred more fragments that the interest of scholars has been centered on. "The five Old Uncials" which date back to the 4th- 5th centuries are:

Manuscript	Century	Location	Contents
1. Aleph Sinaiticus	IV	London	Gospels. Acts, Epistles, Revelation
2. A (Alexandrinus)	V	London	Gospels, Acts, Epistles, Revelation, (minus portions of Matthew, John, II Corinthians)
3. B (Vaticanus)	IV	Rome	Gospels. Acts Epistles (minus portions of I Timothy, Philemon, Hebrews)
4. C Ephraemi Rescriptus	V	Paris	Portions of all the books of the New Testament

5. D Bezae Cantabrigiensiss	V	Cambridge	Portions of the Gospels. Acts. James and Jude

These five manuscripts are the primary reason why we have so many modern versions today, which are *alleged* to be: "based on older and better manuscripts than the Authorized Version."[1]

CORRUPTED READINGS WERE KNOWN AND REJECTED

The translators of the King James Bible from the original language texts of their day have been accused of not having the above codices and is a major reason modern critics justify the adoption of readings from the five uncials above. This could not be further from the truth! **They did have the readings and rejected them.** God is so good to provide answers if we are just diligent to work and search. The following quote will confirm that the able, excellent, godly men who translated the Received Texts to the English of the KJB *did have* and *knew* the readings.

"The following words from Dr. Kenrick, Catholic Bishop of Philadelphia, will support the conclusion that the translators of the King James knew the readings of Codices Aleph, A, B, C, D, where they differed from the Received Text and denounced them. Bishop Kenrick published an English translation of the Catholic Bible in 1849. I quote from the preface:

"Since the famous manuscripts of Rome, Alexandria, Cambridge, Paris, and Dublin, were examined... a verdict has been obtained in favor of the [Latin] Vulgate.

"At the Reformation, the Greek Text, as it then stood, was taken as a standard, in conformity to which the versions of the Reformers were generally made; whilst the Latin Vulgate was depreciated, or despised, as a mere version."

In other words, the readings of these much boasted manuscripts, recently made available, are those of the Vulgate. The Reformers **knew of these readings and rejected them,** as well as the Vulgate."[2] [my emphasis]

The next obvious question is: "Why did they reject the readings?" Although we will never know all the reasons, there are some facts that have been learned

---

[1] Ibid. p. 82

[2] Fuller, DD., David Otis; *Which Bible?*; pp.254-255

about the manuscripts the Latin vulgate is based upon, particularly those that Drs. Hort and Westcott, Tischendorf, Tregelles, and most modern critics favor, codex Aleph (Sinaiticus) and codex B (Vaticanus). The following quotes and information comes from an unusual source. One of our greatest lawyers for the bar of the Supreme Court, and for the U.S. patent court, prepared a work in 1928 that addressed many of these questions. A brief sketch of his life, and the report of the salvation of Philip Mauro, the lawyer, can be found in a book by David O. Fuller D.D., *True or False?*. After his salvation, Mauro recognized the importance of the text of Scripture and noticed the significant differences between the Revised Version of W/H and the KJB. He determined to investigate those differences and wrote a book entitled *Which Version? Authorized or Revised.* The complete work can be found in *True or False?* Philip Mauro said:

PHILIP MAURO, A LAWYER, COMMENTS ON REJECTION OF THE ALEXANDRIAN READINGS AND WHY

"Dr. Scrivener published (in 1864) "A Full Collation of the Codex Sinaiticus," with an explanatory introduction in which he states, among other facts of interest, that "the Codex is covered with such alterations"–i.e., alterations of an obviously correctional character–"brought in by at least ten different revisers, some of them systematically spread over every page, others occasional, or limited to separate portions of the Ms., many of these being contemporaneous with the first writer, but for the greater part belonging to the sixth or seventh century."

We are sure that every intelligent reader will perceive, and with little effort, the immense significance of this feature of the Sinaitic Codex. Here is a document which the Revisers have esteemed (and that solely because of its antiquity) to be so pure that it should be taken as a standard whereby all other copies of the Scriptures are to be tested and corrected. Such is the estimate of certain scholars of the 19th century. But it bears upon its face the proof that those in whose possession it had been, from the very first, and for some hundreds of years thereafter, esteemed it to be so impure as to require correction in every part.

... But more than that, Dr. Scrivener tells us that the evident purpose of the thorough-going revision which he places in the 6th or 7th century was to make the Ms. conform to manuscripts in vogue at that time which were "far nearer to our modern Textus Receptus

...Thus, there are internal evidences that lead to the conclusion that it was the work of a scribe who was singularly careless, or incompetent, or both. In this Ms. the arrangement of the lines is peculiar, there being four columns on each page, each line containing about twelve letters–all capitals run together. There is no attempt to end a word at the end of a line, for even words having only two letters as *en, ek*, are split in the middle, the last letter being carried over to the beginning of the next line, though there was ample room for it on the line preceding. This and other peculiarities give us an idea of the character and competence of the scribe.

But more than that, Dr. Scrivener says: "This manuscript must have been derived from one in which the lines were similarly divided, since the writer occasionally omits just the number of letters which would suffice to fill a line, and that to the utter ruin of the sense; as if his eye had heedlessly wandered to the line immediately below." Dr. Scrivener cites instances "where complete lines are omitted," and others "where the copyist passed in the middle of a line to the corresponding portion of the line below."

From this it is evident that the work of copying was done by a scribe who was both heedless and incompetent. A careful copyist would not have made the above and other mistakes so frequently; and only the most incompetent would have failed to notice, upon reading over the page, and to correct, omissions which utterly destroyed the sense.

Dr. Scrivener's judgment on this feature of the case is entitled to the utmost confidence, not only because of his great ability as a textual critic, but because, being impressed, as all antiquarians were, with the importance of Tischendorf's discovery, it was solely from a sheer sense of duty and honesty, and with manifest reluctance, that he brought himself to point out the defects of the manuscript. Therefore, the following admission made by him carries much weight:

"It must be confessed indeed that the Codex Sinaiticus abounds with similar errors of the eye and pen, to an extent not unparalleled, but happily rather unusual in documents of first rate importance; so that Tregelles has freely pronounced that 'the state of the text, as proceeding from the first scribe, may be regarded as very rough.'"

Speaking of the character of the two oldest Mss. Dean Burgon says:

"The impurity of the text exhibited by these codices is not a question of opinion but of fact .... In the Gospels alone Codex B (Vatican) leaves out words or whole clauses no less than 1,491 times. It bears traces of careless transcription on every page. Codex Sinaiticus 'abounds with errors of the eye and pen to an extent not indeed unparalleled, but happily rather unusual in documents of first-rate importance.' On many occasions 10, 20, 30, 40 words are dropped through very carelessness. Letters and words, even whole sentences, are frequently written twice over, or begun and immediately cancelled; while that gross blunder, whereby a clause is omitted because it happens to end in the same word as the clause preceding, occurs no less than 115 times in the New Testament."

In enumerating and describing the five ancient Codices now in existence, Dean Burgon remarks that four of these, and especially the Vatican and Sinaitic Mss. "have, within the last twenty years, established a tyrannical ascendancy over the imagination of the critics which can only be fitly spoken of as blind superstition."

Dean Burgon, whom we shall have occasion to quote largely because of his mastery of the entire subject, after having spent **five and a half years** "laboriously collating the five old uncials throughout the Gospels," declared at the completion of his prodigious task that

"So manifest are the disfigurements jointly and exclusively exhibited by the two codices (Vatican and Sinaitic) that, instead of accepting them as two independent witnesses to the inspired original, we are constrained to regard them as little more than a single reproduction of one and the same scandalously corrupt and comparatively late Copy."

... As a sufficient illustration of the many differences between these two Codices and the great body of other Mss. we note that, in the Gospels alone, Codex Vaticanus differs from the Received Text in the following particulars: It omits at least 2,877 words; it adds 536 words; it substitutes 935 words; it transposes 2,098 words; and it modifies 1,132; making a total of 7,578 verbal divergences. But the Sinaitic Ms. is even worse, for its total divergences in the particulars stated above amount to nearly nine thousand.

... These are strong statements, but the facts on which they are based seem fully to warrant them. Therefore it matters not what specific excellencies might be attributed to the Revised Version of the New Testament, the fact that the underlying Greek Text was fashioned in conformity to the Mss. referred to in the above quoted paragraph is reason enough why it should be shunned by Bible users.

But let it be remembered in the first place that it is for the supporters of the two ancient Codices, as against the Received Text, to establish their case by a preponderance of testimony; for the burden of proof rests heavily upon them. It is for them to show, and by testimony which carries thorough conviction, that God left His people for fifteen centuries or more to the bad effects of a corrupt text, until, in fact, the chance discovery by Constantine Tischendorf, in the middle of the 19th century, of some leaves of parchment so slightly valued by their custodians that they had been thrown into the waste paper basket, and until (for some mysterious and as yet unexplained reason) the Codex Vaticanus was exhumed from its suspicious sleeping place at the papal headquarters.

It is for them to explain, if they can, the concurrence of a thousand manuscripts, widely distributed geographically, and spread over a thousand years of time, and of the many Versions and writings of "Fathers" going back to the second century of our era. That there were corrupt and defective copies in the early centuries—many of the alterations having been made with deliberate intent-is well known; and to account for the survival of a few of these (three at the most) is not a difficult matter.

Indeed there is good reason to believe that they owe their prolonged existence to the fact that they were known to be, by reason of their many defects, unfit for use. [my emphasis]

It is easy to understand why the Codex Vaticanus Ms. is cherished at the Vatican; for its corruptions are what make it valuable to the leaders of the papal system. We can conceive therefore the satisfaction of those leaders that their highly prized Ms. has been allowed to play the leading part in the revision of the English Bible [KJV], than [and] which there is nothing on earth they have more reason to fear. On the other hand, may not this be one of the causes why God, in His overruling providence has frustrated the attempt to displace the A.V. [KJV] by a new version, based upon such a sandy foundation? But, on the other hand, the fact (as is admitted) of the existence everywhere of a Text represented now by over a thousand extant manuscripts, and agreeing with the Received Text, can be accounted for only upon the supposition that that is the true Text.

... Briefly then, to sum up the matter thus far, we observe:
That the most important and deplorable of the departures of the New Greek Text from the Received Text have been made **with the support of less than one percent of all the available witnesses;** or in other words, the readings discarded by the Revisers [Westcott and Hort] have the support of over 99 percent of the surviving Greek Texts (besides Versions and Fathers).

That the two Mss. which had the controlling influence in most of these departures are so corrupt upon their face as to justify the conclusion that they owe their survival solely to their bad reputation."[1]

Having read the sections above written by a lawyer, Philip Mauro, skilled in evidence, and one of the best textual scholars to live, William J. Burgon, review Metzger's comments above about Dean John Burgon, Westcott and Hort, and the manuscripts. Am I missing something? I don't think so. I believe men like W/H, Metzger, and Aland are missing God's promises of preservation. I believe they are relying on their rationalism. Jack Moorman says scholars have called codex B, the Vaticanus, "the best text", "the most perfectly preserved text", "highly legible", etc.[2]

Herman Hoskier, a student of Burgon, went on to do some of the best textual work that has ever been done.

"He said in *Codex B and its Allies,* ... **"There are over 3000 real differences between Aleph and B in the Gospels alone!"** This is the kind of "foundation" that one has in the new versions".[3] [my emphasis]

Yes, that's right. All the new popular versions in most homes today are based on these corrupt manuscripts!! We will come back to this in a later section.

One final comment by Dean Burgon, who you noticed above, studied these MSS (Aleph and B) for five and one-half (5 ½) years said:

"It is in fact easier to find two consecutive verses in which these two MSS differ, than two consecutive verses in which they entirely agree."[4]

---

[1] Fuller, D.D., David Otis; *True or False?; selected quotes from* pp. 56-80

[2] Moorman, Jack; *Forever Settled;* p. 85

[3] Ibid. p.85

[4] Ibid. p. 85

OTHER POPULAR ALEXANDRIAN UNCIALS

Codex Alexandrinus (A) was probably written in the early 5th century. It has two apocryphal books attached and has much of Matthew missing and only part of John and II Corinthians. Kenyon, who is an Alexandrian-type textual scholar and who is a former curator of the British Museum, said that the Gospels that are the Byzantine Text were revised. The rest of the document is Alexandrian.

"Codex Alexandrinus (A), 450 AD, British Museum, Unger says it follows Origen's Hexapla."[1]

Codex Ephraemi Rescriptus gives a hint as to its nature by the name. It is a classic palimpsest, meaning the original text was 'washed' away and another text was written on top in the 12th century. The text written on top was some of the works of Ephriam Syrus. Experts in the field say most of the original text has been recovered.

Codex Bezae (D) is said to be "the worst of the lot". The MS is said to be from the 5th or 6th century and is in Latin. It has readings entirely different from any other MSS.

Now we approach the reason for taking you through a description of these old uncials. They differ from each other and from the Received Text. Without specifics here are some totals from Dean Burgon.

"Here then are the "five old uncials" that modern scholarship would have us base our Bibles upon. Burgon gives the following summary:

The serious deflections from the Received Text in:

Alexandrinus - 842
Ephraemi Rescriptus - 1798
Vaticanus - 2370
Sinaiticus - 3392
Bezae - 4697

Each deflection may include anything from one word, to a phrase, to a verse, to several verses, etc. In the previous comparison between B, Aleph and the TR, the total number of words was counted. Also as each of these uncials do not have in every instance the same portion of Scripture remaining; the comparison is drawn only from those portions where all are extant. Notice how the above graphically proves not only their

---

[1] Ibid. p. 15

conflict with the TR but also with each other. Burgon's comment on that evidence sums up the sordid state of affairs that modern textual criticism has brought us to. "We venture to assure you, without a particle of hesitation, that Aleph, B and D are three of the most scandalously corrupt copies extant. They have become the depositories of the largest amount of fabricated readings, ancient blunders, and intentional perversions of truth, which are discoverable in any known copies of the word of God." How does Stewart Custer's statement "the Alexandrian text is older and better attested than the others (namely the TR) square with the above evidence ?"[1]

We have come to a section in Jack Moorman's excellent work that can only be presented as he wrote it. It is used with permission. I have not found any better presentation of this material than missionary Moorman's arrangement.

Investigating this section carefully will demonstrate **the extreme bias** of the naturalist, neutral, Alexandrian textual scholar. They have very little regard for the doctrine of preservation, verbal and plenary inspiration, infallibility or inerrancy. Please remember we are still investigating the history of the patient (Bible), which is in the subjective portion of the SOAP acronym. My professors in medical school said repeatedly to the students, "The route [way] to a proper diagnosis begins with an excellent history." That's what we are trying to do here. We have not examined the patient yet. We will arrive at that point when we reach the 'O', objective. We are still gathering information about the original language texts. THE REASON FOR THIS WORK PRESENTING THE INFORMATION IN THIS FASHION IS: 1. TO DEVELOP THE FOUNDATION (CORNERSTONE) ONE NEEDS TO COMPREHEND THE TWO STREAMS OF MODERN DAY GREEK AND HEBREW TEXTS. 2. TO SLOWLY BUILD THE KNOWLEDGE AND UNDERSTANDING NEEDED TO APPRECIATE WHY WE HAVE SO MANY TRANSLATIONS (VERSIONS) FROM THE ORIGINAL LANGUAGE TEXTS. 3. TO UNDERSTAND THE INFLUENCE THESE FACTS HAVE HAD IN THE MODERN WORLD, WHICH WILL BE PRESENTED UNDER THE SECTION: THE PLAN. The highlighted areas in Jack Moorman's work are my doings.

---

[1] Ibid. p. 89

"OTHER IMPORTANT UNCIAL MANUSCRIPTS"

Sir Frederick Kenyon's "Our Bible and the Ancient Manuscripts" is an authoritative presentation of the transmission of Scripture from **the naturalistic position**. It first came out in 1895 and has gone through a number of revisions and editions. The copy that I am referring to is the fifth edition that was revised and enlarged by A. W. Adams D. D. in 1958. Along with its sister volume "The Text of the Greek Bible", it is the classic text book on the subject.

The Bible believer will be very interested to hear what Kenyon (or his reviser) has to say on Page 213. After discussing in detail "the five old uncials", he first discusses three others:

1) Claromontanus (D2), 6th century. It has the epistles of Paul in Greek and Latin. Containing as it does the Latin, it falls into the Western camp, but does not have the striking type of additions that Bezae does.

2) Basiliensis (E), 8th century, 4 Gospels, Byzantine (Received) Text.

3) Laudianus (E2), 7th century, Acts in Greek and Latin, the Greek is Byzantine.

We now come to the statement:

"Of the remaining manuscripts, we shall notice only those which have some value or interest. Many of them consist of fragments only, and their texts are, for the most part less valuable. **Most of them contain texts of the Syrian (Received) type, and are of no more importance than the great mass of cursives.** They prove that the Syrian text was predominant in the Greek world..."

Despite his bias against the Received Text ("less valuable", "not important"), he is forced to concede that "most" of the uncials are of that kind of text. In fact, of the 267 extant uncials, it is overwhelmingly so.

To be more specific, in surveying both of Kenyon's books I could only find that the following MSS were said by him to be of the Alexandrian type (i.e. in basic alignment with Aleph, B, or A).

Aleph, Sinaiticus, 4th century.

B, Vaticanus, 4th century.

A, Alexandrinus, 5th century, Epistles, Gospels are TR.

I , Washingtonianus, 7th century, Fragments of Epistles, "Agrees with Aleph and A more than B. "

L, Regius, 8th century, Gospels, "Often agrees with B."

R, Nitriensis, 6th century, Palimpsest of half of Luke, "Akin in character to Aleph and B."

T, Borgianus, 5th century, Portions of Luke and John, "Closely associated with Aleph and B."

Z, Dublinensis 6th century, Palimpsest containing 295 verses of Matthew, "many agreements with Aleph."

Xi , Zacynthius, 8th century, Palimpsest containing most of Luke 1 - 11 "Its text is akin to B."

Now there may be others and there were one or two instances where a smaller portion of a MS had some Alexandrian readings (i.e. Codex Laurensis). **But out of well over two hundred uncials, these were all that Kenyon and his later revisers were prepared to mention. Further, the very marked conflict between Aleph, B and A is magnified much further when support is sought from these other six uncials.**

Nine conflicting MSS, which early Christians didn't bother to use, out of over two hundred uncials doesn't present any stronger use than the nine papyri that Custer mentions, or the eight conflations that Hort talks about.

At Marquette Manor Baptist Church in Chicago (1984), Dr. Custer said that God preserved His Word "in the sands of Egypt." No! God did not preserve His Word in the sands of Egypt, or on a library shelf in the Vatican Library, or in a wastepaper bin in a Catholic Monastery at the foot of Mt. Sinai. God did not preserve His Word in the "disusing" but in the "using". He did not preserve the Word by it being stored away or buried, but rather through its use and transmission in the hands of humble believers. The good copies were worn out, the corrupted ones were put on the shelf. And to repeat what Kirsopp Lake said, "It is hard to resist the conclusion that the scribes usually destroyed their exemplars when they had copied the sacred books."

Yet despite this, there is the same clear evidence from the earlier Uncials as there is from the Papyri. Kenyon's books list the following pre-7th century MSS as being on the side of the Received Text. Though as his statements show, he doesn't seem to be very happy to admit it.

1) A, Alexandrinus, 5th century, "'The Gospels," says Kenyon, "show signs of the Antiochan revision." (!!)

Hills says, "Another witness to the early existence of the Traditional text is Codex A (Codex Alexandrinus). This venerable manuscript, which dates from the fifth century, has played a very important role in the history of New Testament textual criticism. It was given to the King of England in 1627 by Cyril Lucar, patriarch of Constantinople, and for many years was regarded as the oldest extant New Testament manuscript. In Acts and the Epistles Codex A agrees most closely with the Alexandrian text of the B and Aleph type, but in the Gospels it agrees generally with **the Traditional text**. Thus in the Gospels Codex A testifies to the antiquity of the **Traditional text**." [Byzantine]

2) C, Ephraemi, 5th century, Strouse speaks of its mixed text, but also describes it as being **"pro-Byzantine"**. Kenyon speaks of its Byzantine portions as being due to its "correctors".

3) W, Washingtonianus, 4th or 5th centuries.

It is now housed in the Freer Gallery of Art in Washington, DC. It contains the four Gospels in the Western order, Matthew, John, Luke, Mark. In John and the first third of Luke the text is Alexandrian in character. In Mark the text is of the Western type in the first five chapters and of a mixed "Caesarean" type in the remaining chapters. The especial value of W, however, lies in Matthew and the last two thirds of Luke. Here the text is **Traditional (Byzantine)** of a remarkably pure type. According to Sanders, in Matthew the text of W is of the Kappa 1 type, which von Soden (1906) regarded as the oldest and best form of the Traditional (Byzantine) text.

The discovery of W tends to disprove the thesis of Westcott and Hort that the Traditional text is a fabricated text which was put together in the fourth century by a group of scholars residing At Antioch. For Codex W is a very ancient manuscript. B. P. Grenfell regarded it as "probably fourth century." Other scholars have dated it in the 5th century. Hence W is one of the oldest complete manuscripts of the Gospels in existence, possibly of the same age as Aleph. Moreover, W seems to have been written in Egypt, since during the first centuries of its existence it seems to have been the property of the Monastery of the Vinedresser, which was located near the third pyramid. If the Traditional text had been invented at Antioch in the 4th century, how would it have found its way into Egypt and thence into Codex W so soon thereafter? Why would the scribe of W writing in the 4th or early 5th century, have adopted this newly fabricated text in Matthew and Luke in preference to other texts which (according to Hort's hypothesis) were older and more familiar to him? Thus the presence of the Traditional text in W indicates that this text is a very ancient text and that it was known in Egypt before the 4th century. (Hills).

4) N, Purpureus, 6th century, Portions of the four Gospels, "The text is of **Byzantine type**, in a rather early stage of its evolution". (Kenyon)

5) O, Sinapensis, 6th century, Matthew 13 - 24, **Byzantine**, "Akin to N."

6) Signa, Rossanensis, 6th century, Matthew and Mark, **Byzantine**, "A sister V6 of N."

7) Phi, Beratinus, 6th century, Matthew and Mark, **Byzantine**.

To these we may add the vast majority of the remaining uncial MSS (latest total number is 267) and most of several hundreds of uncial fragments. I believe the number was 320 in 1980."[1] [All Byzantine]

WHY SOME UNCIALS SURVIVED; AND THE MINUSCULE WITNESSES

We have now arrived at the 8th to the 10th century when the uncial (majuscule) script was traded in for the minuscule (cursive) script. Some would have us believe that this change in script was "bad" because 1. It was a "change", and 2. The wrong Received Text-type was handed down. Therefore, the older uncial manuscripts would be a better representation of the 'true' text-type. Just because the older text-type has a higher percentage of THE naturalist's preferred text-types does not make them closer to the 'true ' text-type. The most likely possibility is that the old uncials were not used because they were recognized as a corrupted text and placed on the shelf.

"Burgon regarded the good state of preservation of B and Aleph in spite of their exceptional age as a proof not of their goodness but of their badness. If they had been good manuscripts, they would have been read to pieces long ago. Thus the fact that B and Aleph are so old is a point against them, not something in their favor. It shows that the Church rejected them and did not read them. Otherwise they would have worn out and disappeared through much reading. Burgon has been accused of sophistry in arguing this way, but certainly his suggestion cannot be rejected by naturalistic critics as impossible. For one of their own poets (Dr. Hills refers to Kirsop Lake in the *Harvard Theological Review*, Vol. 21, 1928, pp. 347-349) favored the idea that the scribes **'usually destroyed their exemplars when they had copied the sacred books."[2]** [my emphasis] This completes Dr. Moorman's section.

The question that needs to be asked of the reader at this point is, "How is your modern Bible printed on better paper holding up?" If you have been reading your Bible a lot it probably shows a lot of wear.

The latest count available to me shows there are 2764 minuscule (cursive) MSS. Even the naturalist Kenyon reports the vast majority is the common

---

[1] Ibid. pp. 89-92
[2] Fuller, D.D.; David Otis; *True or False?;* p. 14

ecclesiastical text. [Received Text].[1]

The naturalist textual scholar would also have one believe that all the text-type of the Received Text are copied from the alleged 4th century recension of Lucian, which is part of Westcott and Hort's textual theory. In other words they report direct genealogy based on the flawed W/H theory. Wilbur Pickering reports on the studies and conclusions of Lake, Blake, and New.

"They looked **for evidence of direct genealogy and found virtually none.** I repeat their conclusion:

...the manuscripts which we have are almost all orphan children without brothers or sisters. Taking this fact into consideration along with the negative result of our collation of MSS at Sinai, Patmos, and Jerusalem, it is hard to resist the conclusion that the scribes usually destroyed their exemplars when they had copied the sacred books."[2]

MANY WITNESSES TO THE RECEIVED TEXT

It sounds like the Alexandrian [naturalist] textual scholars have "shot themselves in the foot", and they are going to continue hopping around trying to find a solution to the Traditional [Received] Text. We will put one more nail into the coffin of the "late" recension and give additional support to the universality of the Received Text among the cursives [minuscules]. Pickering believed a reading should be attested to by a wide variety of witnesses meaning "in the first place, many geographical areas, but also different kinds of witnesses—MSS, Fathers, Versions, and Lectionaries." He said Burgon addressed the idea of variety in regards to both aspects:

"Variety distinguishing witness massed together must needs constitute a most powerful argument for believing such Evidence to be true. Witnesses of different kinds; from different countries; speaking different tongues:--witnesses who can never have met, and between whom it is incredible that there should exist collusion of any kind:--such witnesses deserve to be listened to most respectfully. Indeed, when witnesses of so varied a sort agree in large numbers, they must needs be accounted worthy of even implicit confidence... Variety it is which imparts virtue to mere Number, prevents the witness-box from being filled with packed deponents, ensures genuine

[1] Moorman, Jack; *Forever Settled; p. 93*
[2] Pickering, Th.D., Wilbur; *The Identity of the New Testament Text;* p.129

testimony. False witness is thus detected and condemned, because it agrees not with the rest. Variety is the consent of independent witnesses,...

It is precisely this consideration which constrains us to pay supreme attention to the combined testimony of the Unicials and of the whole body of the Cursive Copies. They are (a) dotted over at least 1000 years: (b) they evidently belong to so many divers countries,--Greece, Constantinople, Asia Minor, Palestine, Syria, Alexandria, and other part of Africa, not to say Sicily, Southern Italy, Gaul, England and Ireland: (c) they exhibit so many strange characteristics and peculiar sympathies: (d) they so clearly represent countless families of MSS., being in no single instance absolutely identical in their text, and certainly not being copies of any other Codex in existence,--that their unanimous decision I hold to be an absolutely irrefragable evidence of the Truth."[1]

LESS THAN 1% OF MINUSCULES ARE ALEXANDRIAN TEXT-TYPE

The preceding quote plus the following final information concerning the cursives (minuscules) should put two nails in the coffin of the naturalist, neutral textual critic's apparatus. Notice that in 1948 Kenyon's classic work mentioned above listed only 2401 cursives. The number now is 2764. There is not any known increase in the number of Alexandrian-type text in the newly found minuscules. He tried to depreciate Dean Burgon's information above by again saying in his [Kenyon's] work that the Received Text was a recension in Syria at the end of the fourth century. Kenyon could find only 22, yes, 22 minuscules which support their Alexandrian 'New' Testament Greek Text. Wilbur Pickering's rejoinder is:

"Assuming that when Kenyon says, "A good text of" he means that there is a fair amount of agreement with Vaticanus, or the Alexandrian text, and assuming that there are some similarities between the so-called Caesarean text and Alexandrian (Origen went to Caesarea after he left Alexandria), Kenyon is prepared to list only 22 that give even partial support to the "best" text. Twenty-two out of 2401!!

Are we to believe that in the language in which the New

---

[1] Ibid. p. 143

Testament was originally written (Greek), that only twenty-two examples of the true Word of God are to be found between the 9th and 16th centuries? How does this fulfill God's promise to preserve His Word? Why at that juncture when the uncial script was replaced by the minuscule were an overwhelming number of copies of the Received Text made, but practically none of the Alexandrian? We answer with a shout of triumph, God has been faithful to His promise. Yet in our day, the world has become awash with translations based on MSS similar to the twenty-two rather than the two and a half thousand."[1] [my emphasis]

HOW DID THE MANUSCRIPTS GET CORRUPTED

Now that we have established the two gates through which the MSS have passed, we need to review some more information. One naturally wonders how the corruption occurred and why. We have reviewed in a little detail at the beginning of this work the men of the wide gate, but there is a lot more information available. This information presents evidence as to how the text was corrupted and why. We will need to present a few more details and then we will examine the route or the path the 'new' Greek text took after Westcott and Hort.

Some other men who corrupted the Scripture besides Clement Of Alexandria, Origen, and Marcion were Justin Martyr and Tatian. Justin Martyr was a pagan philosopher who mixed pagan ideas with Christianity. He was born in 100 A.D. about the time of the Apostle John's death. He had a very limited view of the work of the cross in regard to atonement and propitiation.

"Newman indicates that to Justin, Christ's work on the cross was not so much to satisfy the Divine justice, but rather through such an example to enlighten men and turn them from the worship of demons to God."[2]

Justin Martyr taught Tatian who in turn committed many atrocities to the Scripture. Tatian wrote the *Diatessaron*:

"a Harmony of the Gospels,... meaning four in one. The Gospels were so notoriously corrupted by his hand that in later years a bishop of Syria, because of the errors, was obliged to throw out of his churches no less than two hundred copies of this Diatessaron, since church members were mistaking it for

---

[1] Moorman, Jack; *Forever Settled; p. 95*

[2] Ibid. p. 66

the true Gospel."[1]

After Justin's martyrdom Tatian became a follower of the Gnostic heresy. He instructed Clement of Alexandria who started the school at Alexandria which taught gnosticism.

"Clement expressly tells us that he would not hand down Christian teachings, pure and unmixed, but rather clouded with precepts of pagan philosophy. All the writings of the outstanding heretical teachers were possessed by Clement, and he freely quoted from their corrupted manuscripts as if they were the pure words of Scripture. His influence in the depravation of Christianity was tremendous. But his greatest contribution, undoubtedly, was the direction given to the studies and activities of Origen, his famous pupil.

When we come to Origen, we speak the name of him who did the most of all to create and give direction to the forces of apostasy down through the centuries. It was he who mightily influenced Jerome, the editor of the Latin Bible known as the Vulgate."[2]

The reader needs to remember that the original language MSS of the Received Text were translated into the language of most countries so that they would have access to the Words of God. The Wide Gate MSS were translated into other languages, also. The major representative of these translations is the Latin translation of Jerome called the Vulgate. This is the version which influenced many Bibles and affirmed Westcott and Hort's readings. We must add quickly, however, that this is the version whose readings were rejected by Erasmus and the KJB translators except for a limited number. Since this Bible is so important in the history of the two routes, MSS, and other translations, we will look at its author and his work carefully.

JEROME, ORIGEN, EUSEBIUS, AND THE ALEXANDRIAN TEXT

Jerome followed Eusebius by just a few years. Please recall Eusebius used the library at Caesarea established by Origen's student, Pamphilus. He was most likely the original author of the Vaticanus and Sinaiticus MSS which were copies the twenty-five Bibles prepared for Emperor Constantine around 325 A. D.

---

[1] Ibid. p. 98

[2] Ibid. p. 98

Jerome (b. 340 A. D.)closely followed Eusebius with the instructions by the Bishop of Rome to translate the Bible into Latin.

The following information by David Cloud is used with permission.

"Jerome (Sophronius: Eusebius Hieronymus) (340-420) was called upon by his friend Damasus, the Bishop of Rome (who was already exalting himself above his fellows and calling himself the pope), to produce a standard Latin Bible. This was completed between A.D. 383 and 405. JEROME "WAS BROUGHT UP WITH A DISLIKE FOR THE VULGAR [COMMON] EDITION OF THE GREEK, AND WITH A PREDILECTION FOR THE CORRECTED TEXT OF EUSEBIUS; having imbibed an early partiality for this edition, through Gregory of Nazianzum" (Nolan, p. 151).

Jerome rejected old Latin texts **which differed from** Eusebius and thus perpetuated certain textual corruptions in his version. His completed translation included nine spurious apocryphal books. Modern textual critic Bruce Metzger admits that the Greek manuscripts used by Jerome "APPARENTLY BELONGED TO THE ALEXANDRIAN TYPE OF TEXT" (Metzger, The Text of the New Testament, p. 76). THIS MEANS THEY WERE IN THE SAME FAMILY AS THOSE UNDERLYING THE MODERN VERSIONS. F.G. Kenyon, another influential 20th century textual scholar, affirms this by noting that the Vaticanus manuscript so preferred by Westcott and Hort and the English Revised Version of 1881 was the same type of text as that used by Origen and Jerome. "It [the Vaticanus] is the leading representative of the type of text which scholars associate with Alexandria, and of which Westcott and Hort thought so highly that they dubbed it 'neutral', and indeed made the Vaticanus the sheet-anchor of their edition. Powerfully supported in the main, by the quotations in Origen, and by Jerome in his revision of the Latin New Testament" (Kenyon, The Text of the Greek Bible, p. 88). Another 20th century textual critic, H. Wheeler Robinson, says that Jerome's translation was "corrected with the aid of ancient Greek codices of the Aleph B [Vaticanus] type" (Robinson, Ancient Versions of the English Bible, p. 113). **ALL OF THESE TEXTUAL SCHOLARS TELL US THAT THE JEROME LATIN VULGATE REPRESENTS THE SAME TYPE OF TEXT AS THE MODERN CRITICAL GREEK TEXT.** [my emphasis]

It is important to understand that Jerome was deeply infected with false teaching. As for his spirit and character, Jerome is described, even by a historian who had high respect for him, with these words: "such irritability and bitterness of temper, such vehemence of uncontrolled passion, such an intolerant and persecuting spirit, and such inconstancy of conduct" (Schaff, History of the Christian Church, III, p. 206).

Jerome followed the false teaching of asceticism, believing the state of celibacy to be spiritually superior to that of marriage, and demanding that church leaders be unmarried. James Heron, author of The Evolution of Latin Christianity, observed that "no single individual did so much to make monasticism popular in the higher ranks of society" (The Evolution of Latin Christianity, 1919, p. 58). Jerome believed in the veneration of "holy relics" and the bones of dead Christians (Heron, The Evolution of Latin: Christianity, 1919, pp. 276,77). He "took a leading and influential part in 'opening the floodgates' for the invocation of saints," teaching "distinctly and emphatically that the saints in heaven hear the prayers of men on earth, intercede on their behalf and send them help from above (Heron, pp. 287,88). Jerome taught that Mary was the counterpart of Eve, as Christ was the counterpart of Adam, and that through her obedience Mary became instrumental in helping to redeem the human race (Heron, p. 294). He also taught that Mary was a perpetual virgin (Heron, pp. 294,95). He believed in the blessing of water (Heron, p. 306).

Jerome had a particularly hateful attitude toward those who followed the simple apostolic Faith. His writings against these men, whom he falsely labeled "heretics," were characterized with the most vicious sort of language. He was "engaged in many violent and bitter controversies" (Heron, p. 58). Vigilantius, Jovinian, and Helvidius were some of the men upon whom Jerome railed. These men rejected the false traditions which were being added by the early leaders of the Roman Church, including enforced celibacy, worship of martyrs and relics, and the sinlessness and perpetual virginity of Mary. For such "heresies" Jerome heaped upon these men angry labels, calling them dogs, maniacs, monsters, asses, stupid fools, two-legged ass, gluttons, servants of the devil, madmen, useless vessels which should be shivered by the iron rod of Apostolic authority. He said Helvidius had a "fetid mouth, fraught with a putrid stench, against the relics and ashes of the martyrs." "The pen of Jerome was rendered very offensive by his grinding tyranny and crabbed temper. No matter how wrong he was, he could not brook contradiction" (Armitage, A History of the Baptists, I, p. 207). It is no wonder that a man with such a vicious tongue justified the death penalty for "heretics" (Heron, The Evolution of Latin: Christianity, p. 323).

It is interesting to note that Vigilantius, one of the men against whom Jerome railed, was identified by George Faber, diligent historian of the Waldenses and Albigenses, with the Waldensian Christians of northern Italy. In the year 406 Vigilantius published "a most uncompromising and decisive Treatise against the miserable growing superstitions of the age." "In this Treatise, he attacked the notion, that Celibacy is the duty of the Clergy: censured, as idolatrous, the excessive veneration of the Martyrs and the idle unscriptural figment that they are potent intercessors at the throne of grace: ridiculed the blind reverence, which was paid to their senseless and useless relics: exposed the gross folly of burning tapers, like the Pagans, before their shrines in broad day-light, detected the spurious miracles, which were said to be wrought by their inanimate remains, vilified the boasted sanctity of vainly gratuitous monachism, and pointed out the useless absurdity of pilgrimages, either to Jerusalem or to any other reputed sanctuary" (Faber, History of the Ancient Vallenses and Albigenses, 1838, pp. 291,292).

Jerome composed a reply to Vigilantius "in which, it is hard to say, whether illogical absurdity or brutal scurrility is the most predominant."George Faber makes the following important remarks about the conflict between Vigilantius and Jerome "To the ecclesiastical student, the sentiments of Vigilantius are familiar and their complete identity with those of the Vallenses, in all ages, cannot have escaped his notice. He wrote from a region, situated between the waves of the Adriatic and the Alps of King Cottius . Now this district, on the eastern side of the Cottian Alps, is the precise country of the Vallenses. Hither their ancestors retired, during the persecutions of the second and third and fourth centuries here, providentially secluded from the world, **they retained the precise doctrines and practices of the Primitive Church endeared to them by suffering and exile;** [my emphasis] while the wealthy inhabitants of cities and fertile plains, corrupted by a now opulent and gorgeous and powerful Clergy, were daily sinking deeper and deeper into that apostasy which has been so graphically foretold by the great Apostle and, here, as we learn through the medium of an accidental statement of Jerome, Vigilantius took up his abode, at the beginning of the fifth century, among a people, who, Laics [laity] and Bishops alike, agreed with him in his religious sentiments, and joyfully received him as a brother.

Jerome, nurtured in the adulterate Christianity of opulent cities and fanatic monks and lordly prelates, is amazed, yea horrified, at the alpine audacity of Vigilantius. 'What,' cries Jerome, scandalized to the last pitch of endurance, 'does the Roman Bishop, then, do ill, who offers sacrifices to the Lord over the bones of dead men; the bones, I trow, of Peter and of Paul bones, in our estimation, venerable; bones, in thy estimation, a mere worthless portion of dust? Does the Bishop of Rome do ill, who deems their tombs the altars of Christ? Are the Bishops, not merely of a single city, but of the whole world, all mistaken because, despising the huckster Vigilantius, they reverently enter into the stately cathedrals of the dead?'" (italics in original) (Faber, History of the Ancient Vallenses, pp. 293,94,98).

We would gladly answer Jerome's question. Yes, a thousand times, yes. Vigilantius, and his Christian friends in the Alps, were correct, and your apostate bishops were all wrong! We do not believe Vigilantius was a huckster. It is more likely that he was a sincere man of God who was being faithful to the Lord Jesus Christ and the Faith once delivered to the saints.

This is a fascinating bit of information. New Testament prophecies describe two separate streams of "Christianity" operating side by side through the church age. First, there will be true apostolic churches, against which the gates of hell shall not prevail. They will be persecuted, hated, despised, yet they will continue century by century until Christ's return. Jesus promised His faithful ones: "Lo, I am with you alway, even to the end of the world" (Matthew 28:20). Second, there will be apostate churches, which will increase and grow worse and worse as the centuries pass (2 Thess. 2:3; 2 Tim. 3:13; Matt. 24:4,5,11,24; 2 Pet. 2:1-22; 1 John 4:1-6; Jude 4-19; Rev. 17:1-18). The parables of Christ in Matthew 13 depict the course of this present "church age," and they describe a progression of apostasy. **The parable of the leaven, for example, depicts a woman putting leaven into three measures of meal, "till the whole was leavened." Leaven in Scripture stands for sin and error (1 Cor. 5:6; Gal. 5:9). Thus the parable tells us that the error which was introduced by false teachers during the days of the Apostles will gradually increase through the centuries until all the churches are leavened. The ultimate fulfillment of this we see in Revelation 17.**[my emphasis]

Returning to the battle between the Bible-believing Vigilantius and the pre-Romanist Jerome: in the early fifth century, in this one event we see the two aspects of prophecy pertaining to the course of the "church age" being fulfilled side by side: On the one hand, there were genuine New Testament Christians, seeking to maintain the apostolic faith, and standing boldly against apostasy. On the other hand, there were apostates, fearlessly adding their extra-biblical traditions and practices to the Word of God, and persecuting those who resisted their heresies.

It is obvious that Jerome had imbibed many of the false teachings and attitudes which eventually became the entrenched dogmas and practices of the Roman Catholic Church. It was not possible, therefore, that he possessed the Holy Spirit discernment necessary to transmit the purest version of the Scriptures. Even so, the Jerome Latin Vulgate became the Bible adopted by the Roman Catholic Church. The Council of Trent eventually declared it to be the one and only authoritative edition of the Bible, and other versions were condemned. This does not mean that the Jerome Vulgate was accepted by all Christians. Far from it. "Notwithstanding the high reputation of Jerome it was but slowly adopted by the Western Churches, which still persevered in retaining the primitive version" (Nolan, Inquiry into the Integrity of the Greek Vulgate, p. 152). "Jerome was reviled throughout the West for his labors, and it was not until after Gregory the Great had given it his formal approval (about 600

A.D.) that his recension came into general use in the Roman Church" (Vedder, Our New Testament, 1908, p. 297). The separated Christians kept the old Latin versions: "the older Latin remained popular for centuries. German Christians still quoted from these versions in the ninth century; the English and Spaniards in the tenth; and in the French: province of Languedoc the Old Latin Psalter was still in use in the twelfth century. Indeed, Jerome's Latin Bible was not given its familiar label 'Vulgate' (implying common use) until the thirteenth century" (Frank, The Bible through the Ages, p. 138). "THE OLD LATIN VERSIONS WERE USED LONGEST BY THE WESTERN CHRISTIANS WHO WOULD NOT BOW TO THE AUTHORITY OF ROME e.g., the Donatists; the Irish in Ireland, Britain, and the continent; the Albigenses, etc." (Jacobus, Roman Catholic and Protestant Bibles Compared, 1908, p. 200, note 15). "Commentators such as Aelfric and Dunstan in the tenth century employed [the old Latin translations] as the basis of their commentaries" (Robinson, Ancient Versions of the English Bible, p. 116). There are copies of Old Latin manuscripts and fragments in existence which date to the 13th century, "thus proving that the Old-Latin was still copied long after it had gone out of general use" (Robinson, The Bible in Its Ancient and English Versions, p. 104). Furthermore, as we shall see, the separated Christians were not dependent completely on Latin, for they often had their own translations in the vernacular languages.

We must emphasize that the term "Latin Vulgate:" has been used in a number of different ways. The term "vulgate" itself means "common" or "received." It originally applied to the old Latin translation(s) which predated the Jerome version. In modern times, though, it has most frequently been used to describe the Jerome version and its successors. For our purposes we can summarize these modern usages into two general categories. First, the term "Latin Vulgate" is used to refer to the Jerome Latin translation itself. Beyond generalizations, it is difficult to know the precise form of that version. The oldest copy of a Latin Vulgate fragment (the Gospels) alleged to be of the Jerome type dates to 500 A.D. The oldest complete New Testament of the Jerome type that we have dates to 546 A.D. [the Codex Fuldensis (F), written by Victor of Capua; Robinson, p. 120]. Second, the term "Latin Vulgate" commonly refers to the tradition of the Latin Bible within the Roman Catholic Church. In a general sense the Roman Catholic Latin Vulgate dates back to Jerome's version, but it never had a settled form. One of the chief features of Rome's Latin Vulgate, in fact, was that it was constantly changing.

In describing Catholic history in the centuries following the creation of the Jerome Vulgate, Albert Gilmore notes, "The languages of the early Bibles, Hebrew and Greek, were no longer of interest. So marked did this lack of interest become that when, after the Renaissance, Cardinal Ximenes published his Polyglot edition with the Latin Vulgate between the Greek and Hebrew versions of the Old Testament, he stated in his preface that it was 'like Jesus between two thieves'" (Gilmore, The Bible: Beacon Light of History, 1935, p. 170).

A few centuries after the Apostles, the Latin language became a dead language in regard to the common man, and only the very educated could understand it. Even so, Rome continued century after century to use only Latin for its theological training, its liturgy, and its Bible. Its attitude toward those who would put the Bible and sound Bible teaching into the language of the people is evident in the following pages. Rome did not authorize any vernacular language translations in the major languages of Europe until the 17th century (and these were not widely distributed), and it did not allow the mass to be performed in the common languages until the latter half of the 20th century! The Holy Spirit at Pentecost gave the wonderful message of God in the manifold tongues of the people, but Rome has sought to hide the Word of God in a dead language. (We aren't implying, of course, that Rome's liturgy is the true Word of God, but that is a separate issue.) It is also important to note that the Latin Vulgate was not in a settled state until the end of the 16th century, long after Rome had pronounced it authentic, and the text has remained fluid until today. We have mentioned this in passing, but we want to emphasize the point. Bruce Metzger describes the history of the Jerome: Vulgate in this way: "It was inevitable that, in the course of the transmission of the text of Jerome's revision, scribes would corrupt his original work, sometimes by careless transcription and sometimes by deliberate conflation with copies of the Old Latin version. In order to purify Jerome's text a number of recensions or editions were produced during the Middle Ages; notable among these were the successive efforts of Alcuin, Theodulf, Lanfranc, and Stephen Harding.

Unfortunately, however, each of these attempts to restore Jerome's original version resulted eventually in still further textual corruption through mixture of the several types of Vulgate text which had come to be associated with various European centers of scholarship" (Metzger, The Text of the New Testament, p. 76). Metzger assumes that the Jerome Vulgate was a pure text and that it gradually became impure through intermixing with the old Latin translations and other sources. We believe it is more likely that the Jerome edition was impure because it was based upon impure texts similar to the corrupt Vaticanus and the Sinaiticus manuscripts.

In spite of the pontifications of the Council of Trent, which proclaimed the Vulgate the sole authentic edition of the Scriptures, it was not until more than forty years later that a settled edition of the Latin

Vulgate appeared. A papal commission worked for more than 40 years after Trent, but failed to produce an authentic edition. Frustrated by the slow progress of this commission, Pope Sixtus V (1585-1590) took matters into his own hands and produced his own revision, which appeared in May 1590. This edition of the Latin Vulgate was prefaced by a papal bull which identified the Sixtus edition as "true, legitimate, authentic, and undoubted in all public and private debates, readings, preachings, and explanations; and that anyone who ventured to change it without papal authority would incur the wrath of God Almighty of the blessed apostles Peter and Paul" (Jacobus, p. 12). Sixtus died three months later, and, as we shall see, his successors were not impressed with his papal threats! There was a small problem. The Sixtus Latin Vulgate was full of errors, "some two thousand of them introduced by the pope himself" (Janus, The Pope and the Council, 1870). In September 1590 the College of Cardinals stopped all sales and bought up and destroyed as many copies as possible! [It is interesting to note in passing that the Vaticanus Greek manuscript from the Vatican library was "fully used by Carafa for Pope Sixtus V's Septuagint in 1587" (Kenyon, The Text of the Greek Bible, p. 87).] The three popes which followed Sixtus did not live long enough to accomplish much. Urban VII was pope for only two weeks. Gregory XIV lasted ten months. Innocent IX died after only two months in office. Clement VIII (1592-1605) followed, and it was he who issued a new edition of the Latin Vulgate in 1592. The names of both Sixtus V and Clement VIII appeared on the title page. This is known as the Clementine Bible. It contained "more than 3,000 alterations from the text of Sixtus whole passages being omitted or introduced, and the verses being divided differently" (Jacobus, p. 13). The Clementine Bible came with its own papal bull "which specified among other things that, as before, no words of the text might be altered, that no various readings might be registered in the margin, and that all copies were to be conformed to it" (Jacobus, Roman Catholic and Protestant Bibles, p. 13). This is exactly what Pope Sixtus had pontificated some two years and three thousand changes earlier! The point is that Rome's Latin Vulgate, that alleged "authentic edition of the Scriptures," was in a constant state of flux throughout the centuries."[1]

    This concludes Dr. Cloud's section on Jerome and the Latin Vulgate, which

---

[1] Cloud, David; *Rome and the Bible: The History of the Bible Through the Centuries and Rome's Persecution of It;*, 1996; Way of Life Literature, Port Huron, MI. The various texts concerning Jerome are confusing. As the author of this work was preparing information on Jerome, the confusion in the texts caused him to utter a prayer; then my computer indicated an e-mail had arrived, and it was this quote on Jerome. Full, complete and the right Words!

was used with permission.

THE WESTCOTT/HORT TEXT-TYPE OF 1881 IS THE TEXT-TYPE OF ORIGEN, EUSEBIUS, AND JEROME TRANSMITTED TO THE 'NEW' VERSIONS

Returning to "The Wide Gate: The Manuscripts" and the 'new' Greek text of Westcott and Hort in 1881, which was constructed from the handful of corrupted texts coming out of Egypt, we will trace the route of the W/H text. The manuscripts that the Latin Vulgate was based upon are the same manuscripts used by Westcott and Hort. How the text of Westcott and Hort became so widely accepted is still a mystery to me. I can only remind the reader that the Scripture specifically warns of those who would lead one astray contrary to the doctrine taught in the Scripture "by good words and fair speeches".

Since Westcott and Hort held such prominent scholarly positions they were probably able to woo, threaten and challenge those near and far. Once other scholars start down that slippery slope, it becomes a mountain in the way of turning back.

Romans 16:17-18 *Now I beseech you, brethren, mark them which cause divisions and offences **contrary to the doctrine** which ye have learned; and avoid them. For they that are such serve not our Lord Jesus Christ, but their own belly; and by good words and fair speeches deceive the hearts of the simple.* [my emphasis]

After Westcott and Hort published and released the [English] Revised Version (ERV), five days later they released the 'New' Greek Text they had spent 10 years constructing. The critical apparatus that they used in 'developing' the Greek Text had taken them 30 years to construct. That apparatus allowed them to overthrow the Received Text and to base their Greek text on the handful of old MSS. Therefore the ERV is a translation based on **their** Greek Text. In order for a translation to be anywhere near what God would want His people to know, the translation would have to be based on the right foundation or Greek Text or the preserved Words of God in the original languages. The course their Greek Text took is interesting but at the same time sad. To help with this part of the history of the patient, a chart was constructed called, *Bible Societies and the Route of the 'New' Testament Greek Text,* which may be found in the appendix.

AMERICA GETS INVOLVED

An agreement had been reached between the English (Great Britain) Revision Committee and the American Revision Committee which, to say the least, was interesting. The agreement stipulated that the American Standard Version (ASR) could not be released in America for 14 years.[1] This is astounding if Westcott and Hort had "recovered" the lost Words of God. How could one who loves the Lord Jesus Christ keep information from lost or hurting people? Was there a motive such as money involved? Was the delay agreed upon to allow the ERV time to get a toe-hold? We will never know for sure but an "arranged delay" is significant.

The ASR[2] (American Standard Revision) based on W/H Greek text was released on schedule in 1901, twenty years after the release of the ERV's New Testament and 16 years after the ERV' Old testament . You will recall from earlier discussion in this work, Philip Schaff was the chairperson of the ASR and has been cited with others on the committee for their apostasy. Dr. D. A. Waite said:

> **"The False Statement** of Dr. Philip Schaff about DOCTRINE Being Affected. Regarding "variant readings" in the Greek text, Dr. Schaff wrote:
> *"Only about 400 affect the sense; and of these 400 only about 50 are of real significance for one reason or another, and NOT ONE OF THESE 50 AFFECT AN ARTICLE OF FAITH or a precept of duty which is not abundantly sustained by other and undoubted passages, or by the whole tenor of Scripture teaching." [In his Companion To The Greek Testament And English Version as quoted in Bible Translations by Evangelist R. L. Sumner, p. 8, March, 1979]....* this is a completely untrue and misleading statement. Many of these variant readings "affect" many "ARTICLES OF FAITH" whether or not they are "sustained by other and undoubted passages." Schaff was an apostate in doctrine and practice; yet he was the Chairman of the AMERICAN STANDARD VERSION of 1901."[3]

---

[1] Hills, Th.D., Edward F.; *The King James Defended;* p. 226

[2] The ASV was further revised and republished in 1954 as the Revised Standard Version

[3] Waite, Th.D., Ph.D., D.A.; *Defending the King James Version;* p. 133

BIBLE SOCIETIES, VERSIONS, PERVERSIONS, AND THE GREEK TEXT

Now it is time to introduce the reader to the history of "Bible Societies" and their influence on the transmission of the "Wide Gate: Manuscripts", Greek Texts, and Bible Versions (translations). [please refer to the chart in the appendices, appendix 6] The British Foreign Bible Society (BFBS) was founded in 1804 at London Tavern on March 7. The BFSC has supported the Roman Catholic agenda from its inception.[1] The other incredible findings were: 1. They accepted the Unitarians, who **deny** the divinity of Jesus Christ, into their organizations. 2. They also refused to allow public prayer or Bible quotations at any of their meetings. The importance of this is such that the following two quotations will establish the truth of these statements. The first quotes are in regards to the Unitarians.

"When the constitution of the British and Foreign Bible Society was first formulated, it was understandably not foreseen that the question of Unitarianism would have much relevance to the society's work. Before long, however, UNITARIANS GAINED SUBSTANTIAL INFLUENCE UPON THE AFFAIRS OF THE BIBLE SOCIETY, PARTICULARLY IN EUROPE, WHERE SOME AUXILIARY SOCIETIES WERE RUN ALMOST EXCLUSIVELY BY PERSONS OF UNITARIAN BELIEFS" (Brown, *The Word of God Among All Nations,* p. 12).

It was the failure to secure a provision in the society's constitution to remove the Unitarian heretics which led to the formation of a separate organization in 1831, the Trinitarian Bible Society.

"The Trinitarian Bible Society was founded in 1831 after a period of controversy among supporters of the British and Foreign Bible Society regarding the constitution and policy of that Society. Deep concern was expressed over the lack of a Scriptural doctrinal basis sufficiently explicit to ensure that 'Unitarians' denying the Deity of the Lord Jesus Christ could not be admitted to membership or hold office in the Society. A motion recommending the adoption of such a basis was the subject of a prolonged and heated debate in Exeter Hall in the Strand, London, at the Annual Meeting. THE MOTION WAS

[1] Cloud, David, *Unholy Hands on God's Holy Book;* Way of Life Literature, Port Huron, MI; 1999 edition; Part 1, p. 3

REJECTED BY A LARGE MAJORITY, but those who were deeply convinced that the decision was wrong from 'Provisional Committee' ... When it became clear that there was no prospect of bringing this about [the changing of the BFBS's unscriptural policies], the 'Provisional Committee' convened a meeting to establish a Bible Society on Scriptural principles" (*Trinitarian Bible Society Quarterly Record*, No. 475, April-June, 1981, p. 3)."[1]

Incidentally, the Trinitarian Bible Society has gone on to become a respected group and to adhere to godly principles. The second issue of prayer and Bible reading was addressed on May 5th, 1831 by the BFBS.

"There arose a question over the desirability of offering up prayer to God at meetings of the society, concerning which there was no provision in the society's constitution. Lack of such provision would perhaps not have led to serious disagreement were it not for the simultaneous problem about Unitarians. There was a feeling that public prayer to God, offered in the name of Christ, was being avoided for fear of giving offence to Unitarian members. ...

The committee was urged to call a special meeting of the society to settle the matter, but it refused to do so. Since the society's rules did not provide for the requisitioning of special meetings by the members, there was no option but to raise the matter at the next Anniversary Meeting, in May 1831. ... It was to be expected that, with these emotive issues occupying the minds of many people, the Anniversary Meeting would run into stormy weather. The meeting took place on Wednesday, May 4th, 1831, at the newly built Exeter Hall in the Strand. ...

On this occasion the annual report included a recommendation that oral prayer should not be introduced at meetings of the society, but made no explicit reference to the problem about Unitarians. ... At the conclusion of the seconder's speech, a degree of excitement seemed to pervade the Meeting ... J.E. Gordon immediately advanced from the northern end of the platform, and took his place on the right of the chair, amidst loud and continued applause. Several minutes passed before order was restored, and then Gordon spoke:

"If, instead of thus clapping your hands, you would lift up your hands to the throne of grace, I must take the liberty of saying, you would perform an act more becoming a Christian Society. ... The first portion which I seek to establish is, that the

---

[1] *Ibid.* p. 3

British and Foreign Bible Society is preeminently a religious and Christian Institution, and that no person rejecting the doctrine of the triune Jehovah. ..." --interrupted by thunders of applause, which lasted several minutes, BUT WHICH WERE IMMEDIATELY REPLIED TO BY MOST DETERMINED HISSING FROM VARIOUS PARTS OF THE MEETING.

When order was restored, Gordon resumed his speech: "...That no person rejecting the doctrine of the triune Jehovah can be considered a member of a Christian institution. Thirdly, that in conformity with this principle, the expression 'denominations of Christians' in the Ninth General Law of the Society, by distinctly understood to include such denominations of Christians only as profess their belief in the doctrine of the Holy Trinity."

He went on to say that he would not at present raise the question of opening meetings with prayer, as this would be an utter waste of time if the proposition about non-Trinitarians was not at first accepted. When he sought to justify his arguments by quoting from Scripture, HE WAS MET BY REPEATED INTERRUPTIONS AND HECKLING FROM PART OF THE AUDIENCE. THE CHAIRMAN, LORD BEXLEY, SIDED WITH THE INTERRUPTERS AND RESTRAINED GORDON FROM CITING SCRIPTURE, ON THE GROUNDS THAT TO COMMENT ON THE SCRIPTURE WAS "TO GO AGAINST THE PRINCIPLE OF THE INSTITUTION."

A general uproar ensued which the Rev. William Howels vainly tried to calm ... Gordon was seconded by the Rev. George Washington Phillips ... Amid scenes of wild disorder, one speaker after another failed to make themselves heard. ... AT THE END OF THE MEETING, WHICH LASTED FIVE AND A HALF HOURS, GORDON'S PROPOSALS WERE VOTED ON BY A SHOW OF HANDS, AND REJECTED BY A MAJORITY ESTIMATED AT 6 TO 1 (Brown, *The Word of God Among All Nations,* pp. 12-16, quoting *The Record*, May 5th, 1831).

Could anything be stranger than this true history of the British Bible Society? What a shameful, sad account! Here we have professing Christians hissing at and heckling a man of God who had made a simple proposition that those who deny the Triune God should have no part in that God's business! Do not forget that these were supposed Christian leaders and men involved in Bible translation and distribution. Here we have a Bible Society refusing to allow the Bible to be quoted, saying such is against their principles! Here we have a Bible Society having to fight a great battle just to have public prayer allowed in their meetings! And here we have a Bible Society, within 30 years of its founding, voting 6 to 1 against separating from Bible- and Christ-denying Unitarians!"[1]

The American Bible Society (ABS) did not do any better. There were continuous arguments concerning Baptizo (Baptism) and the need for revision of the "common English translation", the KJV, as reported by Thomas Armitage in his 1890 work, *History of the Baptist* in his section on Bible Societies. That this would happen is not surprising since the Roman Catholics were involved from the very beginning in 1816 with the ABS, also.

"It is also acknowledged that Roman Catholic churchmen were invited to participate in the founding of the American Bible Society in 1816" ("The Bible Societies," *Trinitarian Bible Society Quarterly Record*, Jan.-Mar., 1979, pp. 13-14)."[2]

The British Foreign Bible Society and the American Bible Society joined forces in 1946 to become the United Bible Society (UBS). The Greek Text that this organization has supported has been the Greek Text that is a descendant of the Westcott/Hort Greek Text. The UBS has supported the continued revision of this Greek Text. Its third edition of the Greek Text was amalgamated with the descendant of Erdhard Nestle's 1898 Greek text called the Nestle-Aland 26th Edition. So when you hear someone speak of the UBS 3rd Edition or the Nestle-Aland 26th Edition, they are speaking of the same Greek Text. Why is this so important? There are several reasons:

1. The Nestle-Aland Text has undergone 26 editions in 81 years or the average of a new edition every 3.1 years. Wow!

2. The NASB, prior to Nestle's 26th edition, was based on Nestle's 21st edition. That edition [the 21st] has been discarded because the findings of the newest papyri have shown that in over 500 places the Received Text was the right reading all along.[3]

3. The editions of the UBS or the Nestle-Aland Greek text or the W/H text are the 'original language' texts used by all modern versions such as: the NASB (New American Standard Bible), NIV (New International Version), TEV (Todays English Version or aka the Good News Bible, NEB (New English Bible), The Living Bible, The Message, Revised Standard Version, New Living Translation, New Revised Standard Version, Revised

---

[1] Ibid. p. 4

[2] Ibid. p. 3

[3] Riplinger, Gail, *Which Bible is God's Words?*; Hearthstone Publishing, Ltd, Oklahoma City, OK; ISBN 1-879366-81-9; p. 69

English Bible, and all modern common language versions. The magazine, *Christianity Today,* recently called for yet another translation even though one new version is coming out every 6 months. The only redeeming thought in the article was that they criticized the new versions saying:

"The problem with...(i.e., most modern translations) is that they prevent the reader from inferring biblical meaning because they change what the Bible said."[1]

4. It is very important that the reader know and understand who the editors of the UBS 'New" Greek Text are and what they believe. The editors are:

EDITOR'S OF THE 'NEW' GREEK TEXT; SURPRISE; ROME; AND APOSTASY

1.   Carlo Maria Martini:

He is the current Roman Catholic Archbishop of Milan. His diocese is the largest in the Roman Catholic Church containing over 2000 priests and five million parishioners.

"*Time* magazine article reported that **Martini brought together a syncretistic convocation of over 100 religious leaders from around the world to promote a new age, one-world religion.** In addressing this meeting, Mikhail Gorbachev said, "We need to synthesize a new religion for thinking men that will universalize that religion for the world and lead us into a new age.... He is Professor of New Testament Textual Criticism at the Pontifical Biblical Institute in Rome. He is also President of the Council of European Bishop's Conferences. *Time* magazine, December 26, 1994, listed him as a possible candidate in line for the papacy"[2]

Surprise, he is the chairman!

2.   Bruce Manning Metzger:

He is the professor of New Testament Language and Literature, Princeton Theological Seminary, and is on the board of the ABS. He is head of the translation committee for the RSV. The RSV was condemned in 1952 for its 'modernism'. "Today its chief editor sometimes is invited to speak at Evangelical forums. The RSV hasn't changed, but Evangelicalism certainly

---

[1] Christianity Today, *We Really do need Another Translation;* Oct, 2001 issue
[2] Cloud, David; *Unholy Hands on God's Holy Bible*; p. 8

has!"[1]

He was the chairman of the Reader's Digest Condensed Bible which was so horrible. Metzger questioned almost every sacred belief about the books of the Bible. He questioned the inspiration and authorship of Daniel, Peter, and the Pentateuch. Here are some of his statements:

"**Genesis**: "Nearly all modern scholars agree that, like the other books of the Pentateuch, [Genesis] is a composite of several sources, embodying traditions that go back in some cases to Moses."

Exodus: "As with Genesis, several strands of literary tradition, some very ancient, some as late as the sixth century B.C., were combined in the makeup of the books" (Introduction to Exodus).

Deuteronomy: "It's compilation is generally assigned to the seventh century B.C., though it rests upon much older tradition, some of it from Moses' time."

Daniel: "Most scholars hold that the book was compiled during the persecutions (168-165 B.C.) of the Jewish people by Antiochus Epiphanes."

John: "Whether the book was written directly by John, or indirectly (his teachings may have been edited by another), the church has accepted it as an authoritative supplement to the story of Jesus' ministry given by the other evangelists."

1 Timothy, 2 Timothy, Titus: "Judging by differences in style and vocabulary from Paul's other letters, **many modern scholars think that the Pastorals were not written by Paul**."

James: "Tradition ascribes the letter to James, the Lord's brother, writing about A.D. 45, but **modern opinion is uncertain**, and differs widely on both origin and date."

2 Peter: "Because the author refers to the letters of Paul as 'scripture,' a term apparently not applied to them until long after Paul's death, **most modern scholars think that this letter was drawn up in Peter's name** sometime between A.D. 100 and 150."

NOTES ON PSALM 22: "22:12-13: ... **the meaning of the third line [they have pierced my hands and feet] is obscure**." [Editor: No, it is not obscure; it is a prophecy of Christ's crucifixion!] [my emphasis]

Bruce Metzger is a heretic. He piously claims on one hand that the Bible is the inspired Word of God; but out of the other

---

[1] Ibid. p. 10

side of the mouth he claims the Bible is filled with myth and error. He denies the Bible's history, its miracles, and its authorship, while, in true liberal style, declaring that this denial does not do injustice to the Word of God, because, he says, the Bible is not "written for history but for religion" and is not to be read "with a dull prosaic and literalistic mind"! Metzger has been called an Evangelical by some who should know better, but upon the authority of the man's own writings, I declare that Bruce Metzger is an unbeliever. He is a false teacher. He is an apostate. He is a heretic. Those are all Bible terms. Having studied many of the man's works, I am convinced those are the terms that must be applied to him. One Baptist writer cautiously defended Metzger to me with these words—"he did write a superb pamphlet in 1953 refuting the Jehovah's Witnesses and defending the full and absolute deity of Christ." Even the Pope of Rome defends the full and absolute deity of Christ. A man can defend the deity of Christ and still be a false teacher. A man who denies the written Word also denies the Living Word. They stand or fall together. If the Bible contains error, Christ was a liar. If Christ is perfect Truth, so is the Bible."[1]

3. <u>Eugene Nida</u>:

"**As to the atonement of Jesus Christ**, Nida says, "Most scholars, both Protestant and Roman Catholic, interpret the references to the redemption of the believer by Jesus Christ, not as evidence of any commercial transaction by any *quid pro quo* between Christ and God or between the 'two natures of God' (his love and his justice), but as a figure of the 'cost,' in terms of suffering" (Eugene Nida and Charles Taber, *Theory and Practice*, 1969, p. 53). In *A Translator's Handbook on Paul's Letter to the Romans*, Nida (with co-author Barclay Newman) says, "...'blood' is used in this passage [Romans 3:25] in the same way that it is used in a number of other places in the New Testament, that is, to indicate a violent death. ... Although this noun [propitiation] (and its related forms) is sometimes used by pagan writers in the sense of propitiation (that is, an act to appease or placate a god), it is never used this way in the Old Testament."

Nida is wrong. The sacrifice of Christ was not just a figure; it WAS a placation of God, of His holiness and of the righteous demands in His law. Christ's sacrifice WAS a commercial transaction between Christ and God, and was NOT merely a

---

[1] Ibid. p 11-12

figure of the cost in terms of suffering. The sacrifice of Calvary was a true sacrifice, and that sacrifice required the offering of blood—not just a violent death as Nida says. Blood is blood and death is death, and we believe that God is wise enough to know which of these words should be used. Romans 5:8-10 teaches us that salvation required BOTH the blood and death of Christ. Had Christ died, for example, by strangulation, though it would have been a violent death, it would not have atoned for sin because blood is required. Those, like Nida, who tamper with or reinterpret the blood atonement often *claim* to believe in the cross of Christ and in justification by grace, but they are rendering the Cross ineffective by reinterpreting its meaning. There is no grace without a true propitiation. This word means "satisfaction" and refers to the fact that the sin debt was satisfied by the blood atonement of Christ. The great difference between the heathen concept of propitiating God and that of the Bible is this—the God of the Bible paid the propitiation Himself through His own Sacrifice, whereas the heathen thinks that he can propitiate God through his own human labors and offerings. The fact remains, though, that God did have to be propitiated through the bloody death of His own sinless Son.

...Nida says **Bible language was not given of God** but was determined by the writers of the Bible.

"Nida and Taber state that Paul, if he had been writing for us rather than for his original audience, would not only have written in a different language-form, but also would have said the same things differently" (Jakob Van Bruggen, citing Nida and Charles Taber, *Theory and Practice of Translation*, p. 23, n. 3).

Nida does not believe the Bible's own confession about its nature. In 2 Peter 1:21 we read that "the prophecy came not in old time by the will of man: but holy men of God spake as they were moved by the Holy Ghost." Since the Bible writers did not choose their words, it is heretical to say they would write in a different language form if they were writing today. Paul's words did not arise from his own will and context but were Revelations from Heaven and were written in words chosen by God. "But I certify you, brethren, that the gospel which was preached of me is not after man. For I neither received it of man, neither was I taught it, but by the revelation of Jesus Christ" (Gal. 1:11-12). See also 1 Corinthians 2:10-13, where Paul states that the very words of New Testament Revelation are of God."

Nida says there are **no absolutes in Christianity** except

God.

"The only absolute in Christianity is the triune God. Anything which involves man, who is finite and limited, must of necessity be limited, and hence relative. Biblical culture relativism is an obligatory feature of our incarnational religion, for without it we would either absolutize human institutions or relativize God" (Eugene Nida, *Customs and Cultures*, New York: Harper & Row, 1954, p. 282, footnote 22).

Nida puts everything which man has touched in the category of imperfection, even the Bible and the institutions of described in Scripture, such as the tabernacle, the priesthood, and the church. Nida is wrong. The Bible, though written by fallible man, is infallible Revelation.

Nida says **Bible translation is to be tested by the response of non-Christians and by youth**.

"Nida and Taber describe the difference between an earlier concept of translating and their own concept as a shift of the focus from the 'form of the message' to the 'response of the receptor'; therefore the translator must now determine in particular the response of the receptor to the translated message (p. 1). Here it is not a matter of an abstraction, such as 'The English-speaking person,' but it is a matter of real individuals that appears when Nida and Taber desire that translations be attuned to non-Christians and to youth (pp. 31-32), and be tested by the potential users (p. 163)" (Van Bruggen, citing Nida and Taber, *Theory and Practice of Translation*).

Nida has things backwards. How could unsaved people and young people determine if a Bible is an accurate translation of the preserved Greek and Hebrew text of Scripture? They don't have the ability, spiritually or educationally, to make such a determination. The Bible plainly says the unsaved cannot understand God's Word (1 Cor. 2:12-14). It is the translator's job to make an accurate Bible translation. It is then the job of evangelists and teachers to help people understand the Bible.

Nida's erroneous view of the Bible is his foundational heresy, and this heresy alone is justification for God's people to mark and avoid him (Romans 16:17). It is very strange to see people who profess to accept the Bible as the inerrant Word of God following the teachings of men who deny this precious doctrine."[1]

---

[1] Ibid; selections from p. 8-10

Eugene Nida is the person most responsible for abandoning the concept of verbal equivalent (VE) and formal equivalent (FE) translation. This concept is: the priority of the translator is to translate God's Words as close to the meaning of the original language text as possible. It downplays even changing the Word order.

"The KJV basically uses the technique of verbal equivalence and formal equivalence. Verbal equivalence means that the very words, wherever possible, are brought over from Hebrew into English and from Greek into English. The KJV also uses the technique of formal equivalence, that is, the translators brought over, wherever possible, the very forms of the Hebrew and Greek words into English. They didn't transform the grammar. They didn't take a noun and make a verb out of it. They brought a verb into a verb and a noun into a noun wherever possible. They were skilled craftsmen who had a proper concept of what "translation" really is. It comes from *translatus* which in turn comes from two Latin words, *trans* ("across") and *latus which is the past participle of fero ("to carry"). It means to "carry across" from one place to another, or from one language to another. It does not mean to CHANGE, or to ADD, or to SUBTRACT!*"[1]

This concept is very much opposed to the dynamic equivalent (DE) scheme used today in almost all modern translations. The DE puts emphasis on choosing words and phrases that 'modernize' the language and on including only the thought of the sentence or phrase. This is similar to a paraphrase which makes no attempt to translate the words of one language into another, but to interpret or translate by re-stating. It should be obvious the DE is fraught with danger. If a translation is being made by heretics, or apostates, or those with an agenda, the true meaning and purpose could be slanted, or worse, lost entirely. Satan used DE in the Garden of Eden in his encounter with Eve. Reviewing his words will show Satan changed, added, and subtracted from the exact Words of God. When he did, the sentences he used implied entirely different suggestions from what was intended by God. Nida promoted this method of DE translation in most countries of the world:

"The new method of Bible translation is also called "common language translation," "idiomatic translation," "impact translation," "indirect transfer translation," and "thought translation." While some would make a distinction between some of these methods, for the most part we can say they are

---

[1] Waite, Th.D., Ph.D., D. A; *Defending the King James Version*; p. 104, but the book has an excellent discussion of the diabolical dynamic equivalence in several places throughout the book.

used synonymously."[1]

Examples of DE translations would be the *Good News Bible, The Living Bible,* and most of the *New International Version.*

Nida was the man most responsible for the DE translation technique. There are many books and articles by this man on translation methods. He has had a profound influence on adding, subtracting, and changing God's Words. Personally, when I sit down to read God's Words, I want it to be as close to what He said as it can be. I don't want someone else telling me what He said in my personal time with Him. Now if someone wants to paraphrase the Words of God or use DE in the translation technique, that's probably all right, but don't call the book the Holy Bible. Call it a COMMENTARY!!

3. Kurt Aland:

We have already commented on him extensively. He is the co-editor of the Nestle-Aland Greek Text. He does not believe in the verbal inspiration of the Bible nor of the canon of the Scripture. He believes everything about the Bible is up for grabs.

4. Matthew Black and Allen Wikgren:

These men do not believe in the infallibility of the Bible.

Another note of interest is that the UBS Vice-president is Roman Catholic Cardinal Onitsha of Nigeria and on the executive committee is Roman Catholic Bishop Alilona of Italy. Also, the recent Catholic New American Bible was translated directly from the UBS/Nestle Greek text.[2]

NO SURPRISE IN THE TEXT CHANGES

We will conclude the 'New' Greek Text section with a comparison made by Dr. D. A. Waite between the Received Text and the W/H Greek Text. The UBS Greek Text does not do much better although as indicated they have made changes in that text back toward the RT.

---

[1] Cloud, David, *Dynamic Equivalency;* 1994; Way of Life Literature, Electronic Edition, May 2000; Port Huron, MI

[2] Riplinger, Gail; *New Age Versions;* p. 497-498

The N.T. Greek Text
Textual Battle Ground

Textus Receptus	W/H Changes in T.R.
Has 140,521 Greek word	Changes 5,604 places in the N.T.
Has 647 pp. in Greek Text	Changes include 9,970 Gr. words
Has 217 Greek wds. Per page	Changes 15.4 Gr. Wds. Per page
Has 100 % of the Gr. words	Changes 7% of the Greek words
Has all 647 pp. unchanged	Changes total 45.9 pp in Greek Text[1]

SURPRISE IN THE HEBREW TEXTS, PERHAPS NOT

In the last segment of "The Broad Gate: The Manuscripts" we will examine the Hebrew texts that were used by most of the modern translations as the foundation for the Old Testament. I was absolutely shocked to learn some of the following information. You will be, too.

Gerhard Kittel was a theologian during Hitler's reign of terror. He and Hitler have been linked to the occult and anti-Semitism by many people. Most of the information comes from the evidence found at Hitler's bedside, which included Madame Blavatsky's *The Secret Doctrine.* Madame Blavatsky was a Satanist. She and her disciples, particularly Dietrich Eckart, had a profound influence on Hitler and his loyal followers, including Gerhard Kittel. Gerhard told the war crimes trial that "his actions had been "imposed upon him by God"[2] Hitler heard voices that informed him he had been selected by God to be Germany's 'messiah'.

Anti-Semitism is rampant in Blavatsky's writing's and Hitler's scribe, Kittel, who transposed them into theological doctrine. Kittel pushed a new Bible version for Hitler called *Die Heilige Schrift.* The new version was to replace the good old Luther's Bible that had been around since the Reformation. The year

---

[1] Waite, Th.D., Ph.D., D.A.; *Defending the King James Version;* p. Xii
[2] Riplinger, Gail; *New Age Versions;* p.595

Kittel joined the Nazi party he started writing the *Theological Dictionary of the New Testament.* Robert G. L. Waite, a **secular** historian, writing in his book, *Theologians Under Hitler,* said:

> "The potential for trouble suddenly became concrete in 1933. Ego involvement...must have played a role in Kittel's career after 1933. After 1933 Kittel's work changed in tone. Before 1933 Kittel defended Judaism, afterward he attacked it. Kittel produced a body of work between 1933 and 1944 filled with hatred and slander toward Jews...The bulk of Kittel's research between 1933 and 1945 was devoted to a rigorous and harsh anti-Jewish stance...[I]t corresponded to the worst of Nazi propaganda."[1]

It was between those years mentioned in the quote that Kittel was writing his famous *Theological Dictionary.* He was also involved in Nazi publications and organizations.

We went through all the above to reach this astounding conclusion. Gerhard Kittel's corruption of the Hebrew Masoretic Text, Biblia Hebraica Leningrad of **1937** or its Stuttgart Edition of 1967/77, are followed by the NASB, NKJV and all new versions.[2] These editions differ from the Masoretic Received Text in **20,000 to 30,000 places according to Dr. D.A. Waite.**[3]

Now someone can find in the preface of most of the modern translations statements that they used many references such as the Dead Sea scrolls, the Latin Vulgate, the Samaritan Pentateuch, the Septuagint, Jerome's Juxta Hebraica, and lexicographies which are 'dictionaries' like *Brown-Drive-Briggs Hebrew Lexicon* and the *New Thayer's Greek Lexicon.* The liberal Presbyterian Church defrocked Briggs for his liberalism, and J. Henry Thayer was a Unitarian who vehemently denied Christ's divinity.[4] The prefaces also report using cognates, meaning related [corrupt] manuscripts. The modern translations then claim they have used an 'eclectic' text or in other words 'many sources'. This would seem to be the case but many authors report the translation committees departed from a particular text with reluctance.

> "It is common today to read that a given modern translation (see N.I.V. preface) or Greek text is based on an "eclectic" text. This is to give the impression that the "best reading" from many different sources were used including the TR. This must be exposed as being totally misleading. When

---

[1] Ibid. p. 596-597

[2] Ibid. p. 594; This same information is found in Dr. Waite's excellent work, *Defending the King James Version,* pp. 20-21

[3] Waite, Ph.D., Th.D., D.A.; *Defending the King James Version;* pp. 20-21

[4] Riplinger, Gail; *New Age Versions;* p. 601

the critical [meaning by textual criticism] text was first produced by Westcott and Hort, so also today the primary pillar is Codex B and it is only departed from with the greatest reluctance."[1]

The scripture was corrupted from the very beginning in the Garden of Eden and particularly in the first 100 years after Immanuel. Even Bruce Metzger states:

"Irenaeus, Clement of Alexandria, Tertullian, Eusebius and many other Church Fathers accused the heretics of corrupting the Scriptures in order to have support for their special views".[2]

The Words of God continue to be corrupted even into modern times, and perhaps even worse today. As the Scripture indicates—There will be *many* who corrupt the Words of God.

2 Cor. 2:17 *For we are not as **many, which corrupt the word of God**: but as of sincerity, but as of God, in the sight of God speak we in Christ.*

The Scripture also warns us to shun and reject persistent heretics. This should be extended to their writings as well.

Titus 3:10 *A man that is an heretick after the first and second admonition reject;*

The Scripture has a stern warning for those who corrupt the Words of God. Those who associate with dishonest, fraudulent corrupters may be in significant danger also. Read what God says about this issue.

Rev. 22:19 *And if any man shall take away from the words of the book of this prophecy, God shall take away his part out of the book of life, and out of the holy city, and from the things which are written in this book.*

B.F. Westcott said:

"No one now, I suppose, holds that the first three chapters of Genesis, for example, give a literal history—I could never understand how anyone reading them with open eyes could think they did."

Dr. Hort said:

"(1) that eternity is independent of duration; (2) that power of repentance is not limited to this life; (3) that it is not revealed whether or not all will ultimately repent."[3]

Now one last quote made by the Cambridge professor who has hastened the world along the time-line to Armageddon. In light of what the reader has learned from the preceding this quote should appall those who understand.

Hort said:

---

[1] Moorman, Jack; *Forever Settled; p. 84*

[2] Ibid. p. 67

[3] Grady, PhD., Th.D, D.D., William P.; *Final Authority;* pp. 233, 242

"There are no signs of deliberate falsification of the text for dogmatic purpose."[1]

Of course the real reason he insisted that the text had not been falsified was because he knew that his entire critical apparatus must be based on a 'clean' genealogy. Any falsification would make his theory of families fall apart. Why? How can one trace a route laced with lies? There would be too many rabbit trails that would lead to a dead end.

John 8:44 *Ye are of your father the devil, and the lusts of your father ye will do. He was a murderer from the beginning, and abode not in the truth, because there is no truth in him. When he speaketh a lie, he speaketh of his own: for he is a liar, and the father of it.*

The next section will be the last in the history of the 'patient'. We have taken a history of most of the negative and positive aspects of the chief complaints concerning the transmission of the text and how the Bible was produced. Of course, whether one accepts a negative point as negative depends on your view. This is the same in medicine. I have had patients think a six-pack of beer per day was positive, especially construction workers after a long day on the job, until they developed cirrhosis of the liver. Some patients thought multiple sex partners was "no big deal" and "enjoyable" until they acquired a STD (sexual transmitted disease). Other patients thought smoking was a way to be "sociable" and was "their business" and "I've got to die from something." The number of times I had to break the news about a lesion on a smoker's chest x-ray, which may have been cancer, was several hundred. I cannot tell you how often the patient would reach into their pocket, pull out the pack of cigarettes and throw them in the garbage. Of course, invariably it was too late. I hope those reading this, who are on the fence or undecided, will not wait too long to decide in favor of the OOO God. Remember throughout the history of man there has only been a remnant of true believers. It is the remnant *priesthood of believers* who have completely believed and trusted in the Living Word and His 'quickened' Message. They have believed that He is able to do all He has promised and more, even preserve His pure Words forever.

The preceding section can be summed up by this verse:

Galatians 5:9   *A little leaven leaveneth the whole lump.*

---

[1] Pickering, Th.D., Wilbur; *The Identity of the New Testament Text*, p. 41

The Strait Gate: The Manuscripts

Matthew 7:13-14 *Enter ye in at the strait gate: for wide is the gate, and broad is the way, that leadeth to destruction, and many there be which go in thereat: Because strait is the gate, and narrow is the way, which leadeth unto life, and few there be that find it.*

Matthew 7:21-22 *Not every one that saith unto me, Lord, Lord, shall enter into the kingdom of heaven; but he that doeth the will of my Father which is in heaven. Many will say to me in that day, Lord, Lord, have we not prophesied in thy name? and in thy name have cast out devils? and in thy name done many wonderful works?*

SACRED REVIEW VERSES TEXTUAL CRITICISM

We will begin this section back at the time of the New Testament manuscripts and work toward modern times. A brief discussion of an opposite method from Westcott and Hort et al's "scientific" textual criticism called **sacred review** established by Dean Burgon will be accomplished first. However, one will note in reviewing the literature about textual criticism that previously the overall field has been called sacred science. This author has problems with this title, as has already been presented, because of calling it "science." The field is broken into "higher" and "lower" criticism. *Higher criticism* refers to theological concerns and *lower criticism* to textual concerns. This work has dealt primarily with "lower" criticism, but it cannot be divorced from "higher" concerns. Some of the items in this section of the work have already been partly covered by necessity for understanding, such as the formation of the canon, papyrus fragments, and uncial and minuscule manuscripts. There has been some discussion of the patristic documents, but we will cover more information in this history which is part of the subjective of the SOAP acronym. We will need to examine the manuscripts that Erasmus used and the early translations of the Received Text into other languages. When this subjective section is finished we will see what effect all this has had on the "Bible". That will be the objective. When we finish that section we will make an assessment which is similar to a doctor's diagnosis.

Westcott and Hort were the first persons to record exactly how they went about lower criticism. Dean Burgon and others have soundly attacked their presentation or method, but they were ignored by "silence" on the issues which were raised. Instead, Dean Burgon et al could be isolated by "spin," which is a redirecting of pertinent issues to personal attacks on individuals raising appropriate questions. In addition, the matters addressed by Burgon and his rebuttals were very potent. We will now discuss in limited fashion what Dean Burgon laid out so eloquently in his treatise, *The Traditional Text of the Holy Gospels.*

DEAN BURGON'S METHOD OF MANUSCRIPT REVIEW

The field of sacred review is concerned with evaluating a product that is Divine. The Divine Agent [the Holy Ghost] gave to us the Holy Scriptures as Jesus said He would, the words that are for ever settled.

Ps 119:89 LAMED. For ever, O LORD, thy word is settled in heaven.

Dean Burgon says:

"There exists no reason for supposing that the Divine Agent, who the first instance thus gave to mankind the Scriptures of Truth, immediately abdicated His office and took no further care of His work; that He abandoned those precious writings. That a perpetual miracle was wrought for their preservation, that copyists were protected against the risk of error, or evil prevented from shamefully adulterating copies of the Deposit, it is presumed that no one is so weak as to suppose. But it is quite a different thing to claim that all down the ages the sacred writings must have been under God's peculiar care; that the Church under Him has watched over them with intelligence and skill; that it has recognized which copies exhibit a fabricated text, and which an honestly transcribed text – that it has generally sanctioned the one, and generally disallowed the other. I am utterly disinclined to believe – so grossly improbable does it seem – that at the end of 1800 years [now 1920] 995 copies out of very thousand, suppose, will prove untrustworthy; and on the contrary that one, two, three, four, or five remain whose contents were until yesterday as good as unknown should be found to have retained the secret of what the Holy Spirit originally inspired. I am utterly unable to believe that God's promise has so entirely failed, that at the end of 1800 years much of the text of the Gospel had in point of fact to be picked by a German critic out of the waste-paper basket in the convent of St. Catherine, and that the entire text had to be remodeled after the pattern set by a couple of copies which had remained in neglect during fifteen centuries, and had probably owed their survival to that neglect while hundreds of others had been thumbed to pieces, and had bequeathed their witness to copies made from them.

...If the objection be made, and it probably will be, **Do you mean to rest upon the five manuscripts used by Erasmus?**

I reply, that the copies employed were selected because they were known to represent with accuracy the Sacred Word, that the descent of the text was evidently guarded with jealous care, just as the human genealogy of our Lord was preserved; that it rests mainly upon much the widest testimony; and that where any part of it conflicts with the fullest evidence attainable, there I believe that it calls for correction.

...Strange as it may appear, it is undeniably true that the whole of the controversy may be reduced to the following narrow issue: does the truth of the Text of Scripture dwell with the vast multitude of copies, uncial and cursive, concerning which nothing is more remarkable than the marvelous agreement which subsists between them? Or is it rather to be supposed that the truth abides exclusively with a very little handful of manuscripts, which at once differ from the great bulk of the manuscripts, and also widely differ among themselves?

...Now textual criticism occupies itself chiefly with two distinct branches of inquiry: (1) Its first object is to collect, investigate, and arrange the evidence supplied by Manuscripts, Versions, Fathers. And **this is an inglorious task which demands prodigious labor, severe accuracy, unflagging attention, and can never be successfully conducted without considerable amount of solid learning.** ["*Lower Criticism*"] (2) Its second object is to draw critical inference; in other words, to discover the truth of the text, the genuine word of Holy Writ. And this is altogether a loftier function, and calls for the exercise of far higher gifts. Nothing can be successfully accomplished here without large and exact knowledge, freedom from bias and prejudice.["Higher Criticism"]

...The critics of this century have been in too great a hurry. They have rushed to conclusions, trusting to the evidence which was already in their hands, forgetting that only those conclusions can be scientifically [reasonably] sound which are drawn from *all* the materials that exist.

...I. From the very necessity of the case, copies of the Gospels and Epistles in the original Greek were multiplied to an extraordinary extent all down the ages and in every part of the Christian Church...(a) produced in different countries; (b) executed at intervals during the space of one thousand years; (c) copied from originals no longer in existence....More than 2000 MSS copies are now known to exist. It should be added that the practice of reading Scripture aloud before the congregation – a practice which is observed to have prevailed from the Apostolic age – has resulted in the increased security of the Deposit.

...II. Next, as the Gospel spread from land to land, it became translated into the several languages of the ancient world. For, though Greek was widely understood, the commerce and the intellectual predominance of the Greeks, and the conquests of Alexander having caused it to be spoken nearly all over the Roman empire, Syriac [essentially the same as Aramaic] and Latin Versions were also required for ordinary reading, probably even in the age of the Apostles. **And thus those three languages in which the title of His accusation was written above His cross.**

...Before the 4th and 5th centuries the Gospel had been further translated into the peculiar idioms of Lower and Upper Egypt, in what are now called the Bohairic and Sahidic Versions, of Ethiopia and of Armenia, of Gothland [France and Bohemia].

...III. But the most singular provision for preserving the memory of what was anciently read as inspired Scriptures remains to be described. Sacred Science boasts of a literature without a parallel in any other department of human knowledge. The Fathers of the Church, the bishops and doctors of primitive Christendom, were in some instances voluminous writers, whose works have largely come down to our times.

SACRED REVIEW'S SEVEN NOTES OF TRUTH

A reading then should be attested by these **SEVEN NOTES OF TRUTH:**
1. Antiquity, or Primitiveness.
2. Consent of Witnesses, or Number
3. Variety of Evidence, or Catholicity [universality]
4. Respectability of Witnesses, or Weight
5. Continuity, or Unbroken Tradition.
6. Evidence of the Entire Passage, or Context.
7. Internal Considerations, or Reasonableness."[1] [numbers

---

[1] Green, Jay P.; *Unholy Hands on the Bible;* Section: *The Traditional Text of the New Testament* by John William Burgon, B.D., Dean of Chichester; p. 5-15;

added by the author.]

LECTIONARIES

Lectionaries [comes from Latin meaning to read] have not been mentioned. They were Scripture readings put together by the early church to be read in the church service.

"Another important class of Greek New Testament manuscripts are the lectionaries. These are service books which contain in proper sequence the text of the passages of Scripture appointed to be read at the worship services of the Church. Those lectionaries are of two kinds, the synaxaria, which begin the year at Easter, and the menologia, which begin the year at September 1. Aland sets the number of the lectionaries manuscripts at 2143."[1]

There is not one lectionary which supports the W/H or the Nestle-Aland Greek text!!!

PESHITTA AND THE SEPTUAGINT

Peshitta is a Bible of the early Syrian Church which is still used today. It was translated very early and even Bishop Ellicot, the chairman of the Southern Convocation, believes that the Apostle John may have seen portions of it. The Peshitta was believed to have been translated from the original languages at the Antiochian Church which spoke Syriac that is very similar to Aramaic. The controversy rages over when the O.T. and the N.T. translations were done. Some believe the O.T. portion was believed to be a targum, an Aramaic paraphrase of

---

edited by Edward Miller, "who was often busily engaged with Dean Burgon, and when the Dean died suddenly, his papers were left in charge with [Miller] the object of having him edit and complete the Dean's studies as much as was possible under the circumstances".; p. 3; Miller was Prebendary of Chichester, editor of Dr. Scrivener's [remember he was on the council of the Southern Convocation] *Plain Introduction to the Textual Criticism of the New Testament,* and author of *A Guide to the Textual Criticism of the New Testament*

[1] Moorman, Jack; *Forever Settled;* p. 49

the Hebrew. Hebrew by the closing centuries was not very well understood or spoken, hence an Aramaic translation or version was produced. Eventually the Peshitta became corrupted. By the middle of the 3rd century when Origen developed his Caesarian school, and on to the time of Eusebius and Pamphilus, well known corruptions took place. Eventually revisions took place such as the Philoxean (508), the Harclean (616) and the Jerusalem Syriac (c.6th century). The Jerusalem revision was produced from the Septuagint, which will be our next item to discuss.[1] First, we need to make one further comment regarding the Peshitta. Since there are so many extant versions which lend support for the early presence of the RT, the neutral camp has attempted to set a late date for this witness. This shouldn't surprise anyone.

"The Peshitta Syriac version, which is the historic Bible of the whole Syrian Church, agrees closely with the Traditional text found in the vast majority of the Greek New Testament manuscripts. Until about one hundred years ago it was almost universally believed that the Peshitta originated in the second century and hence was one of the oldest New Testament versions. Thus because of its agreement with the Traditional text the Peshitta was regarded as one of the most important witnesses to the antiquity of the Traditional text. In more recent times, however, naturalistic critics have tried to nullify this testimony of the Peshitta by denying that it is an ancient version. Burkitt (1904), for example, insisted that the Peshitta did not exist before the fifth Century but "was prepared by Rabbula, bishop of Edessa (the capital city of Syria) from 411 - 435 AD, and published by his authority."[2]

The Septuagint's (The LXX) history is so controversial that in passing we will only mention comments by Dr. Hills from *The King James Version Defended* and Peter Ruckman's comments in his book, *The Christian's Handbook of Manuscript Evidence* concerning it. Although Ruckman is "tough" in the way he presents material, who is to say in light of the Alexandrian's fabrications and attacks he is not vindicated. He says:

"The whole legend of the LXX is based on one *writing* called "The Letter of Aristeas." [a letter which is probably a fraud]

There is one mention of the Pentateuch only, being translated into Greek...and the passage is doubtful.

Philo of Alexandria, a Bible-denying Jewish Gnostic, mentions the translating of (2) [the Pentateuch] and intimates that the translators were "inspired".

The writer of the "Letter to Aristeas" was NOT who he

---

[1] Ibid. The information in this section, re: The Peshitta, was obtained from *Forever Settled*

[2] Ibid. p. 117

claimed to be..[Ruckman goes on to explain]

Professor Kahle (1875-1964) said that *there never was any such thing as Pre-Christian "LXX!"*

...To this day no Greek scholar has produced one copy of the Old Testament written before 300 A.D.

The Legend of the Septuagint rests on flimsy support that the manuscripts written 200-400 years AFTER the death of Christ *match the New Testament quotations.* Why shouldn't they? *All the writers had the New Testament.* [This means the Greek writings after the N.T. were copies of the New Testament, not the other way around, as many would have us believe. The alleged Septuagint copied the New Testament, not the New Testament copying the Septuagint]

The way [Alexandrians] W/H get out of this bear trap is by insisting that [the LXX] was a revision of a revision, which was a *revision of the original "LXX".*

[Do you remember a similar 'scheme' called the Lucian recension of 350 A.D. for the R.T.]

There is no more evidence that this "recension" took place than the Lucian "recension".[1]

Ruckman goes on to explain how the alleged recension caused the Hebrew text to be allegedly altered so that now the Hebrew Masoretic Text could be changed because it did not match the [original] LXX which would be more accurate. He goes through considerable documentation of this tragedy, another Alexandrian ploy.

Dr. Hills relates the ideas of the prompting of the Septuagint translation for the king of Egypt, Ptolemy Philadelphus by the "seventy". He quickly discounts the 'story', also, and surmises the Scripture was probably translated in Alexandria to meet the "needs" of the Jews living there. He also relates being struck by the inspired wisdom of the Apostles upon using this version in the N.T. He says:

"Sometimes they cited the Septuagint verbatim, even when it departed from the Hebrew in non-essential ways, and sometimes they made their own translation directly from the Hebrew or used their knowledge of Hebrew to improve the rendering of the Septuagint."[2]

Dr. Hills then goes on to describe three O.T. quotations which have given rise to much debate. The debate centers around the writer in the N.T. quoting a

---

[1] Ruckman, Dr. Peter; *The Christians Handbook of Manuscript Evidence;* Pensacola Bible Press, Palatka, Fl.; 1970; 4th printing 1976; pp. 40-44

[2] Hills, PhD., Edward F.; *The King James Defended*; p. 94

verse not found in Scripture, but in a Greek paraphrase, the Septuagint.

Well, it seems Dr. Ruckman's presentation is the best. The Septuagint **copied** from the N.T. and not the other way around. The Septuagint had to be discussed in this section because of the controversy, but the information about this paraphrase, the Septuagint, is certainly not on solid ground!

Dr. D.A. Waite informed me via a telephone interview that he believes the LXX (Septuagint) is an A.D. production.

OLD LATIN MANUSCRIPTS AND THE PRIESTHOOD OF BELIEVERS

Latin was the 'official' language of the Roman empire. Greek, Syrian, Coptic, Aramaic, Hebrew, and others were the 'common' languages. By the time the corrupt Latin Vulgate was finally accepted around 1300 A.D. by force, the 'old' Latin Bibles of the common people, called their vulgate Bible [meaning common and not the Latin Vulgate, which stole the name], and the Latin language were "dying out" or laid aside. Other languages were becoming more prominent as German, French, Celtic, etc. early on however, [and I mean very early in the NT era and on into the early reformation] the Old Latin [translation] MSS are an invaluable record of the Received Text. In general the Latin MSS can be divided into the North African and Northern "Italia" or Italy. As one would expect the N. African MSS were corrupted over and over. The Latin "Italia" (also called Italic) manuscripts remained purer and became the translation most used by the Waldensians, members of the **priesthood of believers**.

"The Reformers held that the Waldensian Church was formed about 120 AD from the apostles. The Latin Bible, the Italic, was translated from the Greek not later than I57 AD. We are indebted to Beza, the renowned associate of Calvin, for the statement that the Italic Church dated from 120 AD. From the illustrious group of scholars which gathered round Beza, 1590 AD, we may understand how the Received Text was the bond of union between great historic churches. That Rome in early days corrupted the manuscripts while the Italic Church handed them down in their apostolic purity, Allix, the renowned scholar, testifies. He reports the following as Italic articles of faith: "They receive only, saith he, what is written in the Old and New Testament. They say, that the Popes of Rome, and other priests, have depraved the Scriptures by their doctrines and glosses."[1]

So important is the Italia Bible that it took the combined effort of corrupt Rome's Popes, famous "fathers", and emperors to keep "It" silent. Looking back through history we can now say they couldn't successfully do that either. The account goes like this:

> "In the fourth century, Helvidius, a great scholar of northern Italy [who was probably a Vaudois[2]], accused Jerome, whom the Pope had empowered to form a Bible in Latin for Catholicism, with using corrupt Greek manuscripts. How could Helvidius have accused Jerome of employing corrupt Greek manuscripts if Helvidius had not had the pure Greek manuscripts? And so learned and so powerful in writing and teaching was Jovinian, the pupil of Helvidius, that it demanded three of Rome's most furious fathers - Augustine, Jerome and Ambrose to unite in opposing Jovinian's influence. Even then, it needed the condemnation of the Pope and the banishment of the emperor to prevail. But Jovinian's followers lived on and made the way easier for Luther."[3]

It was these old Latin and Greek manuscripts, which found their way into the remotest part of Europe and Great Britain. They were carried by the **priesthood of believers**. There is an account of a Celtic priest in Northern Britain who led thousands to Jesus using the descendants of these MSS. The **priesthood of believers** carried the Words with them as they migrated. The famed (or infamous) church father and allegorist Augustine (354-430 A.D.) later came to England and ordered the slaughter of many of these primitive Christians who would not yield to Rome in the 5th century.

> "**Augustine**, now at the head of a hierarchy composed of twelve bishops, immediately made the bold attempt to bring **the ancient British church** [the Puritans brought the gospel to Britain first] under the Roman jurisdiction. Through the influence of Ethelbert he obtained a conference with some of the British bishops at a place which from that time was called Augustine's oak, on the Severn. There the Roman and the British clergy met for the first time; and Augustine's first and imperious demand was, "Acknowledge the authority of the bishop of Rome." "We desire to love all men," they meekly replied, "and whatever we do for you, we will do for him also whom you call the Pope."
> Surprised and indignant at their refusal, **Augustine**

[1] Moorman, Jack; *Forever Settled;* p. 107
[2] Ibid. p. 112
[3] Ibid. p. 106-107

exhorted them to adopt the Roman usages as to the celebration of Easter, the tonsure, and the administration of baptism, that a uniformity of discipline and worship might be established in the island. This they positively refused to do.

Having received Christianity at first not from Rome but from the East [Antioch and Lyons, my addition], **and never having acknowledged the Roman church as their mother, they looked upon themselves as independent of the See of Rome.** A second and a third council were held, but with no better results. **Augustine** was plainly told that the British church would acknowledge no man as supreme in the Lord's vineyard. The archbishop demanded, argued, censured, wrought miracles; but all to no purpose — the Britons were firm. At last he was plainly told that they could not submit either to the haughtiness of the Romans, or to the tyranny of the Saxons. Aroused to wrathful indignation at their quiet firmness, the angry priest exclaimed, "If you will not receive brethren who bring you peace, you shall receive enemies who bring you war. If you will not unite with us in showing the Saxons the way of life, you shall receive from them the stroke of death." The haughty archbishop withdrew, and is supposed to have died soon after (A.D. 605); but his ill-omened prophecy was accomplished soon after his decease."[1] [Augustine personally approved the slaughter, my addition]

CHURCH INSTRUCTION MANUALS AND CODICES

Another document that deserves mentioning is *The Didache (Teaching) of the Twelve Apostles*, which is a manual of church instruction in two parts: (1) instructions for new believers before baptism and (2) a series of directions for worship. The instruction booklet is believed to survive from the beginning of the 2nd century. It is an important witness to the RT Lord's prayer.

There are several codices which contain the RT. One is the Freer Manuscript, Codex W, named after the man who purchased it near Cairo. It is an eclectic text but contains the RT in Matthew and the last two thirds of Luke. Most likely this MS is from the 4th century and indicates the RT was known before the 4th century. Codex A (Alexandrinus) was probably written in Egypt in the early 5th century and contains the RT in the Gospels. It is another witness to an early RT even though the neutral, natural scholars have used it extensively. Many of the readings that favor the early existence of the RT are explained away by the "scholars" in this way: They report without any evidence that the texts in these MSS were brought back in line with the RT by copyist after the alleged recension theory of Lucian around 350 A.D. by W/H without any evidence.[1]

EARLY BIBLES AND CHURCH FATHER WITNESSES

An interesting account of the Armenian Bible deserves to be recounted. The heretic Nestorius had corrupted the Scripture in this country, Armenia, which lies east of Asia Minor [Turkey] and North of Mesopotamia in the area of modern Georgia, Azerbaijan and Armenia by the Caspian Sea.

"Nestorius denied the union of the two natures of God and man in the one Person of Christ. He was accused of teaching that there were two distinct persons--the Person of God the Son and the Person of the man Christ Jesus. This teaching was condemned by the Council of Ephesus in A.D. 431 at which Cyril of Alexandria presided. (Cyril himself witnesses in favour of "God" in 1 Timothy 3:16.)"[2]

After Nestorius was condemned, correct copies of the Greek Bible from Constantinople [Byzantium] were obtained by the Armenians and their translation was revised accordingly. Their new revision would probably have been from MSS of the Byzantine text-type as the MSS confirm.[3]

In the Caucasus lies Georgia, north of Armenia. The Georgian version of the Bible agrees with the Armenian version except for a few MSS called the Adysh MSS which reflect Origen's text from Caesarea. The Armenian, Georgian, and Goth alphabets were developed to specifically record the Words for these people in their language and thus become a forerunner of future missionary efforts at translation. The question always remains, however, will the missionaries be acquainted with the discrepancies in the two paths the original language texts have taken? Will they be taught to use the RT or the KJB as the basis for the translation?

---

[1] Hills, Th.D., Edward F.; *The King James Defended;* p. 172

[2] Fuller, D.D., David Otis; *True or False?;* p. 127

[3] Moorman, Jack; *Forever Settled;* p. 127

The Gothic versions testify to the RT, but show the Arian influence because the missionary to the Goths, Ulfilas [means "little wolf"], had been infected with the Arian heresy. Arianism denied the pre-existence of the Son of God, claiming that He was created by God and not of one substance with the Father. Moorman reports Kenyon says the text-type is:

> "that which is found in the majority of Greek manuscripts."[1]

Two brothers, Constantine and Methodius, were sent as missionaries to the Slavonic people from Constantinople in the 9th century. They also devised an alphabet for these people of East Central Europe and used the Byzantine Text-type[2].[Moorman, *Forever Settled.*, p128]

An extensive report by Jack Moorman categorized the church fathers quotes in his work, *Early Church Fathers and the Authorized Version.* Moorman reflects his disgust at the continued attempt by natural, neutral scholars to:

> "demonstrate how adept our opponents are in performing a "vanishing act" with the early manuscript and versional evidence for the TR. They have been no less adept with the Fathers, and their chief means has been to tell (!) us about "the modern critical editions."[3]

He goes on to blast them for reporting a critical edition of church fathers quotes about to be released in 1936 would show the church fathers quotes had been "assimilated" [adjusted] to the TR. The "edition" to this day has not been "released". The reason it has not been released Moorman surmises is that the quotes favor the TR. Would it surprise the reader that they probably favor the TR?

A summary of the early church fathers and the information from Moorman's work will be presented next. An asterisk (*) means that an incomplete quote was just given to Aleph-B category. This gives absolutely no information as to why the verse or quotation occurred in their writings. Someone needs to make a study of that aspect of the writings of the fathers because some were staunch defenders of the RT and may have quoted Aleph-B in order to refute it. Additionally, many quotes are most likely made from "memory" rather than getting out valuable manuscripts and risking damage to them. My understanding is that the quotes are often "all over the place" and do not reflect consistency or exactness or one particular "book" or manuscript or alleged "family."

---

[1] Ibid. p. 127
[2] Ibid. p. 128
[3] Moorman, Jack, *Early Church Fathers and the Authorized Version;* The Bible For Today, #2136; p. 4

NAME	Number of TR Quotes	Number of Aleph-B Quotes
1. Alexander, Alexandria (273-328)	1	0
2. Ambrose, Milan (339-397)	16	15 (*2)
3. Aphrahat, Syria (d.367)	1	0
4. Athanasius, Alexandria (296-373)	16	15 (*2)
5. Athenagoras, Athens © 177)	1	0
6. Basil the Great, Cappadocia in Asia Minor (330-379)	7	6 (*1)
7. Clement , Alexandria (150-215)	5	10
8. Cyprian, Carthage, N. Africa (200-258)	18	14 (*2)
9. Cyril, Jerusalem (315-386)	11	3
10. Dionysius the Great, Alexandria (200-264)	1	0
11. Ephraem Syrus, Syria (306-373)	0	1
12. Eusebius, Caesarea (260-339)	1	(*2)
13. Gregory, Nazianzen in Cappadocia (329-394)	7	(*2)
14. Gregory, Nyssa in Cappadocia (330-394)	6	1
15. Gregory-Thaumaturgus, Pontus in Asia Minor (213-270)	1	1
16. Hilary, Potiers in France (315-367)	8	7 (*1)

17. Hippolytus, Rome (170-235)	6	0
18. Ignatius, Antioch (35-110)	3	0
19. Irenaeus, Lyons (130-202)	15	5 (*1)
20. Martyr, Justin, Palestine, Ephesus, Rome	1	0
21. Malchion, Antioch (270)	0	1
22. Methodius, Patarta in Asia Minor (other places) (260-312)	4	(*1)
23. Novatian, Rome (210-280)`	2	1
24. Origen, Alexandria and Caesarea (185-254)	18	13 (*1)
25. Polycarp, Smyrna (69-156)	4	1
26. Pontius the Deacon, Carthage (3rd century)	1	0
27. Tatian, Mesopotamia and Rome	66	11
28. Tertullian, Carthage in N. Africa (160-220)	36	8 (*2)
28. Tertullian, Carthage in N. Africa (160-220)	36	8 (*2)
29. Victorinus, Pettau near Lyons (d 304)	1	1
TOTALS	231 (66%)	121 (14 OF THIS NUMBER ARE THE PARTIAL QUOTES INDICATED BY THE ASTERISK *) (34%)

Looks to me like the RT had been received early and used by the Church Fathers! Some of these men have been white washed by the neutral natural scholars and the Roman Catholic church. Many of them were Alexandrians, corrupters of text, and Nicolatians (lorded it over the common people). Others were members of the **priesthood of believers** and were used by the Spirit to ensure many accurate copies of the text were passed on, as we have already documented and noted.

THE REAL MESSENGERS OF THE WORDS

In spite of the notoriety of the church fathers mentioned above, they were not the ones who carried the Words in MSS to the villages and towns of the post-Apostolic period and into the Reformation. Men *like* Helvidius, a Vaudois, in the early period, Peter Waldo, a Waldensian, in the middle period, and George Morell, Olivetan, and Walter Lollard, Waldensians in the early Reformation period, were responsible for this great achievement. Remember George Morell was a Waldensian bard [pastor with a beard] who spent time with several of the great reformers such as Ecolampadius, an assistant to Zwingle, in Basel, Switzerland and Luther in Germany. The following quotes concerning the influence of Morell are fascinating.

"One of the Waldensian bards, George Morell, who formed part of the deputation to Germany in 1533, and who published Memoirs of the History of their Churches, states, that at the time of his writing, there were more than eight hundred thousand persons professing the religion of the Waldenses."[1]

"In the year 1530, Ecolampadius, one of the reformers, then resident at Basel, in Switzerland, was visited by George Morell, one of the pastors among the Waldenses, by whom, on his return to Provence, he addressed a letter "to his well-beloved brethren in Christ, called Waldenses," and it is as follows:

"We have learned with great satisfaction, by your faithful pastor, George Morell, the nature of your faith and religious profession, and in what terms you declare it. Therefore, we thank our most merciful Father, who hath called you to so great light in this age, amidst the dark clouds of ignorance which have spread themselves over the world, and notwithstanding the extravagant power of Antichrist. Wherefore we

---

[1] Orchard, G. H.; *A History of the Baptists;* Way of Life Literature, Port Huron, MI, ; Fundamental Baptist CD-ROM Library 2000b, ISBN 1-58319-065-6; p. Chapter 2, Section 25

acknowledge that Christ is in you: for which cause we love you as brethren; and would to God we were able to make you sensible in effect of that which we shall be ready to do for you, although it were to be done with the utmost difficulty. Finally, we desire that what we write may not be regarded as though through pride we arrogated to ourselves any superiority over you, but consider it as proceeding from that brotherly love and charity which we bear towards you. The Father of our Lord Jesus Christ hath imparted to you an excellent knowledge of his truth, beyond that of many other people, and hath blessed you with spiritual blessings. So that if you persevere in his grace, he hath much greater treasures wherewith to enrich you, and make you perfect, according to your advancement in the measure of the inheritance of Christ."[1]

"Now it should be known, that this was made after that "Peter Masson and George Morell were sent into Germany in the year 1530, as Morland says, to treat with the chief ministers of Germany, viz. Occolampadius, Bucer, and others, touching the reformation of their churches; but Peter Masson was taken prisoner at Dijon." However, as Fox says, Morell escaped, and returned alone to Merindol with the books and letters he brought with him from the churches of Germany; and declared to his brethren all the points of his commission; and opened unto them, how many great errors they were in; into the which their old ministers, whom they called barbs, that is to say uncles, had brought them, leading them from the right way of true religion." [2]

Please recall from the section on "The Strait Gate: The Men" that Olivetan was responsible for leading Calvin to Jesus Christ. What I didn't point out in that section was the fact that **Olivetan was a Waldensian.** These people more than anyone else were responsible for preserving the manuscripts that catapulted the Reformers into the Reformation.

"Wilkinson says more particularly: Four Bibles produced under Waldensian influence touched the history of Calvin: namely, a Greek, a Waldensian vernacular, a French and an

---

[1] Jones, William; *The History of the Christian Church, from the birth of Christ to the 18th Century: including the very interesting account of the Waldenses and Albigenses;* 5th edition Way of Life Literature, Port Huron, MI; Fundamental Baptist CD-ROM Library 2000b; p. Chapter 5, Section 4

[2] Ivimey, Joseph; *A History of the English Baptists;* 1811; Way of Life Literature, Port Huron, MI; Fundamental Baptist CD-ROM; p. Section : "The Divine Right of the Infant Baptism examined and Disproved"

Italian. **Calvin himself was led to his great work by Olivetan, a Waldensian.** Thus was the Reformation brought to Calvin, that brilliant student of the Paris University. **Farel, also a Waldensian**, besought him to come to Geneva and open up a work there. Calvin felt that he should labour in Paris. According to Leger, Calvin recognized a relationship to the Calvins of the Valley of St. Martin, one of the Waldensian Valleys (From Leger, History of the Voudois). Finally, persecution at Paris and the solicitation of Farel caused Calvin to settle at Geneva, where, with Beza, he brought out an edition of the Textus Receptus - the one the author now used in his college class rooms, as edited by Scrivener. Of Beza, Dr. Edgar says **that he "astonished and confounded the world" with the Greek manuscripts he unearthed.** This later edition of the Received Text is in reality a Greek New Testament brought out under Waldensian influence. **Unquestionably, the leaders of the Reformation German, French and English were convinced that the Received Text was the genuine New Testament, not only by its own irresistible history and internal evidence, but also because it matched with the Received Text which in Waldensian form came down from the days of the apostles**.

The other three Bibles of Waldensian connection were due to three men who were at Geneva with Calvin, or when he died, with Beza, his successor, namely, Olivetan, Leger and Diodati. How readily the two streams of descent of the Received Text, through the Greek East and the Waldensian West, ran together, is illustrated by the meeting of the Olivetan Bible and the Received Text. Olivetan, one of the most illustrious pastors of the Waldensian Valleys, a relative of Calvin, according to Leger, and a splendid student, translated the New Testament into French. Leger bore testimony that the Olivetan Bible, which accorded with the Textus Receptus, was unlike the old manuscripts of the Papists, because they were full of falsification. Later, Calvin edited a second edition of the Olivetan Bible. The Olivetan in turn became the basis of the Geneva Bible in English which was the leading version in England in 1611 when the King James appeared."[1]

And so I pray that you sense the great achievement of the Waldensians of old who gave their lives by the hundred of thousands to preserve and pass on the

---

[1] Moorman, Jack; *Forever Settled;* p. part five, Section C: "A Survey of English Bible History; 9. Foreign Language Versions"; p. 171-172

infallible, inspired, inerrant Words of God, no matter what your professors, seminary teachers, or others may have told you. These men and women with certain others, members of **the priesthood of believers,** are responsible for the manuscripts selected by Erasmus to collate and produce the famed Greek text from copies of the originals. This great achievement, which had to be providentially overseen by the OOO God, went on to be edited by others and became the basis for the incomparable King James Version.

Isaiah 35:8 *And an highway shall be there, and a way, and it shall be called The way of holiness; the unclean shall not pass over it; but it shall be for those: the wayfaring men, though fools, shall not err therein.*

THE MANUSCRIPTS OF THE MESSENGERS WERE FOR THE PRINTING PRESS AND THE SCHOLARS

"When Desiderius Erasmus (1466-1536), the great scholar at the beginning of the Reformation, "came to Basle [sic] in July 1515, to begin his work, he found five Greek N.T. manuscripts ready for his use. These are now designated by the following numbers: 1 (an 11th-century manuscript of the Gospels, Acts, and Epistles), 2 (a 15th-century manuscript of the Gospels), 2ap (a 12th-14th-century manuscript of Acts and the Epistles), 4ap (a 15th-century manuscript of Acts and the epistles), and 1r (a 12th century manuscript of Revelation). Of these manuscripts Erasmus used 1 and 4ap only occasionally. In the Gospels, Acts, and Epistles his main reliance was on 2 and 2ap. **Did Erasmus use other manuscripts beside these five in preparing his Textus Receptus? The indications are that he did.** According to W. Schwarz (1955), Erasmus made his own Latin translation of the N.T. at Oxford during the years 1506-16. His friend, John Colet, who had become Dean of St. Paul's, lent him two Latin manuscripts for this undertaking, but nothing is known about the Greek manuscripts which he used. He must have used some Greek manuscripts or other, however, and taken notes on them. Presumably therefore he brought these notes with him to Basle [sic] along with his translation and his comments on the N.T. text. It is well known also that Erasmus looked for manuscripts everywhere during his travels and that he borrowed them from everyone he could. Hence although [Erasmus'] Textus Receptus was based mainly on the manuscripts which Erasmus found at Basel, it also included readings taken from others to which he had access. It agreed with the common faith because it was founded on manuscripts which in the providence of God were readily available."[1]

Herman Hoskier, one of our great textual scholars who lived and worked in the early part of the 20th century, wrote the two-volume work, *Codex B and its Allies: A Study and an Indictment* and his two-volume work, *Concerning the Text of the Apocalypse.* He carefully collated the similar MSS of the Received Text into groups. One reason he did this was to refute the Lucian recension theory of W/H. Another way to state this is to say his evaluation of the thousands of minuscules available was done to determine if they were all copied from a singular revision made in the 4th century or from diverse copies from various regions. After years of labor he makes the following amazing statement which shows the almighty hand of God at work in preserving His inspired, inerrant, infallible Words. Listen:

"I may state that if Erasmus had striven to found a text on the largest number of existing MSS in the world on one type, he would not have succeeded better, since his family MSS occupy the front rank in point of actual numbers..."[2]

Although I cannot find the quote at the time of writing this work, Hoskier states in another place the precise MSS used by Erasmus and how a guiding hand assisted Erasmus. Moorman says:

"There were hundreds of manuscripts for Erasmus to examine, and he did; but he used only a few".[3]

The sad accounts concerning Erasmus and his amazing work relates to the criticism from the neutral natural textual critics. They accuse Erasmus of rushing to print the first Greek Text in order to be first after the printing press was invented. They try to implicate him in sloppy scholarship from hastily obtained MSS. They charge him with making a lot of mistakes. There were errors in the first edition by Erasmus, but they were almost all invariably typographical (spelling) caused by newly invented printing machines rather than textual errors. The second edition corrected many of the spelling-type errors. The great controversy over a few verses in the book of Revelation has been argued ad infinitum in the literature and is not worth repeating here.

Dean Burgon said:

"Through his study of the writings of Jerome and other Church Fathers Erasmus became very well informed

---

[1] Hills, Th.D; Edward F.; *The King James Version Defended;* p. 198
[2] Moorman, Jack; *When the King James Version Departs from the Majority Text;* The Bible For Today, Collingswood, NJ; B.F.T. #1617; p. 16
[3] Moorman, Jack; *Forever Settled; p. 148*

concerning the variant readings of the N.T. text. *Indeed almost all the important variant readings known to scholars today were already known to Erasmus more than 460 years ago and discussed in the notes (previously prepared) which he placed after the text in his editions of the Greek N.T.* Here, for example, Erasmus dealt with such problem passages as the conclusion of the Lord's Prayer (Mt. 6:13), the interview of the rich young man with Jesus (Mt. 19:17-22), the ending of Mark (Mk. 16:9-20), the angelic song (Lk. 2:14), the angel, agony, and bloody sweat omitted (Lk. 22:43-44), the woman taken in adultery (Jn. 7:53 - 8:11), and the mystery of godliness (1 Ti. 3:16). ...

"But if Erasmus was cautious in his notes, much more was he so in his text, for this is what would strike the reader's eye immediately. Hence in the editing of his Greek N.T. text, especially, *Erasmus was guided by the common faith in the current text. And back of this common faith was the controlling providence of God.*"[1]

SOMEONE'S TERRIBLY MISTAKEN

Does this sound like Erasmus hastily put together the Greek New Testament? Of course not! Yet modern scholars such as James White accuse Erasmus of carelessness in the production of the text because of his haste. Listen to White's words and then listen to Kirsopp Lake tell the truth about the manuscripts.

James White comments:

"Erasmus' interest in the text of the Bible, seen in his publishing of Valla's work, prompted him to begin work on the publishing the first printed edition of the Greek New Testament. Up to that time (around 1511) no one had printed the entirety of the Greek New Testament. Everyone was still utilizing hand-copied manuscripts. Up to the summer of 1514 Erasmus worked in England on this project, and then moved back onto the Continent to Basel, Switzerland, where he hoped to find many excellent Greek manuscripts. He was **disappointed** when he found only five, but he set to work with these. [Where is White's reference for this disappointment?] He obtained the

---

[1] Hills, Th.D., Edward F.; *The King James Version Defended;* p. 198-199

assistance of John Froben, a printer there at Basel. Froben encouraged Erasmus to hurry with his work, **possibly** because he had heard that Cardinal Ximenes had already printed his *Complutensian Polyglot,* which included the Greek New Testament, and was merely waiting for approval to arrive from Rome before publishing his work. [Please note the 'possibly' above which means this is conjecture and that the next several sentences build on that conjecture.] Time was running out to be the first to actually publish the Greek New Testament. As a result, the first edition of Erasmus' *Novum Instrumentum* ("The New Instrument") was hardly a thing of beauty, and as soon as it was printed Erasmus had to get to work editing the second edition."[1][my emphasis]

Note what White says above: that Erasmus was disappointed that he found only five (5) manuscripts. David Cloud writes in the *Way of Life Encyclopedia of the Bible and Christianity: Bible Versions:*

"Among the next generation of Greek scholars was Erasmus of Rotterdam, who prepared an edition of the Greek N.T. from five manuscripts in repute at that time.[DWC: **While Erasmus used only a few manuscripts for his work, he had knowledge of a considerable number of Greek texts and ancient versions, including the Vatican codex. See *Erasmus.***]"

Someone is either lying or terribly mistaken about so important an issue. I might add James White does not reference his comments, whereas David Cloud does in his section on Erasmus. David Cloud quoting Dr Hills:

"Did Erasmus use other manuscripts beside these five in preparing his Textus Receptus? The indications are that he did." [This was quoted above but is so important I put it in again!]

White goes on to say in other places in his book that Erasmus used the same textual critic's methods as modern critics. I could not find the principles of textual criticism in his book to confirm these statements, nor could I find anywhere in his book that Erasmus relied on the Alexandrian texts as his foundation which modern critics use, nor could I find a reference. Everything I have read and everything that I have quoted in this work concerning Erasmus is that he rejected the Latin Vulgate foundation which is based primarily on the Alexandrian texts, although he did consult it and used a few readings from the Latin Vulgate. Dr. Hill in his book , *The KJV Defended,* discusses these readings in detail and concludes the discussion by saying the readings from the Latin Vulgate:

"are also found in other ancient witnesses, namely, old

---

[1] White, James; *The King James Only Controversy;* p. 15

Greek manuscripts, versions, and Fathers."[1]

Dean Burgon wrote:

"The God who brought the N.T. text safely through the ancient and medieval manuscript period did not fumble when it came time to transfer this text to the modern printed page. *This is the conviction which guides the believing Bible student as he considers the relationship of the printed Textus Receptus to the Traditional N.T. text found in the majority of the Greek N.T. manuscripts. These two texts are virtually identical.* [emphasis mine]

Kirsopp Lake and his associates (1928) demonstrated this fact in their intensive researches into the Traditional Text or Received Text (which they called the Byzantine text). Using their collations, they came to the conclusion that in the 11th chapter of Mark 'the most popular text in the manuscripts of the tenth to the fourteenth century' differed from the Textus Receptus only four times. This small number of differences seems almost negligible in view of the fact that in this same chapter *Aleph* (Codex Sinaiticus), B (Codex Vaticanus), and *D* (Codex Bezae) differ from the Textus Receptus 69, 71, and 95 times respectively. Also add to this the fact that in this same chapter, B differs from Aleph 34 times and from D 102 times and that Aleph differs from D 100 times.

"There are, however, a few places in which the Textus Receptus differs from the Traditional text found in the majority of the Greek N.T. manuscripts. The most important of these differences are due to the fact that Erasmus, influenced by the usage of the Latin-speaking Church in which he was reared, sometimes followed the Latin Vulgate rather than the Traditional Greek text.

"...Are the readings which Erasmus thus introduced into the Textus Receptus necessarily erroneous? By no means ought we to infer this. For *it is inconceivable that the divine providence which had preserved the N.T. text during the long ages of the manuscript period should blunder when at last this text was committed to the printing press.* According to the analogy of faith, then, we conclude that the Textus Receptus **was a further step in God's providential preservation of the N.T. text** and that these few Latin Vulgate readings which were incorporated into the Textus Receptus were genuine readings which had been preserved in the usage of the Latin-speaking Church. Erasmus, we may well believe, was guided providentially by the common faith to include these readings in his printed Greek N.T. text. In the Textus Receptus God

---

[1] Hills, Th.D., Edward F.; *The King James Defended;* p. 200

corrected the few mistakes of any consequence which yet remained in the Traditional N.T. text of the majority of the Greek manuscripts. ... "It is customary for naturalistic critics to make the most of human imperfections in the Textus Receptus and to sneer at it as a mean and almost sordid thing. ... But those who concentrate in this way on the human factors involved in the production of the Textus Receptus are utterly unmindful of the providence of God. For in the very next year, in the plan of God, the Reformation was to break out in Wittenberg, and it was important that the Greek N.T. should be published first in one of the future strongholds of Protestantism by a book seller who was eager to place it in the hands of the people, and not in Spain, the land of the Inquisition, by the Roman Catholic Church, which was intent on keeping the Bible from the people"[1]

The reader might like to know that, according to *The Way of Life Literature,* Erasmus went to great lengths in his Greek text to make dozens of comments which condemned the Roman Catholic perversions of Scripture and the Catholic Priest's perverted way of life. He remained a priest but tried to change the Roman Catholic Church from the inside. His most important contribution, however, has been the printed Received Text or Traditional Text. The first edition was in 1516 and over the course of the next few years he produced several more editions. After Erasmus' death in 1536, Robert Stephanus (1503-1539) continued his work. Stephanus had to leave the Catholic Church because of persecution and became a Reformed Reformer. His fourth edition had verses for the first time. Stephanus' 3rd and 4th editions agreed closely with Erasmus' 5th and final edition. Dr. Hills reported that Erasmus' 5th edition became a restraining force to further variant readings by the common faith. Following Stephanus came Theodore Beza (1519-1605) who was Calvin's disciple. He produced ten (10) editions of the Greek New Testament entirely faithful to the TR (RT). The reader needs to be reminded that an edition is a reissue of a work with minimal changes related to spelling, typos, etc. The editions of the men above were all based on the RT.

"The translators that produced the King James Version relied mainly, it seems, on the later editions of Beza's Greek New Testament, especially his 4th edition (1588-9). But also they frequently consulted the editions of Erasmus and Stephanus and the Complutensian Polyglot. According to Scrivener (1884), out of the 252 passages in which these sources differ sufficiently to affect the English rendering, the King James Version agrees with Beza against Stephanus 113

---

[1] Ibid. pp. 194-203

times, with Stephanus against Beza 59 times, and 80 times with Erasmus, or the Complutensian, or the Latin Vulgate against Beza and Stephanus [Scrivener, Authorized Edition of the English Bible, p. 60]. Hence the King James Version ought to be regarded not merely as a translation of the Textus Receptus but also as an independent variety of the Textus Receptus."[1]

One should not leave this discussion of the Received Text without several additional comments:

THE PRIESTHOOD OF BELIEVER'S MANUSCRIPTS "RECEIVE" THEIR NAME

First, the name for "the textus Receptus" [Received Text] came from the printers who followed Beza, the Elzevir family of Dutch printers. Their 2nd edition contained this statement in the preface:

"You have therefore the text now received by all (*textum ab omnibus receptum*) in which we give nothing changed or corrupt."[2]

However, the name really came from:

Joh 17:8 For I have given unto them the words which thou gavest me; and they have **received** them, and have known surely that I came out from thee, and they have believed that thou didst send me.

THE MANUSCRIPTS WERE FAITHFULLY TRANSMITTED

Second, the sacred reviewer (SR) is responsible for overseeing every Word of the Received Text. The word "keep" used throughout the Bible places that responsibility on the saints. If there is a question about a "letter," then the Received Text manuscripts must be consulted by the qualified men God gave the local churches. The number of differences in words may seem large to the uninitiated but in reality they are few as compared with the Alexandrian textual

---

[1] Ibid. p. 220

[2] Ibid. p. 208

foundation. Dr. Hills makes this very clear in his great work, *The KJV Defended*. He reviewed the very qualified works of Dr. Scrivener's (1884) and Dr. Hoskier's (1890) that listed the differences in the **Received Text** [textus Receptus] editions. Dr. Hills states that only 9 differences are of any consequence whatsoever. He goes on to say:

"This comparison indicates that the differences which distinguish the various editions of the Textus Receptus from each other are *very minor*. They are also very few. According to Hoskier, the 3rd edition of Stephanus and the first edition of Elzevir differ from one another in the Gospel of Mark only 19 times. Codex B, on the other hand, disagrees with Codex Aleph in Mark 652 times and with Codex D 1,944 times. What a contrast!"[1]

The TR is the end point of the transmission of God's Words in the original languages in MSS that were hand-written. This text became the basis of most of the EARLY English Bibles and the KJB, and certainly, the only Bibles that I would be comfortable using.

We will examine several English Bibles in this section on *"The Strait Gate: The Manuscripts"* for completeness. One Bible was not based on the TR foundation; another one was allegedly corrupted from the TR foundation to the Alexandrian text-type. One was produced for the wrong reasons, the other, for the right reasons. There were only two [Alexandrian] English Bibles of any consequence before the debacle of Westcott and Hort in 1881 and the production of the [English] Revised Version of 1881-1885 based on the Alexandrian Greek text.

BIBLES AND THEIR RELATIONSHIPS TO MANUSCRIPTS

The first "Bible" of the two mentioned above was the Jesuit Douay-Rheims (1609).

Harry A. Ironside said:

"Wherever the Authorized Version has "repent," the Douay-Rheims translation reads, "Do penance." There is no excuse for such a paraphrase"[2]

---

[1] Ibid. p. 222

[2] Ironside, Harry A.; *Except You Repent;* American Tract Society, 1937; Way of Life Literature, Port Huron, MI; Fundamental Baptist CD-ROM Library

We do not need to say any more except that the new 'modern' KJV21 (King James Version 2100), which was supposed to be an updating of the vocabulary of KJB, but changed 2200 verses out of 3,779 and some significantly, is the basis of the 'modern' Douay-Rheims Bible. The KJV21 and the Douay-Rheims Bible were combined to form the *Third Millennium Bible.* So, the tradition of changing God's Words to fit "tradition" rather than preservation continues.

Note the following amazing statement from the Third Millennium Bible web site:

"The Douay-Rheims Version and the King James Version have provided English-language Bible readers world-wide with intrinsically similar, though not identical, wording for well over four centuries. These two historic versions in turn are the only universally accepted English Bible translations developed over the past four hundred years. One of these need only be minimally updated to furnish all believers with a truly universal text. This has now been accomplished. The Third Millennium Bible presents the updated modern recension of the A.D. 1611 King James Version. It stands markedly closer to the Douay-Rheims Version than does either the King James Version or the Douay-Rheims Version to any contemporary Bible. The balance of this preface will focus on how a suitably modern biblical text in the English language **for all of Christendom** has come to be developed and published" (Publishers of the Third Millennium Bible)."[1] [my emphasis]

This Bible, the Third Millennium Bible, is an ecumenical book pulling the world closer to the "one-world government".

A BIBLE FOR THE RIGHT REASONS: THE WYCLIFF BIBLE

Returning to the other [alleged Alexandrian based] Bible, which had an extraordinary influence in the days prior to the publication of the KJB, was the

2000b, ISBN 1-58318-065-6

[1] Cloud, David; *21ˢᵗ Century King James Version Confusion;* 6/2/98; Way of Life Literature, Port Huron, MI; Fundamental Baptist CD-ROM Library 2000b, ISBN 1-58318-065-6

Wycliff Holy Bible of 1388. This Bible was produced for the right reason: to get the Words of God into the hands of the people even though it was alleged to be based on Jerome's work, the Latin Vulgate, but apparently it was not (see above). John Wycliff, "the morning-star of the Protestant Reformation", was not skilled in the languages of Hebrew or Greek, but he was skilled in Latin. Therefore Wycliff was alleged to produce the Wycliff translation from the Latin Vulgate into an Anglo-Saxon type English Bible. Our 'modern' generation could not read but perhaps every fourth (4th) to fifth (5th) word because of the type of English used. The importance of this Bible is the rejection of Romanism by the author and translator, and the placement of 'Scripture' into the hands of the common people. Remember: the value of Wycliff's translation mentioned elsewhere in this work was worth a 'hard days labor' just to have a few hours with it.

The Roman Catholic Church, which was not in power in England at the time of the writing of John Wycliff, so abhorred the man that 41 years after his death his bones were exhumed and burned by the Papacy.

"After encountering many prosecutions and persecutions, having however a powerful protector in John of Gaunt, (or Ghent, in Flanders, his native place,) the famous old Duke of Lancaster, Wiclif [this is the old English spelling] peacefully closed his devout and laborious life, at his rectory of Lutterworth, in 1384. Forty-one years after, by order of the popish Council of Constance, his bones were unearthed, burned to ashes, and cast into the Swift, a neighboring brook. "Thus," says Thomas Fuller, "this brook has conveyed his ashes into Avon, Avon into Severn, Severn in to the narrow seas, they into the main ocean. And thus the ashes of Wiclif are the emblem of his doctrine, which is now dispersed all the world over."[1]

And so Wycliff's work, and its value to **the priesthood of believers,** qualifies it to be placed with the **strait gate** manuscripts.

---

[1] McClure, Alexander; *Translators Revived: Biographical Notes of the King James Version Bible Translators;* c.1850; Way of Life Literature, Port Huron, MI; Fundamental Baptist CD-ROM Library 2000b, ISBN 1-58318-065-6; p. from the preface

COMPLUTENSIAN POLYGLOT BIBLE

The first printed work, which used the TR and, which has been mentioned in some quotes but not explained, was the *Complutensian Polyglot*. This work was printed in 1514 before Erasmus' Greek New Testament in 1516, but it was not distributed without the approval of Rome until 1522.

The following information also alludes to the number of manuscripts available to the men who were involved in the early publications of the printed Greek New Testament such as Erasmus. Erasmus':

> "edition was printed in 1516 and was followed by four later editions [some sources say 5 editions]. At Alcala (Complutum) University in 1502 Cardinal Ximenes gathered manuscripts and men under the direction of Stunica, who published the Complutensian Polyglot in 1522 ... Robert Stephens, relying largely upon Erasmus and Stunica, and with at least fifteen manuscripts at his disposal, produced editions of the Greek text in 1546, 1549, 1550, and 1551."[1] "It was called a "polyglot" because it contained a number of languages in addition to the Greek."[2]

DR. WAITE'S LIST OF BIBLES BASED ON THE RECEIVED TEXT

The following list is from Dr. Waite's great book, *Defending the King James Bible*. All of these Bibles that are listed gave evidence for the RT. We will pick several from the list to examine more closely. Please notice the list builds until the KJB is reached.

> "d. Historical Evidences for the *Received Text* During the Early Modern Period (1453--1831 A.D.)
> (18) The churches of the Reformation all used the

---

[1] Trinitarian Bible Society; *The Divine Original;* as recorded in *Modern Bible Versions* by David Cloud; Way of Life Literature, Port Huron, MI; Fundamental Baptist CD-ROM Library 2000b, ISBN 1-58318-065-6

[2] Waite, Th.D., Ph.D., D.A.; *Defending The King James Version;* p. 221

Received Text.

(19) The Erasmus Greek New Testament (1516) used the Received Text.

(20) The Complutensian Polyglot (1522) used the Received Text. A Roman Catholic Cardinal named Ximenes, edited it, yet it was based, not on the texts which most Roman Catholic Bibles used, the Westcott and Hort text, but on the Received Text.

(21) Martin Luther's German Bible (1522) used the Received Text.

(22) William Tyndale's Bible, (1525), used the Received Text. Tyndale was a great Bible translator who was martyred because of his Bible translation.

(23) The French Version of Oliveton (1535) used the Received Text.

(24) The Coverdale Bible (1535) used the Received Text.

(25) The Matthews Bible (1537) used the Received Text.

(26) The Taverners Bible (1539) used the Received Text.

(27) The Great Bible (1539-41) used the Received Text.

(28) The Stephanus Greek New Testament (1546-51) used the Received Text.

(29) The Geneva Bible (1557-60) used the Received Text.

(30) The Bishops' Bible (1568) used the Received Text.

(31) The Spanish Version (1569) used the Received Text.

(32) The Beza Greek New Testament (1598) used the Received Text. That is the Greek text that the KING JAMES BIBLE was based on, using the 1598, 5th edition of Beza.

(33) The Czech Version (1602) used the Received Text.

(34) The Italian Version of Diodati (1607) used the Received Text.

(35) The KING JAMES BIBLE (1611) used the Received Text."[1]

---

[1] Ibid. p. 47

THE PRIESTHOOD OF BELIEVERS AVOIDED
THE LEAVEN

Before moving into this next discussion, I want to remind the reader of the importance of *contact* in the transmission or lack of transmission of disease. Recall the Scripture tells us a "little leaven, leaveneth the whole lump". Every hospital has an isolation room to prevent spread of transmissible diseases. Every operating room has facilities to scrub hands and arms prior to surgery. Every newborn nursery has strict rules to prevent transmission of disease to newborns. It is foolish for one to expose himself or others to a transmissible disease. Yet, in the instance of many bacterial and viral illnesses such as AIDS, infectious mononucleosis, tuberculosis, pneumococcal, staphylococcus, streptococcus, exposure happens every day. This is foolish. It is no less foolish to expose ourselves to sin that is preventable. The Scripture is replete with examples, and cautions severely against slackness in this area. Yet, modern evangelicals and fundamentalists believe they can "expose" themselves to denominations and persons which hold false or wrong doctrine and come away unscathed. Their modern mantra seems to be "love, love, love" at the expense of "doctrine, doctrine, doctrine." Which do you believe is most important? The truth is that the Words of God are protective; they offer protection. Therefore, to help someone see the "protection" of the doctrines of the Bible is truer love than those who "tolerate" anything. This stand for the Word of God has caused men and women to be "cursed" through the centuries and has led to the martyr's fires. What do you think these verses mean?:

Proverbs 4:14-15 *Enter not into the path of the wicked, and go not in the way of evil men. Avoid it, pass not by it, turn from it, and pass away.*

Romans 16:17 *Now I beseech you, brethren, mark them which cause divisions and offences contrary to the doctrine which ye have learned; and avoid them.*

1 Cor. 15:33 *Be not deceived: evil communications corrupt good manners.*

The men who COPIED the manuscripts of the strait gate understood these instructions in the Scriptures. They became aware of the great travesty of "the doctrines of men" of the wide gate and did everything they could to separate themselves.

2 Cor. 6:17 *Wherefore come out from among them, and be ye separate, saith the Lord, and touch not the unclean thing; and I will*

receive you,

Even the Lord did this, though many tell us he did not because he visited in the house of sinners. He may have been in **their house,** but they were not in **"His House."** See Mark 2:15 and Luke 5:29. However, they did press into His house in Capernaum (Mk. 2:1-2). The sad part of the story is that they did not realize who it was that sat in **their house** across from them. The bottom line in all of this is to separate in worship, obedience, Scripturally, spiritually, and so much as possible, even in your home (2John 1:10).

Hebrews 7:26 *For such an high priest became us, who is holy, harmless, undefiled,* **separate from sinners,** *and made higher than the heavens;*

Many of the men of the strait gate held to the beliefs above so strongly that they went to the fires rather than recant, no matter what the cost. **These men went to the fires fighting for the Received Words of God and their translations based on the PRESERVED WORDS.** They were certainly members of the priesthood of believers. Many more would have been martyred were it not for God raising up some to come along side and protect them.

THE ENGLISH BIBLE AND ITS FATHER, THE APOSTLE OF ENGLAND

William Tyndale's Bible used the Received Text and he was called 'the father of the English Bible. God raised up this man just as the printing was coming of age.

"The most important change of all, though, in Tyndale's time had to do with the printing press. Just 22 years before Tyndale's birth, the city of Mentz was invaded and the knowledge of printing could no longer be kept a secret by its founders. Gutenberg had died only 16 years before Tyndale was born. Only eight years before Tyndale's birth, a printing press had been set up in England by William Caxton. By Tyndale's birth, printing presses had been set up in more than 120 cities of Europe. By the time Tyndale was 32 years old, the Greek New Testament had been printed.

Tyndale yearned to see the Scriptures translated into English directly from the original Hebrew and Greek and to see the English Bible printed and made available to the common man. The historian John Foxe tells us that Tyndale was "singularly addicted to the study of the Scriptures." While debating the need for ecclesiastical reform and theological purity, Tyndale exclaimed, "If God spare my life, ere many years I will cause a boy that driveth a plough shall know more of the Scriptures than thou doest." When he said this, he was addressing a Catholic priest who had stated that "we are better without God's laws than the pope's."

It is evident that God had enflamed Tyndale's heart with a passion to produce a pure English translation of the Scriptures, and to the fulfillment of this noble purpose he dedicated his life, willingly suffering great privations, forgoing the joys of marriage and a settled family life, for the sake of endowing his beloved people with the eternal Word of God."[1]

Tyndale was able to ready his translation of the New Testament for the printer in Cologne in spite of much harassment and persecution by 1525. You will recall that many of his New Testaments were smuggled into England in barrels. In 1531, Tyndale published the Prologue and newly translated book of Jonah for the English people.

"He had already commenced with "the first book of Moses called Genesis, newly corrected and amended by W.T. MDXXXIIII."[2]

"After six editions of the Testament had been issued, he published Genesis and Deuteronomy, in 1530 [It is recognized that this conflicts with the above date which probably has to do with dates of publishing]; and next year the Pentateuch. In the year 1535 was printed the entire Bible, under the auspices of Miles Coverdale, who mostly followed Tyndale as far as he had gone; but without any other connection with him. Of Coverdale, [see below] further mention will be made. But in the year 1537 appeared a folio Bible, printed in some city of Germany, with the following title,--"THE BYBLE, which is the Holy Scripture; in which are contayned the Olde and Newe Testament, truly and purely translated into Englysh-- by Thomas Matthew.--MDXXXVII." [The Matthews Bible] This is substantially the basis of all the other versions of the Bible into English, including that which is now in such extensive use. [The King James Bible] It contains Tyndale's labors as far as he had gone previous to his martyrdom by fire about a year before its publication. That is to say, the whole of the New Testament, and of the Old, as far as the end of the Second Book of Chronicles, or exactly two-thirds of the entire Scriptures, were Tyndale's work. The other third, comprising the remainder of the Old Testament, was

---

[1] Cloud, David; *William Tyndale: The Father of Our English Bible;* Nov. 30, 1999; Way of Life Literature, Port Huron, MI; Fundamental Baptist CD-ROM Library 2000b, ISBN 1-58318-065-6

[2] Anderson, Christopher; *Annals of the English Bible;* 1861; Way of Life Literature, Port Huron, MI; Fundamental Baptist CD-ROM Library 2000b, ISBN 1-58318-065-6; p. Section: *England—Reign of Henry VIII, 1534*

made by his friend and co-laborer, Thomas Matthew, who was no other than John Rogers, the famous martyr, afterwards burnt in the days of "bloody Mary;" and who, at the time of his immortal publication, went by the name of Matthew."[1] [my emphasis]

There can be no doubt that Tyndale was a member of the **priesthood of believers**. The number of martyrs surrounding Tyndale's life and work is staggering. One would benefit greatly from a thorough study of this man, his friends and his life. He became known as the **"Apostle of England"**, so greatly was he respected by the common people. It was his Bible which became the basis of the first ever printed Bible in England. The following quote is placed here as a testament to the man and his work. This quote followed the description of his burning, and a lament about there being no monument on earth to so great a man.

"But there is a better world, where he is not forgotten. "Also now, behold, his witness justly calls Tyndale "the Apostle of England," gives the following beautiful sketch of the man--"First, he was a man very frugal, and spare of body, a great student and earnest laborer in setting forth the Scriptures of God. He reserved or hallowed to himself, two days in the week, which he named his pastime, Monday and Saturday. On Monday he visited all such poor men and women as were fled out of England, by reason of persecution, unto Antwerp; and these; once well understanding their good exercises and qualities, he did very liberally comfort and relieve; and in like manner provided for the sick and diseased persons. On the Saturday, he walked round the town, seeking every corner and hole, where he suspected any poor person to dwell; and where he found any to be well occupied, and yet overburdened with children, or else were aged and weak, these also he plentifully relieved. And thus he spent his two days of pastime, as he called it. And truly his alms were very large, and so these might well be; for his exhibition [i.e. pension] that he had yearly of the English merchants at Antwerp, when living there, was considerable, and that for the most part he bestowed upon the poor. The rest of the days of the week he gave wholly to his BOOK, wherein he most diligently travailed. When the Sunday came, then went he to some one merchant's chamber, or other, whither came many other merchants, and unto them would he read some one parcel of Scripture; the which proceeded so fruitfully, sweetly, and gently from him, much like to the writing of John the Evangelist, that it was a heavenly

[1] McClure, Alexander, *The Glorious History of the English* Bible; c 1850; p. preface, Translators Revived, Way of Life Literature, Port Huron, MI; Fundamental Baptist CD-ROM Library 2000b, ISBN 1-58318-065-6

comfort and joy to the audience, to hear him read the Scriptures; likewise, after dinner, he spent an hour in the same manner. He was a man without any spot or blemish of rancor or malice, full of mercy and compassion, so that no man living was able to reprove him of any sin or crime; although his righteousness and justification depended not thereupon before God; but only upon the blood of Christ, and his faith upon the same. In this faith he died, with constancy, at Vilvorde, and now resteth with the glorious company of Christ's martyrs, blessedly in the Lord." The good man's work did not die with him. During the last year of his life, nine or more editions of his Testament issued from the press, and found their way into English "thick and three-fold." But what is strangest of all, and is unexplained to this day, at the very time when Tyndale by the procurement of English ecclesiastics, and by the sufferance of the English king, was burned at Vilvorde, a folio-edition of his Translation was printed at London, with his name on the title-page, and by Thomas Berthlet, the king's own patent printer. This was the first copy of the Scriptures ever printed on English ground."[1] [my emphasis]

Now, the strait gate manuscripts and Bibles will continue being published one after another!!!

THE MATTHEWS BIBLE AND COVERDALE BIBLE

The Matthews Bible led the way for the first licensed English Bible to be sold in Great Britain. This great accomplishment can be attributed to two men: 1. Thomas Cranmer, and 2. Thomas Cromwell. Cranmer was a linguist at Cambridge who shook off the darkness of scholasticism [Neoplatonism]. Unknowingly and by providence, he helped the King of England, Henry VIII, divorce Queen Catherine and marry Queen Anne Boleyn.

"Cranmer had enunciated the religious principle that the Bible is above the Pope, and now Cromwell brings forward the political one that England is wholly an independent State, and owes no subjection to the Papacy."[2]

---

[1] Ibid. p. Section: William Tyndale

[2] Wylie, J.A.; *The History of Protestantism;* Cassell and Company, 1899; Way of Life Literature, Port Huron, MI; Fundamental Baptist CD-ROM Library 2000b, ISBN 1-58318-065-6; p. Book 23, Chapter 8

All the intrigue in England brought the Coverdale Bible to the point of the being circulated in England without hindrance, which was followed by the licensed Matthew Bible, and the Anglican Church was born.

"Tyndale was burnt; but he ...might say that he had lighted such a candle, by God's grace, in England, as should never be put out. His own New Testament had been rigorously excluded from England, so far as those in authority could exclude it; but the case for which he gave his life was won. Even before his death he might have heard that a Bible, partly founded on his own, had been issued in England under the protection of the highest authorities. In 1534 the Upper House of Convocation of Canterbury had petitioned the King to authorize a translation of the Bible into English, and it was probably at this time that Cranmer proposed a scheme for a joint translation by nine or ten of the most learned bishops and other scholars. Cranmer's scheme came to nothing; but Cromwell, now Secretary of State, incited Miles Coverdale to publish a work of translation on which he had been already engaged. Coverdale had known Tyndale abroad, and is said to have assisted him in his translation of the Pentateuch; but he was no Greek or Hebrew scholar, and his version, which was printed abroad in 1535 (probably, according to the latest expert view, at Marburg) and appeared in England in that year or the next, professed only to be translated from the Dutch (i.e. German) and Latin. Coverdale, a moderate, tolerant, earnest man, claimed no originality, and expressly looked forward to the Bible being more faithfully presented both "by the ministration of other that begun it afore" (Tyndale) and by the future scholars who should follow him; but his Bible has two important claims on our interest. Though not expressly authorized, it was undertaken at the wish of Cromwell, and a dedication to Henry VIII, printed apparently by Nycholson of Southwark, was inserted among the prefatory matter of the German-printed sheets, which were no doubt imported unbound. It is thus the first English Bible which circulated in England without let or hindrance from the higher powers. It is also the first complete English printed Bible, since Tyndale had not been able to finish the whole of the Old Testament. In the Old Testament Coverdale depended mainly on the Swiss-German version published by Zwingli and Leo Juda in 1524-9, though in the Pentateuch he also made considerable use of Tyndale's translation. The New Testament is a careful revision of Tyndale by comparison with the German. It is to Coverdale therefore that our English versions of the poetical and prophetical books are primarily due, and in handling the work of others he showed great skill. **Many of Coverdale's phrases have passed** into the Authorized Version. **In one respect he departed markedly from his predecessor - namely, in bringing back to the English Bible the ecclesiastical terms which Tyndale had banished.** The demand for the Bible continued unabated, and a further step had been made in the direction of securing official authorization. Two revised editions were published in 1537, this time printed in England by Nycholson; and one of these, in quarto, bore the announcement that it was "set forth with the king's most gracious license." The bishops in Convocation might still discuss the expediency of allowing the Scriptures to circulate in English, but the question had been decided without them. The Bible circulated, and there could be no returning to the old ways."[1] [my emphasis]

THE GREAT BIBLE, THE BISHOPS BIBLE, AND THE GENEVA BIBLE

So the Coverdale Bible was circulated, and the Matthews Bible was licensed by the influence of Cranmer and Cromwell. Cromwell became the Secretary of State and Cranmer, the Anglican Archbishop. Their increased authority allowed them to issue an order for a new version by Coverdale that would be placed in every church. This became known as the Great Bible. Cromwell was anxious to place another version in the hands of the people because he was so much involved in the Matthews Bible, which contained remarks in the side-notes offensive to the King and which was produced with Tyndale's influence.[2]

Cromwell was eventually executed and Cranmer died at the stake.[3] The reaction of King Henry against all Reformers and, especially, any Bible that was influenced by Tyndale, caused many translators to flee to Geneva. Under the guiding hand of great Reformers and scholars in Geneva such as Beza, W. Whittingham, and Calvin, the Geneva Bible was produced.[4] Theodore Beza was the distinguished looking Reformer with the long white beard who assisted Calvin until his death, who edited 10 editions of the Greek Text [the 5th edition is the Greek text used for the KJB], who defended the Reformers so eloquently

---

[1] Moorman, Jack; *Forever Settled;* p. 174

[2] Ibid. p. 177

[3] Ibid. P. 177, 180

[4] Ibid. p. 180

at the Council of Poissy, September 9th, 1561,[1] and who had "held the office of Greek professor and theological lecturer at Lausanne"[2]. William Whittingham (1524-1579) was a Greek scholar, married the sister of Calvin, and was the chief translator of the Geneva Bible which was based on Tyndale's work. It is also the first English Bible to be divided into verses.[3] This is the Bible that came to the 'new' world in 1609 with the settlers of Jamestown.

The Bishops Bible was produced under Queen Elizabeth whose reign was friendly to Protestantism. Fifteen bishops made the version and thus the name, Bishop's Bible. It immediately followed the Great Bible as the 'official' Bible in 1568, but the Geneva Bible could not be replaced in the hearts of the people. "In the forty-three years which elapsed before the appearance of the Authorized Version, nearly 120 editions of the Geneva Bible issued from the press, as against 20 of the Bishop's Bible."[4]

THE KING JAMES BIBLE

The next Bible that we will examine, which is based on the Received Text, is the "glorious" King James Bible. Much of the following information came from the book by Pastor D. A. Waite, Th.D., Ph.D., *Defending the King James Version.*

---

[1] Wylie, J. A.; *The History of Protestantism;* Cassell and Company, 1899; Way of Life Literature, Port Huron, MI; Fundamental Baptist CD-ROM Library 2000b, ISBN 1-58318-065-6; p. Book 13, Chapter 6
[2] Ibid; p. Book 14, Chapter 18
[3] McClure, Alex; *Glorious History of the English Bible;* p. Section: "The Geneva Bible"; Way of Life Literature, Port Huron, MI; Fundamental Baptist CD-ROM Library 2000b, ISBN 1-58318-065-6;
[4] Moorman, Jack; *Forever Settled;* p. 171

First, let's review the support for the Received Text (TR) and the Alexandrian Text (W/H) from the Manuscript evidence.[1]

	TOTAL	Number of MSS: W/H	Number of MSS: TR	% of MSS: W/H	% of MSS: TR
Papyrus Fragments	81 (88)	13	75	15%	85%
Uncials	267	9	258	3%	97%
Cursives	2764	23	2741	1%	99%
Lectionaries	2143	0	2143	0%	100%
Totals	5255	45	5210	1%	99%

*TR = Received Text
*W/H = Westcott/Hort Greek Text

Just looking at this table tells a person a lot. Just remember, this does not include the patristic evidence and the translations into other languages such as Syrian, Italian, etc. which adds literally volumes of support for the TR. Without any other information I would want a Bible based on the text with the majority of MSS for support. However, the overwhelming information contained in the SUBJECTIVE, the "S" of the SOAP acronym, precludes desiring any other textual basis for a Bible and indicates God preserved His Words in the TR by providence.

THE HEBREW TEXT OF THE KJB

The Old Testament Text used by the 1881 'revisers' and by the translators of 'modern' versions was presented earlier. The Hebrew and Aramaic text used by the earlier translators in the 15th and 16th centuries had not been corrupted by men like Kittel. The O.T. text had been faithfully copied by the Masoretic scribes as commanded by God and noted by Paul in the N.T.
Romans 3:1-2 *What advantage then hath the Jew? or what profit is*

[1]Waite, Th.D., Ph.D., D. A.; *Defending the King James Bible;* p. 57 This table was made possible by Dr. Waite' figures.

there of circumcision? Much every way: chiefly, because that unto them were committed the oracles of God.

The Jewish scribes had devotedly transcribed the text from copy to copy and they took God's commission of handling His oracles very seriously. The last group of Jewish priests and family to honor God's commandment was the Masoretic scribes who continued until the late Middle Ages [about 1000 A.D.]. After that period the hand copied Hebrew text was machine printed just like the New Testament Text.

"What about the Hebrew text used by the KING JAMES BIBLE translators? Here's some background on it. The **Daniel Bomberg edition**, 1516-1517, was called the *First Rabbinic Bible.* Then in 1524-25, **Bomberg** published a second edition edited by Abraham Ben Chayyim (or Ben Hayyim) iben Adonijah. This is called the **Ben Chayyim edition** of the Hebrew text. Daniel Bomberg's edition, on which the KING JAMES BIBLE is based was the **Ben Chayyim Masoretic Text.** This was called the *Second Great Rabbinic Bible.* This became the standard Masoretic text for the next 400 years. This is the text that underlies the KING JAMES BIBLE. For four hundred years, that was the Old Testament Hebrew text. Nobody translated the Old Testament except by using this text. [This is from *Biblical Criticism Historical, Literal, Textual* by Harrison, Walkie and Guthrie, 1978, pages 47-82.]"[1]

The reader may be questioning if the 10th century Masoretic text was transcribed [copied] correctly and maintained its reliability to the O.T. text before the time of Jesus. We can be assured that what faithful men have told us over the years prior to the following discoveries is true. In other words, trustworthy sacred reviewers such as John Burgon have reassured us the Words of God have been preserved, even before the Dead Sea scrolls at Qumran were discovered in the 20th century.

"Much more recently, at Qumran, two manuscripts of Isaiah have been found. One of them is complete, and dates from the 1st century before Christ. The surprising and amazing thing about this textual evidence, is that the 10th century A.D., Masoretic text is in substantial agreement with the text of Isaiah, that has been buried for two thousand years. **The two texts are in amazing agreement, except for a number of minor punctuation-type variations.**"[2] [my emphasis] [WOW!!!!]

---

[1] Ibid. p. 27

[2] Green, Jay P.; *Unholy Hands on the Bible;* Vol. II; Sovereign Grace Trust Fund, Lafayette, Indiana, 1992; ISBN 1-878-443-65-1; p. 364

The next bit of information will add significant support to why the King James Bible is preferred as a translation, which used the Received Text and the Bomberg second edition Ben Chayyim Masoretic Text. Most of this material was taken from Dr. D. A. Waite's book, *Defending the King James Version.*

THE SUPERIOR KING JAMES BIBLE

Dr. Waite pointed out clearly that the KJB is a superior translation based on God's Words for the following reasons:

    I.   **The translators** whom we have examined briefly earlier in this work were **superior**. Several authors such as Alexander McClure and Gustavus S. Paine have agreed with Dr. Waite and have suggested that a team as qualified as these men will never be put together again. Dr Waite quotes McClure on this issue:

"As the capability of those men, we may say again, that, by the good Providence of God, their work was undertaken in a fortunate time. Not only had the English language, that singular compound, then ripened to its full perfection, but the study of Greek and of the oriental tongues, and of Rabbinical lore, had then been carried to a greater extent in England than ever before or since…It is confidently expected that the reader of these pages will yield to the conviction, that all the colleges of Great Britain and America, even in this proud day of boastings, [about 1857 A.D.] could not bring together the same number of divines equally qualified by learning and piety for the great undertaking. Few indeed are the living names worthy to be enrolled with those mighty men. It would be impossible to convene out of any one Christian denomination, or out of all, a body of translators, on whom the whole Christian community would bestow such confidence as is reposed upon that illustrious company, or who would prove themselves as deserving of such confidence."[1]

    II.   **The texts** of the New Testament and Old Testament previously reviewed in this work that the translators used were **superior**.

    III.   **The technique** the translators used to develop the translation was **superior**. The translation technique was superior because of the team approach that was used.

    First, every member of the six (6) teams had to do his own translation. The total number of men was "up to fifty-seven men". There were 6-7 men per team. There were two teams at each location consisting of a N.T.

---

[1] Waite, Th.D., Ph.D., D.A.; *Defending the King James Version;* p. 81

and O.T. group located at Westminster, Oxford, and Cambridge. Each translator had to defend his work. The names of the men and the section of the Scripture for which they were responsible may be found in Dr. Waite's book.

After the individual translators had defended their work in the group then each company would send it to the other 5 groups. Finally, a group of 12 men reviewed the work one last time. The bottom line is that:

"this makes fourteen times the Bible from Genesis to Revelation was translated, analyzed, and corrected".[1]

Then there were continuing rules concerning areas of additional disagreement, and additional scholars were to be consulted.

The translation technique was superior because the translator used verbal and formal equivalent translation as opposed to dynamic equivalent translation. Dr Waite has an excellent discussion of the "diabolical" dynamic equivalent (DE) translation technique in his book from page 89-132.

IV.   The King James Bible is God's Words kept intact because its **theology** is **superior.** Dr. Waite reports the theology is affected in other versions in two ways:

a.   Doctrinal changes occur because the texts of the new versions are translated by a paraphrase or

b.   The wrong Greek text with doctrinal changes intentionally inserted is used .

There are nine well-known men, Dr. Waite reports, who make false statements about the theology of the new versions. They report that doctrine was not affected by 'modern' versions paraphrasing and by a different Greek text. Those men were: Philip Schaff, Arthur T. Pierson, Louis T. Talbot, Robert L. Sumner, Robert L. Thomas, H. S. Miller, Stanley Gundry, and Ernest D. Pickering.

I have selected one quote from the men listed above to give the reader a sense of all their various statements. Louis T. Talbot states:

"Yet, to repeat for emphasis, for all practical purposes, we still cling to the King James Version, using the **REVISED** [that is the ENGLISH REVISED VERSION of 1881, or the AMERICAN STANDARD VERSION of 1901] as a kind of commentary for analytical study. And let me add that **NO FUNDAMENTAL DOCTRINE HAS BEEN CHANGED IN THE LEAST BY THE LATER VERSION.**"[2]

Oh My! How wrong this statement is, as we will see.

This concludes the history of the issue before us. We have arrived at the section called the Objective, the "O" in the SOAP acronym, where we will

---

[1] Ibid. p. 87
[2] Ibid. p. 134

examine the patient. Examination of a "patient" requires careful observation. In the objective section we will observe some of the effects of all the preceding history and information in this work as it applies to the doctrine and theology in the 'new' versions. Sometimes the effects are subtle, and casual examination will not suffice. Put on your thinking cap.

THE OBJECTIVE

"VANQUISHED BY THE WORD INCARNATE, SATAN NEXT DIRECTED HIS SUBTLE MALICE AGAINST THE WORD"
(By Dean John William Burgon, 1881)

BLINDED GUIDES

Dean Burgon wrote the quote above. He understood the real source of the "corrupter's" motivation to mutilate the Scriptures, to deny preservation, and to create confusion by the lies and faithlessness at every level in modernistic textual criticism. Satan is the father of lies and confusion. Modernistic text critics have been blinded. Jesus said it this way:

Mt 23:24 "Ye blind guides, which strain at a gnat, and swallow a camel."

Modernistic textual "scholars" have gotten so wrapped up in history, archaeology, naturalism, evolution, environmentalism, pridefulness, positions in academia, and one-up-manship (the first to report a "new" finding), that they have forgotten or have deliberately failed "to see" the "big" picture. They have become "blind guides." It is physically nauseating to hear grown men who are allegedly "scholars" proclaim that the changes to Scripture pointed out in this section make "no difference."

This entire work was not written to them, because they will fail to see the truth and "will fall." This work is for those who are suffering because of the confusion wrought by "the blind guides." Jesus said it like this:

Mt 15:14 "Let them alone: they be blind leaders of the blind. And if the blind lead the blind, both shall fall into the ditch."

APOSTATE BELIEFS AND CHANGES IN SCRIPTURE

A brief review of the major theological beliefs of many of the persons who have been involved in textual criticism is in order as one begins this examination. A physician keeps in mind the major points that have been garnered from the history of the patient as he begins his exam.

The modernistic textual critic (as opposed to a sacred reviewer) may believe one, several, or all of the following:

1. The deity of Jesus Christ is either:
   a. Denied or
   b. Subordinated to an inferior position to the Father.
2. The work of Jesus Christ is devalued by
   a. Denying that the death of Jesus was to satisfy God's demand for justice and to atone for man's sin
   b. Substituting a perverted view that the cross simply moved man's heart toward God.
3. The virgin birth is denied.
4. Eternal life is regarded as the knowledge of God here and now on earth.
5. Heaven and Hell are not believed to be real places.
6. The Second Coming of the Lord is taught as having happened in 70 A.D. at the fall of Jerusalem or as occurring at the death of the believer or at the time of salvation.
7. Verbal inspiration of the Scripture is denied, and its authority is restricted.
8. Doctrines are consciously de-emphasized.
9. The incarnation is taught as a "type" of union with all men, which would eventually lead to redemption for all men.
10. Darwin's theory of evolution is accepted, and the accounts of creation are denied. Closely related to this concept is that the Bible contains "mythology" and that multiple books were written by multiple authors.
11. Sin is defined as selfishness.

Most of the heresies mentioned above and at the beginning of this work are the beliefs in the early centuries of the Gnostics, variants of Gnosticism such as Arianism and Montanism, and the Broad Church adherents in the 1800's. Those beliefs are reflected in the altered Scripture in the 'new' versions due to heretical influence as you will see by examining the "Scripture" citations and the changes in words, phrases, and verses.

One of the worst heretics was the Gnostic, Marcion. Marcion deleted all the gospels except Luke. He only allowed ten (10) of Paul's epistles. Many books were corrupted by him. Dr. Moorman reports the following:

"As Irenaeus said concerning Marcion, the Gnostic: "Wherefore also Marcion and his followers have betaken themselves to mutilating the Scriptures, not acknowledging some books at all; and, curtailing the Gospel according to Luke, and the epistles of Paul, they assert that these alone are authentic, which they have themselves shortened."[1]

Many other groups such as the Ebionites, and individuals such as Origen corrupted the Scriptures. Some "scholars" try to show that they were just another group of early Christians who varied in their beliefs.[2] However, anyone with so little respect for the Words of God that they could mutilate them or even change one letter has to be suspect as to their true loyalties.

Now, we will examine specific verses, the changes in those verses, and explain why they are wrong.

THE "O" IN SOAP—AN OBJECTIVE LOOK AT THE SCRIPTURES

Specific words and verses that have been changed in the Bible will be inspected next. The MSS changes will be noted first and then the translations of the corrupted MSS to produce Bibles will be evaluated. Although there are thousands of changes only a few will be examined. **Most new versions reflect some of these changes, if not all of them.** The Scripture quotes are from the KJB. The information was obtained from *Unholy Hands on the Bible,* Vol 2, pp.403-406

Example 1.   In Isaiah 7:14 the word 'virgin' was changed to 'young woman'. This disturbs the rendering by Matthew in 1:22-23, and suggests the virgin-birth of Christ did not occur.

Isaiah 7:14 *Therefore the Lord himself shall give you a sign; Behold, a virgin shall conceive, and bear a son, and shall call his name Immanuel.*

Matthew 1:22-23 *Now all this was done, that it might be fulfilled which was spoken of the Lord by the prophet, saying, Behold, a virgin shall be with child, and shall bring forth a son, and they shall call his name Emmanuel, which being interpreted is, God with us.*

Example 2.   In John 1:18 the phrase "only begotten God"' was substituted for "the only begotten Son". This lowers the 'Son' to a begotten 'God' making Him lower than the other two members of the Trinity. This lowers His deity. Only four manuscripts are known to have used this perverted phrase: Sinaiticus, Vaticanus, P66, and P75.

John 1:18 *No man hath seen God at any time; the only begotten*

[1] Moorman, Jack; *Forever Settled;* p. 97
[2] Ehrman, Bart D.; Lost Christianities; Oxford University Press; New York; 2003; pp. 1-7

Son, which is in the bosom of the Father, he hath declared him.

Example 3.   In Acts 20:28 the phrase "church of God" was changed to "church of the Lord". This lowers Christ's deity by distorting the fact Jesus was God and He purchased the Church with His blood.

Acts 20:28 *Take heed therefore unto yourselves, and to all the flock, over the which the Holy Ghost hath made you overseers, to feed the <u>church of God</u>, which he hath purchased with his own blood.*

Example 5.   Philippians 2:6 "...who being in the form of God, thought it not robbery to be equal with God..." is changed in the *Translators New Testament* (From the BFBS, British Foreign Bible Society) to "but he did not consider that he must cling to equality with God"; and the TEV (Todays English Version) substituted "...He always had the very nature of God, but he did not think that by force he should try to become equal with God." These renderings degrade the deity of Christ and are major departures from the MSS.

Philip. 2:6 *Who, being in the form of God, thought it not robbery to be equal with God*:

Example 6.   1Tim. 3:16 "God" is changed to "He who". I'll give you the verse first this time.

1 Tim. 3:16 And without controversy great is the mystery of godliness: <u>God</u> was manifest in the flesh, justified in the Spirit, seen of angels, preached unto the Gentiles, believed on in the world, received up into glory.

This is one of the greatest verses in the Bible. The support for this verse is so firm that any change is an obvious attempt to denigrate our Lord. Changing an obvious reference to Jesus as "God" to "he who" demotes Christ to not being equal with God. Listen! **"He" does not appear in any MSS** and "who" is found in only one uncial, three lectionaries, and two versions. No Church Father quoted "He who". Even the Alexandrian [Egyptian] texts do not support it. The *Majority Text* [RT] is sustained by A, C, F/G, K, L, P, Phi, over 300 cursive manuscripts and lectionaries, and two versions. The removal of "God" from the text and the placing of "He who" is an obvious attempt to dethrone our Lord! I just got my old NASB off the shelf and looked up this verse. My heart was broken to see the NASB has rendered this as "He who". May God have mercy on the souls of the perverters! Anyone who would take away from the glory of the Lord Jesus Christ, His position, and His name does not understand the following verse and has no fear of God:

Php 2:9 "Wherefore God also hath highly exalted him, and given him a name which is above every name:"

The next several verses omit or remove from Scripture verses or words that are supported by the majority of witnesses.

Example 7.   Matt 6:13 The following doxology is removed from the Lord's Prayer: "for thine is the kingdom, and the power, and the glory, forever.

Amen." This is the prayer taught by Jesus to his disciples. Removing this phrase lowers the respect for God's power and authority.

Example 8. Matt. 18:11 "For the Son of man is come to save that which was lost" is omitted.

The Gnostics want to regulate Jesus to an inferior status to conform to their beliefs. The Vaticanus and Sinaiticus MSS omit this phrase. The majority text [Received Text, Traditional Text] contains this phrase.

Matthew 18:11 For the Son of man is come to save that which was lost.

Luke 19:10 For the Son of man is come to seek and to save that which was lost.

Example 9. In Mark 1:1 the statement "The beginning of the gospel of Jesus Christ, the Son of God", "Son of God" is omitted in the original Sinaiticus palimpsest [a manuscript, which cleaned and used again]. A later scribe added "Son of God" back in, but several versions use this as a reason to add a marginal note indicating "other ancient authorities lack 'the Son of God'. This kind of marginal note causes confusion in the body [church] of the Lord Jesus Christ and is in reality nothing but masquerading lies! They must stop and they will!! Judgment is coming as prophesied, just as sure as hundred of other prophecies have been fulfilled to the letter. Even the Alexandrian text contains the Son of God, just as the RT does.

Example 10. In Mark 9:24 the word "Lord" is omitted. Jesus was not considered 'Lord" by many heretics. Therefore, the Alexandrinus, Sinaiticus, and Vaticanus manuscripts remove "Lord". Modern Bibles as ERV, ASV, RSV, NEB, NASB, NIV, NRSV, follow this lead.

Mark 9:24 And straightway the father of the child cried out, and said with tears, <u>Lord</u>, I believe; help thou mine unbelief.

Example 11. In John 3:13 the phrase "which is in heaven" is deleted. The obvious reason is because many do not believe in a literal heaven or hell; and do not believe Jesus came down from heaven and went back to heaven. The Egyptian texts remove it and the RT retains it.

John 3:13 And no man hath ascended up to heaven, but he that came down from heaven, even the Son of man <u>which is in heaven</u>.

Example 12. John 7:53-8:11 is the woman caught in the adultery pericope. The section indicates that Jesus can forgive sin and so this may have been the reason it was left out of the Sinaiticus, P66, and P75. The RT keeps it. There are reports in the literature that this may have been left out because many lectionaries stopped just before John 7:53. Other authors say the reason is that this particular passage of Scripture was not believed to be true, because Jesus forgave a woman caught in adultery and is not consistent with the Old Testament. I rather believe this passage may have been inappropriate for public reading, and the word placed in the margin to indicate to the public reader to "stop here" was misinterpreted.

Example 13.   John 21:25 refers to the many miracles Jesus did. They were so numerous that the world would overflow with books if they were all recorded. This demonstrates Jesus' authority as God. The Sinaiticus drops the verse and, interestingly, Tischendorf removed it from his 8th edition. The RT keeps it.

John 21:25 *And there are also many other things which Jesus did, the which, if they should be written every one, I suppose that even the world itself could not contain the books that should be written. Amen.*

Example 14.   Acts 8:37 is the Ethiopian's confession of Christ's deity. It is not found in the majority of MSS, Sinaiticus, Vaticanus, Alexandrinus, and others. Through God's providential care it is found in Irenaeus' writings, *Against Heresies,* from the 2nd century, the old Latin from the 2nd – 4th centuries, Floriacansis from the 5th century, Harclean Syriac from the 4th – 7th century, Coptic MSS of the Sahidic and Bohairic from the 3rd and 4th centuries, and in the Textus Receptus. Therefore, it was retained as a reading in the KJB.

Acts 8:37 *And Philip said, If thou believest with all thine heart, thou mayest. And he answered and said, I believe that Jesus Christ is the Son of God.*

TWO HUNDRED EXAMPLES OUT OF 8000 CHANGES

The following information was collected from Biblebelievers.com, a website which defends the RT and the KJV. There are 8,000 places where the Greek Textus Receptus has been changed by modern 'scholarship'.[1] The following verses or words bracketed are either omitted, changed, or added to, by the versions listed at the beginning. You may want to take your Bible and go through the list. There are 200, but this will truly be an "eye opener" for you. The words changed were "not authentic" (they were not in the original manuscripts), **according** to modern scholarship. Remember, most of the changes presented here were because of the 'worship' by modernistic textual scholars of the Aleph and B manuscripts. This work asserts that most of the changes made in manuscripts and versions are clearly explained in light of the corrupted "belief systems" of heretics from all ages. Perhaps you can explain why they left out, added to, or changed the wording by the doctrine heretics and

---

[1]Moorman, Dr. Jack; *8,000 Difference Between the Textus Receptus and the Nestle-Aland NT Greek Texts;* Bible For Today Press; B.F.T. #3084, Collingwood, NJ.

apostates believe as you examine the examples to follow. A brief summary of those beliefs was presented at the beginning of this section to assist the reader.

The list of versions presented below show how many changes are reflected in each version of the 200 verses to follow.

MATTHEW

1. 1:25--(FIRSTBORN) is out. Speaking of the Lord Jesus.
    Matthew 1:25 And knew her not till she had brought forth her firstborn son: and he called his name JESUS. [I'll give you a hint for the reason they left out "firstborn," then you try and figure out the rest of the verses. They denied the virgin birth, and the pre-eminence of the Lord Jesus Christ as the "firstborn" son. This adds evidence that He was the first to open the womb, and therefore is "heir" with all the rights of the "King" and seat of David as prophecies predicted.]
2. 5:44--(BLESS THEM THAT CURSE YOU) is out.
    Matthew 5:44 But I say unto you, Love your enemies, bless them that curse you, do good to them that hate you, and pray for them which despitefully use you, and persecute you;

3.   6:13--(KINGDOM, POWER, GLORY) is out.
     Matthew 6:13 And lead us not into temptation, but deliver us from evil: For thine is the kingdom, and the power, and the glory, for ever. Amen.
4.   6:27--(STATURE) is changed to span of life.
     Matthew 6:27 Which of you by taking thought can add one cubit unto his stature?
5.   6:33--(OF GOD) is out. Referring to the kingdom—
     Matthew 6:33 But seek ye first the kingdom of God, and his righteousness; and all these things shall be added unto you.
6.   8:29--(JESUS) is out. As Son of God.
     Matthew 8:29 And, behold, they cried out, saying, What have we to do with thee, Jesus, thou Son of God? art thou come hither to torment us before the time?
7.   9:13--(TO REPENTANCE) is out. Calling sinners—
     Matthew 9:13 But go ye and learn what *that* meaneth, I will have mercy, and not sacrifice: for I am not come to call the righteous, but sinners to repentance.
8.   12:35--(OF THE HEART) is out. Good treasure—
     Matthew 12:35 A good man out of the good treasure of the heart bringeth forth good things: and an evil man out of the evil treasure bringeth forth evil things.
9.   12:47--(VERSE IS OUT) About Christ's mother.
     Matthew 12:47 Then one said unto him, Behold, thy mother and thy brethren stand without, desiring to speak with thee.
10. 13:51--(JESUS SAID UNTO THEM, and LORD) is out.
     Matthew 13:51 Jesus saith unto them, Have ye understood all these things? They say unto him, Yea, Lord.
11. 15:8 --(DRAWETH UNTO ME WITH THEIR MOUTH) is out.
     Matthew 15:8 This people draweth nigh unto me with their mouth, and honoureth me with *their* lips; but their heart is far from me.
12. 16:3 --(O YE HYPOCRITES) is out.
     Matthew 16:3 And in the morning, *It will be* foul weather to day: for the sky is red and lowring. O *ye* hypocrites, ye can discern the face of the sky; but can ye not *discern* the signs of the times?
13. 16:20--(JESUS) is out.
     Matthew 16:20 Then charged he his disciples that they should tell no man that he was Jesus the Christ.
14. 17:21--(VERSE IS OUT). About prayer and fasting.
     Matthew 17:21 Howbeit this kind goeth not out but by prayer

and fasting.
15. 19:9 --(LAST 11 WORDS ARE OUT). About adultery.
Matthew 19:9 And I say unto you, Whosoever shall put away his wife, except *it be* **for fornication, and shall marry another, committeth adultery: and whoso marrieth her which is put away doth commit adultery.**
16. 19:17--(GOD) is out. None good but (God).
Matthew 19:17 And he said unto him, **Why callest thou me good?** *there is* **none good but one,** *that is,* **God: but if thou wilt enter into life, keep the commandments.**
17. 20:7 --(WHATSOEVER IS RIGHT RECEIVE) is out.
Matthew 20:7 They say unto him, Because no man hath hired us. He saith unto them, Go ye also into the vineyard; and whatsoever is right, *that* **shall ye receive.**
18. 20:16--(MANY BE CALLED BUT FEW CHOSEN) is out.
Matthew 20:16 So the last shall be first, and the first last: for many be called, but few chosen.
19. 20:22--(BAPTIZED WITH CHRIST'S BAPTISM) is out.
Matthew 20:22 But Jesus answered and said, **Ye know not what ye ask. Are ye able to drink of the cup that I shall drink of, and to be baptized with the baptism that I am baptized with?** They say unto him, We are able.
20. 21:44--(VERSE IS OUT) About Christ the stone.
Matthew 21:44 And whosoever shall fall on this stone shall be broken: but on whomsoever it shall fall, it will grind him to powder.
21. 23:14--(VERSE IS OUT) Woe scribes and hypocrites.
Matthew 23:14 Woe unto you, scribes and Pharisees, hypocrites! for ye devour widows' houses, and for a pretence make long prayer: therefore ye shall receive the greater damnation.
22. 25:13--(WHEREIN THE SON OF MAN COMETH) is out.
Matthew 25:13 Watch therefore, for ye know neither the day nor the hour wherein the Son of man cometh.
23. 27:35--(FULFILLED SPOKEN BY THE PROPHET) is out.
Matthew 27:35 And they crucified him, and parted his garments, casting lots: that it might be fulfilled which was spoken by the prophet, They parted my garments among them, and upon my vesture did they cast lots.
24. 27:54--(THE SON OF GOD) is A SON of God.
Matthew 27:54 Now when the centurion, and they that were with him, watching Jesus, saw the earthquake, and those things that

were done, they feared greatly, saying, Truly this was <u>the</u> Son of God.

25.   28:2 --(FROM THE DOOR) is out.
Matthew 28:2 And, behold, there was a great earthquake: for the angel of the Lord descended from heaven, and came and rolled back the stone from the door, and sat upon it.

26.   28:9 --(THEY WENT TO TELL HIS DISCIPLES) is out.
Matthew 28:9 And as they went to tell his disciples, behold, Jesus met them, saying, All hail. And they came and held him by the feet, and worshipped him.

MARK

27.   1:1 --(SON OF GOD) is out in Williams, Goodspeed, Panin, Nestle, New

World, Westcott & Hort.
Mark 1:1 The beginning of the gospel of Jesus Christ, the Son of God;

28.   1:14--(OF THE KINGDOM) is out. Jesus gospel—
Mark 1:14 Now after that John was put in prison, Jesus came into Galilee, preaching the gospel of the kingdom of God,

29.   1:31--(IMMEDIATELY) is out. The fever left—
Mark 1:31 And he came and took her by the hand, and lifted her up; and immediately the fever left her, and she ministered unto them.

30.   2:17--(TO REPENTANCE) is out. Call sinners—
Mark 2:17 When Jesus heard *it,* he saith unto them, They that are whole have no need of the physician, but they that are sick: I came not to call the righteous, but sinners to repentance.

31.   6:11--(MORE TOLERABLE FOR SODOM & GOMORRHA) is out.
Mark 6:11 And whosoever shall not receive you, nor hear you, when ye depart thence, shake off the dust under your feet for a testimony against them. Verily I say unto you, It shall be more tolerable for Sodom and Gomorrha in the day of judgment, than for that city.

32.   6:16--(FROM THE DEAD) is out. John is risen—
Mark 6:16 But when Herod heard *thereof,* he said, It is John, whom I beheaded: he is risen from the dead.

33.   6:33--(HIM) is changed to them.
Mark 6:33 And the people saw them departing, and many knew him, and ran afoot thither out of all cities, and outwent them, and came together unto him.

34.   7:8 --(WASHING OF POTS AND CUPS) is out.
Mark 7:8 For laying aside the commandment of God, ye hold the tradition of men, *as* the washing of pots and cups: and many other

such like things ye do.

35. 7:16--(VERSE IS OUT) About having an ear to hear.
Mark 7:16 If any man have ears to hear, let him hear.
35. 9:24--(LORD) is out. A believer called Him Lord.
Mark 9:24 And straightway the father of the child cried out, and said with tears, Lord, I believe; help thou mine unbelief.
36. 9:42--(IN ME) is out. Little ones that believe—
Mark 9:42 And whosoever shall offend one of *these* little ones that believe in me, it is better for him that a millstone were hanged about his neck, and he were cast into the sea.
37. 9:44--(VERSE IS OUT) About fire not quenched.
Mark 9:44 Where their worm dieth not, and the fire is not quenched.
38. 9:46--(VERSE IS OUT) Where worm dieth not.
Mark 9:46 Where their worm dieth not, and the fire is not quenched.
39. 9:49--(EVERY SACRIFICE SHALL BE SALTED) is out.
Mark 9:49 For every one shall be salted with fire, and every sacrifice shall be salted with salt.
40. 10:21--(TAKE UP THE CROSS) is out. Jesus said—
Mark 10:21 Then Jesus beholding him loved him, and said unto him, One thing thou lackest: go thy way, sell whatsoever thou hast, and give to the poor, and thou shalt have treasure in heaven: and come, take up the cross, and follow me.
41. 10:24--(FOR THEM THAT TRUST IN RICHES) is out.
Mark 10:24 And the disciples were astonished at his words. But Jesus answereth again, and saith unto them, Children, how hard is it for them that trust in riches to enter into the kingdom of God!
42. 11:10--(IN THE NAME OF THE LORD) is out.
Mark 11:10 Blessed *be* the kingdom of our father David, that cometh in the name of the Lord: Hosanna in the highest.
43. 11:26--(VERSE IS OUT) If ye do not forgive, etc.
Mark 11:26 But if ye do not forgive, neither will your Father which is in heaven forgive your trespasses.
44. 13:14--(SPOKEN BY DANIEL THE PROPHET) is out.
Mark 13:14 But when ye shall see the abomination of desolation, spoken of by Daniel the prophet, standing where it ought not, (let him that readeth understand,) then let them that be in Judaea flee to the mountains:
45. 13:33--(AND PRAY) is out, or in italics.
Mark 13:33 Take ye heed, watch and pray: for ye know not when the time is.
46. 14:68--(AND THE COCK CREW) is out.

Mark 14:68 But he denied, saying, I know not, neither understand I what thou sayest. And he went out into the porch; and the cock crew.

47.   15:28--(VERSE IS OUT) Scripture was fulfilled, etc.
Mark 15:28 And the scripture was fulfilled, which saith, And he was numbered with the transgressors.

48.   15:39--(THE SON OF GOD) is A SON of God.
Mark 15:39 And when the centurion, which stood over against him, saw that he so cried out, and gave up the ghost, he said, Truly this man was the Son of God.

49.   16:9-20--(12 VERSES ARE OUT) in some Bibles.

LUKE

50.   1:28--(BLESSED ART THOU AMONG WOMEN) is out.
Luke 1:28 And the angel came in unto her, and said, Hail, *thou that art* highly favoured, the Lord *is* with thee: blessed *art* thou among women.

51.   2:33--(JOSEPH) is changed to father.
Luke 2:33 And Joseph and his mother marvelled at those things which were spoken of him.

52.   2:43--(JOSEPH AND HIS MOTHER) is changed to parents.
Luke 2:43 And when they had fulfilled the days, as they returned, the child Jesus tarried behind in Jerusalem; and Joseph and his mother knew not *of it.*

53.   4:4 --(BUT BY EVERY WORD OF GOD) is out.
Luke 4:4 And Jesus answered him, saying, It is written, That man shall not live by bread alone, but by every word of God.

54.   4:8 --(GET THEE BEHIND ME SATAN) is out.
Luke 4:8 And Jesus answered and said unto him, Get thee behind me, Satan: for it is written, Thou shalt worship the Lord thy God, and him only shalt thou serve.

55.   4:41--(THE CHRIST) is out. The Son of God.
Luke 4:41 And devils also came out of many, crying out, and saying, Thou art Christ the Son of God. And he rebuking *them* suffered them not to speak: for they knew that he was Christ.

56.   6:48--(FOUNDED UPON A ROCK) 'is well built' is inserted.
Luke 6:48 He is like a man which built an house, and digged deep, and laid the foundation on a rock: and when the flood arose, the stream beat vehemently upon that house, and could not shake it: for it was founded upon a rock.

57.   7:31--(AND THE LORD SAID) is out.
Luke 7:31 And the Lord said, Whereunto then shall I liken the men of this generation? and to what are they like?

58. 9:54--(EVEN AS ELIAS DID) is out.
Luke 9:54 And when his disciples James and John saw *this,* they said, Lord, wilt thou that we command fire to come down from heaven, and consume them, even as Elias did?
59. 9:55--(YE KNOW NOT WHAT MANNER OF SPIRIT) is out.
Luke 9:55 But he turned, and rebuked them, and said, Ye know not what manner of spirit ye are of.
60. 9:56--(SON OF MAN IS COME TO SAVE LIVES) is out.
Luke 9:56 For the Son of man is not come to destroy men's lives, but to save *them.* And they went to another village.
61. 11:2-4--(MUCH IS OMITTED FROM THE LORD'S PRAYER)
Luke 11:2-4 And he said unto them, When ye pray, say, Our Father which art in heaven, Hallowed be thy name. Thy kingdom come. Thy will be done, as in heaven, so in earth. 3 Give us day by day our daily bread. 4And forgive us our sins; for we also forgive every one that is indebted to us. And lead us not into temptation; but deliver us from evil.
62. 11:29--(THE PROPHET) is out. About Jonah.
Luke 11:29 And when the people were gathered thick together, he began to say, This is an evil generation: they seek a sign; and there shall no sign be given it, but the sign of Jonas the prophet.
63. 17:36--(VERSE IS OUT) One taken, another left.
Luke 17:26 And as it was in the days of Noe, so shall it be also in the days of the Son of man.
64. 21:4 --(CAST IN UNTO THE OFFERINGS OF GOD) is out.
Luke 21:4 For all these have of their abundance cast in unto the offerings of God: but she of her penury hath cast in all the living that she had.
65. 22:20--(VERSE IS OUT) Out in NEB, and RSV.
Luke 22:20 Likewise also the cup after supper, saying, This cup *is* the new testament in my blood, which is shed for you.
66. 22:31--(AND THE LORD SAID) is out.
Luke 22:31 And the Lord said, Simon, Simon, behold, Satan hath desired *to have* you, that he may sift *you* as wheat:
67. 22:64--(THEY STRUCK HIM ON THE FACE) is out.
Luke 22:64 And when they had blindfolded him, they struck him on the face, and asked him, saying, Prophesy, who is it that smote thee?
68. 23:17--(WHOLE VERSE IS OUT) in many Bibles.
Luke 23:17 (For of necessity he must release one unto them at the feast.)
69. 23:38--(LETTERS OF GREEK, LATIN, HEBREW) is out.
Luke 23:38 And a superscription also was written over him in

letters of Greek, and Latin, and Hebrew, THIS IS THE KING OF THE JEWS.

70. 23:42--(LORD) is out. Remember me, etc.
Luke 23:42 And he said unto Jesus, Lord, remember me when thou comest into thy kingdom.

71. 23:45--(SUN WAS ECLIPSED) placed into Moffatt and NEB.
Luke 23:45 And the sun was darkened, and the veil of the temple was rent in the midst.

72. 24:3 --(OF THE LORD JESUS) is out.
Luke 24:3 And they entered in, and found not the body of the Lord Jesus.

73. 24:6 --(HE IS NOT HERE, BUT IS RISEN) is out.
Luke 24:6 He is not here, but is risen: remember how he spake unto you when he was yet in Galilee,

74. 24:12--(VERSE IS OUT) Peter's testimony.
Luke 24:12 Then arose Peter, and ran unto the sepulchre; and stooping down, he beheld the linen clothes laid by themselves, and departed, wondering in himself at that which was come to pass.

75. 24:40--(VERSE IS OUT) Christ showed them hands, feet.
Luke 24:40 And when he had thus spoken, he shewed them *his* hands and *his* feet.

76. 24:49--(OF JERUSALEM) is out.
Luke 24:49 And, behold, I send the promise of my Father upon you: but tarry ye in the city of Jerusalem, until ye be endued with power from on high.

77. 24:51 (CARRIED UP INTO HEAVEN) is out.
Luke 24:51 And it came to pass, while he blessed them, he was parted from them, and carried up into heaven.

JOHN

78. 1:14--(BEGOTTEN) is out in 1:18, 3:16, 3:18.
John 1:14 And the Word was made flesh, and dwelt among us, (and we beheld his glory, the glory as of the only begotten of the Father,) full of grace and truth.

79. 1:27--(PREFERRED BEFORE ME) is out.
John 1:27 He it is, who coming after me is preferred before me, whose shoe's latchet I am not worthy to unloose.

80. 3:13--(WHICH IS IN HEAVEN) is out.
John 3:13 And no man hath ascended up to heaven, but he that came down from heaven, *even* the Son of man which is in heaven.

81. 3:15--(SHOULD NOT PERISH) is out.
John 3:15 That whosoever believeth in him should not perish, but have eternal life.

82. 4:42--(THE CHRIST) is out.
    John 4:42 And said unto the woman, Now we believe, not because of thy saying: for we have heard *him* ourselves, and know that this is indeed the Christ, the Saviour of the world.
83. 5:3 --(WAITING FOR MOVING OF THE WATER) is out.
    John 5:3 In these lay a great multitude of impotent folk, of blind, halt, withered, waiting for the moving of the water.
84. 5:4 --(VERSE IS OUT) Pool of Bethesda.
    John 5:4 For an angel went down at a certain season into the pool, and troubled the water: whosoever then first after the troubling of the water stepped in was made whole of whatsoever disease he had.
85. 6:47--(ON ME) is out. He that believes—
    John 6:47 Verily, verily, I say unto you, He that believeth on me hath everlasting life.
86. 6:69--(THAT CHRIST THE SON) is out.
    John 6:69 And we believe and are sure that thou art that Christ, the Son of the living God.
87. (7:53--TO 8:11) is out, in brackets or italics.
    This is the woman caught in the adultery pericope.
88. 8:29--(FATHER) is out. Changed to He.
    John 8:29 And he that sent me is with me: the Father hath not left me alone; for I do always those things that please him.
89. 9:35--(SON OF GOD) is out. Is Son of Man.
    John 9:35 Jesus heard that they had cast him out; and when he had found him, he said unto him, Dost thou believe on the Son of God?
90. 11:41--(WHERE THE DEAD WAS LAID) is out.
    John 11:41 Then they took away the stone *from the place* where the dead was laid. And Jesus lifted up *his* eyes, and said, Father, I thank thee that thou hast heard me.
91. 16:16--(BECAUSE I GO TO THE FATHER) is out.
    John 16:16 A little while, and ye shall not see me: and again, a little while, and ye shall see me, because I go to the Father.
92. 17:12--(IN THE WORLD) is out.
    John 17:12 While I was with them in the world, I kept them in thy name: those that thou gavest me I have kept, and none of them is lost, but the son of perdition; that the scripture might be fulfilled.
93. 20:29--(THOMAS) is out.
    John 20:29 Jesus saith unto him, Thomas, because thou hast seen me, thou hast believed: blessed *are* they that have not seen, and *yet* have believed.

ACTS

94. 2:30--(ACCORDING TO FLESH RAISE UP CHRIST) is out.
Acts 2:30 Therefore being a prophet, and knowing that God had sworn with an oath to him, that of the fruit of his loins, according to the flesh, he would raise up Christ to sit on his throne;

95. 7:30--(OF THE LORD) is out. Angel—
Acts 7:30 And when forty years were expired, there appeared to him in the wilderness of mount Sina an angel of the Lord in a flame of fire in a bush.

96. 7:37--(HIM SHALL YE HEAR) is out. Christ—
Acts 7:37 This is that Moses, which said unto the children of Israel, A prophet shall the Lord your God raise up unto you of your brethren, like unto me; him shall ye hear.

97. 8:37--(VERSE IS OUT) or in brackets, or italics.
Acts 8:37 And Philip said, If thou believest with all thine heart, thou mayest. And he answered and said, I believe that Jesus Christ is the Son of God.

98. 9:5-6--(MUCH IS OMITTED) Concerning God's call.
Acts 9:5-6 And he said, Who art thou, Lord? And the Lord said, I am Jesus whom thou persecutest: *it is* hard for thee to kick against the pricks. 6And he trembling and astonished said, Lord, what wilt thou have me to do? And the Lord *said* unto him, Arise, and go into the city, and it shall be told thee what thou must do.

99. 10:6 --(WHAT THOU OUGHTEST TO DO) is out.
Acts 10:6 He lodgeth with one Simon a tanner, whose house is by the sea side: he shall tell thee what thou oughtest to do.

100. 15:18--(KNOWN UNTO GOD HIS WORKS) is out.
Acts 15:18 Known unto God are all his works from the beginning of the world.

101. 16:31--(CHRIST) is out.
Acts 16:31 And they said, Believe on the Lord Jesus Christ, and thou shalt be saved, and thy house.

102. 17:26--(BLOOD) is out.
Acts 17:26 And hath made of one blood all nations of men for to dwell on all the face of the earth, and hath determined the times before appointed, and the bounds of their habitation;

103. 20:25--(OF GOD) is out. The kingdom—
Acts 20:25 And now, behold, I know that ye all, among whom I have gone preaching the kingdom of God, shall see my face no more.

104. 20:32--(BRETHREN) is out.
Acts 20:32 And now, brethren, I commend you to God, and to the

word of his grace, which is able to build you up, and to give you an inheritance among all them which are sanctified.

105. 23:9 --(LET US NOT FIGHT AGAINST GOD) is out.

Acts 23:9 And there arose a great cry: and the scribes *that were* of the Pharisees' part arose, and strove, saying, We find no evil in this man: but if a spirit or an angel hath spoken to him, let us not fight against God.

106. 24:6-8--(MUCH OF THE VERSE IS OMITTED) or in brackets or italics.

Acts 24:6-8 Who also hath gone about to profane the temple: whom we took, and would have judged according to our law. 7But the chief captain Lysias came *upon us,* and with great violence took *him* away out of our hands, 8Commanding his accusers to come unto thee: by examining of whom thyself mayest take knowledge of all these things, whereof we accuse him.

107. 24:15--(OF THE DEAD) is out. Resurrection—

Acts 24:15 And have hope toward God, which they themselves also allow, that there shall be a resurrection of the dead, both of the just and unjust.

108. 28:16--(HALF OF VERSE IS OUT) in italics or brackets.

Acts 28:16 And when we came to Rome, the centurion delivered the prisoners to the captain of the guard: but Paul was suffered to dwell by himself with a soldier that kept him.

109. 28:29--(VERSE IS OUT) in italics or brackets.

Acts 28:29 And when he had said these words, the Jews departed, and had great reasoning among themselves.

ROMANS

110. 1:16--(OF CHRIST) is out or in italics, brackets.

Romans 1:16 For I am not ashamed of the gospel of Christ: for it is the power of God unto salvation to every one that believeth; to the Jew first, and also to the Greek.

111. 1:29--(FORNICATION) is out.

Romans 1:29 Being filled with all unrighteousness, fornication, wickedness, covetousness, maliciousness; full of envy, murder, debate, deceit, malignity; whisperers,

112. 5:2 --(BY FAITH) out in Moffatt, RSV, and NEB.

Romans 5:2 By whom also we have access by faith into this grace wherein we stand, and rejoice in hope of the glory of God.

113. 8:1 --(LAST 10 WORDS ARE OUT) or in italics.

Romans 8:1 *There is* therefore now no condemnation to them which are in Christ Jesus, who walk not after the flesh, but after the Spirit.

114. 9:28--(IN RIGHTEOUSNESS) is out.
Romans 9:28 For he will finish the work, and cut *it* short in righteousness: because a short work will the Lord make upon the earth.
115. 10:15--(OF PEACE) is out. Gospel--
Romans 10:15 And how shall they preach, except they be sent? as it is written, How beautiful are the feet of them that preach the gospel of peace, and bring glad tidings of good things!
116. 10:17--(OF GOD) is out. Christ is substituted.
Romans 10:17 So then faith *cometh* by hearing, and hearing by the word of God.
117. 11:6 --(LAST 18 WORDS ARE OMITTED)
Romans 11:6 And if by grace, then *is it* no more of works: otherwise grace is no more grace. But if *it be* of works, then is it no more grace: otherwise work is no more work.
118. 13:9 --(SHALL NOT BEAR FALSE WITNESS) is out.
Romans 13:9 For this, Thou shalt not commit adultery, Thou shalt not kill, Thou shalt not steal, Thou shalt not bear false witness, Thou shalt not covet; and if *there be* any other commandment, it is briefly comprehended in this saying, namely, Thou shalt love thy neighbour as thyself.
119. 14:6 --(15 WORDS ARE OUT) Regarding the day.
Romans 14:6 He that regardeth the day, regardeth *it* unto the Lord; and he that regardeth not the day, to the Lord he doth not regard *it.* He that eateth, eateth to the Lord, for he giveth God thanks; and he that eateth not, to the Lord he eateth not, and giveth God thanks.
120. 14:21--(OFFENDED, MADE WEAK) is out.
Romans 14:21 *It is* good neither to eat flesh, nor to drink wine, nor *any thing* whereby thy brother stumbleth, or is offended, or is made weak.
121. 15:29--(OF THE GOSPEL) is out.
Romans 15:29 And I am sure that, when I come unto you, I shall come in the fulness of the blessing of the gospel of Christ.
122. 16:24--(WHOLE VERSE IS OUT) in italics or brackets
Romans 16:24 The grace of our Lord Jesus Christ *be* with you all. Amen.

I CORINTHIANS

123. 1:14--(I THANK GOD) is out in many Bibles.
1 Cor. 1:14 I thank God that I baptized none of you, but Crispus and Gaius;
124. 5:7 --(FOR US) is out. Christ sacrificed—

1 Cor. 5:7 Purge out therefore the old leaven, that ye may be a new lump, as ye are unleavened. For even Christ our passover is sacrificed for us:

125. 6:20--(LAST 7 WORDS ARE OUT) Your spirit, etc.

1 Cor. 6:20 For ye are bought with a price: therefore glorify God in your body, and in your spirit, which are God's.

126. 7:5 --(FASTING) is out. Joined with prayer.

1 Cor. 7:5 Defraud ye not one the other, except *it be* with consent for a time, that ye may give yourselves to fasting and prayer; and come together again, that Satan tempt you not for your incontinency.

127. 7:39--(BY THE LAW) is out. The wife is bound—

1 Cor. 7:39 The wife is bound by the law as long as her husband liveth; but if her husband be dead, she is at liberty to be married to whom she will; only in the Lord.

128. 10:28--(THE EARTH IS THE LORD'S) is out, and more.

1 Cor. 10:28 But if any man say unto you, This is offered in sacrifice unto idols, eat not for his sake that shewed it, and for conscience sake: for the earth *is* the Lord's, and the fulness thereof:

129. 11:24--(TAKE EAT) is out. This is my body—

1 Cor. 11:24 And when he had given thanks, he brake *it,* and said, Take, eat: this is my body, which is broken for you: this do in remembrance of me.

130. 11:29--(LORD'S) is out, referring to the body.

1 Cor. 11:29 For he that eateth and drinketh unworthily, eateth and drinketh damnation to himself, not discerning the Lord's body.

131. 15:47--(THE LORD) is out. Lord from heaven.

1 Cor. 15:47 The first man *is* of the earth, earthy: the second man *is* the Lord from heaven.

132. 16:22--(JESUS CHRIST) is out.

1 Cor. 16:22 If any man love not the Lord Jesus Christ, let him be Anathema Maranatha.

133. 16:23--(CHRIST) is out.

1 Cor. 16:23 The grace of our Lord Jesus Christ *be* with you.

II CORINTHIANS

134. 4:6 --(JESUS) is out.

2 Cor. 4:6 For God, who commanded the light to shine out of darkness, hath shined in our hearts, to *give* the light of the knowledge of the glory of God in the face of Jesus Christ.

135. 4:10--(THE LORD) is out.

2 Cor. 4:10 Always bearing about in the body the dying of the Lord

Jesus, that the life also of Jesus might be made manifest in our body.

136. 5:18--(JESUS) is out, or in italics.

2 Cor. 5:18 And all things *are* of God, who hath reconciled us to himself by Jesus Christ, and hath given to us the ministry of reconciliation;

137. 11:31--(CHRIST) is out, or in italics

2 Cor. 11:31 The God and Father of our Lord Jesus Christ, which is blessed for evermore, knoweth that I lie not.

GALATIANS

138. 1:15--(GOD) is out.

Galatians 1:15 But when it pleased God, who separated me from my mother's womb, and called *me* by his grace,

139. 3:1 --(THAT YE SHOULD NOT OBEY TRUTH) is out.

Galatians 3:1 O foolish Galatians, who hath bewitched you, that ye should not obey the truth, before whose eyes Jesus Christ hath been evidently set forth, crucified among you?

140. 3:17--(IN CHRIST) is out.

Galatians 3:17 And this I say, *that* the covenant, that was confirmed before of God in Christ, the law, which was four hundred and thirty years after, cannot disannul, that it should make the promise of none effect.

141. 4:7 --(THROUGH CHRIST) is out.

Galatians 4:7 Wherefore thou art no more a servant, but a son; and if a son, then an heir of God through Christ.

142. 6:15--(IN CHRIST JESUS) is out.

Galatians 6:15 For in Christ Jesus neither circumcision availeth any thing, nor uncircumcision, but a new creature.

143. 6:17--(LORD) is out.

Galatians 6:17 From henceforth let no man trouble me: for I bear in my body the marks of the Lord Jesus.

EPHESIANS

144. 3:9 --(BY JESUS CHRIST) is out. God created—

Ephes. 3:9 And to make all *men* see what *is* the fellowship of the mystery, which from the beginning of the world hath been hid in God, who created all things by Jesus Christ:

145. 3:14--(OF OUR LORD JESUS CHRIST) is out.

Ephes. 3:14 For this cause I bow my knees unto the Father of our Lord Jesus Christ,

146. 5:30--(OF HIS FLESH AND OF HIS BONES) is out.

Ephes. 5:30 For we are members of his body, of his flesh, and of

his bones.
147. 6:1 --(IN THE LORD) is out. Obey parents—
     Ephes. 6:1 Children, obey your parents in the Lord: for this is right.
148. 6:10--(MY BRETHREN) is out.
     Ephes. 6:10 Finally, my brethren, be strong in the Lord, and in the power of his might.

PHILIPPIANS

149. 3:16 (LET US MIND THE SAME THING) is out.
     Philip. 3:16 Nevertheless, whereto we have already attained, let us walk by the same rule, let us mind the same thing.

COLOSSIANS

150. 1:2 --(THE LORD JESUS CHRIST) is out.
     Col. 1:2 To the saints and faithful brethren in Christ which are at Colosse: Grace *be* unto you, and peace, from God our Father and the Lord Jesus Christ.
151. 1:14--(THROUGH HIS BLOOD) is out, or in italics.
     Col. 1:14 In whom we have redemption through his blood, *even* the forgiveness of sins:
152. 1:28--(JESUS) is out.
     Col. 1:28 Whom we preach, warning every man, and teaching every man in all wisdom; that we may present every man perfect in Christ Jesus:
153. 2:11--(OF THE SINS OF) is out.
     Col. 2:11 In whom also ye are circumcised with the circumcision made without hands, in putting off the body of the sins of the flesh by the circumcision of Christ:
154. 3:6 --(CHILDREN OF DISOBEDIENCE) is out.
     Col. 3:6 For which things' sake the wrath of God cometh on the children of disobedience:

I THESSALONIANS

155. 1:1 --(FROM GOD OUR FATHER AND LORD JESUS) is out.
     1 Thes. 1:1 Paul, and Silvanus, and Timotheus, unto the church of the Thessalonians *which is* in God the Father and *in* the Lord Jesus Christ: Grace *be* unto you, and peace, from God our Father, and the Lord Jesus Christ.
156. 2:19--(CHRIST) is out.
     1 Thes. 2:19 For what *is* our hope, or joy, or crown of rejoicing? *Are* not even ye in the presence of our Lord Jesus Christ at his coming?
157. 3:11--(CHRIST) is out, or in italics.

1 Thes. 3:11 Now God himself and our Father, and our Lord Jesus Christ, direct our way unto you.

158. 3:13--(CHRIST) is out, or in italics.

1 Thes. 3:13 To the end he may stablish your hearts unblameable in holiness before God, even our Father, at the coming of our Lord Jesus Christ with all his saints.

II THESSALONIANS

159. 1:8 --(CHRIST) is out, or in italics.

2 Thes. 1:8 In flaming fire taking vengeance on them that know not God, and that obey not the gospel of our Lord Jesus Christ:

I TIMOTHY

160. 1:17--(WISE) is out. The only wise God.

1 Tim. 1:17 Now unto the King eternal, immortal, invisible, the only wise God, *be* honour and glory for ever and ever. Amen.

161. 2:7 --(IN CHRIST) is out, or in italics.

1 Tim. 2:7 Whereunto I am ordained a preacher, and an apostle, (I speak the truth in Christ, *and* lie not;) a teacher of the Gentiles in faith and verity.

162. 3:16--(GOD) is out. Manifest in the flesh.

1 Tim. 3:16 And without controversy great is the mystery of godliness: God was manifest in the flesh, justified in the Spirit, seen of angels, preached unto the Gentiles, believed on in the world, received up into glory.

163. 4:12--(IN SPIRIT) is out.

1 Tim. 4:12 Let no man despise thy youth; but be thou an example of the believers, in words, in conversation, in charity, in spirit, in faith, in purity.

164. 6:5 --(FROM SUCH WITHDRAW THYSELF) is out.

1 Tim. 6:5 Perverse disputings of men of corrupt minds, and destitute of the truth, supposing that gain is godliness: from such withdraw thyself.

II TIMOTHY

165. 1:11--(OF THE GENTILES) is out.

2 Tim. 1:11 Whereunto I am appointed a preacher, and an apostle, and a teacher of the Gentiles.

166. 4:1 --(LORD) is out.

2 Tim. 4:1 I charge *thee* therefore before God, and the Lord Jesus Christ, who shall judge the quick and the dead at his appearing and his kingdom;

167. 4:22--(JESUS CHRIST) is out, or in italics.

2 Tim. 4:22 The Lord Jesus Christ *be* with thy spirit. Grace *be* with you. Amen.

TITUS

168. 1:4 --(THE LORD) is out, or in italics.

Titus 1:4 To Titus, *mine* own son after the common faith: Grace, mercy, *and* peace, from God the Father and the Lord Jesus Christ our Saviour.

PHILEMON

169. 1:6 --(JESUS) is out.

Philemon 1:6 That the communication of thy faith may become effectual by the acknowledging of every good thing which is in you in Christ Jesus.

170. 1:12--(RECEIVE HIM) is out.

Philemon 1:12 Whom I have sent again: thou therefore receive him, that is, mine own bowels:

HEBREWS

171. 1:3 --(BY HIMSELF) is out. Purged our sins—

Hebrews 1:3 Who being the brightness of *his* glory, and the express image of his person, and upholding all things by the word of his power, when he had by himself purged our sins, sat down on the right hand of the Majesty on high;

172. 2:7 --(SET HIM OVER THE WORKS OF THY HANDS) is out.

Hebrews 2:7 Thou madest him a little lower than the angels; thou crownedst him with glory and honour, and didst set him over the works of thy hands:

173. 3:1 --(CHRIST) is out.

Hebrews 3:1 Wherefore, holy brethren, partakers of the heavenly calling, consider the Apostle and High Priest of our profession, Christ Jesus;

174. 7:21--(AFTER ORDER OF MELCHIZEDEC) is out.

Hebrews 7:21 (For those priests were made without an oath; but this with an oath by him that said unto him, The Lord sware and will not repent, Thou *art* a priest for ever after the order of Melchisedec:)

175. 10:30--(SAITH THE LORD) is out.

Hebrews 10:30 For we know him that hath said, Vengeance *belongeth* unto me, I will recompense, saith the Lord. And again, The Lord shall judge his people.

176. 10:34--(IN HEAVEN) is out.

Hebrews 10:34 For ye had compassion of me in my bonds, and took joyfully the spoiling of your goods, knowing in yourselves that ye have in heaven a better and an enduring substance.

177. 11:11--(WAS DELIVERED OF A CHILD) is out.

Hebrews 11:11 Through faith also Sara herself received strength to conceive seed, and was delivered of a child when she was past age, because she judged him faithful who had promised.

JAMES

178. 5:16--(FAULTS) is changed to SINS. (Wrong Greek text.)

James 5:16 Confess *your* faults one to another, and pray one for another, that ye may be healed. The effectual fervent prayer of a righteous man availeth much.

I PETER

179. 1:22--(THROUGH THE SPIRIT) is out.

1 Peter 1:22 Seeing ye have purified your souls in obeying the truth through the Spirit unto unfeigned love of the brethren, *see that ye* love one another with a pure heart fervently:

180. 4:1 --(FOR US) is out. Christ suffered—

1 Peter 4:1 Forasmuch then as Christ hath suffered for us in the flesh, arm yourselves likewise with the same mind: for he that hath suffered in the flesh hath ceased from sin;

181. 4:14--(LAST 15 WORDS ARE OUT) or in italics.

1 Peter 4:14 If ye be reproached for the name of Christ, happy *are ye;* for the spirit of glory and of God resteth upon you: on their part he is evil spoken of, but on your part he is glorified.

182. 5:10--(JESUS) is out, or in italics.

1 Peter 5:10 But the God of all grace, who hath called us unto his eternal glory by Christ Jesus, after that ye have suffered a while, make you perfect, stablish, strengthen, settle *you.*

183. 5:11--(GLORY AND DOMINION) is out of some Bibles.

1 Peter 5:11 To him *be* glory and dominion for ever and ever. Amen.

II PETER

184. 2:17--(FOR EVER) is out, or in italics.

2 Peter 2:17 These are wells without water, clouds that are carried with a tempest; to whom the mist of darkness is reserved for ever.

185. 3:9 --(US IS CHANGED TO YOU) Destroys meaning.

2 Peter 3:9 The Lord is not slack concerning his promise, as some men count slackness; but is longsuffering to us-ward, not willing that any should perish, but that all should come to repentance.

I JOHN

186. 1:7 --(CHRIST) is out.

1 John 1:7 But if we walk in the light, as he is in the light, we have fellowship one with another, and the blood of Jesus Christ his Son cleanseth us from all sin.

187. 2:7 --(FROM THE BEGINNING) is out.

1 John 2:7 Brethren, I write no new commandment unto you, but an old commandment which ye had from the beginning. The old commandment is the word which ye have heard from the beginning.

188. 4:3 --(CHRIST IS COME IN THE FLESH) is out.

1 John 4:3 And every spirit that confesseth not that Jesus Christ is come in the flesh is not of God: and this is that *spirit* of antichrist, whereof ye have heard that it should come; and even now already is it in the world.

189. 4:9 --(BEGOTTEN) is out in some versions.

1 John 4:9 In this was manifested the love of God toward us, because that God sent his only begotten Son into the world, that we might live through him.

190. 4:19--(HIM) is out, or in italics.

1 John 4:9 In this was manifested the love of God toward us, because that God sent his only begotten Son into the world, that we might live through him.

191. 5:7-8--(MANY WORDS ARE OUT OR CHANGED)

1 John 5:7-8 For there are three that bear record in heaven, the Father, the Word, and the Holy Ghost: and these three are one. 8And there are three that bear witness in earth, the spirit, and the water, and the blood: and these three agree in one.

192. 5:13--(LAST 13 WORDS ARE OUT)

1 John 5:13 These things have I written unto you that believe on the name of the Son of God; that ye may know that ye have eternal life, and that ye may believe on the name of the Son of God.

JUDE

193. 1:25--(WISE) is out. Referring to God.

Jude 1:25 To the only wise God our Saviour, *be* glory and majesty, dominion and power, both now and ever. Amen.

REVELATION

194. 1:8 --(THE BEGINNING AND THE END) is out.

Rev. 1:8 I am Alpha and Omega, the beginning and the ending, saith the Lord, which is, and which was, and which is to come, the

Almighty.
195. 1:11--(TEN WORDS ARE OUT) Alpha and Omega, etc.
    Rev. 1:11 Saying, I am Alpha and Omega, the first and the last:
    and, What thou seest, write in a book, and send *it* unto the seven
    churches which are in Asia; unto Ephesus, and unto Smyrna, and
    unto Pergamos, and unto Thyatira, and unto Sardis, and unto
    Philadelphia, and unto Laodicea.
196. 2:13--(THY WORKS) is out.
    Rev. 2:13 I know thy works, and where thou dwellest, *even* where
    Satan's seat *is:* and thou holdest fast my name, and hast not
    denied my faith, even in those days wherein Antipas *was* my faithful
    martyr, who was slain among you, where Satan dwelleth.
197. 5:14--(HIM THAT LIVETH FOREVER AND EVER) is out.
    Rev. 5:14 And the four beasts said, Amen. And the four *and* twenty
    elders fell down and worshipped him that liveth for ever and ever.
198. 6:1 --(AND SEE) is out in 3, 5, 7 also.
    Rev. 6:1 And I saw when the Lamb opened one of the seals, and
    I heard, as it were the noise of thunder, one of the four beasts
    saying, Come and see.
199. 8:13--(ANGEL IS EAGLE) Greek text says "angel."
    Rev. 8:13 And I beheld, and heard an angel flying through the
    midst of heaven, saying with a loud voice, Woe, woe, woe, to the
    inhabiters of the earth by reason of the other voices of the trumpet
    of the three angels, which are yet to sound!
200. 11:17--(AND ART TO COME) is out.
    Rev. 11:17 Saying, We give thee thanks, O Lord God Almighty,
    which art, and wast, and art to come; because thou hast taken to
    thee thy great power, and hast reigned.
201. 12:12--(INHABITERS OF) is out. The earth.
    Rev. 12:12 Therefore rejoice, *ye* heavens, and ye that dwell in
    them. Woe to the inhabiters of the earth and of the sea! for the
    devil is come down unto you, having great wrath, because he
    knoweth that he hath but a short time.
202. 12:17--(CHRIST) is out.
    Rev. 12:17 And the dragon was wroth with the woman, and went
    to make war with the remnant of her seed, which keep the
    commandments of God, and have the testimony of Jesus Christ.
203. 14:5 --(BEFORE THE THRONE OF GOD) is out.
    Rev. 14:5 And in their mouth was found no guile: for they are
    without fault before the throne of God.
204. 16:17--(OF HEAVEN) is out.
    Rev. 16:17 And the seventh angel poured out his vial into the air;
    and there came a great voice out of the temple of heaven, from the

throne, saying, It is done.
205. 20:9 --(GOD OUT OF) is out. Fire came from—
Rev. 20:9 And they went up on the breadth of the earth, and compassed the camp of the saints about, and the beloved city: and fire came down from God out of heaven, and devoured them.
206. 20: 12--(GOD IS CHANGED TO THRONE)
Rev. 20:12 And I saw the dead, small and great, stand before God; and the books were opened: and another book was opened, which is *the book* of life: and the dead were judged out of those things which were written in the books, according to their works.
207. 21:24--(OF THEM WHICH ARE SAVED) is out. Nations—
Rev. 21:24 And the nations of them which are saved shall walk in the light of it: and the kings of the earth do bring their glory and honour into it.

THOUGHTS, CONCEPTS, OR WORDS PRESERVED

The preceding two hundred (200) examples should cause one to sit "on the edge of the chair" and ask, "What is this?" Well, this is the question many have been asking since the days of John Fell (1675), Richard Bently (1662-1742), John Bengel (1687-1752), Johann Semler (1725-1791), Griesbach, Hug, Lachmann, Westcott, and Hort. [See the chart, "History of Unbelief" in the appendices]. If God's Words are infallible, inerrant, and preserved, how could there be so many readings? The assertion by Alexandrians already mentioned is that the "Words" of Scripture do not matter. As long as the thought, concept, or idea is preserved this is all God expected. According to Dave Hunt:

"God's Word is "forever...settled in heaven" (Ps 119:89) so you will find it there, You would also find it in the original copies (were they available) written by men inspired of the Holy Spirit to give us the Scriptures. God could have preserved the originals, but chose not to for His own reasons. What we now have are thousands of copies, most of them fragments of varying sizes, made from copies of copies of copies of the originals. Copyists do make some errors, no matter how careful they are. The errors are generally very small and can be detected by comparing the many copies we have with one another."[1]

---

[1] Hunt, David; *Berean Call*; Oct. 1997 , The Berean Call Electronic Disc, 1986-2001 Newsletters; p. 397

Dave Hunt, a great defender of the faith, is right. His last sentence sums up the whole matter into one concise statement. The point is that we do have the actual inspired, infallible, inerrant Words of God that have been providentially preserved through men who have been guided by the Holy Spirit. We have the Words of God in the Received Text. Yes, there have been a very few moles, warts, and defects along the way which have been incorporated into some of the manuscripts of the Received Text and translations made from it, but we live in a fallen world; full of sin [leaven], defects, and lesions. We believe they have been identified and, by God's providential care, removed so that we have copies of the original language text. God promised to preserve His Words in many places in Scripture and we believe that He has.

However, Hunt, like so many, miss the point that there were two routes, paths, or streams that the Scriptures took or he failed to mention it.[1] One route, the Alexandrian, corrupted the text. The other route, paved by the blood of martyrs, *has preserved the Words of God virtually intact.* There has been *nothing* in this world that was or is absolutely perfect except the Son of God, the Lord Jesus Christ. This does not remove the concept of verbal plenary preservation, inerrancy, or purity from the Words of God.

INERRANCY EXAMINED

The Webster"s Dictionary[2] from 1828 does not contain the word inerrant or inerrancy, but does have the word, inerringly, meaning: without error, mistake, or deviation. By the time of Websters Dictionary[3] in 1992, the word inerrancy appears which is reported as meaning: 1. The state of being free from error and 2. As applied to Scripture, plenary inspiration. So we see that it is a new word that has been applied to Scripture and means something different than the 1828 definition of inerringly, which means without "any" error. When applied to Scripture, inerrancy means plenary; it does not mean "without error" in regards to typing, copying, or spelling. Plenary inspiration means: 1. full in

---

[1] Ibid. Jan 1995, p. 259-260; Unless I have misunderstood David Hunt, his stand does not reflect the two (2) routes nor the fact all modern translations are based on the corrupt MSS.

[2] Websters Dictionary, 1828; 1st Edition; Reprint granted by G & C Merriam Co., Published by Foundation for American Christian Education, 8th edition, San Francisco, Ca

[3] Webster Dictionary of the English Language, Deluxe Edition, PMC Publishing Co., Inc. NY, NY, 1992

all respects or requisites; entire; absolute; also, complete, embracing all parts or members: plenary authority 2. having full powers: plenary jurisdiction. 3. Fully or completely attended; consisting of the full number of members; said of an assembly. IT DOES NOT MEAN A COMMA, OR SPELLING ERROR, OR TYPOGRAPHICAL ERROR (ORTHOGRAPHY) CANNOT OCCUR. To make a printed Bible by 'man' to hold to the standard of absolute perfection, is asking for heaven to be on earth, a heresy believed by the likes of Westcoot [sic] and Hoot [sic]. Heaven is in another place, and is reserved for those who believe and trust in the Lord Jesus Christ that He will deliver us from this "fallen" and "full of errors" world. I agree with Pastor Dr. Robert Massey who thinks that we need to use a word other than inerrancy when applied to the Scriptures because so many people misunderstand it! However, it appears the word, inerrancy, applied to Scripture for so long will not be rooted out. Incidentally "inerrancy" cannot be used as an excuse to alter the "plenary inspiration" of Scripture just because errors occurred in copying, spelling, or typing. Neither can "scholars"use the excuse of orthography problems as an excuse to "construct" what they consider the "original" text.

When a doctor examines a patient he must keep in mind the meaning of 'healthy' or the concept of 'normal' in order to detect the deviation from 'normal', which, therefore, may be a disease or abnormality. Jesus Christ affirmed the occupation of doctors [Matt. 9:12, Col.4 :14] in the Scriptures in regards to physical health, and the Holy Spirit affirmed the concept of "doctors" of the Scriptures in regards to observation of subtle changes from normal and, therefore, corruption, as reflected so vividly in the writings of Paul [2 CO 2:17, 2 Thes 2:2, Titus 1:9-10, 3:10] and inferred in the writings of others in the New Testament [2 John 1:7, Jude 1:10, Rev 2:2].

DOCTRINES ARE EFFECTED

This discussion brings us to the examination of passages that cause doctrinal corruption by the changes wrought by the 'new' versions. Wilbur N. Pickering, Th.M., Ph.D., has written a treatise entitled, *What Difference Does It Make.* He reports the same argument heard from others that the author of this work has heard over the last ten years:

"that no matter what Greek text one may use it will not affect any doctrine. In my own experience, for over thirty years, when I have raised the question of what is the correct Greek text of the New Testament, regardless of the audience, the usual response has been: What difference does it make?"[1]

Dr. Pickering goes on to reason that if there is a discrepancy in the UBS[3] Greek text of 8 % as compared with the Majority Greek text edited by Hodges and Farstead, that amounts to a difference of 48 pages in a 600 page Greek Text. He reasons that about one-half are admittedly minor, but that leaves 25 pages that are significant. In those 25 pages he reports that no cardinal doctrine [such as eternal judgment, the ascension, and the deity of Jesus] is at risk, but he reports that they are weakened. The most important fact is that the most basic of all doctrine:

"the divine inspiration of the text, is indeed under attack"[2]
[my emphasis]

FAR REACHING CONSEQUENCES

Dr. Pickering continues the discussion by relating that if the eclectic text such as UBS[3] [and I might add the Nestle-Aland Greek Text, 26th edition]:

"incorporates plain errors of fact and contradictions such that any claim that the New Testament is divinely inspired becomes relative, and the doctrine of inerrancy becomes untenable. If the authority of the New Testament is undermined, all it teachings are likewise affected. During this whole century the credibility of the New Testament has been eroded, and this credibility crisis has been forced upon the laity by the modern versions that enclose parts of the text in brackets and have numerous footnotes of a sort that raise doubts about the integrity of the Text. THE CONSEQUENCES OF ALL THIS ARE SERIOUS AND FAR-REACHING FOR THE FUTURE OF THE CHURCH.

It seems unreasonable that individuals and organizations that profess to champion a high view of Scripture, that defend verbal plenary inspiration and the inerrancy of the Autographs, should embrace a Greek text that effectively undermines their belief. (A central part of the current debate is the argument that the text in use

---

[1] Pickering Th.M., Ph.D., Wilbur N.; *What Difference Does It Make;* as recorded in U*nholy Hands on the Bible;* Vol. II, Jay P. Green, editor; 1992, ISBN 1-878-443-65-1, Publishers, Sovereign Grace Trust Fund, Layfayette, Ind.; p. 555

[2] Ibid. p. 555

today in not inerrant.) Since their sincerity is evident, one must conclude that they are uninformed, or have not really looked at the evidence and thought through the implications."[1]

In general the following examination of the factual errors, contradictions, and serious anomalies/aberrations by Dr. Pickering can be analyzed by the following information, which has been presented in this work: Byz = Byzantine; lat = Latin; lect = Lectionary; syr = Syrian; capital letters are uncials; numbers beginning with 0 as 036 are minuscules; Diat = Diatessaron; a number preceded by a p is a papyrus; cop = Coptic; UNC = uncials [therefore +6UNC= plus 6 uncials]; Q=Qumran scrolls; and various 'Bibles' are designated by their common abbreviations. He presents 25 examples, but we will examine only five, and ask the serious inquirer to obtain Dr. Pickering's work, *What Difference Does It Make.*

ERRORS, CONFUSION, AND LOSS OF INERRANCY

I.   **Errors of Fact:**
Example 1: Luke 4:44 *And he preached in the synagogues of Galilee.* Galilee is the correct rendering but the error in the eclectic text or UBS[3] is carried over into the NASB, REBV, NRSV, LB, NIV, GNB, NAB. For example the NASB reads: Luke 4:44 *And He kept on preaching in the synagogues of Judea.* The truth is Jesus was in Galilee, not Judea, and continued there. In the parallel passage, Mark 1:35-39, it confirms the RT reading. Mark 1:35-39 And in the early morning, while it was still dark, He arose and went out and departed to a lonely place, and was praying there. 36And Simon and his companions hunted for Him; 37and they found Him, and said to Him, "Everyone is looking for You." 38And He said to them, "Let us go somewhere else to the towns nearby, in order that I may preach there also; for that is what I came out for." 39And He went into their synagogues throughout all Galilee, preaching and casting out the demons.

The supporting MSS evidence:
LK 4:44 Galilaias (of Galilee) – A, D, E, G, K, M, U, X, Y, 036, 037, 038, 041, 044, 047, 0211, +6UNC, F13, 33, Byz, lat, syrp.
The support for the other reading is not nearly as strong and reflects error.
LK 4:44 Ioudaias (of Judea) – p75vid, 01, B, C.L.Q, R (W)F1, Lect, syrs, h, cop
Example 2: Luke 23:45 *And the sun was darkened, and the veil of the*

---

temple was rent in the midst. There is no error in this passage in the RT, but many versions impose an incorrect reading "the sun was eclipsed" as Mofat, Twentieth Century, Authentic, Philips, NEB. Other versions such as NASB, GNB (TEV), REB and NIV avoid the 'eclipsed' phrasing, but use terminology that does not reflect an OOO God causing the "darkening". The NASB says "the sun being obscured". The problem is that an eclipse of the sun is not possible during Easter which is always during a full moon. That's why the date of Easter moves around.

The supporting manuscript evidence:

LK 23:45 eskotisOh (was darkened) – A, Cc, D, E, G, K, M, Q, R, U, V, W, X, Y, 036, 037, 038, 041, 044, 0117, 0135, +UNC, fl, 13, Byz, Lect, lat, syr, Diat

The support for the other reading:

LK 23:45 eklipontos (being eclipsed) – Aleph, p75, 01, (B, Cvid) L, 0124 (cop)

II. Contradictions:

Example 1: Matthew 19:17 *And he said unto him, Why callest thou me good? there is no one good but one, that is, God: but if thou wilt enter into life, keep the commandments.* This passage is often quoted as causing problems because the way it is rendered in the Alexandrian text favors Gnosticism. Dr. Pickering said that there is no way both renderings could be in the Greek, one or the other has to be correct. He goes on to explain that a conflation of the two readings occurs in the Latin text suggesting the two readings were present in the 2nd century and as a matter of fact the Diasterion of Tatian places the Byzantine reading in the first half of the century.

"That such a "nice" Gnostic variant came into being is no surprise, but why do modern editors embrace it? Most modern versions join UBS in this error."[1]

The NASB renders it thus: Matthew 19:17 *And He said to him, "Why are you asking Me about what is good? There is only One who is good; but if you wish to enter into life, keep the commandments."* The reader should be advised that the RT reading points to Jesus as 1. God and 2. the only one who is good. Jesus was asking the young man to reflect on who he was addressing and to recognize Jesus as God. The Gnostic reading does not point to God nor Jesus because of their Arian beliefs.

Support for the RT:

Matt. 19:17 *Ti me legeis agaOon; oudeis agaOos ei mh eis, o Oeos* (Why do you call me good? No one is good but one, God.) This is supported by—C, E, F, H, K, M, S, U, V, W, Y, 037, 042, 043, 045, f13, 33, Byz, Lect, syr^p.h.; cop^sa, Diat

Support for the other reading: *Ti me erwtas peri tou agaOou; eis estin o*

---

[1] Ibid. p. 561

agaOos (Why do you ask me about the good? One is good.)– 01, L, 038, B, D, f', syr'

III. **Serious Anomalies/Aberrations:**

Example 1: John 7:8 *Go ye up unto this feast: I go not up yet unto this feast; for my time is not yet full come.* This is the RT text. The eclectic [or some call it the critical text] reads like this from the NASB: John 7:8 "Go up to the feast yourselves; I do not go up to this feast because My time has not yet fully come." Look closely at these two texts and you will see the critical text makes Jesus a liar because He did go up to the feast! Pickering reports Metzger says the reason they [Alexandrians] do not follow by far the majority of MSS, and even some of their favorites p75 and B, is because of the "inconsistency" between verses 8 and 10. Now who is confused! Here are the verses.

John 7:8-10 Go ye up unto this feast: I go not up yet unto this feast; for my time is not yet full come. 9When he had said these words unto them, he abode still in Galilee. 10But when his brethren were gone up, then went he also up unto the feast, not openly, but as it were in secret.

The supporting evidence for the TR:
John 7:8 *oupw* (not yet) p[66,75], B, L, T, W, X, 037, 038, 044, f[1,13], Byz, Lect, syr[pt], cop Diat[pt]

The evidence for the eclectic text: ouk (not) – 01, D, K, 041, lat, syr[pt], Diat[pt]

Example 2: John 6:47 *Verily, verily, I say unto you, He that believeth on me hath everlasting life.* This passage is very very important to a person's salvation. It presents very clearly that for a person to be saved, that person has to believe in [on] Jesus Christ. There is no other way. The critical, eclectic text leaves "on me" out. This makes it possible for the Roman Catholics to substitute 'the church' as the saving route, or for Hindus, Muslims, etc. to say "we all believe the same thing". This reading also suggests the Gnostics were at work again very early in the N.T. Church 'messing' things up!

The evidence for the RT reading:
John 6:7 eis eme – A, C°, D, K, 037, 041, 044, f[1,13], Byz, lat, syr[p,h, (c,s)], cop, Diat

The eclectic text support for "on me" being omitted: p[66, 75vid], 01, B, C*, L, T, W, 038

ORTHOGRAPHIC AND PRINTING ERRORS IN THE KJB

One other consideration in this "hands-on" section concerning the text of the Bible is to evaluate a common statement made by many in response to the eclectic [critical] Greek [Alexandrian] text and the many changes it has experienced. [Incidentally, those frequent changes have also been reflected in the translations and their many editions based on the changing 'critical' text]

Pastors, deacons, and one chairman of deacons, Sunday School teachers, and others have stated emphatically to me that the KJB has had many changes and editions, also. The truth is that editions of the KJB have been produced, but the editions of the KJB were not for wording changes but for orthographic [spelling] reasons. The reasons for the changes in the 'critical' [eclectic] Greek [Alexandrian] text are for entirely different reasons as documented earlier in this work.

Pastor David Reagin has investigated this subject more thoroughly than anyone else that I have found to date. He relates the same attacks on God's Words which have been related in this work and then proceeds to say:

"The attack referred to is the **myth** which claims that since the King James Version has already been revised four times, there should be and can be no valid objection to other revisions. This **myth** was used by the English Revisers of 1881 [primarily Westcott and Hort, my addition] and has been revived in recent years by Fundamentalist scholars **hoping to sell their latest translation.**"[1] [Oh, how I agree with this statement. This may be the real root for the many 'new' versions and the 'critical' text: That is, $$$$$$$'s paid for royalties and profits from sales. HDW] [my emphasis]

When the KJB was printed in 1611 the Gutenberg press invented by Johannes Gutenberg in 1450 had not changed much at all. The type was hand carved and had to be set by hand. Everyone expected the first edition to need correcting because of the errors introduced by setting type by hand. These errors were not the "kind" of errors that are found in modern editions. Modern editions are continually making textual alterations.

"The two original printings of the Authorized Version demonstrate the difficulty of printing in 1611 without making mistakes. Both editions were printed in Oxford. Both were printed in the same year: 1611. The same printers did both jobs. Most likely both editions were printed on the same printing press. Yet, in a strict comparison of the two editions, approximately 100 textual differences can be found. In the same vein the King James **critics** can find only about 400 alleged textual alterations in the King James Version after **375**

---

[1] Reagin, David; *The King James Version of 1611, The Myth of Early Revisions;* Trinity Baptist Temple Bookstore, 5709 N. Broadway , Knoxville, Tenn. 37918; Send $1.00 for the pamphlet; Well worth it; Way of Life Literature, Port Huron, MI; Fundamental Baptist CD-ROM Library 2000b, ISBN 1-58318-065-6;

years of printing and four so-called revisions! Something is rotten in Scholarsville!"[1]

Closer examination reveals that the first two **revisions**, not editions, occurred within 27 years of 1611. The first revision occurred in 1629 at Cambridge, but in reality was not a revision, but rather a very careful printing and correction of spelling overseen by Dr. Samuel Ward and John Bois. Remember they had worked on the original translation of the KJB. The second "revision" took place in 1638, but Dr. Scrivener, late 19th century, [remember him] relates the "revision" was in reality simply putting back in words or clauses overlooked by the 1611 printers and amended manifest errors.

"Just as the first two so-called revisions were actually two stages of one process—the purification of early printing errors—so the last two so-called revisions were two stages in another process—the standardization of the spelling."[2]

The first 25-50 years after the first printing, English spelling changed rapidly, necessitating the first two revisions. The revisions were not for textual changes. The second two revisions were only 7 years apart in 1762 and 1769, and in reality the second was just a completion of what had been started in the first.

The "revisions" can be looked at from three points of view. 1. Printing changes 2. Spelling changes 3. Textual changes. Since textual changes seem to be the focus of the 'critical' text opponents or "use-the-excuse" opponents, let's deal with them first.

Textual changes in the KJB were due to:

a.   words being inverted,

b.   plural words were written as singular and vice-versa,

c.   a phrase or a word was omitted. "The omissions were obvious and did not have the doctrinal implications of those found in modern translations. In fact, there is really no comparison between the corrections made in the King James text and those proposed by the scholars of today"[3] [in their 'critical' texts, my addition]

A few examples will suffice. First will be the 1611 reading, then the present reading, and then the date of the correction:

1. requite good, requite me good (1629)
2. the crowned, Thy crowned (1629)
3. which was a Jew, which was a Jewess (1629)
4. a fiery furnace, a burning fiery furnace (1638)
5. now and ever, both now and ever (1638)

---

[1] Ibid. p. 2

[2] Ibid. p. 2

[3] Ibid. p. 3

6. this thing, this thing also (1638)
7. shalt have remained, ye shalt have remained (1762)
8. returned, turned (1769)

THE KJB IS NOT DIFFICULT TO READ

The spelling changes were incurred because spelling had not stabilized by 1611, but grammar and vocabulary had. As a matter of fact essentially the same vocabulary today was that of 1611 English. The argument that the "language" and spelling is archaic is wrong, improper, and mostly secondary to the advertising push for the NASB version released in 1960, and that 'push' persists to this day. I was recently in a 'Christian' bookstore and inquired about Bibles and the various versions. I was given a pamphlet which stated the KJB was:

"Difficult to read due to the 17th century English vocabulary and word order" [1]

The truth is that the KJB has been subjected to multiple computer programs which have shown repeatedly that the reading grade level of the KJB is lower than any bible on the market. Also, parents complain that their children cannot read the KJB. Let me remind everyone that the countries I have visited on mission trips demonstrated to me children can learn 3-6 foreign languages easily. Why can't they learn a few archaic words or use one of the new KJB Bibles, such as the Defined Bible,[2] which has the definitions on each page?

The word **order** is the order given by God in the original language texts that emphasizes certain words, as anyone who has studied the Greek or Hebrew of the Bible will tell you. That's why verbal and formal equivalent as opposed to dynamic equivalent translation technique is so important! David Cloud records in his article, *Modern Bible Versions,* the following comments, and quotes D. A.. Waite, Ph.D. Th.D., a language specialist:

"It is also crucial to understand that **the English of the King James Bible is not merely that of the 17th century. It is not the language of Shakespeare**, but the language of the Hebrew and Greek. "Bishop Lightfoot affirmed that this version was the storehouse of the highest truth and the purest well of our native English. 'Indeed,' he wrote, 'we may take courage

---

[1] Family Christian Store; *Bible Comparison Guide,* Given to the author of this work in Nov., 2001

[2] Available from: The Bible For Today, Collingswood, N.J.

from the fact that the language of our English Bible is not the language of the age in which the translators lived, but in its grand simplicity stands out in contrast to the ornate and often affected diction of the literature of the time'" (*The Divine Original*).

Of the English language used in the KJV, George Marsh, in a lecture of 1870, notes: "It was an assemblage of the best forms of expression applicable to the communication of religious truth that then existed, or had existed, in any and all the successive stages through which England had passed in its entire history. ... Even now [in 1870, the language of the King James Bible is] scarcely further removed from the current phraseology of life and books than it was two hundred years since. The subsequent movement of the English speech has not been in a right line of recession from the Scriptural dialect. It has been rather a curve of revolution around it" (Edwin Bissell, *The Historic Origin of the Bible*, 1873, p. 353).

When the Harvard University Press published *The Literary Guide to the Bible* in 1987, they selected the KJB for the literary analysis of each of the Bible books. "...our reasons for doing so must be obvious: it is the version most English readers associate with the literary qualities of the Bible, and it is still arguably the version that best preserves the literary effects of the original languages" (Theodore Letis, Foreword to *Tyndale's Triumph, John Rogers' Monument: The New Testament of the Matthew's Bible 1537*, 1989, p. ii).

We must keep this in mind when we hear the complaints about the "old antiquated King James English." **The King James Bible is written in beautiful and precise English fitted perfectly to the Hebrew and Greek Scriptures, and it is not difficult to learn the few antiquated terms necessary to read it with understanding. If one is not willing to give diligent study to the Bible, he will not understand it no matter which translation he uses**. And if your Bible reads like the morning newspaper, dear friend, you don't have the Word of God, because the Hebrew and Greek Scriptures do not read as simply and as contemporarily as the morning newspaper! While some parts of the Greek New Testament, such as portions of John's Gospel, are so simple a child could understand them, other parts are very complex.

The first and foremost qualification for a Bible translation is that it be an accurate, readable translation of the right Hebrew and Greek text. [Amen!!]

In overall reading level, the KJV is within the reach of anyone with an average education. It is written on an 8th to 10th grade level. This has been proven from computer analysis made by Dr. Donald Waite (of whom we speak more particularly in Myth Five, "Biblical Scholarship Does Not Support the Received Text."). Dr. Waite ran several books of the KJV through the *Right Writer* program and found that Genesis 1, Exodus 1, and Romans 8 are on the 8th grade level; Romans 1 and Jude are on the 10th grade level; and Romans 3:1-23 is on the 6th grade level. We note, further, that while Shakespeare used a vocabulary of roughly 37,000 English words, the King James Bible employs only 8,000 (John Wesley Sawyer, *The Newe Testament by William Tindale*, p. 10, quoting BBC TV, "The Story of English," copyright 1986). Incidentally, other computer programs have reported the reading grade level at four (4).

Dr. Waite says, "I know hundreds of people whose intelligence and educational levels have not reached as high as some of these ... people who say they can't understand this King James Bible, yet these people do understand it. How do you figure that out? Remember 1 Cor. 2:14 which states, 'But the natural man receiveth not the things of the Spirit of God: for they are foolishness unto him: neither can he know them, because they are spiritually discerned.' This verse is still true, regardless of which translation is used" (*Defending the King James Bible*, pp. 50,51).

Dr. Waite continues: "Some people say they like a particular version because they say it's more readable. Now, readability is one thing, but does the readability conform to what's in the original Greek and Hebrew language? You can have a lot of readability, but if it doesn't match up with what God has said, it's of no profit. In the King James Bible, the words match what God has said. You may say it's difficult to read, but study it out. It's hard in the Hebrew and Greek and, perhaps, even in the English in the King James Bible. But to change it around just to make it simple, or interpreting it, instead of translating it, is wrong. You've got lots of interpretation, but we don't want that in a translation. We want exactly what God said in the Hebrew and Greek brought over into English" (Ibid., pp. 241,242).

The following is taken from the instruction manual of the *Online Bible* version 5.0:

"We have now had enough experience to determine which

translation is most suitable for computer word and phrase searching. If one were to rank the NIV, the NKJV and the AV on this point:
- The AV is the best
- The NKJV is good
- The NIV is fair to good

Much to our surprise the vocabulary has increased, not decreased, with modern translations. Hence the greater inconsistency in the translation, and the greater difficulty in finding what you need through a word search. It seems consistency and readability is quite difficult to achieve using modern English. His Majesty, Prince Charles, the Prince of Wales, addressed the problem when he said: "Ours is an age of miraculous writing machines but not of miraculous writing. Our banalities are no improvement on the past; merely an insult to it and a source of confusion in the present. In the case of a cherished religious writing we should leave well alone, especially when it is better than well: when it is great. Otherwise we leave ourselves open to the terrible accusation once leveled by the true master of the banal, Samuel Goldwyn: 'You've improved it worse.'"[1]

CHANGES IN THE HEBREW TEXT

Lastly, let us examine some of the changes in the 'critical' text that have occurred in the Old Testament. The changes in that section of our beloved Book are just as heart wrenching. Please note the changes are consistent with the belief of many who accept the 'critical' schools belief that there is no "heaven or hell". Heaven exists "here and now" and "hell is not a place". The word heaven is left in Scripture, but the definition is changed. The Word 'hell' is changed or removed.

Rev. 22:18-19

For I testify unto every man that heareth the words of the prophecy of this book, If any man shall add unto these things, God shall add unto him the plagues that are written in this book: And if any man shall take

---

[1] Cloud, David, *Modern Bible Versions,* Part 1 of 2, Updated May 28, 2000; Way of Life Literature, Port Huron, MI; Fundamental Baptist CD-ROM Library 2000b, ISBN 1-58318-065-6;

away from the words of the book of this prophecy, God shall take away his part out of the book of life, and out of the holy city, and from the things which are written in this book.

The information in the following charts is included in Pastor Reagin's brochure:

EXAMPLES OF CHANGES CAUSED BY THE CRITICAL TEXT IN "NEW" VERSIONS COMPARED WITH THE KJB

KJB	NASV	NIV
De 32:22 For a fire is kindled in mine anger, and shall burn unto the lowest hell, and shall consume the earth with her increase, and set on fire the foundations of the mountains.	Deut. 32:22 For a fire is kindled in My anger, And burns to the lowest part of Sheol, And consumes the earth with its yield, And sets on fire the foundations of the mountains.	Deut. 32:22 For a fire has been kindled by my wrath, one that burns to the realm of death below.It will devour the earth and its harvests and set afire the foundations of the mountains.
2 Samuel 22:6 The sorrows of hell compassed me about; the snares of death prevented me;	2 Samuel 22:6 The cords of Sheol surrounded me; The snares of death confronted me.	2 Samuel 22:6 The cords of the grave coiled around me; the snares of death confronted me.
Psalm 16:10 For thou wilt not leave my soul in hell; neither wilt thou suffer thine Holy One to see corruption.	Psalm 16:10 For Thou wilt not abandon my soul to Sheol; Neither wilt Thou allow Thy Holy One to undergo decay.	Psalm 16:10 because you will not abandon me to the grave, nor will you let your Holy One see decay.
Psalm 55:15 Let death seize upon them, and let them go down quick into hell: for wickedness is in their dwellings, and among them.	Psalm 55:15 Let death come deceitfully upon them; Let them go down alive to Sheol, For evil is in their dwelling, in their midst.	Psalm 55:15 Let death take my enemies by surprise; let them go down alive to the grave, for evil finds lodging among them.
Proverbs 23:14 Thou shalt beat him with the rod, and shalt deliver his soul from hell.	Proverbs 23:14 You shall beat him with the rod, And deliver his soul from Sheol.	Proverbs 23:14 Punish him with the rod and save his soul from death.

Isaiah 14:9 Hell from beneath is moved for thee to meet thee at thy coming: it stirreth up the dead for thee, even all the chief ones of the earth; it hath raised up from their thrones all the kings of the nations.	Isaiah 14:9 "Sheol from beneath is excited over you to meet you when you come; It arouses for you the spirits of the dead, all the leaders of the earth; It raises all the kings of the nations from their thrones.	Isaiah 14:9 The grave below is all astir to meet you at your coming; it rouses the spirits of the departed to greet you--all those who were leaders in the world; it makes them rise from their thrones-- all those who were kings over the nations.
Ezekiel 32:21 The strong among the mighty shall speak to him out of the midst of hell with them that help him: they are gone down, they lie uncircumcised, slain by the sword.	Ezekiel 32:21 "The strong among the mighty ones shall speak of him and his helpers from the midst of Sheol, 'They have gone down, they lie still, the uncircumcised, slain by the sword.	Ezekiel 32:21 From within the grave the mighty leaders will say of Egypt and her allies, 'They have come down and they lie with the uncircumcised, with those killed by the sword.

EXAMPLES OF SUBTLE CHANGES, BUT CORRUPTION APPARENT IN THE BOOK OF ECCLESIASTES

The following chart of examples of verses from the book of Ecclesiastes, which were illuminated by Pastor Reagin ,reveal the following important subtle perversions:

1. A trait of godliness, equity, becomes skill in verse 2:21
2. The "world" becomes "eternity" in verse 3:11 Many theologians like Westcott and Hort believe every man is eventually going to arrive in eternity. This is Universalism.
3. Man without God becomes "like" a beast instead of "a beast" in verse 3:18
4. The wonderful phrase and sustainer of deity in verse 5:8 is removed. "he is higher than the highest" is changed to "higher official"
5. The meaning of wisdom "to direct" is perverted to wisdom "brings success" in v 10:10
6. "the master of assemblies" becomes the "scholar" in verse 12:11;

KJB	NKJV	NASV
Eccles. 2:21 For there is a man whose labour is in wisdom, and in knowledge, and in equity; yet to a man that hath not laboured therein shall he leave it for his portion. This also is vanity and a great evil.	Eccles. 2:21 For there is a man whose labor is with wisdom, knowledge, and skill; yet he must leave his heritage to a man who has not labored for it. This also is vanity and a great evil.	Eccles. 2:21 When there is a man who has labored with wisdom, knowledge and skill, then he gives his legacy to one who has not labored with them. This too is vanity and a great evil.
Eccles. 3:11 He hath made every thing beautiful in his time: also he hath set the world in their heart, so that no man can find out the work that God maketh from the beginning to the end.	Eccles. 3:11 He has made everything beautiful in its time. Also He has put eternity in their hearts, except that no one can find out the work that God does from beginning to end.	Eccles. 3:11 He has made everything appropriate in its time. He has also set eternity in their heart, yet so that man will not find out the work which God has done from the beginning even to the end.
Eccles. 3:18 I said in mine heart concerning the estate of the sons of men, that God might manifest them, and that they might see that they themselves are beasts.	Eccles. 3:18 I said in my heart, "Concerning the condition of the sons of men, God tests them, that they may see that they themselves are like animals."	Eccles. 3:18 I said to myself concerning the sons of men, "God has surely tested them in order for them to see that they are but beasts."
Eccles. 5:8 If thou seest the oppression of the poor, and violent perverting of judgment and justice in a province, marvel not at the matter: for he that is higher than the highest regardeth; and there be higher than they.	Eccles. 5:8 If you see the oppression of the poor, and the violent perversion of justice and righteousness in a province, do not marvel at the matter; for high official watches over high official, and higher officials are over them.	Eccles. 5:8 If you see oppression of the poor and denial of justice and righteousness in the province, do not be shocked at the sight, for one official watches over another official, and there are higher officials over them.
Eccles. 10:10 If the iron be blunt, and he do not whet the edge, then must he put to more strength: but wisdom is profitable to direct.	Eccles. 10:10 If the ax is dull, And one does not sharpen the edge, Then he must use more strength; But wisdom brings success.	Eccles. 10:10 If the axe is dull and he does not sharpen its edge, then he must exert more strength. Wisdom has the advantage of giving success.
Eccles. 12:11 The words of the wise are as goads, and as nails fastened by the masters of assemblies, which are given from one shepherd.	Eccles. 12:11 The words of the wise are like goads, and the words of scholars are like well-driven nails, given by one Shepherd.	Eccles. 12:11 The words of wise men are like goads, and masters of these collections are like well-driven nails; they are given by one Shepherd.

NKJV CASTS DOUBTS ABOUT PRESERVATION AND MAKES STATEMENTS THAT CANNOT BE AFFIRMED

In this section the NKJV will be examined because there has been so much said in the literature about this version. The preface of the NKJV has been misleading to say the least. The editors and translators say they are standing in the tradition of the AV and that they are leaning on precisely the same Greek and Hebrew texts of the King James Bible. David Cloud reports:

"The Statement of Purpose issued by Thomas Nelson, publishers of the New King James Bible New Testament (1979), makes the following claim:

"Not to add to, take from, nor alter the communication intended by the original translators, but to convey that communication in 20th century vocabulary and usage."

This says to me that the producers of the NKJV are committed to PRECISELY the same text as that underlying the King James Bible. This is absolutely not the case, though... FIRST, THE EDITORS OF THE NKJV ARE DEFINITELY NOT COMMITTED TO THE RECEIVED TEXT UNDERLYING THE KJV. We have corresponded with some of these men, including the executive editor of the Old Testament portion, Dr. James Price. In April of 1996 he admitted to me that he is not committed to the Received Text and that he supports the modern critical text in general -- [He said:]

"I am not a TR advocate. I happen to believe that God has preserved the autographic text in the whole body of evidence that He has preserved, not merely through the textual decisions of a committee of fallible men based on a handful of late manuscripts. The modern critical texts like NA26/27 [Nestles] and UBS [United Bible Societies] provide a list of the variations that have entered the manuscript traditions, and they provide the evidence that supports the different variants. In the apparatus they have left nothing out, the evidence is there. The apparatus indicates where possible additions, omissions, and alterations have occurred. ... I am not at war with the conservative modern versions [such as the New International Version and the New American Standard Version]" (James Price, e-mail to David Cloud, April 30, 1996)."[1]

---

[1] Cloud, David, *The Doubt-Producing Margins of the NKJV;* Sept 6, 1997, Way

The "Majority Text" [not the TR in this case], which supports the NKJV, has acquired support from Jay Green, Zane Hodges, and Wilbur Pickering. The surprising fact concerning this development is that Green supports the "Majority Text:"

> "even though he certainly knows that 'the vast majority of all manuscripts' have never been collated, so that no one knows what they read in the various passages he cites,"[1]

because they may not be what is contained in the majority of the MSS as they have not been collated. Dr. Waite and David Cloud who document the deficiencies in the 'new' Majority Text are confused as to why these three men who formally supported the RT, have switched sides. Could money be the reason?

---

1 Tim. 6:10   *For the love of money is the root of all evil: which while some coveted after, they have erred from the faith, and pierced themselves through with many sorrows.*

This concludes the "O" which is the objective look at Scripture in this work. Remember, the "O" comes from the acronym SOAP. If the reader desires to examine more evidence of the corruption of Scripture readings there are several websites and many books and articles which demonstrate and illustrate this perversion which has come upon the Church unawares. They may be found in the bibliography at the end of this work.

It is time for us to place before you that portion in the work-up of the patient called the "Assessment," the "A" in SOAP. This is the juncture when the 'working' diagnosis of the patient is recorded. The next step will be the "Plan". The "Plan" lays out laboratory evidence needed to support the diagnosis by collecting evidence from X-rays, blood tests, MRI's, etc. In this work we will go to the laboratory evidence presented to us by the churches, by the society in

---

of Life Literature, Port Huron, MI; Fundamental Baptist CD-ROM Library 2000b, ISBN 1-58318-065-6;

[1] Cloud, David; *Moving Away from Preserved Scripture: Examining the Hodges-Farstad Majority Text;* Way of Life Literature, Port Huron, MI; Fundamental Baptist CD-ROM Library 2000b, ISBN 1-58318-065-6;

which we live, and by the individuals in our society. Much of this information will come from the help of good surveyors of society and its trends. The instrument used to "X-Ray" will be the Sword of the Lord, the discerner of the heart.

Hebrews 4:12 For the word of God is quick, and powerful, and sharper than any twoedged sword, piercing even to the dividing asunder of soul and spirit, and of the joints and marrow, and is a discerner of the thoughts and intents of the heart.

ASSESSMENT

SIGNIFICANT CONCLUSIONS

I.   The Churches of the Living God have the preserved, verbal and plenary inspired, inerrant, infallible, Words of God. The inspired, infallible, inerrant, Words of God have not been lost.

II.   There have been unholy hands on the Bible.

III. There have been two paths the Scripture has taken in history:
   A.   The path that was kept and maintained by the Holy Spirit as He worked in the lives of the *priesthood of believers* who preserved the true text of the Scriptures.
   B.   The path that was influenced by Satan who predisposed man to corrupt the Scriptures and to develop the "critical text".

IV. The authority of the Scriptures has been seriously compromised.

V.   **"THE CONSEQUENCES OF ALL THIS ARE SERIOUS AND FAR-REACHING FOR THE FUTURE OF THE CHURCH," SOCIETY, AND THE INDIVIDUAL.**

PLAN

Jeremiah 25:4 And the Lord hath sent unto you all his servants the prophets, rising early and sending them; but ye have not hearkened, nor inclined your ear to hear.

GOD'S WORDS FOR OUR PROTECTION

When a physician plans the steps needed to treat and/or to continue the evaluation of a patient, he must be aware of side effects, or reactions to drug treatments, or radiation from X-rays, or complications from invasive diagnostics and treatments. The facts are relayed or taught to the patient and family so that they are aware of the dangers of treatments or tests. The same approach must be taken in regards to the Scripture. God has sent us a detailed Message, and one must be aware that the Message is full of warnings and of the consequences of ignoring His admonishments. The cautions are for our protection. Many individuals miss this very important concept. The Creator of the earth, the heavens, and man knows what is best for us. However, most individuals reject His authority, protection, and love. They consider the Biblical rules to be "old," to be "restraining," to be "hateful," or to be "mythological." Similarly, many individuals fail to understand that true love is a commitment to another and may consist of "rules" for protection. This is very much like the very specific command a parent gives a child to "look both ways before crossing the street." What if someone could alter the command and make it proclaim: "*occasionally* look both ways before crossing the street."

This is exactly what has happened in the arena of textual criticism. Words have been added, subtracted, or changed and subsequently the meaning has been changed. Oh how foolish! It is contemptuous to believe a mere man could change the OOO God's Words and have them perfectly applicable throughout the ages. But this is exactly what arrogant, haughty, disdainful, prideful men have done.

SERIOUS CONSEQUENCES RESULT
FROM CHANGING GOD'S WORDS

The third and fourth parts of the assessment, the "A" in the acronym, SOAP listed above, are very serious consequences of the false teaching that only the original autographs are inspired, infallible and inerrant. The leap from the alleged **loss of the words** of the original autographs to the subsequent loss of absolute authority becomes very small. If Christians do not know or believe they have the absolute infallible, inspired Words of God, then individuals are free to claim they can make their own rules for morality in the society in which they live and they can set the rules by which they worship God. This is very much like changing the words in a "legal" contract every month or two to suit your situation, belief, or desire. If this happened, how much faith would individuals have in "legal" contracts? The answer is "none." This is what has happened to the Bible. The constant changes, new versions, doubt producing comments in the side margins, and study Bible notes of "new" versions have subtly caused loss of faith in the absolute words and rules and guidance from the Almighty God.[1]

The proof of this tenet is found in the observation of people, the church, and society. If people do not believe in absolute authority from the absolute Words of God, then they are free to do whatsoever is "right in their own eyes". [Judges 21:25, Isa 5:21]

People have demonstrated by their actions, attitudes, and beliefs the following thinking: (See the information and stats below.)

1.   There are so many Bibles which say different "things"; they "know" that we do not have the Words of God. If the Church does not have the actual Words of God, then how does the Church know what He really said for sure?

2.   Since the Church does not have the actual Words, then the Church does not have the absolute teachings.

3.   If Christians do not have the actual, literal teachings, then they are free to substitute what they believe to be correct by the "feelings" and "emotions" they experience.

---

[1]Price, Robert M.; *The Incredible Shrinking Son Of Man;* Prometheus Books, Amherst, New York; 2003. This book is an example of the type of blasphemy is produced by rationalistic 'new' age thinking.

4.   If they don't have the actual Words of God, then there is no final authority outside of the person because all are untrustworthy. The only authority is the "inner" direction that they receive from experiences and "personal" spiritual direction.

5.   Since they have no absolute "directions," they are free to make their own "directions" based on "whatever" is best for "me" and, everything they decide is based on the situation. This is called "relativism." Therefore, morality is based on "my" situation, which is called "moral" relativism.

In the area of Public Health and immunity, there is a concept called "herd" immunity. This simply means that when enough people are immune to a disease like measles, chicken poxes, or mumps that the disease will not be able to be transmitted from one person to another. Similarly if enough people believe in absolutes of morality (avoiding fornication), then a society is protected from the spread of sexually transmitted disease. Similarly, if enough people have developed a cavalier attitude toward the preserved, precious, protective Words of God, then a paradigm shift in beliefs, attitudes, and life style in a society occurs. There is no "immunity" provided by the Words of God. "Attitudes" are transmitted from one person to another like a disease.

This work puts forth the proposition that a paradigm shift has occurred in many nations as a result of the loss of confidence that the Words of God have been preserved. The confidence has been lost because of destructive *lower criticism*. The comments in modern texts subtly undermine assurance in the absolutes of the Scriptures and therefore, subtly approve the turning to "situational" ethics, morality, and truth. This kind of reasoning can be demonstrated in the individual, the Church, and society and will be explored in this final section. Wilbur Pickering has befittingly and poignantly said:

"THE CONSEQUENCES OF ALL THIS ARE SERIOUS AND FAR-REACHING FOR THE FUTURE OF THE CHURCH"[1], SOCIETY, AND THE INDIVIDUAL. [I added society and the individual, which will be demonstrated below.]

---

[1]Pickering Th.M., Ph.D., Wilbur N.; *What Difference Does It Make;* as recorded in U*nholy Hands on the Bible;* Vol. II, Jay P. Green, editor; 1992, ISBN 1-878-443-65-1, Publishers, Sovereign Grace Trust Fund, Layfayette; p.557

WE HAVE GOD'S WORDS AND THEY ARE PRESERVED

The response to someone reasoning as presented above is this: "<u>Either</u> we have the absolute Scriptures written "not by the will of man; but holy men of God spake as they were moved by the Holy Ghost" (2 PET 1:21), and the teachings that are derived from the Words of God upon which the absolutes are based; <u>or</u> we do not." Those are the only two possibilities. "Destructive" criticism has done its best under the guidance of enemy spiritual forces to destroy the plenary inspired Scriptures and to bring the leaven of serious doubt seeping into the minds of men. The leaven introduced by the rationalism of the modern era, called Humanism, and its offspring called textual criticism, has led many to reject the **authority** of the Words of God. Rationalism has caused some of the best scholars in the world to believe the MSS are so confusing that man needs to reassemble the Words of the Living God, that his promises of preservation were false or misinterpreted, and that many parts of the Scripture are "made up."[1] The evidence presented in this work defeats that position and that reasoning. We do have the Words once committed to faithful men and passed down to us through the **priesthood of believers**, and those Words go back to the very pens of men moved by God. However, if the Words are not God's, then the testimonies of the prophets of the O.T. and of Paul, Peter, and John are false. These men were men of honor, truth, and faithfulness. If one cannot believe their testimonies, then no one can be believed. At the risk of redundancy, in 2 Pe 1:21 Peter states: *For the prophecy came not in old time by the will of man: but holy men of God spake as they were moved by the Holy Ghost.* Holy men of God wrote the Holy Words as they were inspired by God, the Holy Spirit. You cannot get any clearer than that. Paul said in 1 Corinthians 14:37 *If any man think himself to be a prophet, or spiritual, let him acknowledge that the things that I write unto you are the commandments of the Lord.* Paul made it clear he was not speaking or writing *his* thoughts, or words, or doctrine, or commandments, but **instructions** [commandments, words] "of the Lord". We have the actual Words recorded by these men!!! Honest, truthful men making statements like these cannot be ignored. In addition, this work has presented the evidence in preceding sections

---

[1]Ehrman, Bart D.; *Lost Christianities;* Oxford University Press, New York; 2003; This book claims many books of the canon are probably fraudulent and shouldn't be in the Bible.

that God's Words were preserved by the saints down through the ages.

Most of the destructive lower and higher critics of the Scripture do not accept these statements, and they have set out to change the actual Words and meaning of Scripture. The following verse written by the Apostle John says: *"For I testify unto every man that heareth the words of the prophecy of this book, If any man shall add unto these things, God shall add unto him the plagues that are written in this book: 19And if any man shall take away from the words of the book of this prophecy, God shall take away his part out of the book of life, and out of the holy city, and from the things which are written in this book."* [Rev. 22:18-19] There could not be a sterner or more serious warning written. The Scripture is full of plagues consisting of diseases, damage to crops, death of firstborn, and full of disasters such as earthquakes, floods, drought, famine, rebellious and reprobate children, murder, deceit, loss of homes, territories, nations, and income.

After 1600 years of recording the Scriptures, by at least 44 authors who were farmers, fishermen, doctors, kings, etc. and an additional 20+ centuries since the Bible was completed, we have **not one proven reason** to doubt the veracity of these men. We have only speculation by agnostics, atheists, and perverted men that the Words of God are not preserved and "pure." [Psa 12:6-7]

In addition, the Words of God are verified in the lives of men by the "wonderful way in which they [the Scriptures] convince the reason, probe the conscience, and apply healing balm to the wounded spirit, [and this] is in itself an independent attestation to their divine origin"[1] The changed Words of God cannot, do not, and will not accomplish the product of this "balm." The consequences of the disobedience of changing God's Words against His stated will are still accumulating. [my addition]

REJECTION OF GOD'S WORDS BRINGS JUDGMENT

It is necessary "that the offenses come," but if one is the offender may God have mercy. This thought, regarding the offenses and offender, launches us into the sayings of God regarding judgments rendered upon those who offend the Holy Words and therefore, a Holy God. The Words of God are replete with examples and a few will be offered here. We, as a "peculiar people" of God, must understand the consequences of failure to heed and obey. The "winds" of

---

[1] Barnes Notes; *A Commentary on the Book of Genesis;* by James G. Murphy; Baker Books, Grand Rapids, Michigan; Reprinted from the 1873 edition in 2001; ISBN 0-8010-0835-2; p. 10

judgment are beginning to blow. Warnings have been sent. We are being judged for tampering with His Letter to mankind.

The next few pages outline judgments that have been administered in the past, and the rumblings of judgments soon to fall on a rebellious generation. We will see the rebellious attitude toward the precepts, commandments, and authority of the Words of God in our institutions of government, our churches, our families, and our children; and we will explore it. We have undermined the confidence our children should have in the Scriptures. **One of the premises of this work is the belief that we have neglected, damaged, and usurped the authority of the Words of God and that the consequences are beginning to show in our culture and society. The "postmodern" world is a rudderless ship on the high seas. May God help us!**

Next we will examine a few warning Scriptures and then begin to examine the effects of rejecting the Firm Foundation; or in other words, rejecting our Absolute Authority, the Words of God preserved through the **priesthood of believers**. Although many people detest the idea that our nation was founded on God's Words, men who used the principles and precepts of the Words of God did established our government. This work cannot explore all the proof, but it is readily available.

God has been sending us ample warnings because of the rejection of His precepts, and in addition, He is beginning to "crank–up" those warnings, just as he did for the southern half of the Israeli nation, Judah. God said to the people of Judah through the prophet Jeremiah, *"And now, because ye have done all these works, saith the LORD, and I spake unto you, rising up early and speaking, but ye heard not; and I called you, but ye answered not; Therefore will I do unto this house, which is called by my name, wherein ye trust, and unto the place which I gave to you and to your fathers, as I have done to Shiloh. And I will cast you out of my sight, as I have cast out all your brethren, even the whole seed of Ephraim."* (Jer. 7:13-15) God had "spake" unto the people of Judah and had warned them of coming judgment because of their apostasy. Israel (the Northern Kingdom represented by Shiloh and Ephraim) had already been carried into captivity to Assyria and now Judah (the Southern Kingdom) was told that it was going into captivity. It was not long before most of the people of Judah were taken into captivity to Babylon.

TWO PRONGED ATTACK BREWING

Could it be that the U.S. will be placed into captivity? There are ample warnings that the control of the Roman Catholic Church, once a murderous religion based on power, is growing in the U.S. government and is being facilitated by the ecumenical movement. [More on this subject later]. In addition, the numbers of Muslims, who are also members of a militant religion based on power and who demonstrate little respect for the sanctity of life, are increasing dramatically in America. There were 30,000 new converts to Islam in six months after the World Trade Center and Pentagon attacks.[1]

The United States Department of State warns in a fact sheet on *Islam in the United States* that it is "one of the fastest-growing religions in the United States. By the year 2010, America's Muslim population is expected to surpass the Jewish population, making Islam the country's second largest faith after Christianity."[2] There were already 4,175,000 Muslims in the U.S. in mid-2000. Most are immigrants but there are over 17,000/year conversions amongst African-Americans to Islam and African-Americans make up 40% of the total number of Muslims in this country. There are already over 2000 mosques nationwide as well as "numerous" Muslim day schools and Sunday and weekend schools.[3] Newscasts such as *"The O'Reilly Factor"* are reporting currently on the "world war" with Islam. Bill O'Reilly, the top cable news reporter, said on April 15, 2002, that the current situation with the Islamic world is a "serious situation" and that he is "looking at a world war". His guest, Wald Phares, PhD and professor at Florida Atlantic University, said "There is a world war [with Islam] and ....We have a serious problem here in America. The vision of American people...has been blurred for so many decades". O'Reilly answered, "You just made one of the best points that I've heard on *The Factor* in quite some time. Americans do not understand the danger that is being posed by the Muslim world to our way of living right now."[4]

---

[1] Berean Call, April 2002, Bend, Oregon; p. 3

[2] Fact Sheet; *Islam in the United States;* U.S. Department of State; International Information Programs; 2001

[3] Ibid.

[4] O'Reilly, Bill; *The Factor;* Tues, April 16, 2002, *The Top Story,* www.foxnews.com/story/0,2933,50425, 00.html

CONSPIRACIES TO SUBDUE AMERICA ARE NOT RECENT

Nor have Americans understood the danger posed to our way of government by the Roman Catholic Church. For centuries warnings have been issued against "Popery" and have been, in general, ignored. William P. Grady has documented the threat dramatically in his book, *What Hath God Wrought!, A Biblical Interpretation of American History.* There are over 1,043,000,000 Catholics in the world and 62.4 million in the U.S. The 107th U.S. Congress has 150 Roman Catholics and Baptists make up the second largest number at 72. The Roman Catholic Church has been involved for centuries in finding a way to establish control over the United States population. Grady writes in his revealing book, "My readers may be surprised to learn that Dr. Morse [Samuel F. B. Morse] was already an accomplished artist and world traveler by the time he invented the telegraph. However, long before designing the transmission code that would eventually bear his name, Morse was providentially led to uncover a clandestine plot against the American government which moved him to send his endangered countrymen an emphatic warning in the form of two books, *Foreign Conspiracies Against the Liberties of the United States* and *Imminent Dangers to the Free Institutions of the United States through Foreign Immigration.* "[1] Grady goes on to quote Dr. S. Ireneus Prime who wrote in his voluminous work on the life of Samuel F. B. Morse the following:

"While Mr. Morse was in Italy in the years 1830 and 1831, he became acquainted with several ecclesiastics of the Church of Rome, one of whom, a cardinal, made a vigorous attack upon the faith of the young artist. A correspondence between them ensued, and frequent interviews. Mr. Morse was led to believe, from what he learned in Rome, that a political conspiracy, under the cloak of a religious mission, was formed against the United States of America. When he came to Paris in 1832 and enjoyed the confidence and friendship of Lafayette, he stated his convictions to the General, who fully concurred with him in the reality of such a conspiracy. Returning to his country in the autumn of 1832, inventing the Telegraph on his

---

[1] Grady, Th.D.,Th.M., D.D., William P.; *What Hath God Wrought A Biblical Interpretation of American History*; Grady Publications, Inc. Knoxville, Tn.; ISBN 0-9628809-2-2, Seventh printing Dec. 2001 ; *p.221-222*

homeward voyage, he never became so absorbed in his invention as to forget the impressions made in Italy respecting the danger to which his country was exposed. The conviction was so strong that he gave much time in subsequent years to the publication in periodicals, in pamphlets, and in volumes, of the facts and arguments which, in his judgement, were important to a fair understanding of the subject."[1]

Grady goes on to document the background of this conspiracy; and he makes the following most astounding observations; and he quotes Dr. Morse:

"The prospect of a military invasion was, of course, out of the question. Something far more subtle was required if the stream of liberty would be dammed at its source. As previously noted, it was while Dr. Morse was traveling in Italy that he was led of the Lord to discover the framework of this intended Austrian subversion. The godly inventor [Dr. Morse was a great and faithful Christian] felt it more than coincidental that within the year of Schlegel's [a devote Roman Catholic German scholar who favored the 'strengthening of absolute power by the Vatican' in 1828] weighty pronouncement, a powerful society named the St. Leopold Foundation was established in the Austrian capital for the avowed purpose "*of promoting the greater activity of Catholic missions in America*". Dr. Morse elaborates: "But how shall she attack us? She cannot send her armies, they would be *useless*. She has told us by mouth of her Counsellor of Legation, that Popery, while it is the natural antagonist to Protestanism, is opposed in its whole character to Republican liberty, and is the promoter and supporter of arbitrary power. How fitted then is Popery for her purpose! This she can send without alarming our fears, or, at least, only the fears of those "*miserable,*" *intolerant fanatics,*" and "*pious bigots,*" who affect to see danger to the liberites of the country in the mere introduction of *a system* opposed to their own, and whose cry of danger, be it ever so loud, will only be regarded as the result of "*sectarian fear,*" and the plot ridiculed as a "*quixotic dream.*" But is there any thing so irrational in such a scheme? Is it not the most natural and obvious act for Austria to do, with her views of the influence of Popery upon the form of government, its influence to pull down Republicanism, and build up monarchy; I say, is it not her most obvious act to send Popery to this country if it is not here, or give it fresh and vigous

---

[1] Ibid. p. 222

impulse if it is already here?"[1]

Grady proceeds to document the completion of the conspiracy in the remainder of his book with alarming quotes, facts, and information. For example, over 500 books and pamphlets have been written on this topic.[2] Can anyone show where this is being reported in our public school text books or mentioned in our churches? Is there any doubt that the Jesuit influence started by Loyola has continued in all aspects of our society from education in our schools to publications to politics? The greatest danger to this nation is our lack of knowledge and information that is true. A nation that is not informed stands in grave danger of being destroyed. Hosea wrote the following: *"**My people are destroyed for lack of knowledge**: because thou hast rejected knowledge, I will also reject thee, that thou shalt be no priest to me: seeing thou hast forgotten the law of thy God, **I will also forget thy children**."* (Hosea 4:6)

THESE ARE NOT JUST "OLD" FEARS

If you are thinking that the modern and postmodern period has eliminated the two-pronged threat of either an Islamic or a Catholic takeover of our government then I suggest you review the information above and chew on the following facts. John M. Swomley, PhD. in Political Science at Kansas City, Missouri's St. Paul School of Theology and Chairperson of ACLU's Church-State Committee and Associate Editor of *The Human Quest* states:

"The Vatican has had a **tremendous** influence on White House policy with respect to foreign affairs and such issues as abortion and birth control, according to *Time* magazine, Feb. 24, 1992. In an article, "The Holy Alliance," *Time* described the way in which a group of Roman Catholic members of the Reagan administration collaborated with the Polish pope to overthrow the existing government of Poland."[3] In that same article, "reporter Carl Bernstein quotes Reagan's first national security advisor, Richard Allen, a Roman Catholic, as stating, "This was one of the great secret alliances [President Reagan

---

[1] Ibid. p. 225

[2] Ibid. p. 225

[3] Swomley, John M.; *Political Power of Roman Catholic Bishops;* *www.population-security.org/sworn-92-05.htm*

and John Paul II] of all time."[1] Reagan also appointed an official United States ambassador to the Vatican in April of 1984 making a formal exchange which "had been dead for over a century….but the exchange was an equally important event in the Catholicization of the U.S. making the Catholic Church a special religious-diplomatic-political entity operating in the very heart of the U.S."[2]

According to Bill O'Reilly, a Roman Catholic, the:

"Catholic Church thinks in terms of 100's of years in regards to policy."

This work has provided just some of the facts that relate to a long-term ploy by the Roman Catholic See to establish control over the American continent. One of the major factors to assist their goals along these lines has been the laws passed which grant more and more control to the Federal government while more and more control is established by back room political meetings. As a case in-point, William Grady records this very distressing report, which points out the lack of knowledge by the "postmodern" Americans who are too busy watching television to read.

"[T]he myriad of evil ramifications from the Civil Rights Act are not even remotely perceived. Regarding this totalitarian Act [the infamous Civil Rights Act passed June 24, 1964], John C. Satterfield (past president of the American Bar Association) warned, "It will completely destroy democracy as outlined in the Constitution…it is uncontrolled federal executive power….Six members of the House Judiciary Committee signed that statement. The protest ended with the notation that the Civil Rights Act of 1964 is 'a blueprint for total regimentation'. In essence, the Civil Rights Act was the devil's final assault on the historic Baptist distinctive of individual soul liberty. With one stroke of the pen, Americans lost their right to protect their private property from deadbeats, perverts, and criminals."[3]

Anyone who has owned apartments, or hired employees, or dealt with government agencies, whether you are African-American, White, Hispanic, or Asian, in the last 40 years can testify that the prophecy of John C. Satterfield was on the mark.

[1] Grady, Ph.D., Th.M., D.D.; *What Hath God Wrought*; p. 523
[2] Ibid. p. 525
[3] Ibid. pp. 513-514

THE SERIOUS THREAT OF ISLAM

Returning to the second prong of what appears to be a Satan inspired two-pronged attack on America:

"Several years ago Steven Emerson produced for PBS an excellent video titled *Jihad In America*. Its cameras went directly inside cell groups associated with mosques here in America where eager young Muslims were being recruited for *jihad* against the United States. Muslim leaders are shown giving speeches about bringing America to its knees through terrorism and making cold-blooded statements such as the following from Fayiz Azzam in Brooklyn in 1989: "Blood must flow, there must be widows, orphans, hands and limbs must be severed and limbs and blood must be spread everywhere in order that Allah's religion stand on its feet!" At the beginning of the video, Emerson, who had tracked international terrorism for the prior ten years, reported on what he called "networks of Islamic extremists" inside the US. He accurately warned that for these militants jihad is a holy war, an armed struggle to defeat nonbelievers, or infidels, and their ultimate goal is to establish an Islamic [worldwide] empire."[1]

Which political power-based murderous religion, Islam or Roman Catholicism, finally subdues the freedom our country enjoys, and carts us off to "captivity" without moving one foot off the soil of the United States will probably be determined in the near future. God's warning in Hosea 4:6 quoted above is distressful and compatible with the warning signs seen on the horizon. America has rejected God's preserved laws and precepts; and His judgment is coming. Listen to the warnings given to Israel at the base of Mount Horeb in the wilderness and see if it doesn't sound just like what is beginning to happen in America. My comments are inserted to hopefully make clearer the tenets of this work.

Leviticus 26:14-21 *But if ye will not hearken unto me, and will not do all these commandments;* [laws and precepts] *[15] And if ye shall despise my statutes* [e.g. sanctity of life, marriage, honesty] *or if your soul abhor* [hate] *my judgments, so that ye will not do all my commandments, but that ye break my covenant: [16] I also will do this unto you; I will even appoint over you terror* [terrorism], *consumption* [disease such as

---

[1] Hunt, David; *Berean Call;* Oct., 2001, p. 2

tuberculosis], *and the burning ague* [infections such as AIDS], *that shall consume the eyes, and cause sorrow of heart: and ye shall sow your seed in vain* [because of crop destruction secondary to unusual weather conditions such as drought, cold, wind; or destruction of the product from insects (honeybee mites), animals, thieves], *for your enemies shall eat it. [17] And I will set my face against you, and ye shall be slain* [civil war, riots, school shootings, war, terrorist attacks, embassy bombings, earthquakes] *before your enemies: they that hate you shall reign over you* [Muslims, Roman Catholic See, Communists]*; and ye shall flee when none pursueth you* [the economy almost failed after the Sept. 11 terrorist attacks]*. [18] And if ye will not yet for all this hearken unto me, then I will punish you seven times more for your sins.* [more is on the way] *[19] And I will break the pride of your power* [humanism, self]*; and I will make your heaven as iron* [drought, heat], *and your earth as brass* [hard to till or work or contaminated]*: [20] And your strength shall be spent in vain: for your land shall not yield her increase, neither shall the trees of the land yield their fruits.* [sounds like America will be poor soon] *[21] And if ye walk contrary unto me, and will not hearken unto me; I will bring seven times more plagues upon you according to your sins.* [Ebola, small pox, anthrax, mad cow disease or other new viruses and bacteria]

THE CRY: "POLY-SCRIPTURAE," CREATING CONFUSION

This work supports the concept that the confusion created by the modernist position of "Poly-Scripturae" [many Scriptures] has led our culture to embrace many false religions, such as Hinduism, Buddhism, Islam, Satanism, New Age-ism, and perverted Christianity as seen in the Catholic denomination. They are being embraced under the umbrella of ecumenism as a result of the confusion wrought by the dynamic equivalent method of translation and by the Alexandrian text "route." So many Bibles are now on the market that attest: "Thus has God said," but logic says that all of them cannot be God's Words. Is it any wonder that most are beginning to say and believe; "We all worship the same God?" Is it any wonder that many people, especially the Roman Catholics, are saying: "Our Bibles are the same?" Is it any wonder that our judicial system, government, schools, families, and churches are confused? If the confusion brought about by sinister forces intentionally corrupting the Words of God and loosening us from a firm foundation of absolute authority has not been the cause of this confusion, then would someone show us the reason! There are some who would say the reason is the removal of prayer from our schools.[1] This author believes that things like abortion, removal of prayers from classrooms, and confusion are *symptoms* of "*Poly-Scripturae.*"

The confusion is so great that even reporters like Dan Rather on the CBS evening news, April 2002, are beginning to ask for "someone" [like the antichrist?] to step forward and solve the growing international mayhem produced by the Islamic/Jewish-Christian conflict in the Middle East. Sounds like the time is drawing near for the 70th week of Daniel to begin.

2 Thes. 2:8-12 *And then shall that Wicked be revealed, whom the Lord shall consume with the spirit of his mouth, and shall destroy with the brightness of his coming: 9Even him, whose coming is after the working of Satan with all power and signs and lying wonders, 10And with all deceivableness of unrighteousness in them that perish; because they received not the love of the truth, that they might be saved. 11And for this cause God shall send them strong delusion, that they should believe a lie: 12That they all might be damned who believed not the truth, but had pleasure in unrighteousness.*

The lie that there are *many* true and acceptable Scriptures [Poly-Scripturae] is leading to delusions and corruption in many aspects of life in regard to these important factors: 1. The belief around the world that the murder of innocent Christians who hold to absolute truth is "serving God" (such as Rome's murder of hundreds of thousands); 2. The murder of innocent babies in the womb to the tune of over 40 million in the United States is of no consequence; 3. The belief that truth depends on the situation, thus there is no absolute truth;, and, 4. Islamic Jihad [holy war] justifies killing anyone, anywhere, anytime.[2]

The confusion produced by all this mayhem is reflected in the choices being made by our children, our churches, and our society. Although each of these categories "say" they believe in the "principles" and "precepts" presented in the Bible, **their choices reveal just the opposite.** However, they are not even aware that their choices are different from what is in the Bible. Someone should

---

[1]Hovind, Kent; *Creation Seminars;* Pensacola, FL.

[2]Pipes, Daniel; *What is Jihad,* New York Post; Dec. 31, 2002
www.danielpipes.org/article/990"Jihad is "holy war." Or, more precisely: It means the legal, compulsory, communal effort to expand the territories ruled by Muslims at the expense of territories ruled by non-Muslims. The purpose of jihad, in other words, is not directly to spread the Islamic faith but to extend sovereign Muslim power (faith, of course, often follows the flag). Jihad is thus unabashedly offensive in nature, with the eventual goal of achieving Muslim dominion over the entire globe."

stand up and say, "WOW!". In reality, as we shall see, they say they believe the Bible, but they don't even read it and what is even more obvious, they don't have a clue as to what the Bible says. They seem to have more pleasure in unrighteousness than the truth and so God has sent a strong delusion. They don't realize they are being deluded. [Reread 2 Thes. 2:8-12 above] The following facts and figures will demonstrate the confusion and delusions.

POSTMODERNISM: A RESULT OF CONFUSION AND EVEN A REJECTION OF MODERNISM

First, let's look at some of the beliefs our children hold. To understand what our children are accepting as truth, however, we must begin with an understanding of "postmodernism."

Postmodernism began during the middle of the last century in the wake of a French philosopher, Jacques Derrida, who coined the term "deconstructionism" or "postmodernism."[1] This system of man's wisdom has infected all societies with a belief which stresses that all meaning and truth are *relative*. The common tenet of philosophy in the past has started with the premise that "I exist", therefore "I am." This new system states that all is relative, even "I exist." The conclusions that result from the tenets of this postmodern philosophy are important for the Church because the results promote this statement: "Christianity may be true for you but it's not true for me."[2] "It assumes that Christianity may be true for some people, in some places, and at some times, but it is not true for all people, in all places, and at all times. It is relatively true, not absolutely or universally true."[3]

If you think this is just a philosophical presentation and is not what is being taught in our schools and colleges, just talk to the children being educated in the public school systems in the country. A case in point is a recent conversation with my grandson who had been attending a Christian school, Covenant Bible College, and had to switch to a local Junior College for financial reasons. He called us, his grandparents, and related in the course of a long conversation about many "things" that they had a guest speaker visit his class at the college who encouraged the class to believe "that what you think is

---

[1] McDowell, Josh; *The New Evidence That Demands A Verdict;* Thomas Nelson Publishers, Nashville, TN; 1999; ISBN 0-7852-4219-8; p. Xlii

[2] Ibid. p. Xlii

[3] Ibid. p. Xlii

right for <u>you</u> is "OK," because everything is relative."

POSTMODERNISM LINKED TO HUMANISM

How has all of this come about? Modernism from the 1700's to the middle of the 20th century has pushed to replace a reliance on God with Humanism, a religion based on man's reasoning and ability. Postmodernism has usurped modernism by saying there is no "need to be chained even to reason and its resulting responsibilities."[1] Postmodernists reject even foundationalism or the progression of beliefs from a foundational truth or belief to another set of beliefs based on the previous set.

According to Peter Van Inwagen, the author of *Metaphysics*:

"They [postmodernists] are deeply hostile to the thought of anything that in any sense stands in judgment over them. The idea toward which they are most hostile is, of course, the idea of there being a God. But they are almost as hostile to the idea of there being an objective universe that doesn't care what they think and could make their cherished beliefs false without even consulting them."[2]

The author of this work proposes that this is egocentric thinking, which is the hallmark of immaturity. It is just this type of self-centered thinking which led Nazi Germany to define the world by considering their "community" to the exclusion of reality and truth, that led to the slaughter of millions of Jews and soldiers of other countries. This type of belief in a dominant society will lead to a one world government or society. Other nations determined the thinking of Nazi Germany was wrong and that it would lead to world domination by those with a corrupt philosophical view. The result was WWII. This type of community egocentric thinking has returned in force, but is no longer limited to a few nations, but is essentially a world view. Therefore, Islamic communities or rogue dictatorial governmental regimes in Iraq, Afghanistan, and Iran, have determined their view is correct for them and they have the right to force it on the world. The rapist thinks similarly. If his desire for power or sex is right for him then "full steam ahead." If you do not think rape has increased in this nation, think again. Postmodernism fuels this type of extremism; that is the satisfaction of "my" desires, feelings, or emotions above all else.

This type of thinking has infected the people of our nation to the point that

[1] Ibid. p. Xlii
[2] Ibid. p. Xliii

children go into a "fog" or "blank out" when an adult tries to reason with them. Their thinking is: "You believe what you want to believe, but I have the right to believe what I want, no matter what the consequences". They do not always get up and walk away, but they certainly tune you out. Norman Geisler, who is not right on every issue, but neither is this author, points out that this type of thinking results in mental and factual conflict. This is called confusion. Geisler gives this example of postmodernism thinking:

"It would mean Billy Graham is telling the truth when he says, 'God exists,' and Madalyn Murray O'Hare is also right when she claims, 'God does not exist.' But these two statements cannot both be true. If one is true, then the other is false. And since they exhaust the possibilities, one of them must be true. If truth is relative, then no one is ever wrong—even when they are. As long as something is true to me, then I'm right even when I am wrong. The drawback is that I could never learn anything either, because learning is moving from a false belief to a true one—that is, from an absolutely false belief to an absolutely true one."[1] [my emphasis]

This brings us to a crucial statement which if one understands this declaration then deconstructionism or postmodernism will be defeated:

"To assert that 'there is no truth' is both self-refuting and arbitrary. For if this statement (there is no truth) is true, it is not true, since there is no truth."[2]

Postmodernists will not understand the preceding statement because they are so confused. Logic has been cast out and emotion and feeling substituted. Postmodernists have a difficult time "thinking."

Similarly, the problem with postmodern thinking is this: where people formerly were repulsed by deceit, lying, murder, stealing, etc., they now accept as sometimes right. The following charts compare "postmodernism" with "modernism" and "Christianity" and should help solidify the dramatic changes occurring in our society.

---

[1] Ibid. p. XliV
[2] Ibid. p. XIV

MODERNISM VERSUS POSTMODERNISM THINKING

I. MODERNISM
(1700's-the latter 20ᵗʰ century)
Philosophy of scientific rationalism

A. Persons find meaning through personal growth and achievement.
B. Esteem knowledge and excellence.
C. Seek to understand the order of reality and operate within those boundaries.
D. Argues that there must be reason and intellectual honesty to create rules of fair play and to facilitate the potential for healthy coexistence.
E. Turn outward and suggest the best decisions are based on reason and science. People need to have emotion and will controlled by rules and law.
F. Assign value to knowledge for its own sake and maintains it is always valuable whether to the individual or society.
G. Respect individuals although they may not always be right. Fickleness towards heroes is not seen.
H. Pedantic, factual, linear lectures are effective communications and have influence toward insight, knowledge, and discovery.
I. Spirituality is a corporate and individual experience.
J. Faith is centered on the Being in whom faith is based, <u>or</u> faith is solidly based on mankind's ability through science and rationalism known as the religion of "Humanism".

II. POSTMODERISM
(late 20ᵗʰ century until ?)

Philosophy in opposition to scientific rationalism.

A. Contend that all striving is worthless and in vain since there is no meaning to be gained and no absolute truth to be understood.

B. Set their sights on comfortable survival and self-satisfaction.

C. Claim there is no grand design, that all is based on chance, and people therefore need not recognize the limitations and boundaries that circumscribe the world of the moderns.

D. Believe the universe is decentralized and there is no ultimate authority beyond oneself. Moral anarchy rules the day. (This means consistent chaos and selfishness.)

E. Turn inward and suggest that the best decisions are based on human will and emotion. They rely on self.

F. Do not assign value to knowledge for its own sake. Value of knowledge is when the information has practical applications and is personally meaningful.

G. Someone earns their respect and credibility day by day, and few retain that level of acceptance for long. There are no heroes. Only 'people' doing their jobs. (Fireman, movie stars, rock bands, etc. do not retain loyalty, fame, or celebrity very long these days.)

H. Conversation is king and communication is predicated on perceiving it as "being genuine". The goal of communication is participation, acceptance, and belonging.

I. Spirituality is important, but wholly personal.

J. Faith is based on the person who possesses the faith, not the Being. Faith is syncretic—that is a personally pleasing mixture of whatever spiritual elements exist in the known world, resulting in an eclectic brew of beliefs, and practices. Their faith may be given a label such as Christianity, but probably bears no resemblance.*

*The information in this chart was made possible by: George Barna's book, *Real Teens,* 2001

CHRISTIANITY VERSUS POSTMODERNISM

CHRISTIANITY

A. Exhorts people to find meaning in life through the practice of loving God and loving one's neighbor.

B. Recognizes the existence of moral absolutes. Absolutes are determined by God and conveyed through the Bible.

C. Acknowledges the existence of one true God, who created everything, exists eternally, and is holy, omniscient, omnipotent, and omnipresent.

D. The death and resurrection of Jesus is the central episode of human history because it enables humans to be reconciled with God and have an eternal relationship with Him.

E. Place their faith in God and the principles and teachings he delivered through the Bible.

POSTMODERNISM

A. Suggests there is no real meaning to be achieved, so self-love becomes a reasonable, primary focus.

B. Implores each individual to determine what is right and wrong for themselves, given the conditions, their feelings and their past experiences. There is no such thing as sin. Therefore there is no need for a savior or for salvation.

C. Encourages people to define their own understanding of 'God', based on experience and perceptions, without the restraints that religious texts and traditions impose upon the human mind.

D. Accept Christian salvation as valid—along with any of several dozen approaches to understanding eternal outcomes.

E. Would rather rely upon themselves as the ultimate source of meaning, purpose, and value. They live for the moment and have little anxiety about the future; the entire notion of eternal salvation is of little interest to them. *

*This chart is made possible by the information in George Barna's book, *Real Teens,* 2001

THE POLITICALLY CORRECT

Thus Bill O'Reilly reports the "politically correct" today would not condemn:

"Russell Yates, Enron executives, and leaders of the Catholic Church in America. What do they have in common? ....No one is responsible, not Mr. Yates [husband of the psychotic mother who killed her four children by drowning], not Kenneth Lay and his cohorts [Enron executives], not Cardinal Law and Egan [Catholic Cardinals who did not remove pedophile priests from contact with children]. Even though those men had authority when things went bad, none of them agreed to take the fall. Russell Yates is blaming anyone he can think of for the out-of-control home in which he lived. Kenneth Lay says he has no idea his company was corrupt and mismanaged, even though he was being paid tens of millions of dollars to run Enron. And the Cardinals? Well, one of them, Law of Boston, admits he made mistakes by reassigning pedophile priests so they could do even more damage, but when it comes to paying for those mistakes, the cardinal will not resign. He wants to keep his power. The other cardinal, Egan of New York, is hiding in his plush office at St. Patrick's Cathedral, continuing to duck all responsibility for allegedly doing the same thing that Law did. So, there you have it. No one's responsible for anything. Yates, Law, and Egan,... It's no secret that personal responsibility is almost extinct in America. Visit any prison. Most inmates say they're either innocent or victims of some terrible injustice that compelled them to commit crimes. Visit any school and listen to the kids who fail or are caught misbehaving. The litany of excuses would be hilarious if they weren't so frightening. John Gotti, he didn't do anything. Ted Bundy, pornography made him a murderer. O.J. Simpson completely innocent of any and all. The list goes on and on. And those of us who refuse to accept excuses for bad behavior are called arrogant and judgmental and callous....Political correctness [the buzz words for postmodernism] has stamped out outrage in this country. No one is responsible for anything in the politically correct world. All crimes can be explained, all irresponsible behavior excused. There is no right and wrong, only disease and neurosis and miscommunications."[1] [my emphasis]

George Barna's post on an internet site supports O'Reilly's conclusions that no one takes responsibility in America any more and it is because:

"a minority of Americans believes in the existence of absolute moral truth.[a preserved, pure, eternal Bible] Even more surprising, the data from a pair of nationwide studies...showed that less than one out of three born again Christians adopt the notion of absolute moral truth."[2] [my addition]

Not only was this surprising but the fact that only one out of ten or 10% of American "born again" teens[3] believe in absolute moral truth. Mr. Barna's group relates this is the same figure for "non-born again" teenagers:

"The virtual disappearance of this cornerstone of the Christian faith—that is, God has communicated a series of moral principles in the Bible that are meant to be the basis of our thoughts and actions, regardless of our preferences, feelings or situations—is probably the best indicator of the waning strength of the Christian Church in America today."[4]

Just as this section was being completed, Barna Research released updated surveys indicating the situation has deteriorated further:

"[T]he Barna statistics show that the percentage of teens who are evangelicals – i.e., those who are not only born again but also believe in the accuracy of the Bible, personal responsibility to evangelize, believe in salvation by grace alone, and possess orthodox biblical views on God, Jesus and Satan – have declined from 10% in 1995 to just 4% today. This demise is attributable to growing numbers of teenagers who accept moral relativism and pluralistic theology as their faith foundation. This decline parallels a similar drop among adults: 12% were evangelicals in 1994, but just 5% fit the criteria

---

[1] O'Reilly, Bill; *No One Is Responsible;* Fox News; The O'Reilly Factor; Wed., March 20, 2002

[2] Barna Research Online; *Americans Are Most Likely to Base Truth on Feelings;* Press Release of 2/12/02; p. 1 of 7; www.barna.org. All of Mr. Barna's facts in this section were used with his permission.

[3] Born-again Christians are defined in Barna's surveys as "people who said they have made a person commitment to Jesus Christ that is still important in their life today and who also indicate they believe that when they die they will go to heaven because they had confessed their sins and had accepted Jesus Christ as their Savior." www.barna.org

[4] Barna Research Online; *Americans Are Most Likely to Base Truth on Feelings;* Press Release of 2/12/02; p. 3 of 7; www.barna.org

today."[1]

THE CHURCH IS IN TROUBLE

The seriousness of these statistics is reflected in another report by Barna which should create alarm in the "body of Christ." Reporting in his press release of Feb. 12, 2002, George Barna said:

When a majority of Christian adults, including three out of four born again Baby Busters, as well as three out of four born again teens proudly cast their vote for moral relativism, the Church is in trouble. Continuing to preach more sermons, teach more Sunday school classes and enroll more people in Bible study groups won't solve the problem since most of these people don't accept the basis of the principles being taught in those venues. The failure to address this issue at its root, and to do so quickly and persuasively, will undermine the strength of the church for at least another generation, and probably longer."[2] [my emphasis]

"EITHER/OR"   OR   "BOTH/AND" THINKING

This work would add to this thought that the absolute confusion caused by the modernist cry, "Poly-Scripturae", has given considerable impetus to the above abomination that has fallen on America. Without any absolute document that can be handed to someone, and that someone told, "This is what God said," relativism is going to ensue. Satan knew this would happen if attacks on the Received Text and the best translation of that text, the King James Bible, were successful. Anyone who has not studied the issue carefully, can say in this postmodern age, not "This is what God said," but rather, "What has God said?!" "You don't have His Words, only what you think He said!" The postmodernist holding dozens of "Bibles" can say, the "originals" have been lost and only the

---

[1] Barna Research Online; *Teens Change their Tune Regarding Self and Church;* Press Release, April 23, 2002; www.barna.org/
[2] Barna Research Online; *Americans Are Most Likely to Base Truth on Feelings;* Press Release of February 12, 2002; www.barna.org/

originals were "inspired," so what the world now has, because of the "corruption" of the text, is only an approximation or estimate of "What God said." The modernist and postmodernist can say: "The loss of the absolute accurate 'Words of God', if there ever was such a thing, and the guess used by modernistic textual critics called "the ring of truth," is not accurate enough for me to use in a technologically precise 'modern' world." Many go on to demonstrate this belief: "Since society does not have the precise 'Words of God', and many of the Bibles are in reality contradictory to one another, Eastern theology or Zen Buddhism is also an acceptable way of thinking." Why? Because Buddhism does not mind contradicting itself or being inconsistent. It is a mystical way of thinking which denies a dualistic world-view such as truth verses error or right verses wrong. Another way to state this insidious Eastern religion's point of view is to point out they do not accept *"either/or"* way of thinking, but like the postmodern, the *"both/and"* line of argument. They are both right! By now you must realize where this is leading. The postmodern world that has completely lost its firm foundation or absolute authority, and is precariously balanced on sinking sand, says that "no religion is wrong," and that "we all worship the same God,"and that "if you believe something different than this eclectic smorgasbord, you are politically incorrect."

Ravi Zacharias points out just how fallacious the *both/and* line of argument is:

"As a professor waxed eloquent and expounded on the law of non-contradiction [both/and], he eventually drew his conclusion: "This [**either/or**] logic is a Western way of looking at reality. The real problem is that you are seeking...contradiction as a Westerner when you should be approaching it as an Easterner. The **both/and** is the Eastern view of reality." After he belabored these two ideas on *either/or* and *both/and* for some time...I finally asked if I could interrupt his unpunctuated train of thought and raise one question...I said, "Sir, are you telling me that when I am studying Hinduism I *either* use the both/and system *or* nothing else?" There was pin-drop silence for what seemed an eternity. I repeated my question: "Are you telling me that when I am studying Hinduism I *either* use the *both/and* logic *or* nothing else? Have I got that right?" He threw his head back and said, "The *either/or* does seem to emerge, doesn't it?" "Indeed it does emerge," I said. "And as a matter of fact, even in India we look both ways before we cross the street—it is *either* the bus *or* me, not *both* of us."[1]

---

[1] McDowell, Josh; *The New Evidence That Demands A Verdict*; p. XlVii - XlViii

[my emphasis]

This fallacious way of thinking demonstrated by Ravi Zacharias has permeated our culture over the last several hundred years. This type of thinking has invaded the "scholars" who have been responsible for translating the Scriptures. They believe the translations made by them using the dynamic translation technique verses the verbal equivalent technique are *both/and* correct. The tenet of this work is that *both/and* cannot be correct. The correct technique has to be *either/or.* The *both/and* Eastern thinking has caused confusion in regards to selecting an absolute, inspired, infallible Bible. With the loss of a firm foundation and "final authority" such activities as abortion, gay sex, sexual fantasies, cohabitation, drunkenness and viewing pornography are acceptable, whether the person participates or not. In other words, if it is right for you, then do it.

ONE WORD WORLD VIEW: "WHATEVER"

"Without some firm and compelling basis for suggesting that such acts are inappropriate, [from absolutes in a Bible they know is accurate] people are left with philosophies such as 'if it feels good, do it', 'everyone else is doing it' or 'as long as it doesn't hurt anyone else, it's permissible.' In fact, the alarming fast decline of moral foundations among our young people has culminated in a one-word world view, *'WHATEVER!'*[1]   [my emphasis]

The contention of this work is that *"The Lie That Changed The Modern World,"* which began in the 17th century Europe, was exacerbated by mid-19th century English professors, Westcott and Hort, and has culminated in so-called "Bibles" of the 20th and 21st centuries, has contributed greatly to the apostasy of the 'last days'. The following quote from Mr. Barna quoted above is worth repeating here:

WHY THE TRADITIONAL CHURCH WILL FAIL: MOSAICS

---

[1] Barna Research Online; *Americans Are Most Likely to Base Truth on Feelings;* Press Release of 2/12/02; p. 2 of 7; www.barna.org

"When a majority of Christian adults, ...as well as three out of four born again teens proudly cast their vote for moral relativism, the Church is in trouble. <u>Continuing to preach more sermons, teach more Sunday school classes and enroll more people in Bible study groups won't solve the problem since most of these people don't accept the basis of the principles being taught in those venues.</u>"[1] [my emphasis]

This is the postmodern generation. This generation bases its decisions on "whatever will make the most people happy or create the least conflict," "whatever you think your family or friends would expect you to do," "whatever will produce the most positive outcome for you, personally," or "whatever feels right or comfortable in that situation."[2] George Barna's book, *Real Teens,* calls this last generation, the **Mosaics**, based on their belief patterns. Just like the numerous new "Bibles" of this generation are eclectic mosaics, so are the people who make up this latest group. Barna relates from his research the changing generations from the "Seniors", born prior to 1926; the "Builders", 1927-1945; the "Baby Boomers", 1946-1964; the "Baby Busters", 1965-1983; and the "**Mosaics**", 1984-2002. Just as "knowledge" has exploded over the last 100 years, so have "eclectic" beliefs exploded. The prophet Daniel alluded to this change in society in the 'last days' saying: Daniel 12:4 *But thou, O Daniel, shut up the words, and seal the book, even to the time of the end: many shall run to and fro, and knowledge shall be increased.* People have been running "to and fro" looking for a "Bible" which will give them "the answers" in these troubling times. The marketing tools of the modern age for the benefit of "bottom line" has left the Builders, Baby Boomers, Baby Busters, and particularly the Mosaics with confusion. Most of them don't have a clue that it is confusion they are feeling and experiencing. Yes, technical knowledge has increased, but running "to and fro" is at a fever pitch. Families are being torn apart because of the "whatever" attitude. Let Dylan Klebold and Eric Harris, the Columbine school shooters, do there "thing." Let Janet Jackson expose her breast on *international* television—"WHATEVER." Go ahead and tell a lie if it benefits the bottom line, even if it is about the Words of an Almighty God.

The "Mosaics" are confused because: "their lifestyles are an eclectic combination of traditional and alternative activities; they are the first generation among whom a majority will exhibit a nonlinear style of thinking—a mosaic, connect-the-dots-however-you-choose approach [*both/and*]; their core values are the result of a cut-and-paste mosaic of feelings, facts, principles, experiences

---

[1] Ibid. p. 3 of 7

[2] Ibid. p. 1 of 7

and lessons; their primary information and connection—the Internet—is the most bizarre, inclusive and ever-changing pastiche [parody] of information ever relied upon by humankind; the central spiritual tenets that provide substance to their faith are a customized blend of multiple-faith views and religious practices."[1] [my emphasis and comments]

The "Mosaics" have no problem with accepting contradictory beliefs or in other words, they have fallen victim to our society's embracing Eastern mystical thinking, *the both/and* type of thinking. A prime example of this type of thinking is the fact that over 60% of teenagers or

"six (6) out of ten (10) teenagers believe that the Bible is accurate at the same time even larger numbers of them reject many of its core teachings."[2]

In addition, most teens acknowledge that the importance of moral truth is "critical," but there are *few* who take time to investigate and/or seek Godly counsel to arrive at a workable conclusion.

The result is of all of the preceding is that "mosaic" teens say one thing but mean something different from the previous generation's values and absolutes. Their decision-making is:

"made in a truth vacuum."[3]

Other things such as video games, hanging out, music, movies, and television take on more importance than investigating "truth"; and, significantly, the music, movies, and television they participate in, reinforces the poor choices today's teens are noted for making. Surprisingly, today's teens note and are concerned about the significant moral decline of America, but, as usual, the contradictory thinking of "Mosaic" teens enters the picture. They choose to regard these issues as not being a pressing problem with only 1 out of 10 listing spiritual, moral, and ethical issues as urgent. As a matter of fact:

"[v]arious studies among teens demonstrate that they appreciate the concept of integrity but have neither the knowledge of its substance nor a deep commitment to live with integrity. Similarly, while teenagers are enthusiastic about spirituality, relatively few have an abiding faith in God based on a true relationship with Him—and few have either the direction or inclination to pursue such a relationship, in spite of its conceptual appeal."[4]

---

[1] Barna, George, *Real Teens;* Regal Books, a Division of Gospel Light; Ventura, CA; 2001; ISBN 0-8307-2663-2, p. 7

[2] Ibid. p. 62

[3] Ibid. p. 63

[4] Ibid. p. 86

In other words the spiritual condition that began in this century to neglect "walking your talk" has been exacerbated in this generation. The author of this work believes that to accept what someone says in this generation as being true is foolhardy, and must be tempered with observation over a period of time. A person's 'word' is no longer trustworthy until their promises can be confirmed by actions over a period of time. Although this has been true in the past, the situation is much worse in this generation.

Barna says:

"Without a doubt, teen America's **confusion** regarding truth is a reflection of the distorted and contradictory teaching and modeling they receive from adults. The Church has provided little help in this regard: The teaching and exhortation provided to young people to focus them upon moral truth and ethical behavior is surprisingly infrequent and obscure, with limited accountability for the lessons conveyed. Some of the principles we teach are clearly grounded in a truth-based worldview, but the worldview itself is difficult to tease out the larger body of information delivered in our preaching, teaching and relationships." [1] [My emphasis]

He continues by relating that the lack of clear teaching has caused today's "Mosaics" to continue choosing relativism.

The next section will examine the choices of the American people in relation to important ethical and moral choices, which includes America's teens. Before proceeding, however, I would like to quote the last part of Hosea again in case the significance has escaped you. God said:

"I will also forget your children" (Hosea 4:6c)

Has the time arrived that He has forgotten our children? (see below) Their attitudes and life styles are disturbing. The violent crime in our schools [school shootings] and neighborhoods [gang drive-by shootings] may be reflecting this frightening statement in Hosea.

Please recall another basic tenet of this work has been that God's people in the "Age of Grace" are members of "the royal priesthood" or **priesthood of believers**; but also recall Jesus said that: *"if the salt have lost his savour, wherewith shall it be salted? it is thenceforth good for nothing, but to be cast out, and to be trodden under foot of men."* (Mat 5:13) Have the "churches" lost their savour in these latter days and has the adult population in the "churches" taken on the appearance of the "world?" Are the "churches" about to be trodden under the foot of men?

This work has demonstrated the fact that a firm foundation and absolute authority of *one* Greek and Hebrew Text preserved and translated into *one* best

[1] Ibid. p 93-94

translation and passed on by this generation, particularly the latter half of the 20th century and, particularly, by the priesthood of believers has been abandoned. The previous generations of the priesthood of believers have suffered persecution, martyrdom, and reviling rather than give in to an apostate church [the Roman Catholic Church] or to pagan societies. Every dispensation in the Scriptures such as the dispensation of conscience and the dispensation of the law has ended in failure. It appears the church age is ending in failure, also.

"And when these things begin to come to pass, then look up, and lift up your heads; for your redemption draweth nigh." [Lu 21:28]

The recent results reflected in surveys concerning attitudes in the churches and society are disturbing and revealing! They reflect the truth of abandonment of the laws, commandments, and precepts of a Holy God. This generation has abandoned absolute truth like a plague. Listen to the facts and the meaning of the following information, much of which came from a George Barna video, *The State of Morality in the United States and the Church.*

Parents impart morality to children that includes conformity to the rules of right conduct and the distinction between what is right and wrong. The problem is the comfort level with the obvious contradictions, some of which were presented above, between right and wrong moral choices and behavior. At least 50% of the population chooses by "what pleases me the most." The reason for concern is that most moral choices in society and the church are not based on God's principles or Words. Most moral choices and perspectives today are in open conflict with God's principles. Sadly, most people view other people's values and behaviors as the problem. There is little appreciation for Matthew 7:3-5 *And why beholdest thou the mote that is in thy brother's eye, but considerest not the beam that is in thine own eye? 4Or how wilt thou say to thy brother, Let me pull out the mote out of thine eye; and, behold, a beam is in thine own eye? 5Thou hypocrite, first cast out the beam out of thine own eye; and then shalt thou see clearly to cast out the mote out of thy brother's eye.*

The topic of abortion and the views of the churches concerning abortion are very disturbing. Out of all adults in the United States, 41% believe abortion should be legalized and 36 % believe it is morally acceptable. Mainline Protestant churches reflect an even worse view. Fifty percent of mainliners believe that abortion should be legal, and 45% believe that it is morally acceptable. The frightening fact is 23% of born-again believers accept legal abortion and 19% say it is morally acceptable. Born-again believers also believe pornography viewed in a sexually explicit movie is acceptable to the tune of 29% or 3 out of 10 and 21% believe reading a magazine with explicit sexuality is not objectionable. Cohabitation is acceptable to 36% of born-agains or almost 4 out of 10, and 39% believe divorce is not a sin. Mainliners are much worse; 54% believe cohabitation is acceptable and 70% or 7 out of 10 say divorce is not a sin.

Although God calls homosexuality an abomination and frequently refers to this "reprobate" condition in the Old and New Testaments, the beliefs of the Church in regards to this issue are frightening. The percentage of all adults in our society that believe homosexuality should be legalized is 48%, but 49% of all mainliner Protestants believe the same way. Even more surprising is the percentage of born-agains, 34% who believe homosexuality should be legalized and 27% of them say it is an acceptable lifestyle.

Thirty-seven percent (37%) of society and 29% of Protestants accept profanity (a reflection of personal integrity), while, amazingly, 22% of born-agains believe it is acceptable. Barna relates that born-agains are statistically different in most categories, "but not by much". For the difference to be noted by "society" there has to be a 20% difference before anyone takes notice.

"The Barna study also showed that there is a racial component to this issue, as well. Among whites, 60% endorse relativism, compared to 26% who adopt absolutism. Among non-white, however, 74% support relativism and just 15% believe in absolute morality. (Fifteen percent of Hispanic adults and only 10% of African-American adults contend that moral truth is absolute.)."[1]

Has the moral relativism brought on by the "coming off of" a firm foundation [absolutism] to a "free-floating" [relativism], and a "choose your own 'Words of God' society" caused irreparable harm? Yes, it has!! The proof is:

(1) Verified in the statements of those 'committees' choosing, "What God said?"

(2) Demonstrated in the dramatic change in crime stats.

(3) Demonstrated in the striking change in family structure and church apostasy.

The statement from one "committee," which "*chose* what God said," will be presented first, although there are many such statements, then the significant crime stats obtained from the U.S. Department of Justice, and followed by a brief look at the family and church.

Also, there are several significant dates which this work proposes is the culmination of Satan's great "lie" in this age and which is the zenith of apostate "Bible" production and distribution by false and heavily financed advertising.

After the release and publication of the NASB in 1960 and NIV in 1973, the floodgates were opened for "Bible committees" which pick and choose, "What God said?" The previous release of the American Standard Version in 1901 (the same date *glossolalia,* speaking in tongues, arrived in the U.S.) had

---

[1] Barna Research Online; *Americans Are Most Likely to Base Truth on Feelings;* Press Release, Feb. 12, 2002; www.barna.org/

been a failure, although the ASV was heavily promoted.[1] The dates of release of the Revised Standard Version in 1952, NIV in 1973, the NASB in 1960, and the New English Bible in 1961 correlates well with the tremendous beginning of strife and struggle in the life of this nation. Please keep these dates in mind as one reviews the following facts and information.

"With the greater proliferation of the English versions [based on the Alexandrian text] occurring in the second half of this century, discerning believers have observed a distinct parallel between these new arrivals and the nations growing ills. In light of Psalm 33:12a, *"Blessed is the nation whose God is the LORD,"* don't you find it rather interesting that the blasphemous *Revised Standard Version* showed up in 1952, the same year the United Nations [the infant one-world government] occupied its permanent headquarters in New York City? ....Elvis Presley would begin leading America's youth to destruction in another three years. Following the arrival of the *New American Standard Version* (1960) and the *New English Bible* (1961) came the Supreme Court ban on prayer (1962), the Beatles' appearance on the Ed Sullivan Show (1963), and the assassination of President Kennedy (1964). The *Good News for Modern Man* paraphrase (1966) spelled bad news for old-fashioned mothers with sons in *Vietnam.* And should we be surprised that *Roe vs. Wade* (1973) and Watergate (1973) just happened to occur in the same year that the *New International Version* hit the market? An insignificant notice which appeared in a 1961 edition of the *New York Times* speaks volumes; "The Fulton Street prayer meetings held during the noon hour for the past 103 years have been *shut down.*"[2] [not my emphasis]

And now to the quote from the *Trinitarian Bible Society* about a "Bible committee" in 1964 that believes '*they*' can pick and choose "What hath God said?"

"The details of English ecumenical Bible distribution...are just a small part of a worldwide trend that has been gathering momentum over the last twenty years. At a major conference of Bible societies in **1964** it was agreed that a "common text" **should be _prepared_ in the original languages of Greek and Hebrew**, and that this text should be translated into other languages so *as to provide* a **"common Bible"** *acceptable* to Protestants and Catholics alike. On the Catholic side, this

[1] Grady, Th.D., Th.M., D.D., William P.; *Final Authority; p. 59*
[2] Ibid. p. 186

concept of a "common Bible" was encouraged by a decree of the Second Vatican Council, in 1965, explicitly referring to the possibility of "co-operation with the separated brothers" (i.e. Protestants) in translation projects. In 1996 the British and Foreign Bible Society amended its constitution so that it could include the Apocrypha in its translations, to make them acceptable among Roman Catholic readers. The same policy was adopted by the United Bible Societies, including most national Bible societies around the world."[1] [my emphasis]

With the above thoughts, facts, and dates in mind observe the U.S. Department of Justice's (DOJ) information on crime in AMERICA. If these seven (7) charts from the DOJ don't bother you, then you have probably made the transition into the mosaic, "WHATEVER," generation. You also need to be aware that shortly after downloading these charts from the DOJ that they changed their site.

---

[1] Trinitarian Bible Society; *Ecumenism and the United Bible Societies*; Article No. 107, Tyndale House, Dorset Road, London SW 19, 3 NN, England; p. 7

DEPARTMENT OF JUSTICE CHARTS DEMONSTRATED SIGNIFICANT SOCIAL UPHEAVAL.

The number of prisoners on death row has been increasing.

To view data, click on the chart.

Prisoners on death row, 1953-2000

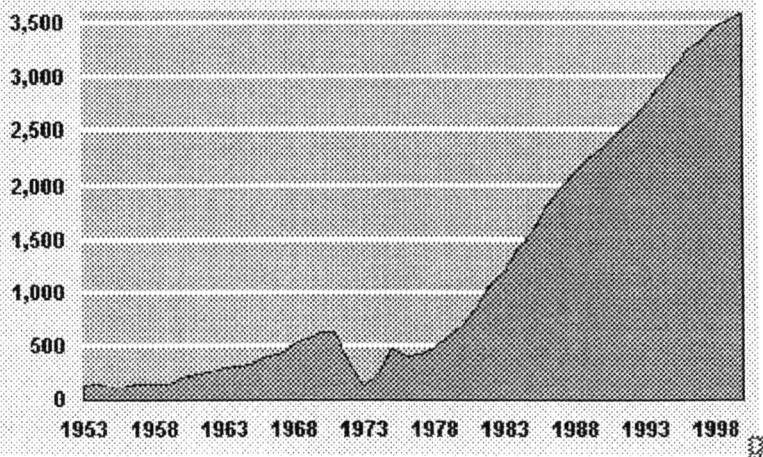

Source: *Capital Punishment 2000*

OJP Freedom of Information Act page
Privacy Statement and Disclaimers
Page last revised on December 11, 2001 [1]

---

[1] U.S. Department of Justice, Bureau of Justice Statistics, *The Number of Prisoners on Death Row Has Been Increasing;* www.ojp.usdoj.gov/bjs/glance/dr.htm

Over half of the increase in State prison population since 1990 is due to an increase in the prisoners convicted of <u>violent offenses</u>.

To view data, click on the chart.

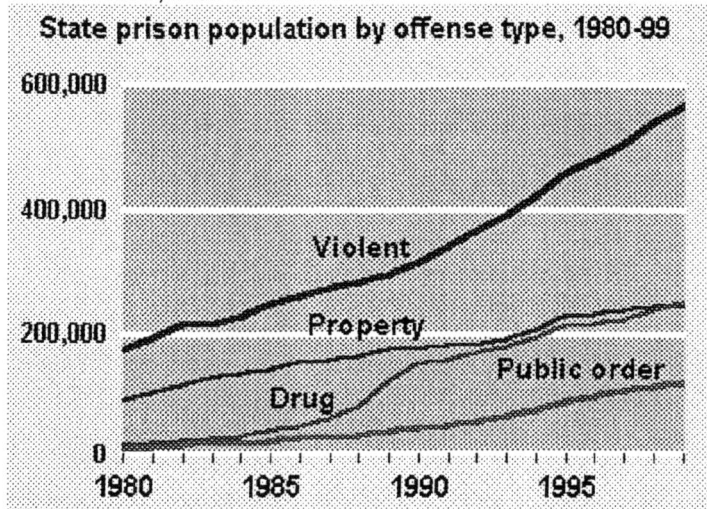

State prison population by offense type, 1980-99

600,000			
400,000		Violent	
200,000	Property		
	Drug	Public order	
0			
1980	1985	1990	1995

Source: <u>**Correctional Populations in the United States, 1997**</u> and **Prisoners in 2000**. Violent offenses include murder, negligent and nonnegligent manslaughter, rape, sexual assault, robbery, assault, extortion, intimidation, criminal endangerment, and other violent offenses. Property offenses include burglary, larceny, motor vehicle theft, fraud, possession and selling of stolen property, destruction of property, trespassing, vandalism, criminal tampering, and other property offenses. Drug offenses include possession, manufacturing, trafficking, and other drug offenses. Public-order offenses include weapons, drunk driving, escape/flight to avoid prosecution, court offenses, obstruction, commercialized vice, morals and decency charges, liquor law violations, and other public-order offenses.

The number of arrests for drug abuse violations increased from 1999 to 2000 for both juveniles and adults.

To view data, click on the chart.

Drug arrests by age, 1970-2000

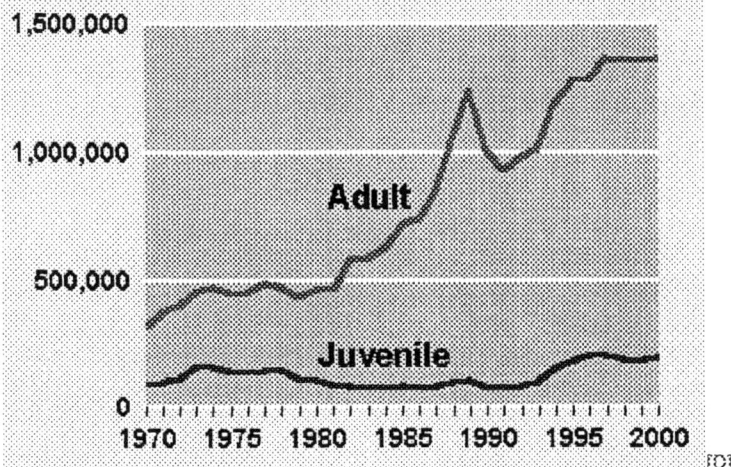

Source: **FBI, The Uniform Crime Reports** (UCR)

Drug abuse violations are defined as State or local offenses relating to the unlawful possession, sale, use, growing, manufacturing, and making of narcotic drugs including opium or cocaine and their derivatives, marijuana, synthetic narcotics, and dangerous nonnarcotic drugs such as barbiturates.

Juveniles are defined as persons under 18 years of age.

Adults are defined as persons 18 years old and older.

The incarceration rate has more than tripled since 1980.

To view data, click on the chart.

Incarceration rate, 1980-2000

Number of offenders per 100,000 population

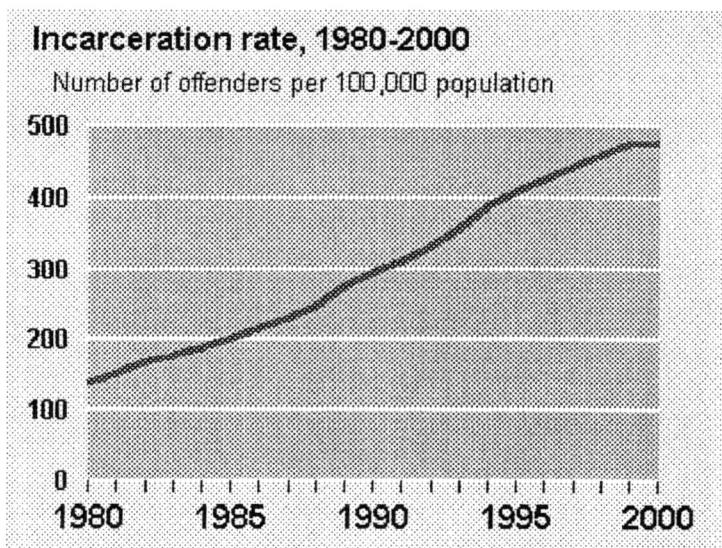

Source: **Correctional Populations in the United States, 1997** and **Prisoners in 2000**.

Note: Number of sentenced inmates incarcerated under State and Federal jurisdiction per 100,000, 1980-00.

Social Statistics Briefing Room

The number of adults in the correctional population has been increasing.

To view data, click on the chart.

Adult correctional populations, 1980-2000

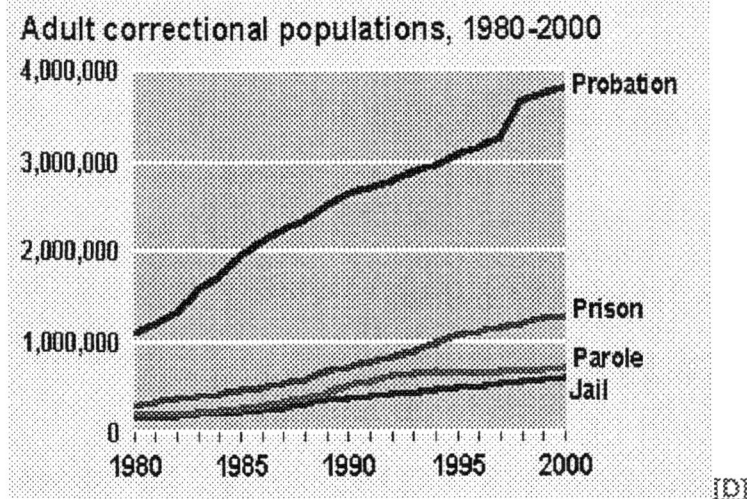

Source: Bureau of Justice Statistics Correctional Surveys (The Annual Probation Survey, National Prisoner Statistics, Survey of Jails, and The Annual Parole Survey) as presented in **Correctional Populations in the United States, 1997** and **Prisoners in 2000.**

In 2000, almost 6.5 million people were under some form of correctional supervision including: Probation - court ordered community supervision of convicted offenders by a probation agency. In many instances, the supervision requires adherence to specific rules of conduct while in the community. Prison - confinement in a State or Federal correctional facility to serve a sentence of more than 1 year, although in some jurisdictions the length of sentence which results in prison confinement is longer. Jail - confinement in a local jail while pending trial, awaiting sentencing, serving a sentence that is usually less than 1 year, or awaiting transfer to other facilities after conviction. Parole -community supervision after a period of incarceration. These data include only adults who are on active or inactive parole supervision or some other form of conditional release, including mandatory release, following a term of incarceration.

More information about the data.

Social Statistics Briefing Room

Direct expenditure for each of the major criminal justice functions (police, corrections, judicial) has been increasing.

To view data, click on the chart.

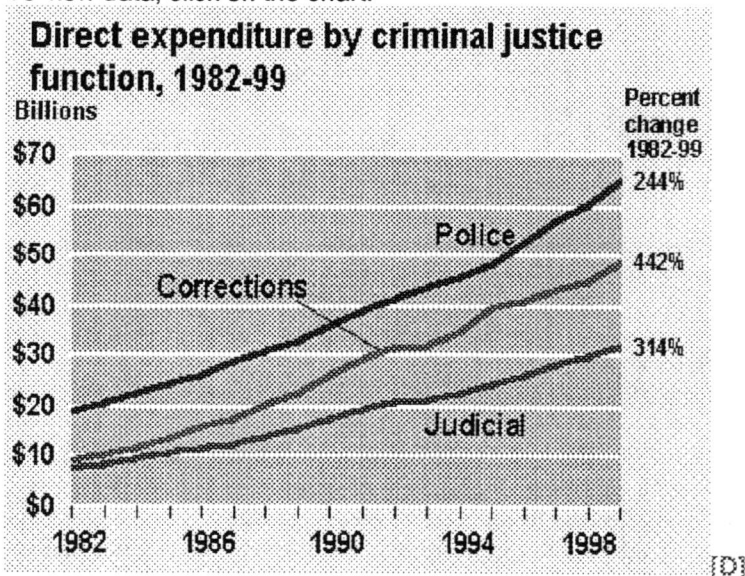

Direct expenditure by criminal justice function, 1982-99

Billions

Percent change 1982-99

$70

$60

244%

$50

Police

$40

Corrections

442%

$30

314%

$20

$10

Judicial

$0

1982   1986   1990   1994   1998

[D]

Source: **Justice Expenditure and Employment Extracts**
Social Statistics Briefing Room

Teens experience the highest rates of violent crime. Violent crime rates declined in recent years for most age groups.

To view data, click on the chart.

Violent crime rates by age of victim

Adjusted victimization rate
per 1,000 persons in age group

Age

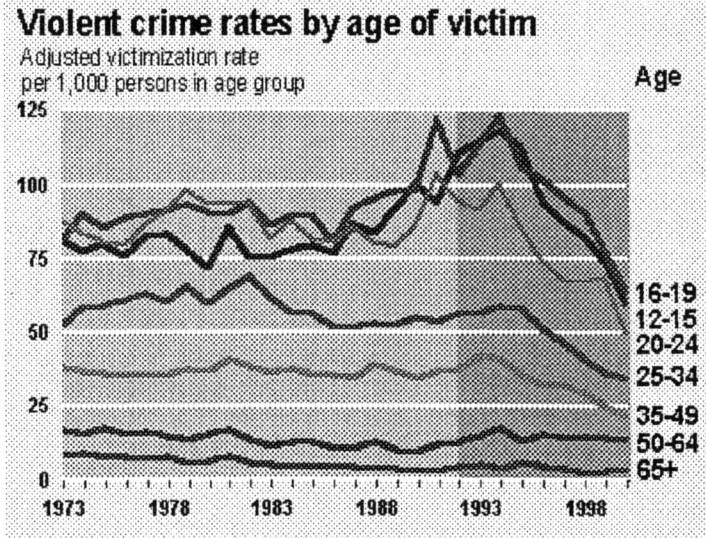

Note: Violent crimes included are homicide, rape, robbery, andth simple and aggravated assault. The National Crime Victimization Survey redesign was implemented in 1993; the areawith the lighter shading is before the redesign and the darker area after the redesign. The data before 1993 are adjusted to make them comparable with data collected since the redesign. The adjustment methods are described in **_Criminal Victimization 1973-95_**. Estimates for 1993 and beyond are based on collection year while arlier estimates are based on data year. For additional information about the methods used, see **_Criminal Victimization 2000_**.

Additional information on this topic can be found in **_Age Patterns of Victims of Serious Violent Crime_**. For related data about homicide trends by age, see **_Homicide Trends in the U.S._** Sources: Rape, robbery, and assault data are from the NationalVictimization (NCVS). Ongoing since 1972, this survey of householdsinterviews about 80,000 persons age 12 and older in 43,000households twice each year about their victimizations from crime.The homicide data are collected by the **FBI's Uniform Crime Reports** (UCR) from reports from law enforcement agencies.

This completes the graphs from the Department of Justice. In light of the information from the DOJ the verse to follow from Hosea is poignant.

Hosea 4:6   My people are destroyed for lack of knowledge: because thou hast rejected knowledge, I will also reject thee, that thou shalt be no priest to me: seeing thou hast forgotten the law of thy God, <u>I will also forget thy children.</u>

The verses to follow also speak of judgment. Although we live in an age of grace, God will not and cannot let justice and judgment be forever set aside.

Joshua 23:15 *Therefore it shall come to pass, that as all good things are come upon you, which the LORD your God promised you; so shall the LORD bring upon you all evil things, until he have destroyed you from off this good land which the LORD your God hath given you.*

Psalm 7:11-13 *God judgeth the righteous, and God is angry with the wicked every day. If he turn not, he will whet his sword; he hath bent his bow, and made it ready. He hath also prepared for him the instruments of death; he ordaineth his arrows against the persecutors.*

Malachi 3:5-6 *And I will come near to you to judgment; and I will be a swift witness against the sorcerers, and against the adulterers, and against false swearers, and against those that oppress the hireling in his wages, the widow, and the fatherless, and that turn aside the stranger from his right, and fear not me, saith the LORD of hosts. For I am the LORD, I change not; .*

Hebrews 13:8 *Jesus Christ the same yesterday, and to day, and for ever.*

MORE EVIDENCE OUR CHILDREN ARE BEING FORGOTTEN

There is much more evidence that God is forgetting our children. According to Barna, the number of children living in homes without two parents has risen dramatically from 19.4% in 1960 to 42.3% in the decade of the 90's. The initial cause was divorce, but more recently the continued climb is due to single mothers and cohabitating couples. However, the number of divorces has increased four fold since 1960.[1]

This work has related the cause of this catastrophe, which is still unfolding, to the loss of a firm foundation or the loss of the belief in absolutism.

---

[1] Barna Research; Barna Updates Released Through 2001 and can be Referenced on the Barna Research Website at www.barna.org

The incongruity of stated beliefs to the moral choices of the last three generations is alarming and disconcerting. Most people today do not even realize they are making diametrically opposed decisions. [Jesus spoke often about 'the blind' and 'blind guides', Jn 9:39, Mat. 15:14, Mat 23:16, and referenced in Zeph 1:17] For example, eighty two (82) percent say they believe the Bible, yet:

"39% of Americans say that Jesus Christ was crucified, but he never had a physical resurrection. Nearly the same proportion of born again Christians (35%) embrace this same thinking"[1].

Six out of ten adults say the devil, or Satan, is not a living being but is a symbol of evil, yet 7 out of 10 are aware the Bible describes Satan, or the devil as an angel who formerly served God in Heaven. Most adults, 70%, state they

"consistently allow their life to be guided by the Holy Spirit, yet 6 out of 10 (60%) agree that the Holy Spirit is a symbol of God's presence or power but He is not a living entity. Over 50% (52%) of all born again Christians reject the existence of the Holy Spirit. Forty-three percent of adults believe that Jesus Christ committed sins while He was on earth. "Compared to two years ago, just half as many Americans believe that absolute moral truth exists, dropping from 38% in January 2000 to only 22% in November of 2001."[2]

In spite of the these facts:

"85% of Americans self-identify as Christians [and] 72% believe in God when described as the all-powerful, all-knowing, perfect creator of the universe who rules the world today. (2001)"[3]

The incongruity extends to born-again Christians who believe the Bible teaches:

"that God helps those who help themselves."[4]

"Four in ten (39%) of the born again segment also

---

[1] Barna Research Online; *Beliefs*; **www.barna.org/cgi-bin/**MainArchives.asp; p. 1 of 2

[2] Ibid.

[3]   Barna   Research   Online;   **www.barna.org/cgi-bin/PageCategory.asp?CategoryID=2**; p. 1 of 2

[4] Ibid. *Born Again Christians Ignorant of Faith;* Survey Also Finds Hell's Description Divides Americans; Could it have something with taking the references to Hell out of Scripture? See this work. **www.barna.org/cgi-bin/PagePressRelease.asp?PressReleaseID=32&Reference=C**; p. 1

maintain that "if a person is generally good, or does enough good things for others during their life, they will earn a place in heaven".[1]

The very surprising comparison is that Christian beliefs parallel non-Christian beliefs, or another way to state this is to say the Church looks and believes like the world.[2] It is not surprising therefore that many Americans believe that hell does not exist.[3]

What do all of these facts, figures, and information mean? It does not mean that truth is irrelevant. The absolute authority is the Scripture. The Scripture teaches that the church in the latter days will be like the Laodicean Church, which was "neither hot or cold" (Rev. 3:15), or in other words says: *"Whatever"*. She looks and sounds like the 'postmodern' world. Jesus Christ said, *"So then because thou art lukewarm, and neither cold nor hot, I will spue thee out of my mouth."* (Rev. 3:16) This is one of the sternest warnings in all of Scripture. The Church today does not take a stand against apostate beliefs, but says, "**Whatever.**" The proof that the "whatever" church exists, lies in the acceptance of "co-operation" or "tolerance" of false beliefs and the desire to "work together". Four out of five or 79% of adults said they would find it:

"preferable for Protestants and Catholics to put aside their differences, focus on the things they have in common, and work together whenever possible"[4].

Have Americans forgotten that the Catholic hierarchy has not rescinded one Vatican council or decree? This is serious business. Someone can proclaim that the Catholic denomination has changed for as long as they want, but the truth is, they have not! The proof is "in the pudding" and is affirmed in the following long quote from *"The Way of Life,"* which used with permission:

"Mel Gibson, producer of The *Passion of the Christ* [movie], says that he accepts the Council of Trent as an authoritative statement of Catholic doctrine. In so saying he is correct and is far more knowledgeable about Catholicism than the evangelicals and Baptists who are supporting him and his movie.

In January 1996, Pope John Paul II commemorated the 450th anniversary of the opening of the Council of Trent by visiting Trento, Italy, and affirming that Trent's declarations "maintain all their value."

The Council of Trent was conducted by four different

---

[1] Ibid. p, 1
[2] Ibid. p. 1-2
[3] Ibid.
[4] Ibid. www.barna.org/cgi-bin/PageCategory.asp?CategoryID=16; p. 2 of 3

popes (Paul III, Julius III, Paul IV, Pius IV) between the years 1545 to 1565, and had the two-fold goal of bringing reform to Catholicism and condemning and hindering the growth of Protestantism. A series of anathamas were issued against Protestant doctrine. The Index of Prohibited Books was set up, condemning authors and writings which were deemed anti-Catholic. During the era of Trent, the barbarous Inquisition was further unleashed against those who dared to reject Roman heresies.

In 1564 the doctrines of Trent were summarized in a papal bull entitled The Tridentine Profession of Faith. Dr. Raymond Surburg notes that "all Roman Catholic clergy and teachers must subscribe to it as well as converts to the faith from Protestantism. The person subscribing to it must swear true obedience to the Pope" (The Christian News, July 10, 1995, p. 6).

An official statement of the doctrines approved at Trent were issued in 1566 in the Roman Catechism.

The Council of Trent denied every Reformation doctrine, including Scripture alone and grace alone. Trent hurled 125 anathemas (eternal damnation) against Bible-believing Christians, including these:

"If any one shall deny that the body and blood together with the soul and divinity of our Lord Jesus Christ, and therefore entire Christ, are truly, really, and substantially contained in the sacrament of the most holy Eucharist; and shall say that He is only in it as a sign, or in a figure, or virtually--let him be accursed" (Canon 1).

"If any one shall say that the substance of the bread and wine remains in the sacrament of the most holy Eucharist, together with the body and blood of our Lord Jesus Christ, and shall deny that wonderful and singular conversion of the whole substance of the bread into the body, and of the whole substance of the wine into the blood, the outward forms of the bread and wine still remaining, which conversion the Catholic Church most aptly calls transubstantiation--let him be accursed" (Canon 2).

"If any man shall say that Christ, the only begotten Son of God, is not to be adored in the holy sacrament of the Eucharist, even with the open worship of latria, and therefore not to be venerated with any peculiar festal celebrity, nor to be solemnly carried about in processions according to the praiseworthy, and universal rites and customs of the holy Church, and that he is not to be publicly set before the people to be adored, and that his adorers are idolaters--let him be accursed" (Canon 6).

"If anyone shall say that the ungodly man is justified by faith only so as to understand that nothing else is required that may cooperate to obtain the grace of justification, and that it is in no wise necessary for him to be prepared and disposed by the motion of his own will ... let him be accursed" (Canon 9).

"If anyone shall say that justifying faith is nothing else than confidence in the divine mercy pardoning sins for Christ's sake, or that it is that confidence alone by which we are justified ... let him be accursed" (Canon 12).

Pope Pius IV (1559-1565) issued a summary of the decisions of the council under the title Pope Pius's Creed. We will quote part of this creed, which has ever since been regarded as an authoritative summary of the Catholic faith:

"I profess also, that there are truly and properly seven sacraments of the new law ... namely, baptism, confirmation, eucharist, penance, extreme unction, orders, and matrimony, and that they confer grace.

"I profess likewise, that in the mass is offered to God a true, proper, and propitiatory sacrifice for the living and the dead; and that, in the most holy sacrifice of the Eucharist, there is truly, really, and substantially, the body and blood, together with the soul and divinity of our Lord Jesus Christ.

"I constantly hold that there is a purgatory, and that the souls detained therein are helped by the suffrages of the faithful.

"Likewise, that the saints reigning together with Christ, are to be honoured and invocated; that they offer prayers to God for us; and that their relics are to be venerated.

"I most firmly assert, that the images of Christ, and of the mother of God, ever virgin, and also of the other saints, are to be had and retained; and that one honour and veneration are to be given to them.

"I also affirm that the power of indulgences was left by Christ in the church, and that the use of them is most wholesome to Christian people.

"I acknowledge the holy Catholic and Apostolic Roman church, the mother and mistress of all churches. And I promise to swear true obedience to the Roman bishop, the successor of St. Peter, the prince of the apostles, and vicar of Jesus Christ.

"I also profess, and undoubtedly receive all other things delivered, defined, and declared, by the sacred canons and general councils, and particularly by the holy Council of Trent.

And likewise, I also condemn, reject, and anathematize, all things contrary thereto, and all heresies whatsoever condemned, rejected, and anathematized by the church.

"This true Catholic faith, out of which none can be saved..." (Miller's Church History, pp. 1081-1082).

These proclamations and anathemas were fleshed out in the murderous persecutions vented upon true Christians by Rome--and Trent has never been annulled. The Vatican II Council in the 1960s referred to Trent dozens of times, quoting Trent's proclamations as authoritative and reaffirming Trent on every hand. At the opening of the Second Vatican Council, Pope John XXIII stated, "I do accept entirely all that has been decided and declared at the Council of Trent." Every Cardinal, Bishop and priest who became a member of the Council also signed that document (Wilson Ewin, You Can Lead Roman Catholics to Christ, Quebec Baptist Mission, 1990 edition, p. 41). The New Catholic Catechism cites Trent no less than 99 times. There is not the slightest hint that the proclamations of the Council of Trent have been abrogated by Rome.

Consider a few examples of how Vatican II looked upon Trent:

"The dogmatic principles which were laid down by the Council of Trent [remain] intact..." (Constitution on the Sacred Liturgy, p. 37).

"Therefore, the following in the footsteps of the Council of Trent and of Vatican I, this present Council wishes to set forth authentic doctrine of divine revelation" (Constitution on Divine Revelation, p. 678). "[Christ] is substantially present there through that conversion of bread and wine which, as the Council of Trent tells us, is most aptly named transubstantiation" (Constitution on the Sacred Liturgy, p. 110).

"For under this form (leaving intact the principles of the Council of Trent, by which under either species or kind there is received the true sacrament and Christ whole and entire), the sign of the eucharistic banquet appears more perfectly" (Constitution on the Sacred Liturgy, p. 124).

"The Roman Missal, promulgated by our predecessor St. Pius V in the Year of our Lord 1570 by decree of the Council of Trent, is universally acknowledged to be among the most useful of the many fruits which that Council brought forth for the good of the Church of Christ" (Constitution on the Sacred Liturgy, p. 138).

"When issuing decrees that the Order of the Mass should be revised, the Second Vatican Council ruled, among other things, that certain rites were to be restored to the vigour which they had in the days of the holy Fathers. These are the very words used by St. Pius V in his Apostolic Constitution Quo primum whereby he promulgated the Tridentine Missal of 1570 [Trent]. The employment of the very same words indicates that the two Missals, though separated in time by four centuries, are nevertheless inspired by and embody one and the same tradition. ... In those troubled days St. Pius V was unwilling to make any changes in the rites except minor ones; he was intent on preserving more recent tradition, because at that time attacks were being made on the doctrine that the Mass is a sacrifice present under the eucharistic species" (Constitution on the Sacred Liturgy, p. 155).

"In this way the liturgical norms of the Council of Trent have in many respects been fulfilled and perfected by those of the Second Vatican Council" (Constitution on the Sacred Liturgy, p. 159).

"This sacred council accepts loyally the venerable faith of our ancestors in the living communion which exists between us and our brothers who are in the glory of heaven or who are yet being purified after their death; and it proposes again the decrees of the Second Council of Nicea, of the Council of Florence, and of the Council of Trent" (Constitution on the Church, p. 377).

"The sacrament of baptism cannot be repeated ... and therefore to baptize again conditionally is not allowed unless there is prudent doubt of the fact, or of the validity, of a baptism already administered (Council of Trent, Session 7, Can. 4)" (Decree on Ecumenism, p. 445).

"The Fathers of the Council, continuing the work begun by the Council of Trent, confidently entrust to superiors and professors in seminaries the duty of training Christ's future priests in the spirit of that renewal promoted by the Council itself" (Decree on the Training of Priests, p. 654).

Those who are flirting with Rome today and who are claiming that Rome has changed are incredibly gullible at best. Rome hasn't changed, except superficially, but those who profess to be Protestants, Evangelicals, and Baptists certainly have."[1]

---

[1]*Pope Affirms Curses Of Trent*; Updated April 8, 2004 (first published January 14, 1996) (David Cloud, Fundamental Baptist Information Service, P.O. Box 610368, Port Huron, MI 48061, 866-295-4143,

Yes, Catholics believe in the deity of Christ, but are heretical on many other doctrines. One example is their teaching that salvation is in, by, and through their denomination and not by belief in Jesus Christ **alone**. The Roman Catholics state: "If you are not a member of the Roman Catholic Church you are not saved." Another example of an apostate belief is that baptism, or even sprinkling saves.

In light of the above, why have so many denominations, evangelicals, neo-evangelicals, fundamentalists, and individuals such as Billy Graham gone after an apostate denomination? They say it is because of trying to win them over to the Lord Jesus Christ and His doctrines. Or they say we must all love one another and exerciser tolerance. Surely they know all the admonitions of the Scriptures.

Ro 16:17-18¶ Now I beseech you, brethren, mark them which cause divisions and offences contrary to the doctrine which ye have learned; and **avoid** them. [18] For they that are such serve not our Lord Jesus Christ, but their own belly; and by good words and fair speeches deceive the hearts of the simple.

1Co 15:33 Be not deceived: evil communications corrupt good manners.

And there are many other verses in the pastoral epistles, which support this same doctrine. But let's put this "bellying up" to apostate denominations and individuals into perspective. What if you had a daughter who was 16-17 years old and she brought home a young man who was: 1. An addict, (to sacramental pomp and other "things") 2. A member of a commune, (exclusive) 3. A greedy, wealthy person, (wealth beyond imagination is corrupting) 4. A ruthless murderer (Just examine the history of the Catholic church. See Dave Hunt's book, *The Woman Rides The Beast.*), and 5. A liar and deceiver, who has no intention to "reform." (Examine the Jesuit history, among many other things.) Would you want your daughter to **avoid** him? Remember, this is part of the "P" in the SOAP acronym. If you understand this work and the characteristics of certain denominations, religions, and persons, who exhibit these traits, should you be their friend? Should you **avoid** them in light of Scriptural pronouncements? Oh yes, you could rewrite the "rules" of Scripture, to bring it into conformity with **your** beliefs, or pretend you did not know.

fbns@wayoflife.org;

BIBLE SOCIETIES AND ALLIANCES ARE
JOINED WITH APOSTATE GROUPS

T
his is exactly what has happened with Bible Socities; they have rewritten the "rules." The Bible Societies all over the world are now **producing** (meaning to edit, change the wording, and/or place catholic doctrine or other heresies in the margins) Bibles in cooperation with apostate or pagan religions. Many "Churches" are using these fabricated Bibles. Documents have been obtained from the various societies, which show "full" co-operation with (for example) the Roman Catholic Church in translation, distribution, and administration since the 1980"s. Here is a list of the countries where this is occurring: (in Africa) Egypt, Algeria, Botswana, Burundi, Cameron, Central African Republic, Ethiopia, Ivory Coast, Kenya, Madagascar, Mauritania, Mozambique, Nigeria, Rwanda, Sudan, Uganda, Zambia, Zimbabwe, (in North and South America) Brazil, Cuba, Netherlands Antilles, Nicaragua, Paraguay, Peru, Canada, U.S.A., (Asia, Australia and the Pacific) Australia, China, India, Indonesia, Iran, Japan, Korea, Malaysia, Micronesia, South Pacific Islands of Fiji, Samoan, Solomon, Tahitian, and the Cook Islands, Papua New Guinea, Philippines, Sri Lanka, Thailand, (in Europe) Yugoslavia, Czechoslovakia, Romania, Lithuania, Belgium, Cyprus, France, Germany, Greece, Italy, Lebanon, Malta, Netherlands, Norway, Portugal, and Spain.[1]

The following information was lifted from the Internet and it is placed here with sadness, with the reality that the Roman Catholic Church "joins hands with" pagans on many fronts, and with amazement that the Southern Baptist Convention contributes money to "The Baptist World Alliance".

"BAPTIST WORLD ALLIANCE DIALOGUES WITH ANGLICANS AND JOINS HANDS WITH ROME AND PAGANS. Friday Church News Notes, February 8, 2002 (David W. Cloud, Fundamental Baptist Information Service, P.O. Box 610368, Port Huron, MI 48061, 866-295-4143, fbns@wayoflife.org) The Baptist World Alliance and the Anglican Church recently stated the goals of their formal dialogue, the Anglican-Baptist International Conversations (ABIC). One of these is "to look for ways to cooperate in mission and community activities and increase our fellowship and common witness to the Gospel." This is disobedience to the Words of God, which requires believers to mark

---

[1] Trinitarian Bible Society; *Ecumenism And the UBS;* Data located throughout the report.

and avoid those who teach contrary to the apostolic faith. Though the Anglican Church is filled with heresy, unbelief, and immorality, the Baptist World Alliance refuses to obey God's Words in its dealings with it. In fact, the Baptist World Alliance affiliates with every sort of apostasy. In January, the head of the Baptist World Alliance, Setri Nyomi, joined hands with the Pope and the leaders of many pagan religions at the Day of Prayer for Peace in Assisi, Italy. The Southern Baptist Convention not only is a member of the Baptist World Alliance, but also contributes the largest share of the finances to this disobedient organization."[1]

And if you are still not convinced that "the lie that changed the modern world" has **produced** Bibles that have contributed to ecumenism by their weakened and often false doctrine, consider this. These perverted Bibles have led the Roman See and Pope to declare:

"we all worship the same God." [See the following quote.]

"In *Global Peace and the Rise of Antichrist* I [Dave Hunt] provide much evidence that John Paul II [the current Pope] is the greatest ecumenist of all time. For example, on page 156, I [Dave Hunt] relate his gathering together in Assisi, Italy, in 1986, the leading figures of 12 world religions to pray "for peace" to whatever "god" each believed in. There were snake worshipers, fire worshipers, witch doctors, Hindus, Buddhists, Muslims praying together. **The Pope declared that they were all praying to the same "God"** and that their prayers were creating a spiritual energy which was bringing about a new climate for peace—that "the challenge of peace...transcends religious differences." Vatican II, *Lumen Gentium*, 21 November 1964, 16, is very specific: "But the plan of salvation also includes those who acknowledge the Creator, in the first place amongst whom are the Muslims: these profess to hold the faith of Abraham, and together with us they adore the one, merciful God, mankind's judge on the last day." That Allah is not the God of the Bible is clear. For an excellent treatment of Islam, I highly recommend *Islamic Invasion*, a book we offer."[2]

The Roman religion is making progress toward bringing all world religions, including Islam, under one 'umbrella,' the Catholic Church. A Bible

---

[1] Cloud, David; Fundamental Baptist Information Service, *Baptist World Alliance Dialogues with Anglicans and Joins Hands with Rome and Pagans;* Feb 8, 2002

[2] Hunt, David; *Berean Call, 1986-2001 Newsletters*; CD-ROM 2002; August, 1992; p. 143

that all religions can embrace is needed to facilitate the movement. The embracing of the Alexandrian Greek text, its descendants, and translations, has done much to further the goal of the one-world government and religion.

"THE CONSEQUENCES OF ALL THIS ARE SERIOUS AND FAR-REACHING FOR THE FUTURE OF THE CHURCH," SOCIETY, AND THE INDIVIDUAL.

The next step in the plan of enemy spiritual forces is to remove certain books from the Bible that are "embarrassing" to certain groups. Great progress has been made toward this goal, but this work cannot address these continuing attacks on His Words.

Much much more could be said, but this work will close with a warning to the Church. The last sentence of a sermon delivered by Dr. Robert Massey at the First Baptist Church in Cleveland, Georgia on April 14, 2002 was related to the issue of not allowing the Holy Spirit to work in the life of the churches. From the information in this work, one can say the churches have quenched the work of the Spirit; God's will is not being accomplished in the Laodician Church of the last days, and Dr. Massey's last sentence is prophetic. He said: "You have heard it said that God will have to apologize to Sodom and Gomorrah if He does not punish this nation, but I tell you, He will have to apologize to Ananias and Sapphira if he does not discipline the Church". Are you ready?

Rev. 22:20-21 *He which testifieth these things saith, Surely I come quickly. Amen. Even so, come, Lord Jesus. The grace of our Lord Jesus Christ be with you all.*
Amen.

H. D. Williams, M. D.

Appendices

Appendix 1
How To Know God

The OOO (omniscient, omnipotent, omnipresent) God is not hard to get to know. He loves you and love is one of His characteristics. 1 **John 4:16** says: *And we have known and believed the love that God hath to us. God is love.* He has demonstrated His love in so many ways that it is hard to decide where to start, except to start where He wants every person to start. Where is that?

I.   *John 10:10* **I am come that they might have life, and that they might have it more abundantly.**

These are the Words of Jesus Christ. Also, He said, "I am He" in John 8:24. What He is saying is that He is God. He gave us innumerable proofs that He is God while He was here. God wants us to "have life", and to "have it more abundantly." Throughout history there have been millions who have testified: He has given me "life more abundantly." You can have 'life more abundantly,' too. God is love and He wants you to know how!

II.   Romans 3:*23 For all have sinned, and come short of the glory of God;*

Sin is missing the mark. The mark is the standard God has set. The standard is reflected in the Ten Commandments. If you miss any one of those standards, you have sinned.

1.   **Exodus 20:3** Thou shalt have no other gods before me.
2.   **Exodus 20:4** Thou shalt not make unto thee any graven image, or any likeness *of any thing* that *is* in heaven above, or that *is* in the earth beneath, or that *is* in the water under the earth:
3.   **Exodus 20:7** Thou shalt not take the name of the LORD thy God in vain; for the LORD will not hold him guiltless that taketh his name in vain.
4.   Exodus 20:8 Remember the sabbath day, to keep it holy.
5.   **Exodus 20:12** Honour thy father and thy mother: that thy days may be long upon the land which the LORD thy God giveth thee.
6.   **Exodus 20:13** Thou shalt not kill.
7.   **Exodus 20:14** Thou shalt not commit adultery.
8.   **Exodus 20:15** Thou shalt not steal.
9.   **Exodus 20:16** Thou shalt not bear false witness against thy neighbour.

10. **Exodus 20:17** Thou shalt not covet thy neighbour's house, thou shalt not covet thy neighbour's wife, nor his manservant, nor his maidservant, nor his ox, nor his ass, nor any thing that *is* thy neighbour's.

God says that <u>all</u> have sinned. (Romans 3:23) He says it this way, also, "All we like sheep have gone astray; we have turned every one to his own way." (Isaiah 53:6) Although we don't understand all the ramifications completely, we do know that when we sin it causes turmoil in our life and in this world. The Bible says it this way: "For we know that the whole creation groaneth and travaileth in pain." (Rom 8:22)

Since God loves us, He wants us to be free of this "pain". He also wants to be where we are because He loves us. He cannot be where sin is found because he is pure and holy. It is like mixing yeast, a symbol for sin, into bread. The yeast spreads throughout the bread like an infection. Therefore, we must be and are separated from God who is sinless and holy. The Bible says it like this: "For the wages of sin *is* death." (Romans 6:23) The infection of sin leads to death. You cannot cure the infection by philosophy, religion, or good works. These are man's efforts to achieve "abundant" life and they don't work. The scourge of sin is so terrible that something only God could do will remove it.

III. But, "God commendeth his love toward us, in that, while we were yet sinners, Christ died for us." (Romans 5:8)

Sin is such a horrible curse in and on this world that the shedding of blood was necessary to save us from the infection. God loves us so "that He gave His only begotten Son, that whosoever believeth in Him should not perish but have eternal life." (Jn. 3:16) Remember the penalty for sin is death. Just as the price for breaking the law has to be paid by a fine or prison time, a price had to be paid for sin.

I once heard a story that makes this point clear. A Roman General was sitting in judgment of "law breakers" when a very elderly man, about 90 years of age, came before the General for adjudication or assigning the penalty. The penalty for the old man's crime was set by law and could not be changed. The penalty was 39 lashes with a whip. The penalty could not be cancelled according to Roman law. The General knew the lashing would kill the old man, so, he stripped off his clothes and substituted for the old man. This is a true story. The following information is true, also. A perfect, sinless substitute is required by God to fulfill the penalty of death because of sin. God was willing to give us His perfect, sinless Son, Jesus Christ, to fulfill the requirement of death. Just as amazing was the willingness of Jesus Christ to die for you and me on the Cross. *John 15:13 Greater love hath no man than this, that a man lay down his life for his friends.*

IV. But God commendeth his love toward us, in that, while we were yet sinners, Christ died for us. (Romans 5:8)

Notice that the Scripture says: "while we were yet sinners" that "Christ died for us". Just like the old man who was still a debtor to the Roman law, the General paid the price for his "sin". Our General, the Lord Jesus Christ asks us to appreciate the gift of eternal life and to turn from our sins. Can't you just imagine that the Roman General told the elderly man to never break the law again.

V. Truly, these times of ignorance God overlooked, but now commands all men everywhere to repent [Acts 17:30]

One must turn from sin (breaking the law) to God, which is repentance. This must be a sincere "turning" in the heart from rebellion to becoming obedient "in the heart" to God. Jesus pointed the way to God.

VI. Jesus saith unto him, **I am the way, the truth, and the life: no man cometh unto the Father, but by me.** (John 14:6)

Jesus who is God set the rules. He paid the price. He pointed the way by the Cross. But He also set the rule that "no man cometh unto the Father, but by me." (Jn. 14:6) You must believe who the Lord Jesus Christ is, the work that He did on the Cross for you, and turn from "your wicked ways." You will not know everything immediately, and God does not require you to know everything before He saves you. He must see that you have a sincere heart, and are willing to set out on a journey with Him as He teaches you.

VII. *For I delivered unto you first of all that which I also received, how that Christ died for our sins according to the scriptures; 4And that he was buried, and that he rose again the third day according to the scriptures: 5And that he was seen of Cephas, then of the twelve: 6After that, he was seen of above five hundred brethren at once; of whom the greater part remain unto this present, but some are fallen asleep.* (1Corinthians 15:3-6)

Jesus said, "I am He", and proved to us that He is God by His resurrection. He proved He loved us by dying for us to pay the penalty of *our* sin. He was our substitute.

VIII. But as many as received him, to them gave he power to become the sons of God, *even* to them that believe on his name: (John 1:12)

We cannot know all the ramifications of sin because we cannot see "everything," just as we cannot see the "wind" or sound waves, or sin. We see the results of sin, but not sin. Similarly, we cannot know all there is to know about God or we would be God. This much we do know. Death in the Words of God is described as separation from God, and results in eternal separation in a place called Hell. He is willing to save you from the penalty of eternal separation by simply receiving the Lord Jesus Christ by faith. You do not have to know everything. There will be a day when everything will be explained, but for now God says "believe on His name," the name of Jesus Christ, and He will give you eternal life. John 3:15 says very clearly: *"That whosoever believeth in him should not perish, but have eternal life.* He repeated this statement in the very next verse to be certain we understand. Eternal life is being present with God where there will be no tears, sadness, sickness, hunger, or pain. You are saved from eternal torment.

IX. *For by grace are ye saved through faith; and that not of yourselves: it is the gift of God: Not of works, lest any man should boast.* (Ephesians 2:8-9)

There is no philosophy, religion, work, or good living that will save you. You simply have to ask God to save you from the penalty of sin because you believe that Jesus Christ is the Son of God, that He died for you, and that He rose from the dead. He loves you and wants to give you this free gift for simply saying and believing in your heart, "that Jesus died for <u>me</u>".

John 5:24 Verily, verily, I say unto you, He that heareth my words, and believeth on him that sent me, hath everlasting life, and shall not come into condemnation; but is passed from death unto life.

It doesn't get any clearer than John 5:24. If you believe Him, simply tell God you do. You will be saved. THAT'S IT! There is not one other thing you have to do. You should also tell someone about your decision. *That if thou shalt confess with thy mouth the Lord Jesus, and shalt believe in thine heart that God hath raised him from the dead, thou shalt be saved.* (Romans 10:9)

When you are saved, God changes you. You will sense the change. The change allows God to see Christ in you. The change also allows God to live in you. Know ye not that ye are the temple of God, and *that* the Spirit of God dwelleth in you? (1Corinthians 3:16)

If you asked God to save you, welcome to the kingdom of God. Join a body of Bible believing saints [a church] and worship the Creator with them.

Appendix 2

HISTORY OF UNBELIEF[1]

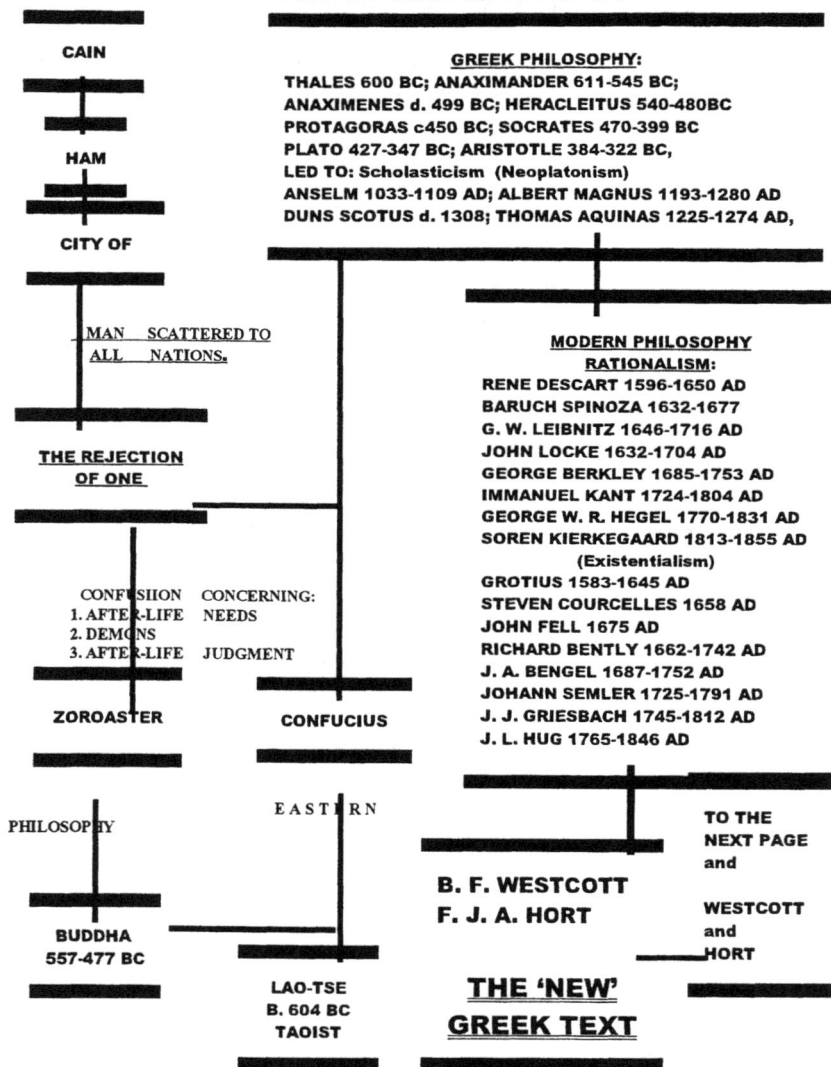

CAIN

HAM

CITY OF

MAN SCATTERED TO
ALL NATIONS.

**THE REJECTION
OF ONE**

| CONFUSION CONCERNING: |
| 1. AFTER-LIFE NEEDS |
| 2. DEMONS |
| 3. AFTER-LIFE JUDGMENT |

ZOROASTER

PHILOSOPHY

**BUDDHA
557-477 BC**

GREEK PHILOSOPHY:
THALES 600 BC; ANAXIMANDER 611-545 BC;
ANAXIMENES d. 499 BC; HERACLEITUS 540-480BC
PROTAGORAS c450 BC; SOCRATES 470-399 BC
PLATO 427-347 BC; ARISTOTLE 384-322 BC,
LED TO: Scholasticism (Neoplatonism)
ANSELM 1033-1109 AD; ALBERT MAGNUS 1193-1280 AD
DUNS SCOTUS d. 1308; THOMAS AQUINAS 1225-1274 AD,

MODERN PHILOSOPHY
RATIONALISM:
RENE DESCART 1596-1650 AD
BARUCH SPINOZA 1632-1677
G. W. LEIBNITZ 1646-1716 AD
JOHN LOCKE 1632-1704 AD
GEORGE BERKLEY 1685-1753 AD
IMMANUEL KANT 1724-1804 AD
GEORGE W. R. HEGEL 1770-1831 AD
SOREN KIERKEGAARD 1813-1855 AD
(Existentialism)
GROTIUS 1583-1645 AD
STEVEN COURCELLES 1658 AD
JOHN FELL 1675 AD
RICHARD BENTLY 1662-1742 AD
J. A. BENGEL 1687-1752 AD
JOHANN SEMLER 1725-1791 AD
J. J. GRIESBACH 1745-1812 AD
J. L. HUG 1765-1846 AD

CONFUCIUS

EASTERN

B. F. WESTCOTT
F. J. A. HORT

**LAO-TSE
B. 604 BC
TAOIST**

THE 'NEW'

GREEK TEXT

TO THE
NEXT PAGE
and

WESTCOTT
and
HORT

---

[1]This chart was made possible by the information in Edward F. Hills', *The King James Version Defended*

Appendix 3
THE DESPISERS

Ac 13:41 Behold, ye <u>despisers</u>, and wonder, and perish: for I work a work in your days, a work which ye shall in no wise believe, though a man declare it unto you.

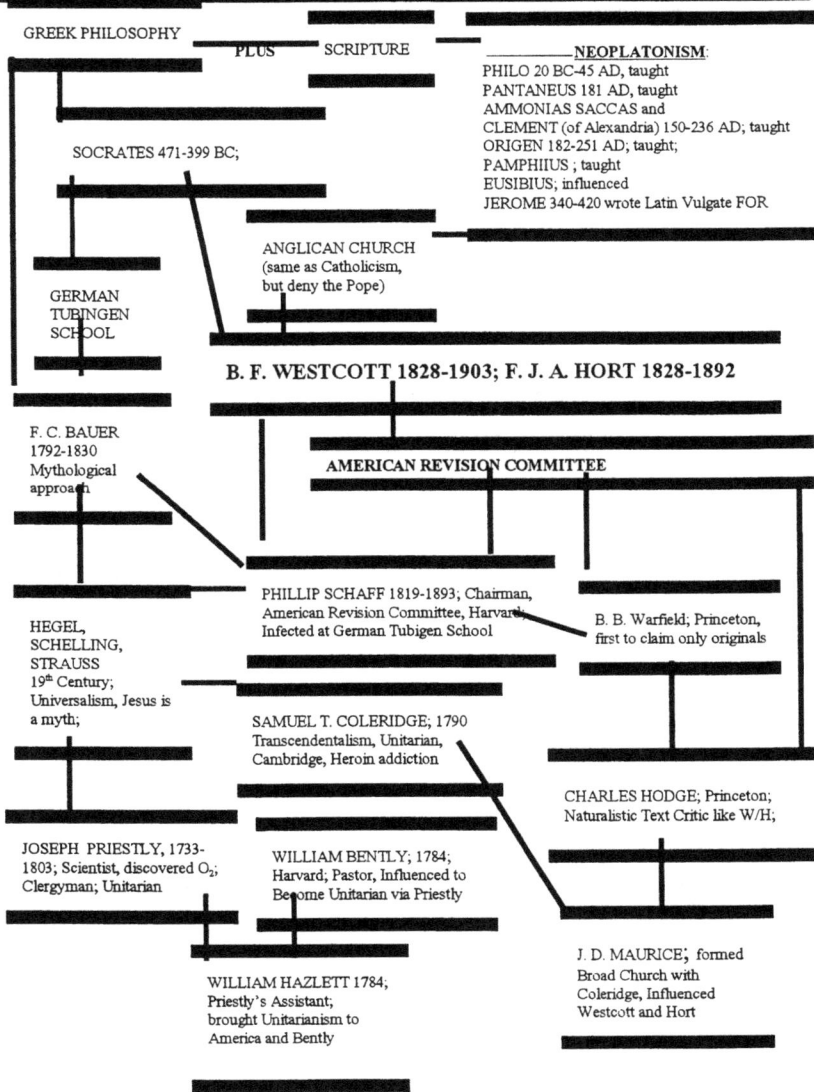

GREEK PHILOSOPHY

PLUS SCRIPTURE

_____NEOPLATONISM:
PHILO 20 BC-45 AD, taught
PANTANEUS 181 AD, taught
AMMONIAS SACCAS and
CLEMENT (of Alexandria) 150-236 AD; taught
ORIGEN 182-251 AD; taught;
PAMPHIIUS ; taught
EUSIBIUS; influenced
JEROME 340-420 wrote Latin Vulgate FOR

SOCRATES 471-399 BC;

ANGLICAN CHURCH
(same as Catholicism,
but deny the Pope)

GERMAN
TUBINGEN
SCHOOL

B. F. WESTCOTT 1828-1903; F. J. A. HORT 1828-1892

F. C. BAUER
1792-1830
Mythological
approach

AMERICAN REVISION COMMITTEE

PHILLIP SCHAFF 1819-1893; Chairman,
American Revision Committee, Harvard;
Infected at German Tubigen School

B. B. Warfield; Princeton,
first to claim only originals

HEGEL,
SCHELLING,
STRAUSS
19th Century;
Universalism, Jesus is
a myth;

SAMUEL T. COLERIDGE; 1790
Transcendentalism, Unitarian,
Cambridge, Heroin addiction

CHARLES HODGE; Princeton;
Naturalistic Text Critic like W/H;

JOSEPH PRIESTLY, 1733-
1803; Scientist, discovered O_2;
Clergyman; Unitarian

WILLIAM BENTLY; 1784;
Harvard; Pastor, Influenced to
Become Unitarian via Priestly

WILLIAM HAZLETT 1784;
Priestly's Assistant;
brought Unitarianism to
America and Bently

J. D. MAURICE; formed
Broad Church with
Coleridge, Influenced
Westcott and Hort

Appendix 4

METHOD OF BIBLICAL PRESERVATION

OLD TESTAMENT ERA

Adam and Eve

Abel

Noah

Job

Moses

Joshua,
Samuel

David

Major
Prophets

Minor
Prophets
(Ezra)

Deut. 31:26
"Writings"
kept in the
Tabernacle
with the Ark
or in the
Temple by
God's
command

De 31:26 Take this book of the law, and put it in the side of the ark of the covenant of the LORD your God, that it may be there for a witness against thee.
De 17:18-19 And it shall be, when he sitteth upon the throne of his kingdom, that he shall write him a copy of this law in a book out of that which is before the priests the Levites: And it shall be with him, and he shall read therein all the days of his life: that he may learn to fear the LORD his God, to keep all the words of this law and these statutes, to do them:
Ps 105:8¶ He hath remembered his covenant for ever, the word which he commanded to a thousand generations.
Jesus said: Mt 24:35 Heaven and earth shall pass away, but my words shall not pass away.
Jesus said: Mt 5:17-18¶ Think not that I am come to destroy the law, or the prophets: I am not come to destroy, but to fulfil. Mt 5:18 For verily I say unto you, Till heaven and earth pass, one jot or one tittle shall in no wise pass from the law, till all be fulfilled.
Jesus said: Joh 12:47-48 And if any man hear my words, and believe not, I judge him not: for I came not to judge the world, but to save the world. He that rejecteth me, and receiveth not my words, hath one that judgeth him: the word that I have spoken, the same shall judge him in the last day.

SCRIBES
COPIED
THE
OLD
TESTAMENT
BY
COMMAND
OF
GOD.
THE
COPYING
CONTINUES
UNTIL
NEAR
THE
END
OF
THE
MIDDLE
AGES

NEW TESTAMENT
James 40ish AD

Mark 40-70 AD
Matthew "
Luke "
John "

Acts

Romans 49-67 AD
1Cor. "
2Cor. "
Galatians "
Ephesians "
Philippians "
Colossians "
1Thess. "
2Thess. "
1Tim. "
2Tim. "
Titus "
Philemon "

1Peter 63-66 AD
2Peter "

Hebrews 64-69 AD.

Jude 70-80 AD

1, 2, 3, Jn. 80-90 AD

Acts 6:7 PRIESTS (SCRIBES) obedient to the faith in the LORD JESUS CHRIST most likely taught the PRIESTHOOD OF BELIEVERS how to copy .

FAITHFUL HAND-WRITTEN
COPIES MADE BY THE
SAINTS IN LOCAL
INDEPENDENT CHURCHES
SUCH AS THE DONATISTS,
NOVATIANS, WALDENSES,
AND OTHERS UNTIL THE
PRINTING PRESS..

Faithful hand-
written copies
made until the

PRINTING

Appendix 5
CHURCH FATHERS

I. APOSTOLIC PERIOD: A. D. 75-150
 A. *Western Region:* Italy, Gaul [France], Greece, Important cities: Rome, Lyons, Thessalonika, Corinth, Athens.
   1. Clement of Rome (30-100 A. D.)
 B. *Antiochian [Eastern] Region:* Syria, Asia Minor (Macedonia, Phrygia), [present day Turkey] Palestine. Important cities: Jerusalem, Caesarea, Antioch, Constantinople [Byzantium], Ephesus, Smyrna
   1. Ignatius 35-107 A. D.
   2. Polycarp 69-155 A. D.
 C. *Alexandrian Region:* North Africa, Egypt. Important cities: Alexandria, Carthage.
   1. None

II. ANTE-NICENE PERIOD: A. D. 150-325
 A. *Western Region:* (see above)
   1. Irenaeus 120-192 A. D.
   2. Hippolytus 170-236 A. D.
   3. Tertullian 150-220 A. D.
   4. Cyprian 200-258 A. D.
 B. *Antiochian Region:* (see above)
   1. Lucian 250-312
 C. *Alexandrian Region:* (see above)
   1. Justin Martyr 100-165 A. D.
   2. Clement of Alexandria 150-217 A. D.
   3. Origin 184-254 A. D.
   4. Didymus 313-398

Council of Nicea = 325 A. D.

III. POST-NICENE PERIOD: 325-500 A. D.
 A. *Western Region:* (see above)
   1. Augustine 354-430 A. D.
 B. *Antiochian Region:* (see above)
   1. Diodorus d. 394 A. D.
   2. Chrysostom 345-407 A. D.
   3. Theodoret 397-457 A. D.
   4. Basil 330-379 A. D.
   5. Gregory of Nazianzen 329-390 A. D.
   6. Gregory of Nyssa 330-395 A. D.
 C. *Alexandrian Region:* (see above)
   1. Athanasius 296-373 A. D.
   2. Cyril 315-386 A. D.

Appendix 6

BIBLE SOCIETIES AND THE ROUTE OF THE 'NEW' TESTAMENT GREEK TEXT OF WESTCOTT/HORT[1]

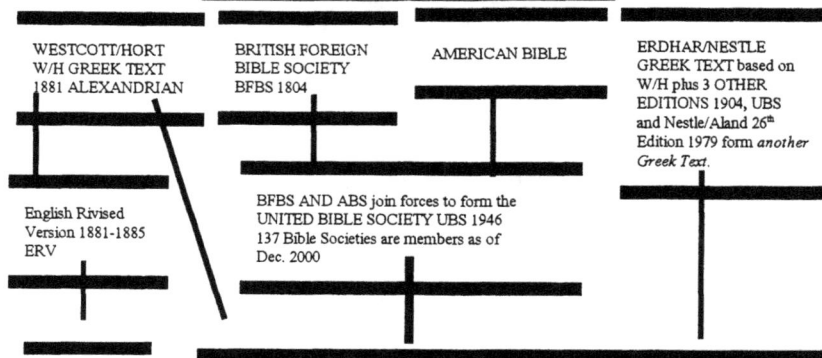

WESTCOTT/HORT
W/H GREEK TEXT
1881 ALEXANDRIAN

BRITISH FOREIGN
BIBLE SOCIETY
BFBS 1804

AMERICAN BIBLE

ERDHAR/NESTLE
GREEK TEXT based on
W/H plus 3 OTHER
EDITIONS 1904, UBS
and Nestle/Aland 26th
Edition 1979 form *another*
Greek Text.

English Rivised
Version 1881-1885
ERV

BFBS AND ABS join forces to form the
UNITED BIBLE SOCIETY UBS 1946
137 Bible Societies are members as of
Dec. 2000

American
Standard
Version ASV
1901

ANOTHER 'NEW' GREEK TEXT
The UBS 3rd and the Nestle/Aland 26th Editon

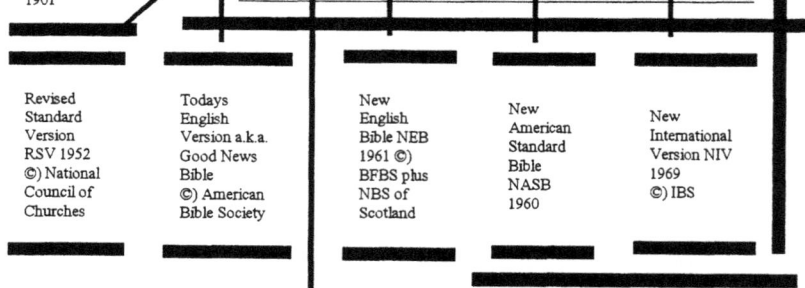

Revised
Standard
Version
RSV 1952
©) National
Council of
Churches

Todays
English
Version a.k.a.
Good News
Bible
©) American
Bible Society

New
English
Bible NEB
1961 ©)
BFBS plus
NBS of
Scotland

New
American
Standard
Bible
NASB
1960

New
International
Version NIV
1969
©) IBS

COMMON LANGUAGE VERSIONS

EDITORS:
1. Roman Catholic Archbishop
   Carlo MariaMartini
2. Bruce Manning Metzger
3. Kurt Aland
4. Eugine Nida
5. Allen Wikgren
6. Matthew Black

[1]This chart was made possible by the information in Dr. D. A. Waite's book,
Defending the King James Version

UBS CREED: Their sole concern is to recruit every believer, whatever his private creed may be...irrespective of denominational divisions and creedal [doctrinal] distinctions. [This is very ecumenical]

Appendix 7

HISTORY OF DISSENTERS FROM ROME

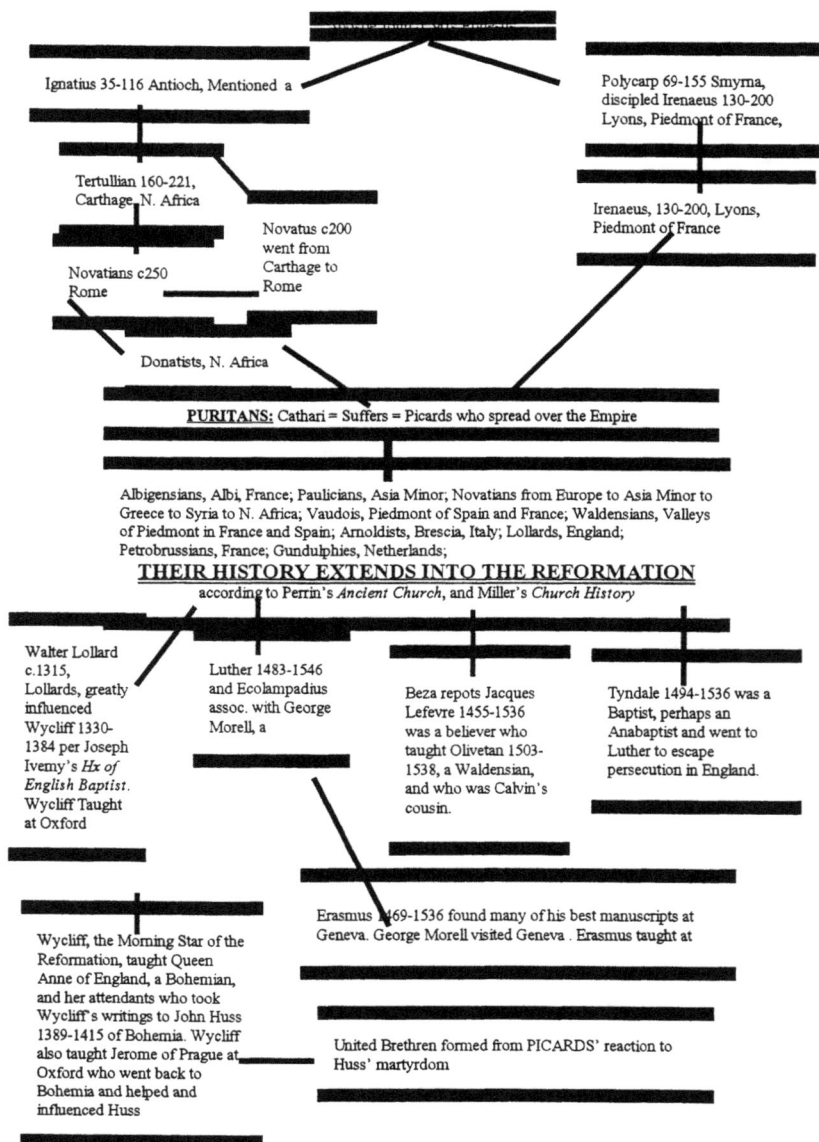

Ignatius 35-116 Antioch, Mentioned a

Polycarp 69-155 Smyrna, discipled Irenaeus 130-200 Lyons, Piedmont of France,

Tertullian 160-221, Carthage, N. Africa

Novatus c200 went from Carthage to Rome

Irenaeus, 130-200, Lyons, Piedmont of France

Novatians c250 Rome

Donatists, N. Africa

PURITANS: Cathari = Suffers = Picards who spread over the Empire

Albigensians, Albi, France; Paulicians, Asia Minor; Novatians from Europe to Asia Minor to Greece to Syria to N. Africa; Vaudois, Piedmont of Spain and France; Waldensians, Valleys of Piedmont in France and Spain; Arnoldists, Brescia, Italy; Lollards, England; Petrobrussians, France; Gundulphies, Netherlands;

THEIR HISTORY EXTENDS INTO THE REFORMATION

according to Perrin's *Ancient Church*, and Miller's *Church History*

Walter Lollard c.1315, Lollards, greatly influenced Wycliff 1330-1384 per Joseph Ivemy's *Hx of English Baptist*. Wycliff Taught at Oxford

Luther 1483-1546 and Ecolampadius assoc. with George Morell, a

Beza repots Jacques Lefevre 1455-1536 was a believer who taught Olivetan 1503-1538, a Waldensian, and who was Calvin's cousin.

Tyndale 1494-1536 was a Baptist, perhaps an Anabaptist and went to Luther to escape persecution in England.

Wycliff, the Morning Star of the Reformation, taught Queen Anne of England, a Bohemian, and her attendants who took Wycliff's writings to John Huss 1389-1415 of Bohemia. Wycliff also taught Jerome of Prague at Oxford who went back to Bohemia and helped and influenced Huss

Erasmus 1469-1536 found many of his best manuscripts at Geneva. George Morell visited Geneva . Erasmus taught at

United Brethren formed from PICARDS' reaction to Huss' martyrdom

Appendix 8
Bibliography

Allix, Peter; *Some Remarks Upon the Ecclesiastical History of the Ancient Churches of the Albigenses*; 1690; Oxford: At the Clarendon Press; Port Huron, MI; Fundamentalist Baptist CD ROM 2000b; Way of Life Literature.

Allix, Peter; *Some Remarks on the Ecclesiastical History of the Ancient Churches of Piedmont*; 1690; Fundamentalist Baptist CD ROM 2000b; Way of Life Literature.

Anderson, Christopher; *Annals of the English;* 1845, 1861; London; William Pickering; Fundamentalist Baptist CD ROM 2000b; Way of Life Literature.

Archer, B.D., LL.B., Ph.D.; Gleason L.; *Encyclopedia of Bible Difficulties*, Grand Rapids, Michigan; Zondervan Corp, 1982.

Armitage, Thomas; *A History of the Baptists Vol I and II*; Originally published in N.Y. in 1890 by Bryan, Taylor and Company; Baptist Standard Bearer, Paris, Arkansas; ISBN 1-57978-353-8, and 1-57978-354-6.

Barna, George; *Real Teens*; Ventura, California; Regal Books; 2001.

Barna Research Online; *Press Releases*; www.barna.org.

Benedict, David; *A General History of the Baptist Denomination in America, and Other Parts of the World*; 1813; London, Printed by Lincoln and Edmonds; Fundamentalist Baptist CD ROM 2000b; Way of Life Literature.

Benedict, David; *A History of the Donatists*; 1875; Nickerson, Pawtucket, RI; Fundamentalist Baptist CD ROM 2000b; Way of Life Literature; Port Huron, MI.

Berean Call, Electronic Disc; 1986-2001 Newsletters.

Bible Comparison Guide; Family Christian Store; Nov., 2001

Bible For Today Press; Many articles and brochures; They have thousands.

Bible For Today Website; www.biblefortoday.org

Braght; Thieleman J. van; *Martyrs Mirror, The Story of Seventeen Centuries of Christian Martyrdom, From the Time of Christ to A.D. 1660*; Scottsdale, Pennsylvania; Herald Press; Translated from the Dutch or Holland language from the edition of 1660 by Joseph F. Sohm.

Brandenburg, Kent, Editor; *Thou Shalt Keep Them*; Pillar and Ground Publishing; El Sobrante, CA; 2003

Bruce, M.A., D. D., F. F.; *The Canon of Scripture*; Downers Grove, Illinois; Intervarsity Press; 1988.

Bruce, M. A., D. D., F. F. ; *Tradition Old and New*; Grand Rapids, Michigan; Zondervan Publishing House; 1974.

Burton, Barry; *Let's Weigh the Evidence*; Ontario, California; Chick Publications, Inc.; 1983.

Burgon, Dean John William; *A Guide to the Textual Criticism of the New Testament*; Dean Burgon Society Press; Collingswood, New Jersey

Burgon, Dean John William; *Inspiration and Intepretation*; Dean Burgon Society Press, Collingswood, New Jersey

Burgon, Dean John William; *The Last Twelve Verses Of Mark;* Dean Burgon Society Press; Collingswood, New Jersey

Burgon, Dean John William; *Revision Revised,* Dean Burgon Society Press, Collingwood, New Jersey

Burgon, Dean John William; *Traditional Text Of The Holy Gospels*; Dean Burgon Society Press, Collingswood, New Jersey

Carson, Ph. D., D. A.; *The King James Version Debate, A Plea for Realism*; Grand Rapids, Michigan; Baker Book House; 1979.

Carter, Cecil J.; *The Collected Works of Cecil J. Carter*; Prince George, British Columbia; 1990

Christian, A.M., D.D. LL.D., John T.; *A History of the Baptists*; Texarkana, Ark-Texas, Baptist Sunday School Committee of the American Baptist Association; 1922.

Christian, John; *The Waldensian Churches*; 1922; Fundamentalist Baptist CD ROM 2000b; Way of Life Literature; Port Huron, MI.

Cloud, David W.; *For Love of the Bible, The Battle for the King James Version and the Received Text from 1800 to Present*; Oak Harbor, Washington; Way of Life Literature; 2nd Edition; 1999.

Cloud, David W.; *Myths about the Modern Bible Versions*; Oak Harbor, Washington; Way of Life Literature; 1999.

Cloud, David W.; *Has the Southern Baptist Convention Been Rescued from Liberalism ?*; Oak Harbor, Washington; Way of Life Literature; 1999.

Cloud, David W.; *Examining "The King James Only Controversy"*; Port Huron, Michigan; Way of Life Literature; 1998.

Cloud, David W.; *William Tyndall : The Father of our English Bible*; November, 30, 1999; Fundamentalist Baptist CD ROM 2000b; Way of Life Literature.

Cloud, David W.; *Fundamentalist Following Textual Critics;* Fundamentalist Baptist CD ROM 2000b; Way of Life Literature.

Cloud, David W.; *Unholy Hands on God's Holy Book, A Report on the United Bible Society;* 1985; Fundamentalist Baptist CD ROM 2000b; Way of Life Literature.

Comfort, Ph.D., Philip W.; *Essential Guide to Bible Versions*; Wheaton, Illinois; Tyndale House Publishers; 2000.

Cruse, C. F.; *Eusebius' Ecclesiastical History*; Peabody,

Massachusetts; Hendrickson Publishers; Reprinted 1998.

Dean Burgon Society Message Books, Dean Burgon Society, Co0llingswood, NJ, Published by Bible For Today.

Dean Burgon Society Website; www.deanburgonsociety.org. Many articles on the website and many books available

Erickson, Ph.D., Millard J.; *The Postmodern World, Discerning the Times and the Spirit of Our Age*; Wheaton, Illinois; Good News Publishers, 2002.

Ehrman, Bart D.;*Lost Christianities,* Oxford University Press; New York, New York

Foxe, John; *Foxe's Christian Martyrs of the World*; Uhrichsville, Ohio; Barbour and Company, Inc.; 1989.

Fuller, D.D., David Otis; *True or False?*; Grand Rapids, Michigan; Grand Rapid International Publications; 1983

Fuller, D. D., David Otis; *Which Bible?;* Grand Rapids, Michigan; Institute For Biblical Textual Studies; 1990.

Fundamentalist Baptist *CD ROM 2000b*; Way of Life Literature; Port Huron, MI.

Glenny, W. Edward; *The Bible Version Debate*; Fundamentalist Baptist CD ROM 2000b; Way of Life Literature.

Gipp, Th. D., Samuel C.; *Gipp's Understandable History of the Bible*; Northfield, Ohio; Daystar Publishing; 2nd Edition; 2000.

Gipp, Th.D., Samuel C.; *The Answer Book, A Helpbook for Christians*; Northfield, Ohio; Daystar Publishing; 2001.

Grady, Ph.D., Th.D., William P.; *Final Authority, A Christian's Guide to the King James Bible*; Schererville, Indiana; Grady Publications, Inc; 1995.

Grady, Ph. D., Th. D., William P.; *What Hath God Wrought! A Biblical Interpretation of American History*; Knoxville, Tennessee; Grady Publications, Inc.; 2001.

Green, Jay P.; Editor, *Unholy Hands On The Bible*, Vol. I and II; Lafayette, Indiana; Sovereign Grace Trust Fund; 1992.

Green, Jay P; The Gnostics, The New Versions, and the Deity of Christ; Lafayette, Indiana; Sovereign Grace Publishers; 1994.

Hills, Th. B., Th. D. Th. M., Edward F.; *The King James Version Defended*; Des Moines, Iowa; The Christian Research Press; 1984.

House, H. Wayne; *Charts of Christian Theology and Doctrine*; Grand Rapids, Michigan; Zondervan Publishing House; 1992.

Holman Bible Dictionary; *Dead Sea Scrolls*; Holman Bible Publisher Database, © Navpress Software; 1997.

Hunt, Dave; *A Woman Rides the Beast*; Eugene, Oregon; Harvest House Publishers; 1994.

Ironside, Harry A.; *Except You Reprint;* American Tract Society; 1937 Fundamentalist Baptist CD ROM 2000b; Way of Life Literature; Port Huron, MI.

Ivimey, Joseph; *A History of English Baptists, Including an Investigation of the History of Baptism in England from the Earliest Period to Which It can Be Traced to the Close of the Seventeenth Century;* 1811; Fundamentalist Baptist CD ROM 2000b; Way of Life Literature.

Jones, William; *The History of the Christian Church, from the Birth of Christ to the 18ᵗʰ Century;* 5ᵗʰ Edition; 1826; Printed by W. Myers, Castles Street, Holbor, London; Port Huron, MI; Fundamentalist Baptist CD ROM 2000b; Way of Life Literature.

Journals: *Christianity Today, Christian Research Journal, Berean Call, O Timothy*

Lewis, Ph. D., Jack P.; *The English Bible from KJV to NIV, A History and Evaluation;* Grand Rapids, Michigan; Baker Book House; 1991.

McClure, Alexander; *The Glorious History of the English Bible;* c1850; Fundamentalist Baptist CD ROM 2000b; Way of Life Literature; Port Huron, MI.

McClure, Alexander; *Translators Revived: Biographical Notes of the King James Version Bible Translators;* c1850; Fundamentalist Baptist CD ROM 2000b; Way of Life Literature; Port Huron, MI.

McDowell, Josh; *The New Evidence That Demands A Verdict;* Nashville, Tenn.; Thomas Nelson Publishers; 1999.

Metzger, Bruce M.; *The Text of the New Testament, Its Transmission, Corruption, and Restoration;* New York, Oxford; Oxford University Press; 3ʳᵈ Edition; 1992.

Millard, Catherine; *The Rewriting of America's History;* Camp Hill, Pennsylvania; Horizon Books; 1991.

Miller, Andrew; *Church History;* London; c1860; Port Huron, MI; Fundamentalist Baptist CD ROM 2000b; Way of Life Literature.

Miller, Andrew; *History of the Inquisition;* c1881; Fundamentalist Baptist CD ROM 2000b; Way of Life Literature; Port Huron, MI.

Moorman, Jack A.; *When the KJV Departs from the "Majority" Text, A New Twist in the Continuing Attack on the Authorized Version;* Collingswood, N.J.; The Bible For Today; B.F.T. # 1617; 1988.

Moorman, Jack A.; *Early Church Fathers and the Authorized Version, A Demonstration!;* Collingswood, N.J.; The Bible For Today; B. F. T. # 2136; 1988.

Moorman, Jack A.; *Early Manuscripts and the Authorized Version, A Closer Look! With Manuscript Digest and Summaries;* Collingswood, N.J.; The Bible For Today; B.F.T. #1825; 1990

Moorman, Jack A.; *Forever Settled, A Survey of the Documents and*

History of the Bible; Collingswood, N.J.; The Bible For Today; B. F. T. # 1428; 1985.

Moorman, Jack A.; *Conies Brass and Easter, Answers to the "Problem" Passages in the Authorized Version*; Collingswood, N.J.; The Bible For Today; B. F. T. # 1737.

Moorman, Jack A.; *Missing in Modern Bibles, Is the Full Story Being Told? An Analysis of the New International Version*; Collingswood, N.J.; The Bible For Today; B. F. T. # 1726; 1989.

Murphree, B. A., M. A., M. Div. Litt. D., Jon Tal; *Divine Paradoxes, A Finite View of an Infinite God*; Camp Hill, Pennsylvania; Christian Publications, Inc.; 1998.

Murphy, James G.; *Barnes Notes: A Commentary on the Book of Genesis*; Grand Rapids, Michigan; Baker Books; 2001.

Orchard, G. H.; *A Concise History of the Baptists*; 1855; Bedfordshire, England, Port Huron, MI; Fundamentalist Baptist CD ROM 2000b; Way of Life Literature.

O'Reilly, Bill; *The Factor;* Fox News Prime Time; April 16, 2002; "The Top Story"

Orr, James; *The Christian View of God and the World*; Grand Rapids, Michigan; Kregel Publications; 1989.

Perrin, Jean Paul; *History of the Ancient Christians, Inhabiting the Valleys of the Alps;* First Published 1618 by the author; 1847; Philadelphia, Pennsylvania; Griffith and Simon; Reprinted Gallatin, Tenn.; Church History Research and Archives; 1991.

Pentecost, J. Dwight; *Things to Come*; Grand Rapids, Michigan; Durham Publishing Company; 1958.

Pickering, Ph.D., Th.M., M.A., B.A., Wilbur N., *The Identity of the New Testament Text*, Nashville, Tenn.; Thomas Nelson Publishers; 1980.

Richardson, Th. D., D. D., Cyril C.; *The Early Christian Fathers*; New York, New York; Macmillan Publishing Company; 1970.

Reagin, David; *The King James Version of 1611, The Myth of Early Revisions;* Knoxville, Tennessee; Trinity Baptist Bookstore.

Riplinger, Gail A.; *Which Bible is God's Words?*; Oklahoma City, Oklahoma; Hearthstone Publishing, Ltd.; 1994.

Riplinger, Gail A.; *New Age Bible Versions*; Munroe Falls, Ohio; A.V. Publications; 1994

Robbins, John W.; *Scripture Twisting in the Seminaries*, Part I: Feminism; Jefferson, Maryland; Trinity Foundation; 1985.

Ross, Ph.D., Dr. Hugh; *The Fingerprint of God*; Orange, California; Promise Publishing; 2nd Edition; 1991.

Price, Robert M. *The Incredible Shrinking Son Of Man, How Reliable Is the Gospel Tradition;* Prometheus Books, Amherst, New York.

Ruckman, Ph.D., Th. M., B.D., M.A., B.A., Peter S.; *The Christian's Handbook of Biblical Scholarship*; Pensacola, Florida; Bible Believers Press; 1998.

Ruckman, Ph.D., Th. M., B.D., M.A., B.A., Peter S.; *How to Teach the "Original" Greek*; Pensacola, Florida; Bible Baptist Book Store; 1992.

Ruckman, Ph.D., Th. M., B.D., M.A., B.A., Peter S.; *The Christian's Handbook of Manuscript Evidence*; Palatka, Florida; Pensacola Bible Press; 1976.

Ruckman, Ph. D., Th. M., B. D., M. A., B. A., Peter S.; *King James Onlyism versus Scholarship Onlyism*; Pensacola, Florida; Bible Believers Press; 1992.

Salliby, (Chick) Rev. Charles; *If the Foundations Be Destroyed*; Taylors, South Carolina; Faith Printing Company; 1994.

Sightler, M.D., James H.; *Tabernacle Essays on Bible Translation*; Greenville, South Carolina; Tabernacle Baptist Church; 1993.

Stone, Nathan; *Names of God*; Chicago, Illinois; Moody Press; 1944.

Swomley, John M.; *Political Power of Roman Catholic Bishops;* **www.population-security.org.**

The Holy Bible, 1611 Edition, Hendrickson Publishers, Inc., Peabody, MA

Trinitarian Bible Society; *The Greek Text Underlying the English Authorized Version of 1611*; London, England; Tyndale House; 2000

Trinitarian Bible Society; *Ecumenism and the United Bible Societies;* London, England; Tyndale House; Article # 107; 1995.

U.S. Department of Justice; *Islam in the United States,* Fact Sheet; International Information Programs; 2001.

U.S. Department of Justice; *Bureau of Justice Statistics;* www.ojp.usdoj.gov/bjs/glance

Vance, Ph. D., Laurence M.; *Double Jeopardy, The New American Standard Update*; Pensacola, Florida; Vance Publications; 1998

Waite, Th. D., Ph. D., Pastor D. A.; *Heresies of Westcott and Hort*; Lubbock, Texas; Plains Baptist Challenger; 1979. Now available from Bible For Today.

Waite, Th. D., Ph. D., Pastor D.A.; *Defending the King James Bible*; Collingswood, N.J.; The Bible For Today Press; 1995.

Way of Life Encyclopedia of the Bible and Christianity; 4th Edition; Way of Life Literature; Port Huron, MI.

Webster's Dictionary; 1828; 1st Edition; Reprint Granted by G & C Merrian Co.; Published by Foundation for American Christian Education, 8th Edition, San Francisco, California.

Webster Dictionary of the English Language, Deluxe Edition; PMC Publishing Co., Inc.; N.Y., N.Y.; 1992

Weldon, John; *Decoding the Bible Code, Can We Trust the Message*; Eugene, Oregon; Harvest House, Publishers; 1998.

White, B.A., M.A., James R.; *The King James Only Controversy, Can you Trust the Modern Translations?*; Minneapolis, Minnesota; Bethany House Publishers; 1995.

Wylie, L.L.D., J. A., *The History of Protestantism*; 1899; London, Paris, New York & Melbourne: Cassell and Co., Limited; Fundamentalist Baptist CD ROM 2000b; Way of Life Literature.

Appendix 9
INDEX

the
BIBLE
FOR
TODAY

900 Park Avenue
Collingswood, NJ 08108
Phone: 856-854-4452
www.BibleForToday.org

B.F.T. #3125

www.ingramcontent.com/pod-product-compliance
Lightning Source LLC
Chambersburg PA
CBHW060315100426
42812CB00003B/789

* 9 7 8 0 9 9 8 5 4 5 2 7 1 *